Off the Cuff

by

Swasie Turner

To My Wife Marjorie

Published By Avid Publications
7 Garth Boulevard
Higher Bebington
Wirral
Merseyside
L63 5LS
United Kingdom
Tel 051 645 2047

Further copies of this book can be obtained from the above.

Edited by William David Roberts - Avid Publications

All Rights Reserved
ISBN No: 0 9521020 4 8

Foreword

by Alison Halford

(Former Assistant Chief Constable of Merseyside .)

In a highly regimented world of police conformity and culture, Swasie Turner (ST) is a decidedly 'one off ' : a colourful, flamboyant exuberant character whose like is now regrettably an endangered species in the world of policing.

His passion for the 'Job' , for the cloth and for smartness in uniform together with his honesty and forthright sense of humour burns through this highly entertaining insight into the world of provincial policing. Swasie's recall for detail is phenomenal as he meticulously recounts with both pathos and humour so many of his encounters during his years in the force.

Swasie's first chief called him a persistent bugger. Doubtless along the years, other bosses have called him by other names because as the story unfolds, his willingness to always put the welfare of his troops first and doing things his way, has ensured that he has not always been ' flavour of the month ' with the powers that be. His crunching description of the 'Armchair Brigade' , those on high who ruled from the lofty pinnacles of force headquarters and of other minor supervisory despots, takes us behind the scenes in a unique way.

We are shown the real side of policing; the ways and means act at work, where rules are broken , niceties ignored but the job still gets done. All types and manner of individual and incident are paraded under Swasie's pen. Each event is graphically brought to life from the author's awesome eye for detail and we are treated to a lively chronology of life in the lower ranks of the police as never exposed before.

ST reached the rank of 'Skipper' , or Sergeant to those unused to Police jargon. Some never achieve even that first rung on the promotion ladder. Never willing to crawl to management, always fully committed to doing the job as he thought best may have got him the label of outspoken maverick. Sometimes perhaps too zealous and over the top in some of his exploits but always his loyalty and professionalism was there for all to see. All this is a matter of opinion.

What is not in doubt is that ST has written a humdinger of a good read with all the virtues and warts of police work rolled up between the pages. When I had read it, he asked me to rate it and it's author. I'd make him Chief Constable, and I should know.......

Although we never met on duty, I was a member of that disdained Armchair Brigade at the same time as Swasie served on the lower deck. So to Skipper Swasie , I say " Well Done. "

Alison Halford

Acknowledgements

I should like to express my gratitude to the following people who have been kind enough to allow me the use of their photographs:-

Mr. Brian Jones of Aintree
Stephen Shakeshaft- courtesy of Liverpool Daily Post and Echo
Mrs Nora Povall, widow of Detective Sergeant Charlie Povall
Mrs Pat Gribbin, widow of Jack Gribbin (Ex - Main Bridewell)
Mrs Nora Lazer of Wallasey

My special thanks to Richard (Sonny) Hempkins, the late Les McHale, Park Sergeant Billy Quick, the late Detective Sergeant Charlie Povall and all those who helped me back in the old days to achieve my ambition of becoming a Police Officer.

Swasie Turner 1994

The Author

Swasie Turner did not want to stop being a member of the Police Force. As he says in his book, the decision was made for him by an horrific incident in the line of his duty. He still lives near where he was born on the Wirral and misses the Police a great deal. He is trying very hard to come to terms with this loss.

Swasie wanted to try and write an account of his working life, and usually Swasie achieves what he sets out to do. He has done it.

He is one of the worlds 'Characters' who stand out from the crowd, (often the source of some of his problems along the way) yet Swasie Turner is also, as Hamlet said " a man, take him for all in all." He is a very human being, with all the frailties that go with it.

Since retiring, the author now spends his time oil painting, writing and continues to visit the various friends made during his convalescent periods at Hove, East Sussex.

His other activities include deep sea fishing. At the time of the completion of his book, he had undergone a total of six operations on the damaged knee and will soon receive a complete new knee joint.

Contents

Chapter One - The Dawn.

Since I was a very small boy my ambition was to become a Police Officer. My late grandfather, George Woods, had served as a Sergeant in the Birkenhead Borough Police and I had an uncle who had served in the same force as a wartime reserve constable. However, as a young boy, for some unknown reason, I was always terrified whenever I saw a policeman appear.

The Author's late Grandfather Sergeant Woods

I was born and bred in Saughall Massie, a small village on the Wirral. My father was a Birkenhead Corporation 'bus driver, my mother, a hard working housewife. Being a small village, everyone knew the local policemen by name. It was a common sight to see the local bobby (and sometimes the Sergeant) pedalling a bicycle around the rural beats. One of our local bobbies I remember vividly. He appeared to be nine feet tall and the same across his shoulders. He was known to young and old alike as 'Monty'. There was never any trouble when he was around. Many times, he alone kept Moreton in order, especially the area surrounding Moreton Cross on a Saturday night. He, like most of his colleagues in those days would not hesitate to administer a sound cuff

1

round the ears to those who sometimes warranted it (including myself).

Sometimes he would take an aggressive adult into a nearby entry where he would offer free 'advice' or 'administer' justice on the spot, thus eliminating the need to arrest the belligerent offender. Monty's 'advice' always worked!. Monty, Cyril Rae and 'Flash Harry' were three well known constables who patrolled the streets of Moreton and kept them safe for law abiding citizens to go about their business. All of these officers were well over six feet tall, as were most policemen of that bygone era.

As a teenager, no doubt like many others, I sometimes received a whack across the back of my head from the cape of one of these three, as my mates and I made our noisy exit from the Moreton Picture House, to ensure that we made our way home quietly. Who was going to argue? With hindsight, there's no doubt that their form of 'chastisement' certainly had the desired effect in diminishing anyone's enthusiasm to misbehave. In those days, to go home and complain to one's parents that a bobby had given one a 'clout' would undoubtedly invoke their wrath, and ensure similar treatment from them.

As I grew up through my school days, my yearning to join the ranks of the police never left me. For some unknown reason, when I subsequently applied to join the Birkenhead Police, my application was turned down?! Undeterred, I then applied to join the Wallasey Borough force, but again my application was unsuccessful. I applied to Liverpool City Police, but again received a negative result. Similar applications to Cheshire County and the Metropolitan Police down in London met with the same fate. To say that I was puzzled (and alarmed) would be a gross understatement indeed. I had never been in trouble with the law, although like most children, I doubt if I could have been described as the most 'angelic' of children! I was certainly not aware of anything of a detrimental nature that would obstruct my becoming member of the Police force.

Therefore, I was truly baffled and worried as to why my numerous attempts were continually being thwarted. Eventually, I decided on a new tack. I applied to become a Special Constable with the Birkenhead Police. To my surprise I was accepted and duly became Special Constable 43 of the Birkenhead Borough Police, even better, I was posted to my local station at Upton. How immensely proud I was having at last become a policeman. I threw myself whole heartedly into my new 'achievement', although I still yearned for the regulars!. I worked very hard as a special, attending every lecture and buying and studying expensive law books in an attempt to further this end. I volunteered to perform duty every day or night that I could.

Some of the regulars thought I was mad, although there was not the childish 'anti-special' attitude then that I was to encounter later on in life!. Armed with my new warrant card, my note book and wearing my sharply pressed uniform (with 'dog collar' tunic) I paraded for my first duty at the lecture room, at Headquarters, Birkenhead at 7-45pm, Wednesday, 18 November 1959, as a fully sworn in Special Constable. I listened intently and hung on to every word uttered by the lecturing Sergeant. Two

2

evenings later, I paraded at Upton before going out to patrol my first beat (in company with an experienced Special).

The Author as Special Constable 43'C'

We lined up and paraded in an ante-room of the station. My Inspector, a middle-aged man who was a very prominent businessman in the fruit importing business in the City, Mr Wilf Briscoe (one of nature's gentlemen) entered the room and the parade Sergeant, Sergeant 'Bob' Butler, a legal executive, brought the parade to attention. We were then inspected and finally given various instructions, criminal intelligence of note and our beat areas to patrol for the evening. The parade was then interrupted by the entrance of the station's 'regular' Sergeant, Sergeant Millington (who, sadly, is no longer with us).

Sergeant Millington was full of his own importance and was not a very friendly man at all. He and his wife lived above the station and it was not unusual to see either of them wandering around the station at various times of the day or night. I was to see Sergeant Millington chastise his constables many times, sometimes quite severely, in the presence of his wife or even us specials, when he was on, or off duty. These occasions were very embarrassing, not least for the poor recipient constable.

Upton Police Station

As time went on, I tried to avoid this man. He was not very obliging when I sought his help and guidance on various matters and he was usually very sarcastic with his comments. It was obvious that he had little time for us specials. His attitude however, was far different towards Mr Briscoe and Mr Butler. Perhaps he and his wife were fond of apples and hoped to purchase their own house some day? I tried to enlist the help of my Sergeant and Inspector with a view to becoming a regular, but they could do no more than seek the help of Sergeant Millington. Although he promised he would 'see what he could do', nothing was ever forthcoming. (I was to find out years later that he did in fact continually thwart my efforts in one way or another, often suggesting that I was not 'suitable police material').

To my knowledge, I never gave any cause for him to adopt the attitude that he did. Perhaps my grandfather had upset someone in the force years before? I was, from the start however, a very keen officer. It was not long before I was bringing in a variety of summonses. I did not know it at the time, but this was just not done by the special fraternity and I found that instead of enhancing my position with my superiors, especially Sergeant Millington, I was, in fact, 'rocking the boat'. One evening I was taken to one side by Sergeant Millington and told in no uncertain terms (within the hearing of my regular and special colleagues) that we specials were there ONLY to assist the regulars if, and when required to do so, and I should leave the 'proper' police work to his men. I was the only special young enough to become a regular, as the remainder of my section were well into middle age. Perhaps they were all content just to be uniform carriers or playing at bobbies, but I was determined that I wanted to become professional police officer.

Special Inspector Wilf Briscoe

My wife was proud that I had become a special but I think that she kept an open mind as to my eventual (hopeful) aspirations. I don't think even she thought that I would make the regulars.

There was one constable , from the regulars, who used to help me a lot, the late Constable Norman Gilfoyle, affectionately known to all as the 'blood orange' (due to his very red complexion). He was a regular of many years standing and continually offered me his help and assistance whenever I sought it. Due to a lot of encouragement from Norman, I bought myself a bicycle and, after he had pestered his Sergeant (Millington), I was able to accompany regular officers on cycle patrol during weekdays (and nights). Eventually, I was allowed to patrol on my own. I relished these 'solo' cycle patrols as I longed to catch a burglar or other 'juicy' job which I thought may enhance my prospects. As time went on, such was my enthusiasm that I was sometimes allowed (when Millington was away) to take my large Alsatian dog out on foot patrol with me.

This would be completely unheard of today. It certainly had the desired effect at various violent incidents outside one or two of the then more notorious pubs in the area, and assisted in the dispersal of the local yobs greatly. (Much to the delight of the licensees and my regular colleagues).

Some of my summonses went through and I was able to gain some valuable court experience. At this time my wife Marje and I lived with

5

my mother and father at the family home in Beech Avenue, Saughall Massie, which was about one mile away from Upton Police Station. I used to feel so proud when I would call home for a cuppa whilst out on patrol with one of my 'regular' colleagues. However, it still wasn't the real thing.

In December 1959 my wife went into Highfield Hospital, Wallasey for the impending birth of our son, Ronald. On Wednesday, 16 December, I was on police duty and given permission to go straight to the hospital to attend the birth, during which I was present, white gown over my uniform, and even assisted Sister Salisbury and Doctor Wallace at the happy event by holding Marje's hand and mopping her brow.

A short time later, I made another application to become a regular member of the Birkenhead force, and this time things started to move. I was instructed to attend the police doctor's surgery in Rock Ferry for a medical examination. At the conclusion of the examination the doctor informed me that there was no reason why I could not become a police officer, in other words, unofficially, he told me I had passed my medical. I remember going home on the 'bus in a jubilant mood. A short time later I sat my written exams and couldn't believe it when I was to learn that I had passed these also. I was told that I would be sent for to attend at the Chief Constable's Office for final interview.

I duly attended for interview by the late Major S J Harvey. Eventually, out of the five of us to reach Major Harvey's office, there were only myself and one other candidate for final consideration. Each of us were individually sent for and, after interview, told to go and await the Chief Constable's final decision. Finally, when we thought we could bear the suspense no longer, we were both sent for and we stood alongside each other in front of the great man's desk. Major Harvey informed us that there was only one vacancy in the force. He had decided therefore, that as I was in employment and the other was out of work the latter unemployed candidate would be given the position.

I was absolutely gutted. I shook hands and congratulated the new Birkenhead Borough Constable 49 Roberts, struggling to hide my acute disappointment, about turned and left the office.

I continued with the specials but the bottom had fallen out of my bucket. I felt devastated.

Sergeant Millington (gleefully) advised me against trying again as there would be no further vacancies for some time to come, and it was obvious now that I should seek something other than a career with the police. I was determined that I would continue my attempts to enter the service. I knew that Millington revelled in my failures so far, but for obvious reasons, I daren't say a word.

I joined the Cheshire County Fire Brigade and duly passed out as Fireman 1633 at the conclusion of my course, which was a three months residential course at Heswall, on the Wirral. I eventually qualified and served as a 'Red Machine' (Fire Engine) driver. The fire service certainly held a large degree of excitement and I was involved in some very nasty, and hair-raising incidents, not least, was a serious explosion at Prices

Candle Works , Bromborough, where I managed to bring one badly burned casualty out alive from the horrific incident in which his two colleagues perished. Although I enjoyed my work, and the company of my colleagues, it was the Police Service that I continued to yearn for.

I was secretly determined that I would persevere in this direction, and hopefully make it one day? My brigade colleagues at Runcorn, Heswall and finally Bebington fire stations, never knew of my ambition to leave their ranks for those of the Police.

Chapter Two - The Turn of the Tide.

One cold, wet January evening in 1963 my wife and I were sitting at home in front of a large, open ,coal fire. My wife was reading the Liverpool Echo. I was browsing through a copy of Police Review. Suddenly, my wife turned to me and informed me that there was an advertisement in the Echo asking for Park Constables in Liverpool. I read the advertisement. It said that constables were required by the City of Liverpool Parks Police and invited applicants to write for an interview. I decided to give it a try and wrote off to Superintendent Buchanan, applying for a position with his force.

I received a reply instructing me to attend at Park Police Headquarters, Calderstones Park, Liverpool for written and medical examinations and, if successful, an interview with the Superintendent.

I attended as instructed.The headquarters were situated in the 'Mansion House' at Calderstones Park. Calderstones is a very up-market area of rural Liverpool, the park itself was very well tended and the Manor House was scrupulously clean and tidy.

The Mansion House Calderstones Park

There were quite a number of candidates present on the day. Although there were, unfortunately, some failures, ten of us made it and were accepted into the force. We were sworn in, kitted out and duly commenced our four week course under the supervision of the Superintendent and instructors in first aid, judo, swimming and, of course, police duty and local by-laws and other legislation.

Our course was held at Calderstones Park but we went on numerous visits to Fire and Police Stations, swimming baths and ambulance stations.

On completion of the course we were all posted to various locations throughout the city boundaries. I was posted as Constable 82 to Sefton Park. This is a very large park which has a number of roads and houses within, together with a lake, bowling greens, cricket and football pitches and their pavilions. We constables had the full powers of a constable in all of the City's parks, gardens and recreation centres, including Liverpool's airport. We were also sworn special constables of the City of Liverpool. I had studied hard on my course and was pleased to have obtained high marks in my final exams at the course's conclusion. I was still determined to get on. By now, Court appearances held no fear for me and I was soon becoming well known on the landings of the Liverpool City (and Birkenhead Borough) Magistrates' Courts. Indeed, most of the Court staff thought that I was a City bobby due to my regular attendances.

Park Police Course (Author centre back row, Sergeant Quick, centre front row)

I was regularly locking up 'flashers' (indecent exposures) but I also made a number of arrests for offences of theft, buggery, gross indecency and, on one occasion, rape. (Some of these offences were only triable at the Crown Court before a jury). I was continually dealing and assisting with various accidents on the roads of the parks and administering

9

first aid to casualties. I had qualified in first aid and life saving on our course at Calderstones. I had, by now, relinquished my position with the Birkenhead Specials, being a Liverpool Special (due to my position with the Parks Police). After six months my next posting was to Stanley Park. This park is situated between the two major Merseyside football grounds of Everton (Goodison) and Liverpool (Anfield). This was to be a busy posting for me, especially at weekends, when one or the other team was playing at home. Again assaults , robberies, thefts, offences involving indecency, drunks and the perpetual and ever increasing vandalism.

There were, of course, periods when things were quiet, I spent many hours secreted in bushes, huts or other suitable places of concealment keeping observations on those whom I had a 'feeling' were up to no good. Sometimes, these observations paid dividends when a wrongdoer thought all was clear and would suddenly 'flash' to an unsuspecting female (sometimes a young girl) or snatch a purse or steal a bicycle. The shock when a bobby suddenly appeared from nowhere and arrested him and recovered the property was worth it all.

Due to my regular 'visits' to Westminster Road Police Station with various types of offender, a lot of my time there was spent with the CID. It was during these dealings that I met and became very friendly with the late Detective Sergeant Charlie Povall. I will be eternally grateful to Charlie for his unrelenting encouragement and help, not only with the arrests that I had made, but in assisting my efforts to join the regular force on his learning of my ultimate ambition.

The late Detective Sergeant Charlie Povall

10

Westminster Road Bridewell

He certainly made a very large contribution and a big impact on my eventual success. I shall never forget Charlie.

One particularly nasty job involving Charlie's help was an arrest I made for an offence of 'gross indecency' involving a little boy. I was standing on the bridge which overlooked the lake in Stanley Park one morning when I noticed a young man in his early twenties enter the park via the Spellow Lane gates. The young man was holding the hand of a small boy and both went into the toilets situated near to the park gates. Although there were no grounds for my thinking that there was anything untoward, I nevertheless decided to follow them in to see if all was well. On my entering the toilets I saw that there were two cubicles, the door to one of these was closed, the other open. As there were no other persons in the toilet, it was obvious where the two were. I heard the rustling of clothing from behind the closed door. Again, no cause for alarm as I assumed the adult was preparing the youngster to use the toilet, as we have all done for our own children. However, I decided to stay for a few minutes. I then heard the child's voice say "No, don't, your hurting me". I jumped onto the toilet seat in the adjoining cubicle and looked over the dividing partition. I saw the man with his trousers round his ankles. He was trying to force the boy to commit an act of oral sex (the boy was just seven years old). I jumped down and kicked the locked door of their cubicle open. I dragged the man out, still with his trousers down.

The poor child was terrified at the sight of a policeman appearing and, although the child's face bore a couple of scratches, he was thankfully saved from further physical harm due to my timely intervention.

I arrested the man and took him (not too gently) through the streets

11

to the nearby Westminster Road Bridewell. (This fine, old building is now a public house and restaurant named 'The Old Bill'). I held the boy's hand and gently reassured him en-route. The police did not have personal radios at this time, nor were there mobile patrols (other than Traffic) so, in many cases, prisoners were walked to the Police Station if there was one near enough. If not, the officer, or someone he requested, would 'phone for a van.

Doctor 'Morrie' Kirwan

As we walked along, the boy screaming aloud what had happened, passers by guessed what had happened and by the time we had reached the Police Station, the offender was covered in spit and had a bloody nose. Obviously, the local people (especially the women) were only trying to explain that they were very vexed at what the man had done to the boy!

On arrival at the station, the boy and the young man were examined by the force Bridewell surgeon, the well known, very efficient and popular Doctor Maurice 'Morrie' Kirwan. Fortunately, the child subsequently recovered from his horrific ordeal. The 'buck' (as we call baddies in Liverpool) subsequently received his come-uppance at Liverpool Crown Court by receiving 18 months' imprisonment, (nowhere near enough in my opinion). I received the utmost help and guidance in taking the matter through to the Crown Court from Sergeant Povall. Every time that I needed help in any way whatsoever with any arrest I made (even if the CID were not involved), I only had to call at Westminster Road to see Charlie, or ring his office. He even gave me his home telephone number, which illustrated just how utterly privileged I was. Nothing was too much effort for him and I like to think that his mannerisms, conduct and politeness, not to mention his ability to take all in his stride, eventually rubbed off onto me?

By now we had left my mother's house and moved into a self-contained ground floor flat a short distance away in West Kirby, amusingly referred to by some of my colleagues as 'debtors retreat'. Next door to our flat was a lovely park with a beautiful lake bearing swans, ducks and moorhens. There were bowling greens, swings and the well known tennis courts. These courts hosted the international tournaments, when many of the famous tennis stars appeared on their courts. We enrolled our son into the local primary school (St. Bridget's). All was going well, Marje had a part-time job as a shop assistant and I really liked my work BUT, I still yearned to be a 'proper' policeman!

I received a further posting to Newsham Park. This was a 'quieter' park than the others but like Sefton Park there were roads , a lake, bowling greens and houses within its boundary. My new Sergeants were as different as chalk and cheese. One, Sergeant Jack Capstick, was a quiet and reserved man. The other. Sergeant Rickart. (also Jack) was a quick tempered man who did not suffer fools lightly. He had a son who was a serving City Police Inspector. Sergeant Rickart was very quick to spot any short-comings in a person, and did not hesitate to let that person know it.

It was not long before both Sergeants became aware of my ultimate ambitions and, when they realised this, they were both very understanding and encouraging although, I did bear the brunt of Sergeant Rickart's cynicism whenever I made a hash of things. Again, at Newsham, I made a number of arrests for the inevitable thefts, criminal (malicious, as it was then) damage and quite a few for indulging in various forms of indecency and gross indecency. I found that a large number of males who involved themselves in gross indecency were commercial travellers, reps and van delivery drivers (well-to-do, a lot of them). They would park their vehicles near to the toilets and await others who would do the same. It never ceased to amaze me how decent, clean, well-dressed men who came from good homes, many with wives and children and who sometimes held quite a high positions , often professionals, in society , would 'hang around' gent's toilets and sometimes, ultimately would find themselves arrested for their disgusting behaviour and finally end up before the courts. I was to deal with this type of person right throughout my police career. Sometimes I would stop the occasional vehicle travelling through the park and on one such occasion, I arrested a man and recovered a number of stolen car radios and lamps from his van, so it wasn't just indecency offences in the parks.

Whilst serving at Newsham Park I had a lengthy chat with Sergeant Capstick, who advised me to try for the City Police as it was obvious that it was that which I wanted.

In January 1965 therefore, I wrote off for my application form. This was duly received, completed and, together with the appropriate references, sent off post haste. On Saturday, 23 January I received a letter from the Liverpool City Police Training School, Mather Avenue, instructing me to attend there the following Friday for attestation and medical examination. I sweated for a full week and come Friday, I was up with the lark.

The full morning was consumed by sitting written examinations of maths, English, dictation, general knowledge, spelling and other equally important topics. After lunch, all of the applicants were taken to the main hall, where, we were informed by the recruiting Sergeant, Sergeant Webster, that those who had successfully passed the morning's exams were now required to undergo a medical examination during the afternoon. Those required to stay were to listen for their names to be called and then go to an adjacent room to await the doctor. Those not called were not required further (they had failed) and could go home. I listened with bated breath for my name to be called but, alas, it was not to be. Eventually, the Sergeant concluded the list of names of those who had made it. I couldn't believe it, I'd dipped! I knew that my maths had let me down. Blast it!

As I made my dejected way from the Training Centre to the nearby 'bus stop in company with a serving Liverpool fireman who had also failed, he remarked, "If they're that short and can afford to be so choosy, bollocks to them". I knew that it must have been my maths so, when I arrived home, (after the sad and humiliating explanation of the day's outcome to my wife), I immediately sat down and wrote off again to the Liverpool City Police. I told them that I knew that my maths left a lot to be desired but respectfully requested that I be given another chance to sit the exams.

To my amazement, I received a letter informing me that I would be allowed to attend Mather Avenue in a month's time to sit the exams once again. Due to this, I immediately purchased a book entitled 'Teach Yourself Mathematics' by the University Press. I then enlisted the aid of a friend who was a Merchant Navy Navigation Officer (who was obviously a 'dab hand' at maths), Richard 'Sonny' Hempkins. He came to my home most evenings and was akin to a very patient school teacher with a very thick pupil. He and I worked into the night on each occasion. Goodness, he must have wondered how anyone could be so thick!

Duty at Newsham had its ups and downs, I received some sympathy from my colleagues but also some stick from others, at my dismal attempt to leave their ranks for those of 'The City'. Just prior to going off duty at II pm one night I was walking alongside a scrap yard adjacent to the railway on the edge of Newsham Park when I heard noises coming from the yard. I climbed over the wall and, although it was dark, I could see by overhead railway lighting, two men attempting to force an entry into the yard's office. On hearing my approach, the two men ran off. I gave chase but they both made good their escape into the darkness. I stumbled and received a cut to my face from a protruding piece of jagged metal and was treated for my injury at nearby Tuebrook Police Station. British Transport Police searched the area with their dogs but found nothing. Never mind, some you win, some you lose.

The following day, one of my 'elderly' colleagues had a violent row at the dinner table with Sergeant Rickart. This particular constable was known as somewhat of a 'skiver' and was renowned for going missing on his beat, but was always inevitably found somewhere hiding in a toilet, pavilion, hut or other similar place of secretion from the Sergeant, reading his paper instead of patrolling his beat. Due to his addiction of toilet hunting, Sergeant Rickart christened him (and for ever onwards referred to him as) 'shit the pan', irrespective of whoever happened to be within earshot. The Sergeant didn't take too highly at having to continually search for his officer in order to 'give him a peg' (record his visit in the constable's note book). The indignant constable took great exception to his 'title', bleating that he was regularly taken short and it always seemed to be when the Sergeant was about. He resented the Sergeant addressing him, a middle aged man, with such a childish and most offensive term as 'shit the pan', as it was very degrading and embarrassing. Needless to say, the rest of us at the table were highly amused at the antics of two grown men behaving in such an undignified manner like a couple of immature children.

Some days later, whilst out on patrol, I saw a man whom I recognised from his ungainly walk and heavy shock of hair, as being one of the two men who had eluded me at the scrap yard the previous week. He admitted to being one of the two responsible for attempting to break into the office but would not name his accomplice. He was arrested and taken to Tuebrook Police Station. What a piece of luck! He appeared before the Liverpool City Magistrates' Court the following day and pleaded guilty. He was fined £20, quite a reasonable fine in those days. The following day, would you believe it, I caught a NUN ! depositing litter. I saw her drop a plastic carrier bag containing dirty linen and other rubbish, behind a hedge in Gardeners Drive, near to the Judges residence. It was very embarrassing having to rebuke a young nun. I went to see the Mother Superior and there let the matter rest with her.

I made frequent visits to the public library prior to my next visit to Mather Avenue, to study the names of the current members of the cabinet in preparation for my forthcoming general knowledge exam. I was leaving nothing to chance. even my wife, Marje, was helping me with my studies by now.

Thursday, 5 March arrived. My big day! I was at the Police Training School ALL DAY! Written exams all morning, and - success!, lunch then, MY turn to go with the others into the ante -room to await our medical examination. This took up most of the afternoon, concluding with the inevitable anxious wait to see if we had passed this also. Eventually, the recruiting Sergeant, our old friend Sergeant Webster, came into the room and informed those fortunate ones of us that had passed. I certainly felt for those who hadn't made it after all this. I had been along that road myself. From the original 35 to 40 of us that morning, there were now about 14 or so. We all sat anxiously waiting to be called to the Chief Constable's office for final interview and selection (or rejection).

Finally, my name was called and I was marched in, left, right, left, right, halt. Stand at ease. Stand easy. I found myself standing in front of the man himself, the legendary Mr Herbert 'Bert' Balmer. He was a very nice man and I was made to feel at ease by him. There was no doubt he was a very knowledgeable man. He seemed fully up to date with regard to my past. He appeared to know more about me than I did. He asked me numerous questions and seemed impressed with my answers. Eventually, he leaned back in his high leather chair, thought for a while, then he said "Well, I'll say one thing Turner, you're certainly a persevering bugger. I'm going to give you a chance." I could have kissed him there and then! I couldn't believe what I was hearing. All the efforts, all the years, all the hard work, I'd finally done it. I hardly remember my journey home on the 'bus and train. I was absolutely jubilant. I started the next Friday!

Once home I couldn't even face my dinner. I took Marje, my dad and his sister, Edie, for a celebratory drink - and how! What a pity what my mother didn't live to see me finally make it, as she had sadly passed away twelve months earlier.

The following day, Saturday, I went on duty feeling on top of the world. This time, when it became known that I had been successful, there was no giggling behind hands, no micky-taking, the lads and the Sergeants were great, some more than a little envious, but they all congratulated me on getting there at long last. The two Sergeants were kindness itself at the good news and wished me well. On Monday, I took my wrist watch for repair as I wanted it in A1 condition for Bruche (the Police Training Centre near Warrington). When I went on duty for the afternoon shift I could sense a completely different atmosphere among my colleagues. Needless to say, I was walking on air. During my time at Newsham I had made a very close friend there, Constable Les McHale.

Les was in his late forties/early fifties and, like myself, he always wanted to be a City bobby but he never made it and, in any case, he was too old now. Les was a real book worm. He studied and studied. I think that he almost knew the current edition of 'Moriartys Police Law' (the Police service 'Bible') from cover to cover, by heart. He was always a thorn in the side of his seniors due to his intimate knowledge of the law and police procedure in general, especially recent legislation as, like me, he took the job very seriously indeed. However, as he was only a park bobby, it was so sad, as all his knowledge and expertise remained untapped and of little use to him as such. He did so wish to be promoted but again, sadly, this was never to be and poor Les was to die suddenly in his middle fifties. Although Les was a frustrated man, I think he saw in my ultimate achievement (being accepted into the regular force) that which had, in his own case, eluded him forever. I looked upon him almost as a 'mentor' as he always tried to channel his knowledge and experience through my work by way of his help and assistance. Although he had a fair number of good arrests, his seniors didn't want to know. To them, he was a 'boat rocker', he 'caused ripples' or, as he was commonly referred to by some of those higher in rank (but inferior in knowledge) in the job, as a 'pain in the arse'. I respected Les very much.

On this particular Monday, Les and I took two hours 'time due' and slid off duty at 9pm. As Les lived nearby, he took me to his local pub for a couple of drinks to celebrate my success. Les was a popular person in his local, almost next to his home in nearby Celt Street. Although many people in the pub were not exactly head over heels in love with the police, Les told every one of his friends in there the reason for our presence that night. Everyone joined in the celebration and, by the time it came for me to leave for my bus home, I was well on the way to becoming well and truly pissed and made my way home on the 'bus and train in a somewhat inebriated state. As it happened, I didn't get ear-ache either when I got home. Obviously, Marje was happy for me too and understood the situation.

I went on duty the following day and met my replacement. He was a young l9 year old constable who assured me that it wouldn't be long before he would be following me into the City Police, just like that! (As it transpired, he never made it.)

On Wednesday, the l0 March l965, I paraded, in uniform, at 6.45am for the last time as a Park bobby. My day was spent with a last patrol with the Sergeant (Capstick), clearing my locker, making sure all pending files were catered for by my colleagues and, in general, drinking tea and nattering.

One Sergeant in particular is worth mentioning, Sergeant Billy Quick, the Parks Training Sergeant. He called in to wish me all the best and promised that he and Les would be there at my passout parade on my big day at Bruche. Again, I received a lot of help and guidance from Bill, another man who willingly gave a lot of his time to help others. The following (and very last) day, I was allowed to go in at 9am in civvies. Sergeant Capstick and I went by 'bus to the stores to hand in my uniform. After this, we had a walk around the City centre. As I intended taking my wife, father and aunt out for a drink and a meal that night, I went to the bank and withdrew the princely sum of £l0-0-0 (more than one week's wages) and certainly more than enough to cater for the evening.

Eventually, Sergeant Capstick said I could go home and he came with me to the underground station (Central) in Ranelagh Street. I said my farewell but promised that I would keep in touch with my pals and colleagues and sincerely thanked him and asked him to convey my thanks to all those who had helped me and had served with me. I felt very emotional indeed, as it was now beginning to dawn on me that my years and years of efforts, even when others were telling me to forget it, were at last going to bear fruit.

Tomorrow, I was, at long last, going to become a 'real' policeman.

Chapter Three - The New Beginning

On Friday, 12 March, 1965, I was up at 6.30 am, washed, shaved and impatiently waiting to board the 8.20am train from West Kirby to Liverpool.

After my train and 'bus journey to Liverpool, I arrived at Police Headquarters and there were the rest of the new 'batch'. We were duly processed and sworn in etc. and this procedure consumed the whole morning. We all had our lunch in the canteen, after which we were taken by police transport to the notorious Liverpool main Bridewell. This was a very old, thickly walled, fortress-like building of seeming Napoleonic vintage, secreted away up a narrow street (Cheapside) in the City centre. This building had housed many very well known members of the criminal fraternity, some spent their last days there before being taken to the scaffold. Many tales could the building tell.

The main entrance to the building consisted of a large, steel barred gate, and on our arrival we were greeted at this gate by a fearsome looking man with black, greasy hair, thick black eyebrows and a thin, black pencil moustache, his shirt sleeves rolled up his thick, hairy arms almost to his armpits, showing his numerous tattoos. The infamous 'Black Jack' Gribbin. One did not need to be police orientated to have heard of him. He was a legend in his own lifetime. the stories that abounded about him were very many indeed, no doubt many had been elaborated upon over the years, enhancing his fearsome reputation in how he dealt with those in need of 'correction' but there was no doubt, even his very appearance would instil fear and foreboding into those who dared to cross him. What a pity there were not some of his ilk today in our present climate of criminal activity. The likes of him would do wonders to some of the disrespectful and 'misunderstood' miscreants who abound in our modern society.

"I suppose you're the new sprogs" was the growl that greeted us from the other side of the steel grille. With a spine chilling rattle of Jack's keys, the gate was unlocked and creaked slowly open. "Through there" Black Jack indicated. Not a smile.

I wished someone would remind him that we were on his side! Even our accompanying Sergeant seemed fearful of him and followed us meekly past the flat capped, smart (and equally fierce looking) Inspector, standing behind the Bridewell counter as if impatiently awaiting the Bridewell's next customer; another 'cry for help from the wilderness' whom society had caused to err! We were taken into the bowels of the building. Some of the cells still had the original iron rings fitted to the walls to restrain the more violent members of our wicked society who, once incarcerated, insisted on still being naughty! The walls were 2 ft thick and were cold and damp. The floors were of stone flags.

The sight, feel and general atmosphere was very sinister and would itself be a certain deterrent to any God fearing, law abiding person. We were told to sit on a long, wooden bench seat in a cell passageway.

Liverpool Main Bridewell Cheapside

Black Jack Gribbin

Opposite this was a room, which in fact were two cells knocked into one. The barred windows embedded high up in the walls and the solitary light bulb protruding from the arched brick ceiling were the room's only form of illumination. Jack left us there, his last growled instruction, "sit there 'til yer name's called" echoed through the corridors. I don't know why, but we sat there talking in whispers. When our voices rose, one of us would say "SHHH', as though to speak or be happy in there would constitute an indictable offence.

Occasionally, we could hear the disenchanted and not very happy utterances of those inmates who were just not pleased to be in there. Someone, somewhere shouted "I know my fucking rights, you can't keep me in here." No doubt this sent Jack scurrying for his keys to go and listen to the prisoner's side of the argument, illustrating his unwillingness to remain until their worships wished to see him in Court.

Eventually, a slim, brown smocked, bespectacled man in his late fifties came round the corner and disappeared into the room. After a few minutes preparing his room, he started to call us in one by one. "Constable Hope", in went Frank. After he was fingerprinted and photographed, he returned to join us on the bench. "Constable Wareham", Ray Wareham then went in to be similarly processed. Eventually, "Constable Turner", good heavens, my new full title! I entered the room and was ushered to a chair situated before a camera mounted on a metal tripod. I sat motionless as I was told and was photographed.

After my photo was taken, I was taken over to a table against the far wall beneath one of the recessed, barred windows. On the table was a heavily ink stained piece of towel, an ink pad and tube of thick, black ink. At the near edge of the table was a short length of 1/2 inch thick copper plate. I was asked to remove my jacket and roll up my shirt sleeves. The man then proceeded to ink the roller on the pad and roll the ink onto the copper plate.   He took my left hand and rolled each of my fingers and thumb, one at a time, on the inked copper pad, then rolled each inked digit in turn onto a large printed form bearing spaces for the imprinting of my finger and thumb tips. This form was folded in a certain way at the edge of the table to enable this to be done. The ink roller was then rolled over the complete palm of my hand from wrist to fingertips, my hand was then in turn rolled over another part of the form, receiving the full print of my hand. The same was done with my other hand. This task completed, I was told to go and wash my hands at the sink in the corner. I then returned to my seat in the corridor to await this while the process was repeated upon the rest of my colleagues.

When we had all been fingerprinted and photographed, we were taken back to Headquarters for what I had waited all these years for, my coveted Liverpool City Police warrant card. A black, folding cardboard wallet bearing the gold embossed words 'POLICE WARRANT CARD' on a simulated black leather skin.

By now, most of the working day had been consumed and we were getting to know each other pretty well. We were all looking forward to

Bruche. The Sergeant told us to report to the canteen and get ourselves a cup of tea. Shortly afterwards, he joined us, telling us to report to the stores at Everton Terrace Police Station the following day to be kitted out with our uniforms and 'appointments' (whistle, truncheon and note book).

With that, he dismissed us for the day.

Going home on the train I was like a kid with a new toy. I kept getting my warrant card out of my pocket to make sure it wasn't all a dream. After dinner, I played with the baby and watched a bit of television then went to bed to await tomorrow.

Saturday morning, I3th March, I arrived at Everton Terrace. This, again, was a very narrow cobbled street, most of the left hand side going up was taken by the large Police Station which incorporated the City Police stores. I arrived at 8.45am for 9 o'clock. This was the standard time to parade for duty, a quarter of an hour before the shift started, (unpaid) and it was a discipline offence to be one second later than the quarter of an hour early mentioned.

The large, burly Bridewell Sergeant (policemen always appeared to be big men in those days) beckoned us through the building to the stores area.

City Police H.Q.

There, we were greeted by a smaller, but older Sergeant and his constable assistant, the former wearing half moon spectacles and a tape measure around his neck. "

Okay you lot, over 'ere" called the balding Stores Sergeant, looking at us over the top of his glasses like an old school ma'am. His

21

tunic breast was adorned with what appeared to be hundreds of medal ribbons covering his large, barrelled chest. We were kitted out with everything except the proverbial kitchen sink. Great coat, 2 mackintoshes, one of which weighed a ton being of thick rubber and canvas material (no amount of rain would ever get through that), our beloved cape, three tunics (one best, one for summer and one for winter), 6 pairs of trousers, summer I, summer 2, best and winter I, 2 and 3. (Woe betide anyone being caught wearing any item at the wrong time of the year.)

The Old City Police Stores Everton Terrace

Shirts (minus collars, pockets and epaulettes) a box of detachable collars (starching for the use of), whistle and chain, truncheon, note book and leather note book wallet, a copy of the 'sacred' 'Moriartys Police Law' (the Policeman's Bible) and other ancillary items. We were given a large paper sack to put in what we could, some were smart enough to have brought large suitcases. I used the paper sack! Once kitted out, we were told that we could go. I remember leaving the building and struggling down the narrow street, with a colleague Frank Hope, until I had to negotiate a steep set of concrete steps to the main road below and make for the 'bus stop. We must have looked like mobile clothes stores. It was one hell of a struggle getting home on public transport. We raised a few eyebrows and caused a few giggles on our way home. However, I didn't give a damn. Frank, a tall, slim lad from the other side of the City, decided he would come home with me that day (including all his kit), and we would have a couple of pints on the Wirral. Frank and I had a few pints in Hoylake before he gathered up his kit from where he'd left it in our flat and made his way back home to Liverpool. We arranged to meet at Lime

Street station and travel to Bruche together by train the following day, Sunday I4 March.

The following day, I met Frank as arranged, there were a number of the 'gang' there also. We travelled to Warrington and from there, we caught a 'bus to the Training Centre at Bruche. We alighted from the 'bus and walked the few hundred yards from the main road to the camp gates. We were all mustered into the main hall and then, after the preliminary speeches of welcome and all the do's and don'ts, we were allocated our various classes and eventually shown to our billets. I was paired off with a lad from Southport Borough, Ian (Jock) Walker. Our billet, 'L' Block (co-incidentally the same as Jock's and my class, 'L' class) consisted of two Nissen huts, joined by a communal front entrance. Going in, our billet was to the left and the other, the women s' billet, was to the right.

Needless to say, those of us allocated to 'L' Block were the envy of the establishment, being nicely tucked away beyond the drill 'square'. I can assure you we were read the riot act regarding the gravity of the heinous 'offence' and its inevitable consequences should any of us dare to wander into the women's quarters. As if any of us would!!?

At first, some of the Sergeants and other instructors took sheer delight in putting the fear of God into those males and females who had never experienced the rigours of iron discipline. They threatened us with what would befall any one of us should we ever be a second late for parade, not come up to scratch at inspections, be caught reading, not in one's bed after lights out (at II pm), and other equally heinous pitfalls for the unwary. Some of the lads and girls were terrified.

There were two drill Sergeants. One, Sergeant 'Andy' Smythe, a man who was soon to convey to us what an efficient and strict drill instructor he was, but also a complete gentleman and an ardent helper to all those who made a genuine effort. He certainly soon endeared himself to all, and won our undivided attention and complete respect.

L Block Billet

23

The other drill instructor was a complete and utter bully, (I think 'bastard' would be a more apt description of the man). Throughout the course he gave those who had difficulty with their lot, one hell of a time. After our formal 'bedding in' I didn't endear myself to the powers that be when I had to inform them that, not only did I have a number of court cases pending in Liverpool which would require my attendance but, I was also due to appear at Liverpool City Magistrates' Court the following morning, Monday the 15th.

Sergeant Smythe was sympathetic and realised that I, the new boy was, to say the least, apprehensive at seeking leave so soon after arriving. He told me not to worry, he would sort things out and let me know what to do shortly. His colleague, the other drill Sergeant asked me, in a very loud voice and in front of all, who the bloody hell did I think I was, asking to be excused my first parade at the start of the course? He made it plain that he was going to keep a bloody eye on me and that I'd better toe the line and watch it. I cursed my having to interrupt my long awaited course so early but there was not a thing I could do about it.

Sergeant Smythe obviously appreciated this but the other Sergeant (who was also the physical training instructor, so I shall call him Sergeant PTi) relished the fact that he'd found someone to pick on so soon. During my evening meal that first day Sergeant Smythe came to the table and said to me, "as soon as you've finished your meal Turner, you can go home, but get back here straight from court tomorrow" I stood up, (one always stood to attention when speaking to an instructor) and thanked him for his assistance with my problem.

The following morning I attended the Liverpool City Juvenile Court to give evidence against a poor, misunderstood cry for help in the wilderness that had fallen off the plank of righteousness into the sea of evil and had been swept away on the tide of nastiness and who needed anointing with the balm of human kindness. The poor mite was found guilty of snatching a 70 year old woman's purse. He was fined £5-0-0 and ordered to pay 25 shillings costs (£1.25), 17 shillings and sixpence of that was for my travelling expenses (87p), to Liverpool and back from Bruche! Although I stood in court and felt 10 feet tall in my new City uniform, nobody noticed the difference due to my regular appearances (the uniform was very similar anyway).

I arrived back at Bruche having missed both lunch and the afternoon's first lecture. Fortunately, the lecture I had missed was all about the course procedure and the issuing of note books, pens etc. so I didn't feel as though I was behind in any way. In any case, Jock was to bring me up to date back at our quarters later on. Jock kept me in touch every time I missed anything due to my court appearances. We helped each other considerably during our studies.

At the evening meal, Sergeant Smythe again came over, "how did your court case go Turner?" Standing up, I replied "very well, thank you Sergeant." The Sergeant then motioned me to sit down and said "well done lad, carry on eating" After dinner, Jock and I did our regular hour or two of study, then to the lounge for a pint where he filled me in with the morning's events and described the 'hassle' all had received on the first parade, from Sergeant PTi. Jock and I finished our drinks and turned in for the night at about 9.30pm.

At II.I0pm that night I was awoken from my sleep by a loud bang on one of the doors along the passage. I nearly jumped out of my skin. "get that bloody light out" screamed the now familiar voice of our 'beloved' Sergeant PTi. "Eleven o'clock walk in the morning, both of you" he went on. II am was the time allocated to defaulters who were to attend the Deputy Commandant's office to learn their fate for whatever misdemeanour that they had the misfortune of being caught perpetrating. "Why doesn't that baldy sod go and fuck himself" grumbled Jock in the darkness, not too happy at being woken so rudely. "Shurrup Jock, he might be outside the door" I whispered. I didn't fancy blotting our copy book for the sake of delighting our bald headed 'friend'.

At 6am the following morning Jock and I were up and to the ablutions for a wash and (cold) shave. Back to our room, dress, then to box our blankets ready for the morning inspection prior to parade. We boxed our blankets and 'nit picked' at each other's uniform whilst the other stood still, then brushed each other down. These jobs done, we stood and awaited inspection. We daren't sit or go near the bed for fear of getting fluff on our uniforms. We awaited inspection with trepidation. We dreaded the 'screaming skull' carrying out the inspection, as he would make damned sure he found something untoward. Whilst we were standing there with our door open, we saw a couple of the WP's next door getting dressed. Goodness grief, how embarrassing! "Look at the bloody tits on her Swasie", said Jock. After five minutes or so, I thought, gawping at my bare-breasted colleague, 'I'm going to have to stop looking in a minute'! This was to happen frequently, last thing at night or first thing in the morning. I started to get worried as I heard that things like that made you go blind!.

At 7am we heard the Sergeant entering the lads' quarters and offering the occasional bit of 'advice' to those unfortunate enough to invoke the Sergeant's displeasure at not having done something correctly. Fortunately, it was Andy Smythe's voice however, (anyone invoking his wrath was soon to get to know Sergeant Smythe was a stickler for everything being correct and would accept nothing less). Any person silly enough to upset 'Andy' usually realised quite quickly that he had done so and the offender usually received the Sergeants sincere terms of endearment and advice, in one. Jock and I received our inspection favourably. Our state of turnout and our room and beds were the subject of Sergeant Smythe's praise. Jock and I had started as we intended to carry on if we could. Sergeant Smythe left with his growl, "don't be late on parade (at 7.40am). He was pleased with us!

The morning parade went okay. Sergeant Smythe was an absolute true professional (ex Guards), striding about, pace stick under his arm, barking out his orders and occasionally asking a not-too-tidy recruit if he had been sleeping out in his uniform. "PARADE, PARAADE

SHUN" he would shout as the senior officers arrived to grace the parade with their presence. "PARAAADE, STAND AT EASE." Sometimes he would continue to a not quick enough police woman, "open your legs woman, you're quite safe here." Those immature enough would grin or giggle at such remarks but heaven help them if they were spotted. "what's so funny officer?" would be the inevitable next line, "Nnnnnothing Sergeant" would be the frightened reply.

After parade, we were dismissed to go to breakfast. I always liked the food there. It was good and those greedy ones of us always had second helpings of one thing or another.

After breakfast it was to our classroom ready for the morning's lectures. We first had to elect a class leader. We chose to elect Sam Fox, a Blackpool Borough man and ex-Army pilot. Sam was a very funny guy and a very able man. He was to prove more than a match for Sergeant PTi's sarcasm. Sam became almost a 'mother hen' to some of the younger, inexperienced element of the class. During our resident Sergeant's absence, he kept the class in order with his non-stop renditions, ditties and anecdotes. He very soon indeed became the brunt of Sergeant PTi's intense dislike.

One rainy start to an afternoon's activities, namely a cross-country run, saw 'L' class lined up in the rain waiting to start our soggy run along the canal bank and over fields before our ultimate return to the fold.

Sergeant 'Andy' Smythe

We were prevented from starting however, due to the non-appearance of one of our somewhat immature members of the class. He was known colloquially as 'Simba' due to a period of time he had spent in Africa. Sergeant PTi was very soon became impatient and, to say the least, irate. He kept looking at his watch and cursing. Eventually, along sauntered Simba as though he had all the time in the world at his disposal. He was very quickly informed that he was on the II o'clock walk the following day. We were soaked before we started. I think it was due to this (as it would appeal to PTi, us getting soaked because of a classmate), that the class itself was saved from communal punishment, as the sight of us all standing there dripping, women and all, would no doubt highly amuse him. The two women we had in our class were Jean Pegg, a very pleasant and friendly young girl and Edie Logan, a warm, matronly woman in her late thirties, married to a police Inspector and a re-join from one of the forces in bonnie Scotland. I think both women were Lancs. County officers. Each was a credit to our class. We all completed the run and after returning, showered and changed back into our uniforms and attended the day's final classroom lecture. Our class instructor was Sergeant Jack Warner of Bolton Borough, a big, strapping late 30 to early 40 year old with a strong Bolton accent. He was a very patient instructor, he needed to be with us, and he devoted a lot of his off-duty time to bringing those slow ones of the class to the level of the others, by giving them 'homework' to do.

Some Fridays, Sergeant Warner would dish out pieces of paper and announce that we were to have a 'slip' test. He would then write a number of questions on the blackboard and announce "right, we'll have a slip test and see who's been paying attention. I'll mark your papers on Monday." The latter remark was guaranteed to really make our weekend! Sometimes, when our instructor was absent or delayed, another instructor would come in to 'mind' us, or Sam would look after the class. It was on one of these occasions that Sergeant PTi entered the room and singled ME out! "TURNER!" I stood up. "Yes Sergeant" I replied, wondering what the hell I had done. "I hear that you're a dab hand in the ring." Boxing and weight-lifting were my two favourite sports. "I've done a bit Sergeant" I replied modestly, wondering how the hell he had found this out. "Right down to the gym at 6.30 tonight in your PT kit" he instructed. He then left the class in the charge of Sam. I was informed that there was a lad from Cheshire County who was a promising ABA boxer and was training for a forthcoming bout at London's Royal Albert Hall.

He was well and truly a prodigy of Sergeant PTi, who used feed him with a continual stream of sparring partners in the gym for his training, some of whom, indeed one of my classmates, a lad named Stenhouse from Lancs County, received a bit of a hiding during which he was given a black eye.

Armed with this knowledge, I nervously attended the gym as instructed and donned a pair of gloves. I was determined that I was not going to be 'ring fodder' and be used as a patsy for this fellow. There were a few of the lads present in various modes of training, and there was Sergeant PTi with his pet thumper. A couple of the lads were put in with Cheshire County s' aspiring champion for a minute or so but I think they were intimidated by his reputation and were subsequently knocked about a bit. Sergeant PTi turned to me, "Okay Turner, in you go" he smirked. I entered the ringed area and squared up. As soon as I heard the dreaded Bong! as PTi hit the bell, I crossed the ring and immediately attacked my opponent before he had chance to set out his stall.

I hit him with two hard left jabs to his body followed by an equally hard right to his face. The latter punch drew a heavy flow of blood from my opponent's nose as he backed off, surprised at the utter ferocity of my attack. Sergeant PTi stepped in and stopped us immediately. "What the hell are you playing at Turner ?, Your only supposed to be sparring!" he screamed, giving me the instant impression that he was vexed at my roughing up his shining light. I was never asked to spar with the lad again, although I did attend the gym throughout my stay at Bruche to indulge in my passion of weightlifting. That night I did not invoke the pleasure of Sergeant PTi that was for sure.

Periodically Sergeant Smythe would organise a stage show, or Ramsammy as they were affectionately referred to. Anyone who cared to volunteer as an act was very much encouraged and appreciated. Some participants sang, played an instrument, juggled, or otherwise entertained in their own various ways, much to the enjoyment of their audience of students, staff and guests. I fancied myself as a stand up comic and impersonator and duly volunteered my services. The first of these Ramsammies took place on the evening of Friday, 19 March. Although I vainly say it myself, I had the audience rolling in the isles as I mimicked some of the instructors, emphasising their individual characteristics. The place fell apart when I took off Sergeant PTi (although he was certainly not amused at the bantered attack on his 'street cred'!). I concluded my act with an impression of the legendary P. J. Proby, including the infamous incident when he split his trousers on stage. I certainly put myself on the course map from then on.

Some evenings, Jock, myself and a couple of classmates, including our two policewomen ,Jean and Edie, would go into Warrington for a drink. We already went into the town twice weekly during lesson times for our swimming training, as at that time the centre did not have a pool of it's own. One day whilst sitting at the dining table eating my evening meal I received a sharp poke in the back. I looked around and saw sergeant PTi standing there. "Haircut, barbers tonight,10 o'clock," he barked. He continued along the tables , ordering a similar fate to others. I wouldn't mind, but my hair was shaved just above my ears as it was, so it was painfully obvious that sergeant PTi was playing silly buggers. Still, I wasn't going to let anyone see that it bothered me. At the time ordered, 10 pm on the dot, I attended and presented myself to the camp barber. " You don't need me son" , he said and waved me away.

Obviously this wasn't the first time that the barber had experienced

PTi's little games. Others there however , didn't fare so well, but some were, like myself, mystified as to why they had been singled out. It didn't bother me as I had experienced sergeants of his ilk before. I sincerely hoped that it had made his day, keeping us from our studies(and bed) for nothing more than his own personal amusement.

In those days most of us recruits didn't have luxuries like a car or phone, but I managed to write home once or twice a week, I certainly looked forward to receiving letters from home, keeping me posted as to the everyday running of the household etc. Another Friday brought another cross-country day ! As usual, prior to our setting off, the class was lined up on the parade ground, in our PT kit, (singlet, shorts and plimsolls). Again the rain was falling, (It nearly always decided to rain when we held our cross-country runs) to add to our discomfort and ensure our eventual cold and wet return to the camp. We were all present, with the exception once again, of 'the late' Simba, yes, the tall, gangly member of Bootle's Borough Force had done the honours yet again and upset the sceaming skull, some people obviously never seemed to learn ! Sergeant PTi finished up dancing with rage. He was Puce! ,We thought that anytime now he was going to have either a 'thrombo' or a miscarriage, or both, Oh Dear ! As the minutes ticked by, the sergeant was beginning to look more and more like a potential candidate for the intensive care unit of Warrington General Hospital, especially when the bold Simba, decide to appear on the horizon, slowly sauntering along completely oblivious to the heavy rain which had by now already reduced us all to wet rags.

Simba also appeared oblivious to the rantings and ravings of the 'skull'. "GET YOUR BLOODY USELESS ARSE OVER HERE THIS MINUTE, NOW!" screamed the near hysterical sergeant, trembling with rage. Simba decided to break into a 'semi' run and joined our sodden ranks.

" THANK YOU FOR DECIDING TO JOIN US AT LAST! , shouted the sergeant, spitting everywhere as he spluttered. Making things worse in all his naivety, Simba innocently , (and foolishly) replied ,"THAT'S ALRIGHT SERGEANT ! " If it were at all possible, there is no doubt whatsoever, that the sergeant would have made an even bigger name for himself by giving birth or miscarrying on the spot! Simba just stood there with a silly grin on his face. That did it! Sergeant PTi screamed hysterically, " Oh, so it's funny arriving late again is it ? " and went on " Well, we'll all join in the fun then. You will all parade here again in full PT kit at 6.30 on Monday morning. That should give you all a laugh! "

That really did make our day. The thought of standing there near naked in the early hours of Monday morning when we would have enough to do getting ourselves and our kit ready for the mornings parade and inspection, just because of one thoughtless and stupid pillock, especially after our weekend leave.

When the opportunity arose, no doubt some of the members of the class, would wish to thank their selfish and inconsiderate classmate for his avoidable indiscretion in one way or another. It seemed however that it was like water of a duck's back trying to chastise Simba. Not a word of regret or apology was forthcoming to his comrades for the unenviable predicament that his lackadaisical attitude had put us all in. Some of the class thought that there the matter rested with Simba, Wrong !

After a pleasant weekends leave the class arrived back at camp early on the Sunday night to prepare our uniform and kit for the following morning , as there wouldn't be much time to spare on the day, as we were due on the parade ground at 6.30 am, and muster parade and inspection was at 7.40 am.

On the Drill Square (Sam Fox leading squad, author 3rd from left)

Oh how we all relished the thought of tomorrow. God bless you Simba! 6.30 am Monday, no rain, but there was a touch of frost, Lovely ! We all made sure that SImba was well and truly on time on this occasion. At 6.55 am the bold sergeant PTi made his appearance.

Donned in full uniform, including his greatcoat and gloves, he strutted along our ranks of shivering men and women, then stood there and addressed us, " Right, now you've had your fun you can all run a couple of circuits around the track." Oh gosh, wasn't this going to be fun. We all started to run along the cinder track. It was here that our class Leader, Sam Fox, was to come into his own, and establish himself as a good leader to his colleagues.

One of our two females was obviously having trouble keeping up with the rest and seemed to be unwell. Sam went to her and asked if she was alright. It transpired that she was having a heavy monthly period and she was near to tears at trying to run, and having to embarrassingly explain the cause of her discomfort. Sam told her to go to her room. He was then called over to the sergeant who enquired what the problem was.

On being told the sergeant shouted to the policewoman to come back, but Sam shouted, " No, you carry on, I'll see to this."

We don't know what went on between Sam and the Sergeant, but we did hear the sergeant shout " II o'clock walk this morning, what's your

'Square Bashing' with Sergeant Smythe

name again lad?" Sam shouted in return " FOX ! sergeant, spelt P-H-O-C_K_S !" and grinned as he resumed his run along the track.

I'm sure that the Sergeant did not even notice Sam's sarcasm in spelling his name as he strode away angrily, but no doubt at the same time pleased that he had secured another victim for the II am defaulters parade.

We finished our run and drifted back to our billets to ready ourselves for the forthcoming parade and inspection, the 'show' over.

The incident concerning Sam and the Skull spread like wildfire throughout the camp and the results of the II 0 am walk were eagerly awaited by all, (including no doubt, some of the staff).

As a result of the furore caused by Simba's misdemeanours, some of the lads were not satisfied that such a 'dick head' should be allowed to get away with it, and so they decided to teach him a lesson that he hopefully would not forget!. After our early morning run we were all about to go on parade in our usual 'mint' condition. Suddenly, as we were walking out of the billet we heard a terrible commotion coming from the ablutions. On returning to see what was wrong, Jock and I saw a few of the lads leaving, and there, in a bath full of water, in full uniform, helmet and all, lay Simba. He was squealing like a little pig, "Look what they've done, look what they've done!". Jock and I helped him out of the bath and he stood there dripping and wailing at what had been (deservedly) meted out to him by his disgruntled colleagues.

31

L Class in classroom

Leaving him to make parade Jock muttered, "perhaps you'll get the fucking message now". We both made our way over to the parade ground to form up into ranks.

Somehow, Simba did make the parade, but he must have took another uniform straight from a suitcase as it was heavily creased and dotted with specks of fluff. He looked just like an unmade bed!. Simba, due to his appearance on parade, made the II o'clock walk without any trouble. He never uttered a word when asked why he had donned the wrong uniform, and nobody else could help, as nobody saw or heard a thing! As for Sam's II o'clock walk ? He was given a mild ticking off by the deputy commandant Mr Dawber for assuming control and daring to pre-empt the situation and go against the Sergeant!. We never knew what, if anything, was said to the Skull!.

We studied hard and had our periodical exams, and after 5 weeks, a new (Junior) intake arrived, elevating ourselves to the promoted status of Intermediates !. Next time, we would become the 'cream; the Seniors!. I had by now established myself as a bit of a personality on the stage and felt quite proud to be in demand for every show by Sergeant Smythe, and other private shows for the staff and their guests. At least this would do me a bit of good if it were to reach the ears of my force back in Liverpool I thought.

My mimicry was by now being honed to a fine art. I had most of the instructors, the camp doctor, the commandant and his deputy really off to a tee. I was pleased to note that they appeared flattered and enjoyed my respectful micky taking. Even the 'Skull' eventually appeared pleased that he was included in my repartee with the others, (in fact it was my portrayal of him that they wanted most of all. It was virtually always assumed that he would be high on my agenda. I found that Sergeant PTi eventually became almost human to me. When Jock and I were busy in our billet studying each evening one of us would go over to the main block and purchase some sandwiches and a drink of pop (alcohol was strictly forbidden in our quarters) as anything stronger would not help our studies, such was the heavy workload of legislation and procedure that we were expected to plough through.

I must admit that due to the close proximity of our female colleagues next door we also regularly did a bit of clandestine study of biology and anatomy, w'hen the opportunities presented themselves!. Many were the times when our studies were diverted due to the curtains not being drawn and strip shows were inadvertently performed.

With the amount of such unofficial study that Jock and I did, there is no doubt we would certainly have gained top marks in any anatomy exams!. One or two of the lads foolishly jeopardised their careers by secretly making illegal nocturnal visits to the girls' quarters next door, obviously for no other reasons than to get to know their female colleagues better!. To my knowledge, nobody was ever caught.

I used to look forward to our weekends when Jock and I would travel to Liverpool by train when I would leave him at Lime Street station and meet him there again on the Sunday evening prior to travelling back. Simba was made to forfeit one of his weekends by being made to perform jankers (fatigues) because of the sloppy way he conducted himself. Sometimes Jock and I met at the Pierhead and travelled back to Warrington by the H5 Crosville bus.

When travelling home, and after leaving Jock at Lime Street on the Saturday, I would board the underground train which would take me under the Mersey to Birkenhead Hamilton Square station where I would be met by my wife. We would cross the road and dine at the well known eating venue of Olivieries. Rough and ready though it was, my wife and I enjoyed many meals in that particular establishment, sadly the premises are no more. They were certainly happy days. The weekend leave did not allow a lot of time at home as we were not dismissed from Bruche until Saturday noon, and we had to be back in camp by 10 pm the following night. We were however, allowed two long weekends when we left Bruche on the Thursday evening and returned next Tuesday morning.

I wrote to my Park Police chums when I had the time, and kept them posted as to my progress, especially Les McHale. I also received letters from Sergeants Quick and Capstick.

On Monday 26 April, one of the Lancashire Constabulary lads, Constable Dilkes, decided that he'd had enough. He said he couldn't take any more and was packing it in. We all tried hard to persuade him to change his mind and see the course through, but he would not be moved and duly left the service. Still, I suppose that it was best to decide then and save the tax payer further expense. I still think that he didn't give it a fair try however, as he left almost before he began. I suppose the saying 'If you can't stand the heat, get out of the kitchen' applies and would be a reasonable epitaph for poor Dilkes's short police career.

The following Friday was another Ramsammy night. I teamed up with a policewoman from Lancs County, Mavis Jackson and together we rehearsed the Peter Sellers routine 'Doctor I'm in trouble " miming it to a record. We went over it again and again until we performed it to perfect timing. We were helped continuously by the show's workaholic manager and producer, Andy Smythe.

On the night of the show I performed my usual mimicry during the first half, and during the second half, Mavis and I performed our Peter Sellers act. I was daubed with brown make up and made to look like an Indian doctor, this went down well because our camp doctor, Doctor Choudry, was himself an Indian. Our successful double act brought the house down. I believe Mavis and I were spoken about long after we had completed our course and left the establishment to return to our respective forces, (the day after the show, Liverpool football team beat Leeds to win the cup.)

On Wednesday, 5 May, I again had to attend at the Liverpool City Magistrates Court to give evidence in one of my previous Park Police cases. In doing so, to my permanent regret, I missed my class being officially photographed for posterity. Although I do have a copy of the photograph it does not have the same sentimentality due to my being excluded from the picture. On Thursday, 20th, our class instructor, Sergeant Warner received the good news that he had passed his own promotion exams enabling him to be eligible for promotion to Inspector rank. We made sure that he stood us all a pint that night. It certainly must have cost him a bob or two by the time he had bought everyone a celebratory drink in the lounge.

It didn't take much to cause the beer to flow. For each qualification or promotion that anyone obtained, it was the 'norm' for him or her to push the boat out'. Whilst I was at Bruche I qualified in First Aid, after which I received the bar to my Royal Lifesaving Bronze medal, I then qualified for the society's Bronze Cross, followed a short time later by the Award of Merit and finally the Instructor's certificate. I was immensely proud to have so qualified for so many awards. These were each christened by the traditional treating of my colleagues to unquenchable quantities of ale! causing acute anaemia to my wallet!.

After again attending court in Liverpool on the 27th I arrived back at Bruche having just missed lunch. I sat and dined solo in the dining hall prior to the afternoons lectures. All the expense of travelling to Liverpool and back for an Indecent Exposure trial, and the defendant , after being found guilty of such exposure to a female, was fined the paltry sum of £5.00. Obviously another sad cry in the wilderness that society should pity!

After our final exams we all anxiously awaited the results. Our exams lasted a couple of days, which included written, practical and oral tests. All were meticulously marked and no quarter was given. When the time came, you either knew it or you didn't!. There were, unfortunately some failures. Some of these were lucky enough to be put back an intake and given another chance, others unfortunately didn't make it.

L Class official photograph (I was at court, so missed it.)

Jock and I passed our exams and the night before our passout parade, the two of us, together with a host of other deliriously happy young men and women, went out and got well and truly inebriated, or, as is more aptly described, pissed as newts!. The day we all had been waiting for finally arrived. Thursday, the l0th of June, the big day! the day of our passout parade.

After breakfast we all donned our best uniforms. Jock and I gave each other one last meticulous brush down before emerging into the sunlight to go on parade. On the square everyone looked resplendent in their immaculate turnout. Each officer's uniform had been double checked by their room mates. Let us hope that all our rehearsals for the parade went well, and nobody made a cock up!

I spotted my wife, dad and Aunt Edie walking towards the parade ground and escorted them to a good seated vantage point at the side of the parade ground next to the Senior Officers and VIP guests' dais. My uniform tunic sleeves and trousers were creased to razor sharp perfection, thickly soaped on the inside so that the wax would hold them stiff, I could almost shave with them. My white cotton gloves were dazzlingly clean, the toe-caps of my boots were polished to mirrors.

What a parade it was. I felt so proud, I was almost moved to tears marching to the sound of the band. We executed our precision drill squad by squad (class by class). Thankfully, nobody put a shiny boot wrong throughout the drill display, not even the amazingly smart Simba?. There was no doubt that his classmates had made sure of his turnout and ensured that he would "gel" on the day!

As they had promised, and true to their word, Sergeant Billy Quick, and Constables Ged Foster and of course my mate, Les McHale from the

Liverpool City Parks Police were there to witness the big event. They hadn't forgotten after all. They were so proud, one would have thought that they were close relatives of mine.

The day was wonderfully sunny and warm and I didn't want it to end. After the parade we were allowed to show our guests around the establishment. Eyebrows were raised when Auntie Edie looked through the window of my room and saw the policewomen in their room opposite!. We finally retired for tea and a snack to the main lounge prior to the staging of a show in the afternoon.

The show proved very successful indeed and again Mavis and I performed our Sellers routine after which I performed my usual mimicry. Everyone had a fabulous day. Each and every one were so proud of their newly qualified Police Officer friend or relative who they had come to see at their moment of triumph.

Eventually, sadly, it was time to say goodbye to Marje, dad and the gang and as soon as they left I turned in for the night, completely shattered but elated. The easy bit was over, now to start justifying myself as a real policeman!

Author with wife Marje on Passing Out Day

We rose at 7-00 am the following morning, our last day at Bruche, being allowed the privilege of a 'lie in" as there was no parade. After breakfast we were all assembled into the main hall for our final address by the Commandant, Mr Ross. Finally, I said goodbye to my many new found friends, some friendships had been formed that would last many years to come, even to the present day. I sadly bade farewell to my class instructor, Sergeant Warner and also to Sergeant Andy Smythe and the other instructors (including the skull!), who, to a man wished all of us every success in our new careers.

We all left the establishment full of pride and elation as we went off to our big cities, and others to their moorlands and shires of the countryside. Now for home and a couple of days well earned rest and lazing about before starting in earnest on Monday next.

With Park Police colleagues after Passing Out Parade.
L to R Sgt Billy Quick author 'Jed' Foster and the late Les McHale

Chapter Four - City Policeman

Monday, 14 June 1965 was the start of my two weeks local procedure course at Mather Avenue. Duties were Monday to Friday, nine to five with the weekends off. We were required to travel to and from duty in full uniform.

The course consisted of (more) lectures, first aid training, swimming, physical training, self defence and cross-country running. We were also given hypothetical and simulated incidents which we were expected to encounter at one time or another during our careers and - EXAMS!

Police Training School Mather Avenue, Liverpool

The course went well during the first week. However, I very nearly came unstuck the following week.

Our weekly pay parade was held on a Wednesday. On Wednesday of the second week I attended pay parade and was handed my sealed wage packet containing (£10-15/-, or £10-75p as it would be now) by the duty officer. Later, as I was entering Central Railway station on my way to catch the train home to West Kirby, I reached into my trouser pocket to retrieve my return ticket. To my horror I felt nothing! My ticket AND my wage packet which should also have been there, were missing. Surely I hadn't suffered the indignity of me, a police officer in full uniform, having my pocket picked? As I was gathering my thoughts as to what I should do next, a woman pushed her way through the homeward bound crowds shouting, "OFFICER! OFFICER! Christ, she meant me!. I wished that

I could have shrivelled up. I wished I could have told her, "Christ love, don't come to me, I'm only in training yet!".

The woman confronted me with, "I've just found this on the pavement outside the station" and handed me a sealed wage packet full of cash, MY wage packet!. being a "highly trained young officer", fresh out of the Police Training academy, and still training locally, I should have known how to deal with (as I had been VERY meticulous on the dreaded subject) of found property. All I could manage to do however, was to stand there like a moron, realising that it was MY pay packet and say, "Thanks love, it's mine!". I then took it from her and rushed to catch my train. I absolutely cringe when I think of the way I completely and blatantly omitted to carry out the rigid and correct procedure when receiving found property from a member of the public.

How utterly open I had left myself to allegations by pocketing the item. I had neglected to obtain the lady's name and address or to present myself at a Police Station. Also. as it was mine, not necessarily hand in the packet, but certainly report the lady's find together with her details, including the date, time and place of the finding, into the station's "found property" book. Once I was comfortably sitting on the train on my way home, the gravity of my failure to conform to the correct procedure dawned on me. Realising what I had (or rather had not) done I pondered, should I say nothing about the incident and hope that the woman wouldn't check to see if the cash had been claimed after the appropriate period had elapsed, or should I report it next morning at Mather Avenue and risk the very real possibility of dismissal, such was the seriousness of my stupid omission of very strict procedures regarding the receiving of found property.

By the time I arrived home I was very worried indeed. I told Marje of the foolish and avoidable predicament I had placed myself in. Although she didn't realise the seriousness of the situation, she didn't hesitate to tell me that honesty must prevail and, as I had nothing to hide (phew!, I'm glad she thought so!) the matter must be duly reported first thing on my arrival at the training school the following morning.

The next day, still in possession of my sealed wage packet, I went to the Superintendent's office and there presented myself to Superintendent Greenham. Mr Greenham listened politely to my tale of woe (or, to put it another way, my story of inefficiency and rank stupidity). As I stood there to attention, he gave me by far the biggest and most humiliating dressing down ever (which I richly deserved!). I started to sweat when he told me that he didn't know whether to send me to the Chief Constable, as, how was he to know that the packet that I had with me was the one that the woman had found and handed to me? Of course I couldn't prove anything. I could now see things through his suspicious policeman's eyes and doubting mind, (an attitude that I was to acquire, and still posses today!). How suspicious things looked.

Eventually, after much thought and deliberation, the Superintendent accepted that I had told the truth about the matter, (he could see that I was really concerned) he looked up at me and said,

"Turner, I'm not at all happy about this. You knew exactly what should have been done when you received the packet from that woman. What's the woman going to think if she tries to claim the cash and is told - Oh, the policeman kept it because it was his!?" Again I could see his justification at making such remarks. How bloody, absolutely, unforgivably stupid I had been. All I could do was to accept that things did look bad and that I had been grossly remiss in dealing with the situation as I was being trained, here at the training school, and previously at Bruche. I sincerely hoped that I could appeal to his better nature regarding his dealing with the matter. The Superintendent, sat there staring at the fingernails of his left hand. He then subjected me to a long and icy stare before saying, "in a nutshell you are a fucking idiot. What are you?" "A fucking idiot sir" I replied. Another pause, then, "get out and join your class. Lets hope she doesn't write in after three months. "(the then period of time before a person was entitled to claim property they had found). That was the conclusion of our "little chat!". I duly (and gratefully) saluted, about turned and marched out, breathing one hell of a sigh of relief. I would NEVER err when dealing with found property throughout the rest of my career, of that there would be no doubt.

I finished my period at Mather Avenue then commenced a period of "inter-departmental" training. This consisted of a further three weeks spent on shifts accompanying colleagues during their various duties. First, I spent some days with the traffic department on both early and late shifts, as crew to mobile traffic patrols. We attended at various incidents such as traffic accidents, fires, domestic disputes and the like. I learned a lot from my more experienced colleagues as to how these matters were dealt with.

During this period, we recruits received our postings. Some were posted out to the sticks at Lawrence Road or Allerton (the posh areas!) in what was then 'F' Division. Others were posted to various other divisions throughout the force area, 'B' Division (Prescot Street), 'C' Division, 'A' Division (City centre). I was posted with Ray Wareham to "Spike Island", 'D' Division, at Rose Hill. This division catered for the notorious Scotland Road area and also covered a number of the city's docks.

During my time spent with the Traffic department I remember my first parade there at Spekeland Street (long since moved to the present site at Smithdown Lane). My day began with Parade at 8.45 am (day duty) and it was still the norm to travel to and from duty in full uniform. I remember well, getting off the train and walking up Ranelagh Street past Lewis'; large department store and on up through the rush hour crowds along Mount Pleasant to the police garage at Spekeland Street. I was hoping to hell that nobody would burden me with any problems en route (AS THERE WERE NO BOBBIES ABOUT!).

Again my turnout was immaculate, it was never to be anything less, nor was my time keeping. After parade I was allocated a patrol and sat in the big black Ford Zodiac alongside my driver. I felt the real McCoy travelling around on mobile patrol from one end of the city to the other.

We had our lunch at the Dog and Gun Police Station in Car Lane East, out in the sticks of Croxteth. This station and others, such as Allerton, Lark Lane, and Hatton Garden, were popular eating places for the traffic crews.

I spent a period with the City Police Hackney Carriage Department (now non-existent). In those days the police were completely responsible for the running of the City's Hackney carriages and the licensing of their drivers. The police were very stringent in the enforcement of the rules and regulations governing such operations, they granted (and revoked) licences to operate as such, what a pity it is not the case today!

Other interesting periods were spent at Headquarters in the Force Information room, CID Headquarters, Fingerprint Department and the force files room where I read the intricate details of some of the most famous crimes and notorious murders, such as the Cameo Cinema murder and other equally enthralling sagas, including photographs and other items. My headquarters period was highly interesting and many of the things that I learned there were always to remain with me. During this local period of familiarisation we were given the weekends off, after which we would go our various ways to our new stations.

Chapter Five - Rose Hill (Spike Island)

Rose Hill Bridewell was a very awesome and impressive looking, large, red brick and sandstone building, as were most of the City's Police Stations. They were built like fortresses. Heavy, thick iron studded timber doors, steel barred windows and stone flagged floors. As the division covered such a rough area of the City the 'esprit de corps' among the men was paramount. Rose Hill Police Station was known throughout the force as "Spike Island". (A book of that name was published many years later referring incorrectly to 'A' division's St. Anne Street Police Station).

Constable Wareham and I arrived at our new station and after the formalities, and introductions to colleagues, senior officers and other members of staff, each of us was placed under the wing of a detective Sergeant, as we were to spend our first two weeks with the CID, prior to joining the ranks of our uniformed section.

Our first day started at 9 am Monday, 26 July 1965 (my seventh wedding anniversary). Ray and I were taken upstairs to meet our new Chief Superintendent, Mr Joe Bodger. At first sight Mr Bodger appeared to be a grumpy individual. He was nearing the end of his police service. However, when I got to know him better, I found him to be a very sincere copper, and kindness itself to a trier. I was to get on well with him (apart from the rare ticking off due to my sometimes over exuberances.) After our meeting with the Chief Super, Ray and I were told to go for the usual cup of tea to the small canteen below, where a CID officer would later collect us.

`On entering the little side passage at the bottom of a flight of stone steps,(well worn by many former generations of the City' s guardians of the peace,) which led down to the vast parade room, we made our way to the little serving hatch at the end and ordered two teas. I knocked on the little counter and a small, stern faced woman in her sixties appeared in her stained white apron, wiping her hands on a cloth. "What d'ya want?" she snapped. "Two teas please" I replied. "You'll 'ave to wait, can't yer see I'm busy" said the grumpy old woman as she turned away and returned to the inner sanctum of her kitchen, amongst her dishes and pans. We had met the fearsome "Aggie" of Spike Island!.

After a quarter of an hour or so we were collected from the canteen by a friendly detective constable, John Edgar, (we never did get our tea!). John introduced himself and took Ray and I up to his CID office and there introduced us both to those of his colleagues that we had not already met. It was obvious that some of them, by their demeanour, resented the intrusion of probationers into their domain.

I was to work with Detective Sergeant Ian Baxter, who was a short (for a bobby!) stocky man, with a black pencil moustache and thick black greasy hair. Ian was an ex-force boxing champion and a very friendly and helpful man. I was to enjoy working with him very much. Ray Wareham was put with another Sergeant. During our short, two week 'stint' with the Rose Hill CID I found that we were tolerated by some and resented by others.

One of the detective constables was well known for being a homosexual. He and another Detective constable thought that they were a couple of Scotland Yard aces, and looked down on us two sprogs as though we were dirt!.

After two weeks with the CID I decided that I would eventually like to become a detective myself. Sergeant Baxter was excellent. I went on numerous jobs with him which included arrests for serious offences such a rape, robbery, theft etc and included the execution of ducks (search warrants bearing the famous Liverpool emblem, the Liver Bird) for the search and (hopefully) recovery of stolen property.

Rose Hill Bridewell (Spike Island)

One morning, in the early hours, I accompanied Sergeant Baxter and Constable Edgar to a house near the City centre, the home of a well known fence (receiver of stolen property). On receipt of Sergeant Baxter's knock we were greeted by a rough looking middle aged man, clad only in his underpants, who asked with the usual pleasantries, "what the fucking hell d'you want?". Sergeant Baxter replied, "you know why we're here Ernie , we've got a warrant to search your house for stolen jewellery". The standard look of hurt disbelief from Ernie was punctuated by the equally standard, "there's fuck all 'ere".

We entered the house and picked our way through the discarded clothing on the downstairs floor and started to search the house. After a thorough search we found nothing incriminating downstairs. We searched drawers, cupboards, boxes and after searching the kitchen also, we made our way up the stairs followed by the now irate Ernie. A female's voice shouted "what the hell's going on Ern ?". Ernie duly informed his wife, "it's the fuckin' busies, they're saying I've got some gear that's pinched". We commenced to search the upstairs rooms and received tirades of abuse as we did so from Ernie, ably assisted by his lady wife, who, by the sound of her oratory, must have come top of the charm school for air hostesses! We eventually entered the bedroom where the woman was. She was still lying in bed, the sheets pulled up to her shoulders. She glared at us and spat out venomously, "you heard what he said, there's fuck all here". Sergeant Baxter said, "there's nothing hidden under there is there? and lifted the covers, "you cheeky bastard!" the woman screeched. "I'm gonna report you" growled Ernie.

Although we didn't find any stolen jewellery we did however find a number of new garden implements hidden in the loft. These were in fact from a recent shop-breaking in the area. As Sergeant Baxter passed the items down to John and I he looked at Ernie and said sarcastically, "the loft insulation needs watering, the lettuce are dying!. We recovered a number of spades, rakes, watering cans and other garden implements.

Ernie was arrested and subsequently fined by the City Magistrates for his momentary lapse in failing to pay for the items obtained after closing ! Once or twice we recovered stolen property during our frequent visits to jewellers, scrap yards and other likely places of disposal. All routine, groundwork policing. Being present during such arrests resulted in my attending court a number of times, including the Liverpool Crown Court, for the more serious offences, such as multi-thousand pound warehouse breaking etc.

On the 5 August, after completing a late shift (3 to II), I was being given a lift to the station to catch my train home by a colleague, Detective Constable Mal Simpson. As we were travelling along Dale Street we saw a man suddenly smash the large display window of Morrows, the gents outfitters. We stopped, got out of the car and ran back to the shop just in time to see the hapless man climb out through the shop as broken display window and into our arms. What an amusing sight it was. There he was wearing three hats on his head with their individual price tags dangling down like an Australian's bush hat. Over his arms were draped a number of expensive suits and a sheepskin coat. Obviously he hadn't realised that the shop was closed and that he should have paid for the items. He had a lot of expensive clothing in his possession and was arrested and charged with shopbreaking.

He was eventually sent to prison by the courts as he had a number of previous, similar, " memory lapses' whilst out shopping at night, or, as they are otherwise, perhaps unfairly referred to, as "similar previous convictions". This was my first, almost solo arrest as a CID officer, albeit only a temporary one. During my CID period I also consumed a fair amount of beer, in keeping with the true traditions of the department!.

Chapter Six - New Constable on the Beat.

On Monday 9 August I started my first day's duty as a uniformed beat Constable. I was posted in Chief Superintendent's orders as Extra, Ist Town Section. My new section Sergeant was John Sankey, Sergeant 7"D". John Sankey was a six foot, well built man with thinning blonde hair and a quiet and soft voice. I was there on parade at 6-45 am ready to go out on foot patrol with my accompanying senior constable, Constable II3"D" Brian McLeod. I was introduced to my section and found that they were a reasonable bunch of lads. I did however, unfortunately experience one or two who were not quite so friendly, as I found that these looked down on recruits for one reason or another (obviously forgetting that they too were once recruits themselves!).

One of those characters was a surly ex-Royal Navy man, who was to say the least, downright rude and he made sure that Ray and I knew that he had no time for us. He would even get up and move to another table in the canteen if a recruit entered and sat at his table. He definitely had an attitude problem. I made sure that I would have as little to do with him and his kind as I could.

My first day went well. It absolutely flew by and in no time Brian and I were back at the station (at dead on 3 pm and no earlier) for Sergeant Sankey to sign us off duty in our note books at the conclusion of our day's duty. The remainder of the week went by with equal speed. During that first week I assisted at a very large warehouse fire. I also had to attend at Mather Avenue training school each Wednesday evening between 6 pm and 9 pm for Probationers class. I was lucky the first week, as my rest days were Friday, Saturday and Sunday.

My second week was night duty, II pm to 7 am the following morning, always parading a quarter of an hour earlier at a quarter to (these I5 minutes were unpaid, and one would commit a disciplinary offence by being late for parade!).

We were still required to travel to and from duty in full uniform, and as I used public transport, it wasn't long before I became involved!. The first time was in fact during this first week of night duty, when I arrested a woman who was drunk in the City centre.

I was leaving Central station to walk to the nearby number three bus stop where I would board the bus and travel the short distance to Rose Hill. As I was leaving the station and walking along Ranelagh Street, a woman who was staggering about the footwalk in front of me suddenly squatted down, lifted her skirt exposing her knickerless posterior and proceeded to urinate onto the pavement in full view of passers by, many of whom were uttering their disgust at the woman's unsocial and drunken behaviour. I had no alternative but to tell her to behave herself and move on. This was silly really as how does one stop a person when they are halfway through relieving themselves ? On being told, the inebriated lady proceeded to shout in her drunken voice "fuck off, I'm having a piss aren't I?" and continued urinating as though I wasn't there. I could see that the late night revellers were waiting to see what was to happen next. I could not ignore the incident and walk on, so I arrested her and took her to the main Bridewell, the City's main place of incarceration for females. It wasn't pleasant walking her through the busy streets, thronged with drunken yobs, baying for the woman's release. Running such a gauntlet, I anticipated an attempt would be made to free her by some enterprising anti-police drunk. Although I anticipated trouble, I managed to make it to the Bridewell without further incident. The woman was held there overnight to facilitate her appearance before their Worships the following morning.

On my arrival at the main Bridewell, I presented my obnoxious and inebriated lady to the duty Inspector. As soon as he saw her, the Inspector sighed and said "Oh No! Not you again Maggie. What's the charge Officer? As if I didn't know!" His constable assistant bent below the counter before reappearing with a large brown paper property envelope in which to place my prisoners' meagre possessions.

"Good evening Sir" I began. "I'm Constable Sixty Nine 'D' Turner, stationed at Rose Hill. I have arrested this woman for being drunk and disorderly. The circumstances are that...". I was rudely interrupted with "I was only having a piss" from my angry female as she banged her left fist onto the Bridewell counter, holding on to it with her other hand to steady herself.

"Quiet Maggie". shouted the Inspector, and turning politely and patiently, added, breathing a long sigh and rolling his eyes to the ceiling 'Carry on Officer'. I resumed my verbal spiel and related the circumstances of the arrest. We were joined by a female wardress and my prisoner was told to go with her to an ante-room to be searched. This procedure was necessary to eliminate the possibility of the prisoner or anyone else being harmed by secreted weapons, and also to ensure that the prisoners property remains in the safe while they are held in detention.

Maggie did not want to be searched and became very aggressive towards the wardress. The constable and the Inspector immediately grabbed my reluctant lady and propelled her to a nearby cell where the necessary search was carried out amid loud protests and abuse. Eventually there was the sound of the heavy cell door being slammed and the three returned to the sanctuary of the charge office.

The Inspector then asked me, "what the hell were you doing in Ranelagh Street Officer?". I informed him that I was on my way to Rose Hill to commence night duty and came across the drunken woman as I was making for my bus. The Bridewell constable, probably a little annoyed because I had interrupted his nocturnal card game, said, "you should have looked the other way you stupid sod!". I requested that my Sergeant be informed at Rose Hill and the Inspector volunteered to do so while I got on with typing my evidence for Maggie's subsequent court appearance the following morning. After completing my evidence and subsequent checks with the Criminal Records Office to establish if there were any outstanding matters regarding my female, as well as completing other administrative procedure, I was eventually able to leave and make my way to Rose Hill.

I arrived at my station and was greeted by Sergeant Sankey. 'So you've met our Maggie have you?" he asked before adding, "you're lucky she didn't smack you in the gob, she usually does!". My "tutor", Constable McLeod had been patiently (and very happily) awaiting my belated arrival down in the canteen with a cup of tea, instead of being out in the wind and rain. After donning my beloved cape (the best item of warm and protective piece of equipment issued) Brian and I made our way out into the night to patrol our beat, making first, for Scotts bakery in Fox Street for a cup of soup from their machine!.

Brian was one of those colleagues who took an interest in his charge and willingly passed on his experience and knowledge. He was a delight to work with, and certainly an asset to the job and those of us who were aspiring young bobbies willing to learn.

Later, during my mid shift meal in the canteen during the early hours, I was subject to a few ribald remarks from the 'anti recruit brigade' those older, more idle, uniform carriers that unfortunately exist, even to this day, who take a delight in ridiculing those of us who take the job seriously. We go out and bring in jobs, and detect and prevent crime while they drink away their time or secrete themselves away out of trouble until it is time to go home. One such officer, referring to my arrest on my way in to duty in town, sarcastically said, "silly sod, getting involved when your 'e not even on duty. You'll learn one day!". Just how else I could have catered for such behaviour when witnessed by all and sundry he didn't say. As my shoulders were broad enough to stand such childish remarks, the remarks fell on stony ground!.

I was happy with my work. I loved the variety each day brought while working from 'Spike Island', especially when I was catching society's felonious deviants!.

One thing I enjoyed while working morning shifts at Rose Hill, was after leaving parade and walking out onto my beat, I would treat myself to the morning 'ritual' and visit Arden House, a large Salvation Army hostel, just off Scotland Road. This establishment not only accommodated long distance lorry drivers, but also the city's homeless and society's drop outs. I would walk along to the place, sneak in through the back door and make my way to the kitchens and tuck into a large bacon and tomato "buttie" and a piping hot mug of tea. What a ritual that was. There's many a generation of bobbies from Spike Island who will remember Arden House with deep affection. What a loss when the beautiful old building was demolished to make way for the new Mersey Tunnel which was to lead through to Wallasey some years later. There were nearly always two or three other bobbies en-route to their beats straight from the morning parade, who would also make a slight detour' to Arden House. Heaven only knows how much we must have cost the 'Sally' Army for those butties and mugs of tea in those days ? I happily plead guilty to my gastronomic sins at Arden House.

Arden House, Scene of many Gastronomic delights.

The Round Counter cafe, Scotland Road Bevington Bush

Another favourite speck was the Roundy !, (the Roundcounter cafe at the Scotland Road junction with Bevington Bush) 300 yards farther on

Whenever we made an arrest on night duty we were allowed to go off at 3 am, as we would have to attend court the same morning to cover the arrest involved. Due to this, no doubt many drunks were locked up on their merry way home from their local hostelry after an evening's embibement to facilitate the welcome "early dart" for the officer concerned. Many a happy night time reveller finished up in the slam to ensure such an early journey home to bed for the bobby. This procedure tended to eliminate the use of initiative by some of the more unscrupulous officers where drunks were concerned, when a friendly escort home would have sufficed, and enhanced relationships!.

From Wednesday, 25 August I was on my own. I was 'flying solo' now. Nobody to hold my hand. As time went on I preferred patrolling my own beat. I went out of my way to get to know as many of my flock as I could. I soon became well known to shop-keepers, local children and the many 'Mary Ellens" who abounded at that time, (Mary Ellen referred to the women of Liverpool who dressed in woollen shawls at the time, and were a common sight on the streets of the City). Due to my large handlebar moustache I soon picked up the name 'Handlebars'. I think that everyone and his dog referred to me by that name from then on.

One such old Mary Ellen I befriended lived in very poor conditions in a first floor 'Scotch Flat' as they were then known, off Great Homer Street. I discovered her whilst I was walking along the landing of the flats to see if all was well with the residents. I saw that the door to one such flat was partly open. I detected the musty smell of acute dampness oozing out from within. I pushed the door further open and looking in I could see into the dimly lit and dingy living room.

Sitting in the far corner of the sparsely furnished room near to a black cast iron fireplace (devoid of a lit fire) was a frail old lady huddled in her proverbial tightly wrapped black shawl. Above the mantelpiece hung a vintage wooden framed oval mirror.

The old 'Scottie' Road

The mantelpiece itself bore an old faded brown photograph, also in a wooden frame, of a young first world war soldier.

I entered the flat and as I did so, what was obviously the old lady's only friend, a large ginger Tom cat, jumped from her lap and walked towards me under the square, wooden topped table bearing a half empty milk bottle, a chipped teapot, an almost empty sugar bowl and a tea cup, minus saucer. A stained teaspoon was on the floor, having been probably dropped by the old girl who couldn't manage to retrieve it. The cat purred loudly as he rubbed himself against my uniform trousers, his tail pointing vertically to the ceiling as he awaited my friendly stroke, (or preferably a boot up the arse!). "Everything alright Ma ?", I asked as I entered her domain. "I'm alright son" came the faint reply.

The flat was tidy but sparse. The smell of dampness abounded. I could see no signs of food. It was cold in that flat also.

I asked the old girl if she was living on her own to which she replied, "aye, I'm all on my own lad. The last of the line. she gave a sigh and looked pensively at the photo of her late husband on the mantelpiece. "I don't half miss 'im" she said. I changed the subject. "Where's the tea then" I asked, looking cheekily at the solitary cup. "I don't think there is any now lad. I think that was the last", she said indicating the chipped, brown teapot now empty on the table. "Let's have a look" I volunteered. I brushed aside the heavy curtain which sealed the room from a very small kitchen which was equally bare. Against the wall was a kitchen cabinet, one of its top two doors minus its frosted glass revealing an empty interior.

The tray was down on which was another spoon, an empty tin tea caddy and a crumpled piece of paper that had once enveloped a block of margarine . Opposite, in the stone sink, was a dirty plate and a knife, alongside a tin lid, which was obviously the cat's plate. "Christ Ma, where's all the food ?" I asked her, I can't find any in here!". There was a rotting half cut cabbage and a couple of old potatoes in a cardboard box beneath the sink's U bend pipe. I returned to her and told her, "I won't be a minute Ma" and went to one of the barrow women on Great Homer Street, Hannah Howard , to buy some items from her barrow for the old girl and some groceries and a loaf from a shop on the corner. I returned to the old lady and put the items of food from Hannah into the cardboard box and the bread, butter and groceries, which included tea and milk, into her cabinet. I found the matches , lit the gas stove and boiled a kettle of water. Finding another (cracked) cup I washed this and the cup from the table and made a fresh pot of tea. As I joined the old girl I said, "here Ma, have this" and gave her a big black plum from a paper bag full that Hannah had given me as I was leaving her. I made her a jam 'buttie' and together we sat down and had a cuppa.

The old girl gave me a right ear bashing for going and buying the few measly items of food for her. "Why isn't the fire lit Ma? I asked. "'Coz I've got no coal" she replied. As she looked in the direction of the empty fireplace she pointed to the photograph on the shiny black mantelpiece. 'That's my husband" she said proudly. "He's been dead eight years and

50

I still don't half miss him" she added. I felt bloody sorry for her. Tomorrow I'd have that fire lit for her and have some coal in the place.

I eventually left her and resumed my beat. There were lots and lots of lonely old people in the same predicament as my new found friend, cold and hungry and living alone. I certainly would do my best for any similar people should I come across them. What annoyed me however, was that many of them had close relatives, sisters, brothers, sons, daughters, many of whom just couldn't give a damn.

The following day I rooted out a coal delivery lorry on my beat. I put my best 'bumming' act on and asked the driver if he could do me a favour and "drop a bit of coal off at ....". "Your'e alright mate, I'll drop her some off later" I was promised. I told the driver how grateful I was and how much it would surely be appreciated. He wouldn't take any money from me. 'I'll fill a couple of buckets by brushing the deck" he said. That'll do me I thought.

When I called at the old lady's later, I saw that, in the kitchen the coalman, true to his word, had left a half full sack of coal on the floor by the sink, next to my box of 'goodies'. In no time I had a nice fire lit, the heavy roar echoing through the room as I held a copy of the Liverpool Echo across the bars to draw the fire. "Your'e a good lad son", the old girl muttered gratefully, "but you shouldn't be doing this".

I continued visiting my new 'girlfriend' regularly dropping bits and bobs in for her. Sometimes on my rest day, my wife and I would go over to Rose Hill on the train for my wages. On such excursions we would go and see if the old lady was okay. "You've got a good 'un there" the old lady once told Marje. I don't know if my wife agreed or not, perhaps Marje thought that the old lady was becoming prematurely senile by uttering such comments about her husband?

My work load of summonses were getting quite heavy. Sergeant Sankey's hair was no doubt prematurely greying each time he set eyes on his increasingly heavy 'cases pending' tray, which contained mostly, MY 'jobs'.

There were occasions when he would 'keep me in' and ensure that I spent a whole day getting the typing down to a reasonable level (as well as allowing his hair to colour again). "Christ Swasie, slow down a bit will you" were his comments. Sergeant Sankey caught me 'red handed' one morning. I was walking up Dryden Street en route to the old lady's to see how she was getting on. I was carrying a string bag containing one or two items for her. Obviously I didn't walk along the main road carrying such things but, nipping up a side street I thought I would be away from prying eyes. Trust the Sergeant to be looking for me just then, and, coincidentally walking down Dryden Street. 'What the bloody hell's this ?" he asked angrily. I told him where I was off to and why. "You don't want to start this" he said, "There's a difference between looking after your beat and buying half of bloody Liverpool for them!" He was absolutely right of course but I had taken to the old girl and took a lot of pleasure in 'seeing that she was alright'. "I don't want to see you walking through the streets like a benevolent bloody Santa Claus again' warned my Sergeant. I realised that of course he was right and took the message as read. I intended to be more discreet in future. Anyway, point taken.

I joined the force concert party. This organisation was run by men and women of all ranks and catered for the entertaining of old age pensioners, sick children and any other charitable cause which had been brought to the attention of the Concert Party's powers that be. Together with the Liverpool Police band, the concert party was well known and raised quite a lot of money for various charities. I resumed my 'Bruche' act of stand up comic and impersonator. We used to meet and rehearse in the officers' dining room at Central Police Headquarters, Hope Street. A prominent member of the organising side of things was a constable Ronnie Irving, a tireless individual who spent many of his off duty hours in locating (and subsequently performing for) many local forms of the establishment. We performed at many venues, such as the David Lewis Theatre, Liverpool's Crane Theatre, hospitals, old peoples' homes, orphanages and many other such deserving venues. Most of the time each of us spent involved at these performances was in fact our own time, sometimes we were granted 'facilities' in the 'firms' time but most of the time we gave was our own, and we were all very happy to so do. Our reward?, the only reward we cherished. 'The happy, smiling, appreciative faces of our audiences, young and old.

I was also now being 'booked' for the force's individual functions, Divisional Christmas parties, CID parties, Promotion 'dos', I liked these, I was always happy with free food, and plenty of free booze. Eventually it was to become the 'norm' to 'get Swasie for the Do'. I was to have many free dinners and free ale in the forthcoming years as a 'performer' for the lads.

One day, dad accompanied me to Liverpool for my wages. After collecting these, and calling for a cuppa to the old girl's, dad and I decided on a bit of a 'pub crawl' and 'have a few pints and a good old Scouse pie. We started at the Rossy', (the Roscommon pub) and after visiting a few more 'places of imbibement, we finally surfaced at the Liverpool City Police Club, Fairfield, on Prescot Road. By now dad and I were quite merry and our financial resources somewhat depleted. Dad decided to invest a tanner (sixpenny piece, two and a half pence now) by feeding one of the clubs two one-arm bandits. Would you believe it?, he won the jackpot, (about £10), then, after feeding the other bandit some minutes later, he touched for the jackpot from that too. Twenty quid, we were absolutely loaded. nearly two weeks wages in near enough half an hour. We were now millionaires. I damn near had to use a block and tackle to help dad onto the rear platform of the bus outside the club when we left for home (pleasantly pissed as the saying goes:) The pockets of dad's mac were nearly ruptured by the weight of coins he was carrying. what a day (and night) that was.

Our section at Rose Hill boasted another Sergeant, Jack Kitto. Sergeant Kitto would accompany new officers on their beat and would subject the bobby to continual hypothetical questions. I was 'caught' regularly by Jack, and as we walked along he would invent an incident and then ask me what I would do to cater for such an incident. I was asked to quote Acts of Parliament and sections of the Act appertaining to the 'incident'. I would be asked for definitions of various offences. At first I used to dread being 'captured' by Sergeant Kitto, but as time went on and I was to get to know him better, I realised that his bark was worse than his bite, and he was in fact a very decent fellow who was trying to assist his recruits to better their knowledge. I must admit that it did assist me and I became very adapt at reciting definitions to him.

At the top end of Scotland Road, a mile or so from Rose Hill, was a little cobbled street called Athol Street. Situated halfway down on the right hand side was another little fortress, Athol Street Bridewell, this station was a favourite for a cuppa when we used to collect our white coats for our school crossings or point duty. We would return our coats afterwards and have a natter with the 'B.P.'(Bridewell Patrol or Station Officer). Athol Street was a haven when we had a fighting drunk so far from Rose Hill at the top end of 'Scottie'.

Similarly there was another bastion of incarceration on the 'bottom ground' near to the docks, Esk Street Bridewell. This station was situate off the main Derby Road, over the border in 'E' Division. On entering this particular building one walked through a little courtyard and into the station. Walking in with a prisoner we would stand before the Sergeant in a little 'dock' just like those in a courtroom. Again, Esk Street was a boon when one had a 'naughty' prisoner down there. All three of these fine, soundly constructed buildings are no longer in being, another loss to our heritage!. The foreboding appearance of the buildings themselves no doubt acted as a deterrent to some and maybe even encouraged some onto the 'straight and narrow' to avoid being taken there.

I called in to see my Park Police pals as often as I could. Unfortunately, due to a few members of the force considering themselves far above, and completely out of touch with the Parks Police, we did not (each organisation) enjoy a very happy relationship with each other, which was very sad. Park Bobbies were looked upon as 'inferior beings' by some of my City Police colleagues, EXCEPT in my presence " .

As I was walking along Great Homer Street one very wet, cold and windy afternoon, I decided to call at the old girl's flat. Ten minutes or so out of the sleet, a nice cuppa and a chat would warm the cockles of my heart before continuing getting wet for the rest of the evening. When I arrived at the flat I saw that the door was closed tight. Very unusual. I pushed the door. It wouldn't open. I pushed again, no, it wouldn't move. "Are you there Ma? I shouted. There was no response. I knew that she must be in there as she could barely get about."Ma, are you alright?" I shouted. Again, no response. There was something wrong.

I stood back then booted the door. It wouldn't move. Again I put my boot to the door, it moved slightly. I stood back again, this time I put my shoulder to the door. It moved a couple of feet, but there was something stopping it opening. I gave the door one more almighty heave and this time I moved it sufficiently to squeeze inside. There, behind the door the

Athol Street Bridewell

Esk Street Bridewell

old girl lay, dead. Her beloved cat was lying by her meowing pitifully as if trying to tell me tearfully what I was by now painfully aware.

She had obviously been dead for some time as she was absolutely stone cold. I lifted her woollen shawl and saw beneath her tatty old cotton blouse that she was wrapped in newspapers for extra warmth, (a common practice among old people, I regularly discovered over the ensuing years). Bloody Hell, would you believe it ?, I didn't even know her name.

After I had informed the various authorities and departments, I awaited the arrival of the doctor and eventually supervised her removal to the City mortuary and arranged for the safe storage of her few pitiful possessions,.

I returned to Rose Hill to complete the paper formalities and other procedural activities. The last thing that I placed into a paper property envelope at her house was her treasured photo of her husband which had taken pride of place on her mantelpiece.

Unfortunately, tragedies such as this were not an uncommon part of a policemans 'lot'. I was determined not to allow myself to become involved to such a similar degree again, although I didn't regret having done so on this occasion.

The Old Scotland Road in the 60's

We now had another Sergeant posted to our section. At first he seemed decent enough. To look at, he resembled the well known cartoon Stone-Age character, Barney Rubble of the television series, the Flintstones. He was instantly christened Barney Rubble by the section the moment that he arrived. He was very untidy, his uniform resembled an unmade bed, his trousers looked as though they had been ironed on

55

a corrugated ironing board, or over an accordion. He was to smartness what chocolate was to fireguard manufacture!

Our new Sergeant tried hard to be 'one of the boys' and in doing so, his familiarity bred constant mickey taking and undue contempt from the lads who, because of his scruffy appearance, had little respect for him. It was not uncommon for him to parade for duty unshaven. Some treated him so disrespectfully at times that it was quite embarrassing. His boots looked as though they had been polished with a pumice stone. When dining in the canteen he nearly always finished up 'wearing' bits of his meal on his lapels or tie. The lads didn't require a menu, they would just 'read' his clothes.

My progress reports were going well. I appeared to be performing my job satisfactorily. My arrest rate was becoming quite impressive. Some of my colleagues christened me 'One a day Turner'. I must admit, I enjoyed my notoriety. I used to creep along back entries ('Jiggers' as they were referred to in Liverpool) or hide in shop doorways, waiting to see if I could catch any potential thieves or burglars. Many times (as it did in the parks) my endeavours bore fruit and I successfully apprehended many villains for various offences. Because of this, I became well known to many advocates, some of whom appeared to take it quite personally when I had the audacity to have their 'innocent' client before the court yet again. Indeed, I was even accused in court by one such barrister of 'having a vendetta against the criminal fraternity', Although yes, I was, (and still am, very much !) guilty of being so.

Some of the 'defences' or mitigation put forward by these, educated, welfare orientated (to their clients, NOT their victims!) defenders, were absolutely unbelievable. "My client has never had a nice new bicycle of his own, that is why he stole the complainants cycle. He only resorted to violence because he (the victim) wouldn't let him have it!

"The old lady's hip would not have been broken if she had let go of her handbag". Please don't impose a prison sentence my Lord, my client's very timid and the other prisoners may attack him" after one such 'client' had sexually abused a three year old boy.

On many occasions, the cross examination of the police or other prosecution witnesses took on a very personal tone. I remember one Crown Court trial where I was the arresting officer, I was accused of 'NOT USING INITIATIVE' because I didn't give the poor, misunderstood yob another chance, as due to his persistent participation in crime, plus his previous bad record of assaults, burglary and theft, when I caught him stealing four cucumbers from the Williamson Square fruit market, it was only 'petty' and it would be obvious to me that he ran a very high risk of a custodial sentence. Surely therefore could I not have made him "Just put the items back and give him another chance? My immediate reply was of course, an emphatic "NO" Many have been the times where I have been portrayed as the 'Villain' for "risking the liberty of my client" due to my persistent obsession for the taking of felons from the streets". Again, I plead an emphatic 'Guilty'. After arresting a very drunk bread delivery van driver when he almost fell out of his vehicle as he was about to drive away from a public house during the Christmas period, I was portrayed by the man's barrister at the Crown Court as "A large sinister black spider, dangling over the city waiting to pounce on any unsuspecting 'fly' that had consumed alcohol. Surely I could have just cautioned him as it was Christmas time". Perhaps people aren't as dead when they are killed by drunk drivers at that time. I really must get a grip of things and stop getting bad people prosecuted, no wonder the courts are so busy!

This particular driver had staggered from a public house at ten o'clock absolutely paralytic. He and his van boy eventually managed to unlock the doors of the vehicle and get into the cab. With considerable difficulty he managed to start the vehicle but he had forgotten to close the driver's door. Fortunately the vehicle stalled, as the driver, in attempting to close the door, almost fell from the vehicle. I witnessed all of this from across the road and by the time I eventually reached the vehicle the driver was attempting to re- start his vehicle. I went to the driver's still unclosed door. The powerful reek of beer greeted my unwelcome arrival. The driver couldn't even focus his eyes properly. "Get out - Now" I ordered. "Are 'ey boss, ish Krishmush" the hapless driver offered. "out "' I again ordered. The driver alighted from the vehicle and almost fell into my arms. he was absolutely stoned. I removed the keys from the ignition and duly arrested him without further ado. I took him the short distance along the road to Rose Hill Police Station and placed him in custody. Dr. Morrie Kirwan was sent for and attended. On the Doctor's arrival he obtained a sample of blood from the defendant. At the time of the arrest, the van boy, a lad of sixteen or so, became abusive and strongly disputed the authenticity of my parents' marriage certificate. However, being a young lad having consumed a pint or two of 'dutch courage' and obviously trying to be loyal to his mate, I overlooked his behaviour and advised him to take my advice as it would definitely be in his own interests if he were to desist in his abuse of me and proceed to make his way home and await the arrival of Father Christmas. He accepted my advice and left me with my very drunk driver.

After his elected Crown Court trial, when he was subsequently found guilty, heavily fined and disqualified from driving for twelve months he was leaving the court building when he spotted me outside. "Satisfied Now? You've cost me my job you bastard" he screamed, "I hope you rot in hell". Right away I knew that he wasn't happy with me at all. Perhaps it was all my fault that he had put himself in such a vulnerable plight that fateful night! Perhaps I should have been more tolerant as his counsel suggested and, seeing as it was Christmas, allowed him to drive off and, hopefully, reach home without having killed someone. I really shouldn't be so heartless, especially at Yuletide.

The days and nights wore on. I was getting to know my patch, it's people and also my colleagues. During the daytime I always called in to the shops to see if all was okay, and to let the local populace see for themselves what they were paying their rates for. I was now also starting to 'sus out' who was who amongst my colleagues.

My eyes were well and truly opened during one of my night shifts.

I was on foot patrol walking alongside what was then the Cazneau Street fruit and vegetable market of the City. It was about three o clock in the morning. All was very quiet. Stacked against the wall of the market along its Cazneau Street length were sacks of farm produce ready for the market to open at around five o clock, when business would commence. Sacks of potatoes, carrots, cabbages, sprouts, and all kinds of fruit had been delivered and stacked by the various wholesale suppliers earlier on, waiting to be taken inside when the gates were opened later.

Cazneau Street was a poorly lit, wide, cobbled street. The market on one side and various business and storage premises on the other. The street still had the old cast iron 'gas type' street lamps (which were in fact electrically illuminated).

Fruit Market Cazneau Street, circa 1949

As I turned into the Street from Great Homer Street I heard the sound of a vehicle's engine coming from further up the street on the market side. Although it was dark I could make out a vehicle parked against the wall of the market further along the street, in the dark patch between street lights.

The vehicle was not displaying its lights. I knew it was too early for the market staff so I tucked myself into the shadow of the high boundary wall of the market premises and crept towards the vehicle. As I got nearer to the vehicle I heard familiar voices from by the vehicle which I now could distinguish as being that of Rose Hill's Landrover (in actual fact it was a Austin Gypsy referred to as the Landrover or Jeep).

I walked up to the vehicle and recognised two of my colleagues, one a recruit . They were loading sacks of vegetables and fruit into the back of the vehicle. I recognised another colleague sitting in the driver's seat. The latter turned round on my arrival. "'What's going on here?' I naively and quite unsuspectingly asked. The driver said, "You haven't seen us here Swas". The two bobbies who had been loading the vehicle then got into the rear alongside the sacks, closed the rear door and the vehicle started up and drove off.

I made my way to Rose Hill for my belated refreshments. On my arrival at the station I went to a Sergeant and told him what I had seen a short time earlier in Cazneau Street. The Sergeant (now deceased) said, "It's one of the perks, you'll get some if you want some". . I told him that I wanted no such part of any 'perk' and I told him that I felt compromised with having such activity take place on my beat. "Keep your fucking eyes shut" said the Sergeant.

When I later mentioned this incident to a fellow constable of some years service whom I trusted, I was informed that this practice had been going on for years and was only 'minor' compared to some of the things that happened. I couldn't believe it. What the hell was I to do, being a brand new bobby, 'straight out of the box? That is a raw recruit, straight out of the box of new policemen. I reluctantly let the matter rest, as I wasn't sure who was 'at it' and who wasn't.

On another occasion at the same venue during a night shift I saw two bobbies, (one of them being the recruit) doing the same thing again, except that they were using one of their own vehicles for the purpose. As we were going off duty from that particular night shift I went to the recruit as he was about to drive home. I voiced my concern and considerable displeasure at what he was up to he was by now, obviously one of the 'clique'. I was spoken to by other officers during my next tour of duty, who included the previously mentioned Sergeant.

This time I was 'warned' to keep my "eyes and trap shut", otherwise there would be "gear found" in my locker. By 'Gear found ' I mean that property of an incriminating nature which could discredit and or compromise me. Word had got around the one or two unsavoury members of the shift who partook in such activities that they were not to let me see or hear anything untoward as I couldn't be trusted. I was therefore very wary of some of my fellow officers and decided to keep myself to myself as much as I could, bearing in mind however, that we may all need each other at some time or another as ours was a very dependable service in times of crisis or when dealing with 'sticky' situations. If I were to completely disassociate myself altogether I could well end up putting myself in a very precarious position. I decided to just not to get involved and steer very clear of such distasteful and dishonest carryings on.

Being a bobby on the beat let us not forget that it is he who is the 'backbone' of the service and the 'first line' of approach by Mr and Mrs Public. The beat officer is expected to deal with anything from childbirth, a major traffic accident, murder, rape, the loss of little Johnny's bike, or even a major incident and is expected to know the law when called upon for legal advice. Not like some lawyers(but not all) who can sit and contemplate their navel whilst picking their nose or reaching for a G and

T from his big plush leather high chair in his comfortable 9 to 5 office or perusing Stones Justices manual in the security of the courtroom. The bobby has very many incidents of a large variety that he could be called to deal with and sometimes make a very important instant decision. One which could very easily make or break him.

One day a very irate woman walked into Rose Hill Police Station dragging her cherubic little offspring of a son. She demanded that someone give the lad a "Bloody good hiding". Apparently the young terror had gathered all his dad's jerseys, pullovers and some shirts, his mother's cardigans and the baby sister's woollen cot blankets and shawls and happily took them to the local rag and bone man who equally happily supplied the little mite with a goldfish in a little plastic bag of water. Oh! she was so thrilled at her son's initiative. It was with considerable difficulty that the Bridewell Sergeant and those others of us present at the time could maintain a serious and sympathetic look on our faces for the poor woman. To keep the woman's trust and keep her happy the Sergeant admonished the child to tears. "That'll teach yer, yer little bastard. All for a bloody goldfish". She thanked us and dragged the by now hapless little bugger out of the building. Another satisfied 'customer', no doubt taking him home to a hiding from his father.

As I paraded for afternoon duty one Saturday I was told that I was to patrol with a new recruit who had just arrived onto the Section. Blimey, the blind leading the blind . I must be well thought of to be given a recruit to take out under my wing '. As we lined up on parade I was quite proud to think of myself as being a 'tutor' constable. Barney Rubble the Sergeant, (still wearing yesterday's menu on his left lapel) handed out the various files and documents for the officers in charge to complete or perform whatever duty the documents required. On reaching me the Sergeant instructed me to leave the parade and go immediately to Athol Street, where a double 'sudden death' had occurred.

I took my new 'charge' and left the building. We both jumped aboard a passing number 3 'bus which would drop us at the top of Athol Street, about I mile along Scotland road. The words of the Sergeant were, 'You take the new lad, Stellafox. there's been a sudden death at _____ Athol Street". ME take the new lad! I was still virtually a new lad myself. Wondering what was to greet us I asked my colleague if he had seen a dead body before. I tried to appear 'matter of fact' and casual as though I had dealt with such cases on a regular basis! "Oh hell aye, I saw loads when I was in the Andrew" (the Royal Navy) he cockily replied. I must admit, I was mystified as to why sailors served their time as 'morticians', still, ours not to reason why!

The scene of the tragedy was a first floor flat. The flat was meticulously clean, indicating the immense pride taken by the occupants in keeping it so. Tastefully decorated, thickly carpeted with pictures and ornaments adorning the walls. The occupants were in fact a mother and daughter.

Both ladies worked at the nearby 'Tate and Lyle factory. As we arrived at the block of flats we saw that quite a large crowd of people had gathered outside in the street blocking the pavement. An ambulance was parked at the kerb, both it's rear doors wide open and one of it's crew standing by awaiting our arrival. "Come away Freddie and behave yourself, show some respect" yelled a woman to her mischievous little 'tinker' of a son who was gawping into the ambulance and generally making a nuisance of his little self. "Ey up! 'Ere's the bobby now" she added, fruitlessly hoping that the added threat would have the desired effect. It didn' t. The police had arrived , (Two probationer constables), so all would be looked after and efficiently dealt with now!! thought the gathered throng. "What's up, Mary?" a woman asked loudly and indiscreetly. "I think someone's dead" "'Mary' authoritatively answered. "Who is it?" was the next question "Dunno, someone in the flats" said 'Mary'.

Stellafox and I climbed the steps up to the landing and made our way along to the flat concerned. The other member of the ambulance crew awaited us at the open door of the premises. On entering I detected a strong sickly smell of gas. The ambulanceman had already opened all of the windows of the flat. I told Stellafox not to allow anyone to enter (unless of course it was established that it was a relative) and to make sure that nobody activated any electrical switches in the flat. I entered the bedroom.

There, lying on the floor was the body of a young woman of approximately 20 years. She was clad only in her nightdress and was lying on her back near to the window. Lying in the bed, was an older, middle aged, woman. What a tragic, sad, sight it was. what a pitiful waste of life.

It was obvious by the position in which the girl lay on the floor near the window, that she had attempted to open the window but must have succumbed to the fumes and suffocated before she could do so and fell onto her back. I saw that underneath the window was a central heating radiator which was duly established to have been leaking gas into the room while the two ladies were sleeping). I was joined by Stellafox after he had summoned the various departments ie, Gas Board, Police Surgeon, and Fire Brigade to attend. As I was required to remove the young lady's necklace and earrings for safe keeping, I asked my colleague to hold the young lady's head while I did so. As I removed her earrings I tilted her head to one side and her mouth dribbled onto Stellafox's hand. he looked at his hand, his eyes rolled, and he then fainted. Spark out. Just as this happened a distraught relative decided to put in an appearance.   How bloody embarrassing. So much for his service in the 'Andrew'.

Once the formalities had been carried out, the bodies were eventually removed to the City Mortuary and the premises secured. Stellafox and I returned to Rose Hill to complete the required paperwork, after which we resumed our beat patrol. It would be a long time before my mate would be so cocky again.

Sometimes, when patrolling one's beat during darkness, an unsuspecting bobby could be subject to various pranks by his colleagues.

61

In the early hours of one morning I was diligently sleuthing' along a deathly silent Great Homer Street, 'milking' shop door handles (checking the properties) when I heard a loud bang from behind me. I damn near jumped right out of my skin. I looked around me. Not a soul in sight, but a pram wheel came careering towards me, bouncing up the pavement and striking a lamp post before spinning to an eventual stop back in the centre of the road. (and there wasn't a toilet in sight!) I stood there wondering where the hell the wheel had come from. It was not uncommon for buckets of ash, bricks or even an old television set to be thrown down at you from some of the flats as you passed). Eventually a voice shouted~ "I bet you shit yourself then didn't you Swas?". It was the bobby on the adjacent beat, who, hiding in a 'jigger' (entry) had decided to have a little fun at my expense and had thrown the wheel to frighten me. Gosh, I was absolutely beside myself with hilarity!

Along Great Homer Street was a Greek fish and chip shop. Time and time again I had requested the proprietors to switch on the lights of his parked vehicle during the night when it was left outside his shop. He continually ignored my requests so I resorted to reporting him for summons. He was summoned and fined on a number of occasions. However, he still would not bother to comply with the law. One of my Sergeants was so fed up with this man's repeated contempt for the law that during one night shift, we were walking past the offender's shop in the early hours when the Sergeant said, "Right, bollocks to this. He's going to have to learn to do as he is told". He made sure that nobody was about then proceeded to remove the valve core from all four of the vehicle's tyres and deflated them before replacing the valve cores. "That should cure the bastard" said my Sergeant. (As it happened, it must have done, because the vehicle was either illuminated or removed during the night time after that. Justice must have eventually been done?)

The entrance of the Mersey Tunnel was quite near to Rose Hill and with me living on the Wirral and sometimes travelling to work via the tunnel with colleagues, I soon befriended a number of the Tunnel Police officers. What a great bunch of lads they were. They were always extremely helpful and would always be more than willing to transport me through the tunnel should I so require. Many a Birkenhead or Liverpool bobby had cause to be grateful to the officers of the Mersey Tunnel Police, for having been given a lift through as well as the occassional tow when our vehicles broke down. . I personally have been very grateful on occasions when, after having been delayed due to making an arrest, or due to some other incident, a kindly officer has given me a lift through, sometimes straight home to my door. I still keep in touch with a number of Tunnel colleagues to this day, some thirty years later. One such old friendship started at that time when Bill Atkins was a young Tunnel bobby, Bill is now the Superintendent in charge of the Tunnel Police Force.

Once, after completing a morning duty I was walking towards James Street station to catch my train home to West Kirby. As I was passing a number of people in a 'bus queue near to the station, I saw that one man standing in the queue had a cement bag at his feet. Protruding from the dirty paper bag, were a number of copper pipes and some lead. I was in full uniform at the time. "Can I have a word with you Mate ? I whispered into his ear. He left the queue and out of earshot, I asked him what it was he had in the bag. "Just some bluey" (Scrap lead) and copper" he replied. I asked him where he had got it from. "I took it from the Town Hall, I work there" the by now very nervous man replied. I asked him if he had been given permission to take the metal, "Not really, but it's only scrap, I thought I'd weight it in for a few bob" he went on. I asked him to accompany me back to the Town Hall, which was a matter of a few hundred yards away from the 'bus stop. He picked up his bag and we set off back to the Town Hall at the end of Castle Street. He took me to a side entrance where we entered and descended a flight of steps.

We went into a room and there was a very large, portly, A Division bobby sitting at a bench table, helmet off and consuming a large mug of tea. "I'm in it now Gerry " my unfortunate possessor of the metal muttered to the officer. The officer turned to me and asked "What's up Officer ?" I informed him of the reason for our return to the Town Hall and my A Division colleague explained that, although he wanted nothing to do with my visit, it wasn't uncommon for workmen employed at the Town Hall to 'remove' any surplus metal to weigh in at local scrap yards. "Yes of course it's illegal," my colleague went on, "but we turn a blind eye. It's up to you what you do now you've brought him here". I was not prepared to overlook the matter and I summoned a van to take my prisoner and I to the main Bridewell after obtaining a statement under caution in which the man admitted stealing the metal, knowing he had no right to take it. I took the man to the main Bridewell where he was charged with the offence. He subsequently appeared before the city magistrates the following morning and was fined £15.

I arrived home three hours late on the day of the arrest and this time was reimbursed as 'time due'.

I was walking past the same spot again from morning duty one Saturday and as I passed the large oak doors of the Scottish Insurance building adjacent to the same bus stop I heard a female voice crying for help. I stopped, there it was again, I realised that the voice was coming from behind the doors of the insurance building. I stooped down and pushed open the brass letter box in one of the doors and peered through. Inside I saw a lady sitting on the stone floor by her mop and bucket. "It's the police love, what's the trouble? ?" I enquired. "I can't get out, I've been locked in here since they closed at I2 o'clock (It was now three thirty). The poor lady was in tears. I reassured her that I would have her out in no time. I rang our Information room and they, in turn summoned the keyholder of the premises to the scene. The lady was then thankfully released, all part of the service!

I was invited to take part in a show at Bruche by my old drill Sergeant 'Andy' Smythe. What a night that was. After the show, I had a nice supper, a few pints and was bedded down for the night, on the house, this was the first of two such invitations to take part in a show there since my leaving. I was highly honoured.

I still needed to study as well as work hard, and still had to attend probationer constable classes, sit exams and I was still subject to regular 'progress' reports. These were submitted by my Sergeants and Inspectors and were deemed very important by the powers that be. I regularly saw some of the "gang' at court and they all appeared to be getting along okay. I was still not happy with some of the 'naughtiness' that continually raised its ugly head in various forms amongst some of my colleagues.

One Sunday morning saw me walking along Scotland Road, intending to sneak into Arden House for a mug of tea and a bacon buttie' before the City awoke. A fellow officer was accompanying me as he made his way to his own beat. He too was going to make a ·quick call' at the hostel. As we passed a chemist's shop we saw that the window had been broken and items scattered about the footwalk. As it was on my beat I would have to deal with the matter. Either the night man had not spotted the break, or it had been done after he had passed.

"Here, does your missus use this?" asked my colleague, passing me a bottle of an expensive well known brand of perfume. At the same time I saw him place a couple of items into his own pocket. "Hey, behave yourself for Christ's sake, put that back, this is my beat" I said angrily. He reluctantly replaced the items back inside the broken display window. He was one of the two, the other being the recruit, who had filled his car boot with goods from the fruit market!

I told him to leave me to it (as I started to make notes of the incident and prepared to summon the proprietor to attend his premises) The keyholder eventually arrived and made a provisional list of property that was missing. I catered for the attendance of the CID and Fingerprint department then left to resume my beat patrol.

Later, whilst having my meal in the canteen, I noticed that some of the lads at the next table were whispering to each other and talking behind their hands, one of whom was the colleague who I made return the property to the Chemist's window display earlier. I saw that he was secreting something under his newspaper when he realised that I was looking at him. I carried on eating my breakfast after which I followed the others into the nearby snooker room for a quiet sit down before returning back out onto my beat.

Whilst I was sitting there relaxing and watching the lads playing snooker a young officer entered the room and made for my colleague who had been secreting whatever it was in the canteen. "Have you got any more of those hairsprays left?" To which he received the reply "Keep your voice down, no, I only got four and they've all gone". I was fuming. I walked across the room and took hold of my 'undesirable' colleague's tie. "You despicable Bastard" I snarled at him and walked out. I am ashamed and sorry to admit that I was apprehensive to do anything at the time because I had no idea to whom I could confide, and so again, I let the matter go. God, I hoped that this lot would get caught one day. (It was not to be, the few officers mentioned went on and some even reached higher rank and remained in the job.

The same two from the Cazneau St. incident were subject to a very near miss however, a short time later.

During one tour of night duty two police officers (our dynamic duo) were seen by a night watchman attending at a garage in Collingwood Street. The garage was near to the premises the watchman was protecting. Later, the watchman saw the same two officers leaving the garage pushing a wheeled tool cabinet which they then placed into the back of a police Landrover parked nearby. The cabinet was obviously full of tools as it took considerable effort to get it into the vehicle. The two officers then got into their vehicle and drove off into the night. (As it happened, to the recruit's house where the tools were deposited into his garage).

The following right, the watchman hosted another officer who had called into his premises for a cuppa and a smoke. During their conversation the bobby casually mentioned that "_____'s garage was screwed (broken into) last night and a load of tools went". The watchman then remembered what he had seen during the night referred to. He didn't say anything to the young bobby but reported it to a CID officer who was known to him the following day at Rose Hill. A search warrant was obtained as the CID intended to search the home of the (easily traced) Landrover driver, and, as they knew that his constant friend was the recruit, his home also. Unfortunately, someone in the CID tipped off a member of the section and he went to the recruit and told him of the developments. The officer was told by the recruit where the tools were and the officer immediately went and recovered the tools with his crew member and took them to the nearby Leeds Liverpool canal, where the incriminating items were deposited forthwith, (where they presumably remain to this day) The 'obliging' Landrover crew then resumed their normal patrol. Needless to say, when the CID arrived a search proved negative and although a number of officers were interviewed with regard to the matter, the matter was never brought to a satisfactory conclusion. A very close shave indeed for the perpetrators, although this 'near miss' didn't cure either officer. (The recruit was eventually promoted to senior rank).

A similar unsavoury incident occurred one Sunday morning as I was patrolling my beat along Scotland Road. It was about 9-30am during a morning shift. As I walked past a recently closed down public house I could hear noises coming from within the premises. I could also hear people talking quietly. I went to a nearby telephone box and dialled 999. As the only person who could be contacted by radio was the Divisional Inspector (and traffic), I requested his assistance. I asked that I be met away from the pub concerned so as not to alert those inside if they were unlawfully on the premises.

My Inspector and two traffic cars arrived simultaneously. I explained the position and the traffic men were strategically placed to prevent any escape. The Inspector and I crept round to the rear of the premises and stood by the rear door and listened, Yes, there was someone in there alright. The door by which we were standing had been forced. We made our way silently into the building. In the spacious lounge, behind the bar, was a large, cut glass ornate mirror set in a carved mahogany wood frame. As the premises had only recently been vacated and ceased trading, the furniture and fittings all still remained in situ.

We saw two beat constables (from other beats). They were trying to unscrew the mirror from the wall. "What in the hell d'you think you're doing?" the Inspector asked the startled two. The two officers (very senior in service) both jumped back and look shamefaced. One finally stuttered, "We were on our way in for scoff sir, (refreshments at 10.00am) and we heard noises so we came in through the broken door to investigate". Ten out of ten for quick thinking I thought! The officer went on "The bastards got away, we were just tightening this mirror they tried to remove". As we all know, every beat constable's itinerary included a screw driver!? It was obvious that the two intended the removal and ultimate collection later of the very valuable mirror.

The Clock Vaults Pub Scotland Road

As there was no evidence to prove otherwise, there was nothing to do but accept their explanation. However, the Inspector, also a policemen of some 'vintage' took both the men to one side and quietly let them know that they were lucky, as he (the Inspector) was not in the least bit 'happy' about the situation. I was later cursed by one of those concerned for almost dropping them right in it! If I could have proved what was painfully obvious,

I would willingly have entered the witness box to give evidence against them. No further action was taken.

Travelling to Rose Hill by 'bus from Central station to parade for night duty was always 'risky'. Being in full uniform at that time of night the buses were nearly always full of late night revellers, many of whom were, on occasion, aggressively drunk. The 'bus conductors were always happy when a bobby boarded his bus, but for the officer, there was always an individual, who, on seeing the uniform, would always want to 'have a go'.

One such incident happened as I boarded the number 3 bound for Rose Hill. I stood back until those boarding from outside the Wine Lodge had done so. I stood on the platform and the conductor shouted "Hold tight please", then rang the bell to signal his driver to move off. "Ding, Ding, Ding' three bells, we were not going to stop until someone wanted to alight, as the bus was fully loaded. "Fares please", the conductor squeezed his way along the packed to standing lower saloon. One inebriated loud mouth spotted me standing on the platform. "Fucking Hell, Jimmy Edwards" he shouted, "If you can't fight, wear a fucking big 'at." At first the conductor told him to be quiet. The man, drawing his bravery via his alcohol consumption, tried to get up from his seat shouting, "'Who's going to fucking make me?". Oh dear! it was obvious that we were going to have to sort him out. "I'll take you bastards any fuckin' time" slurred our articulate elocution instructor. I told the conductor to instruct his driver to make straight to Rose Hill Bridewell. Our 'bus duly pulled up outside the Bridewell where I unceremoniously removed the foul mouthed yob from the vehicle and dragged him inside to the Bridewell counter.

The 'bus, gratefully relieved of its troublesome passenger, drove back onto it's original route. The Bridewell Sergeant, Sergeant Farrell (later to become Assistant Chief Constable in Merseyside) tapped his pen onto the counter, his other hand supporting his head, his elbow resting on the counter and his eyes rolling up to the ceiling. "Okay, Sixty Nine, What's the charge? asked Sergeant Farrell. "Drunk and disorderly Sergeant" I replied, the sweat pouring from me due to my struggle to get my prisoner into the building from the 'bus. "The circumstances are........." I went on to relate my extract from "Gone with the Wind" to the always very laid back Sergeant. My prisoner was searched and, still insisting on being abusive and violent, was taken, not too gently, to a cell for the night. "Christ Swasie, Where d'you find 'em?" asked the Sergeant. I was certainly not going to allow any drunken loud mouthed yob to get away with that behaviour, especially as I was so conveniently going ON duty, so it was no trouble to me. The conductor called into the station the following night and expressed his gratitude and also the gratitude of his passengers for my timely removal of the drunk from the bus the night before, as apparently, this man was a constant 'Thorn in the side' of the 'bus crews and their passengers, so I felt additionally justified in my arresting him, I was to repeat this duty once or twice more during my travels to and from duty over the years.

It wasn't only arrests that were time consuming and deemed the only important type of police work. Summons 'jobs' too could be very involved. Whilst engaged on point duty during the morning peak hour at a very busy arterial junction at Scotland Road and Ellenborough Street

Author on Point Duty. Scotland Road/Ellenborough Street

my attention was drawn to a green Morris Oxford, OKF-7I. This vehicle was at the head of a line of traffic I had stopped to allow the Scotland Road flow to commence.

I saw that the vehicle was not displaying a current excise (Tax) disc. I went to the driver and asked him to get out of the vehicle. I asked him to whom did the vehicle belong. The driver informed me that the vehicle was his. I asked him why the vehicle was not displaying a current Vehicle Excise Licence. He told me that he had "Sent off for it and it was in the post"

Good heavens, I'd never heard that one before. I told him that the tax disc was by now five weeks out of date going by his date when the old disc was alleged to have expired. I asked him for his name and address. He gave me the name William Foat and gave an address in the City.

As he was unable to show me any documents relating to his use of the vehicle, I issued him with the appropriate form to furnish these within the obligatory 5 days. This he failed to do. I went to the address he had furnished me with and my visit established this to have been a false address. There was no such person as William Foat at that address. To coin a phrase, I had been given a 'joey'. On tracing the last registered owner of the vehicle (this took days or even longer in some cases, not the seconds via the P.N.C (Police National Computer) that is the norm with our modern technology), I ascertained that he had sold it to a dealer for scrap, and his name was not William Foat.

It was assumed by Sergeant Sankey and the lads that I had been worked a 'flanker' and that this would be one job 'that had got away'. Not a bit of it. I was determined to catch the smart Alec and bring him before the court. I visited a number of local 'corner shops' (good gossip centres), pubs, betting shops and other likely places in an effort to trace my 'William Foat'. My perseverance paid off. One of my visits was to a local second hand car dealer's premises. On looking through his receipt books, Bingo! I saw a name 'William Foat' and a signature of the same name. The signature matched the William Foat signature endorsed on my copy of the document production form that I had issued to my 'elusive pimpernel'. I was at last getting somewhere.

The receipt in the book was for the sum of £15. My Mr Foat had purchased the car OKF 71 for the sum of £15 but he obviously had forgotten to tax it (and therefore insure it also). Again, the address in the receipt book proved to be false. However, I made a number of door to door enquiries in the area of the address. My systematic enquiries eventually bore fruit. 'With the permission of my Sergeant I was making these enquiries outside my own Division on the neighbouring patch. Eventually I received the breakthrough I was looking for.

Some of the local children knew the car that I described, but they told me that it didn't belong to a Mr Foat. They gave me another name and told me that the man who owned a car like that was the boyfriend of a sister of one of their playmates. They believed that he lived across the city somewhere. On the strength of this information I did in fact trace the girlfriend of the car's owner. I did not approach her, instead I enquired via a friend of hers who worked in a local fish and chip shop, telling her that I had a message for her mate's boyfriend. My ploy worked. I was told that "He lives on Holt Road, near to the Pakki's spice shop". It didn't take me long to find the house. With my Chief Superintendent (Mr. Bodger's) permission, a colleague, Bobby Collins took me to the address straight after morning parade one Sunday morning in the Divisional Landrover.

We were greeted at the door by a shocked middle aged woman in her nightie, her hair in rollers, and obviously still half asleep, and fearing that we were the bearers of bad news. (In a way, to her son, we were going to be!) Not asking her "Do you have a son?" in case she denied this, instead I asked her, "Can I have a word with ___ (naming my quarry) please," "He's in bed, I'll go and get him" the lady replied. Eventually a young man came down the stairs and with a puzzled look on his face, asked us what our early morning visit was all about., I recognised him as being the man who gave me the name William Foat at the junction on that morning when I was engaged on point duty some weeks before. I had found him at last.

I told him that I recognised him and after cautioning him in accordance with the requirements of the then, Judges' Rules, I asked him for an explanation. He strenuously denied being the person concerned and told me that he didn't have a car. He did say that he had a green car a long time ago but he sold it to "Some bloke, I forget his name". It was obvious that he was lying. I again issued him with a H.O.R.T. (Home Office Traffic Form) for the production of his documents to cater for his use of the vehicle OKF 71 on the day that I had stopped him. He was unable to do so, even within the new five day period. He was summoned and successfully prosecuted for driving a motor vehicle on the original date, not having insurance,not displaying a current vehicle excise licence, and giving a false name and address to a Police Officer. On his appearance before the City Magistrates' Court he was heavily fined.

Church Street in the 1960's

Policewoman on Crossing Duty in a busy Clayton Square 1960's

I was summoned to Mr Bodger's office after Sergeant Sankey had brought this, and other various successful prosecutions that I had instigated, to his notice. I received the Superintendent's warm congratulations, was commended for my endeavours and was informed that his sentiments were to be endorsed onto my personal file at Headquarters for the information of the Chief Constable. I was to receive my first Commendation.

Alongside Rose Hill Bridewell was a small block of flats. One of the residents of this block owned a dilapidated and extremely unroadworthy motor scooter. This rusty machine was parked against the pavement for months and months. Eventually I went to see the owner and asked him to move it. He told me it was scrap and he had finished with it. Three times I repeated my journey next door to instruct him to move the offending machine. The owner continued to ignore my requests and the vehicle remained parked at the roadside. I eventually reported and prosecuted him with the offence of 'depositing litter' for which he was fined and instructed by the court to dispose of the machine post haste. Served himeright. It was a bit cheeky leaving it there almost outside the police station.

There was a small garage in Vauxhall Road which traded under the name Boundary Service Station. Outside these premises parked on the forecourt against the road were a number of second-hand cars for sale.

The lads would call while on patrol to browse around the used cars also the garage was the proverbial 'tea speck'. My colleagues used to ask me why I didn't have a car as I lived so far from the station. I gave this matter some thought. We were on our feet now my job was secure the pay wasn't all that bad (approx. £12 per week take home now) so one day whilst having a brew at my 'speck' I asked the boss at the garage if he could recommend anything to me.

"I've got a nice little Ford Pop over there" he said, "It's in bloody good nick". He took me outside and showed me a nice shiny blue Ford Popular (the old sit up and beg type). He sat inside and pulled the starter. The engine popped into life straight away and sounded very quiet and smooth. "How much?" I asked. "Well I always look after the boys" he flannelled, " I'm asking £25 but to you Swasie, I'll take £20". I stroked my chin with my finger and thumb pensively. "Hmmm" I thought out loud. Two weeks pay!

"Would you give it a good once over for me before I took it?" I cheekily asked. "Certainly I'll have it up on the ramp and give it a bloody good service and everything for you" the boss replied adding, "You hard faced sod" as he grinned at me. It was now Tuesday, pay day tomorrow. "Can I pick it up on Friday. I'll square you up then" I asked. "No problem it'll be ready and waiting for you all prim and proper for you to collect Friday".

It was with considerable difficulty that I kept this secret from my wife. We were actually going to own a car of our own. I kept £5 from my wage packet and drew the other £15 from the bank on Friday morning. Every day until Friday I couldn't resist going to have a look at my 'new' car.

Friday arrived, as soon as I was dismissed at 3 pm, I waited for the afternoon jeep patrol to leave the building and bummed a lift down to Vauxhall Road. My car was waiting. The jeep crew came to have a look. I stood there like Baron Rothschild. My car stood there gleaming. "That's her" I proudly indicated to my colleagues.

Marje with new Ford Pop

I went inside to 'do the business', the garage had arranged my insurance and taxed It for me (an extra fiver for the latter). I opened the door and got into the driving seat. The leather upholstery smelled like brand new.

I started up and drove off home, making sure the Tunnel bobbies saw me on my way through, imagining that they would be green with envy! On my arrival at our flat in Dunraven Road, West Kirby, I saw my wife at the gate chatting to a neighbour. As I alighted from 'my' vehicle and walked through the gate my wife said, "You're late, has someone lent you their car to come home?".

I carried on into the house and once inside, turned to my wife. "What do you think of our new car love?" I asked. , Marje was overjoyed, then, suddenly realising that cars cost money asked, "Will we be able to afford it, how much was it, are you sure we'll be alright?". I reassured her that I had thought about committing ourselves very deeply before I made the decision. "We'll be okay" I replied. My wife's apprehension soon gave way to renewed excitement. "Can we go for a ride round as soon as you get changed?" she asked. "You bet, I've got to go and fill her up with petrol anyway" I said. In a few minutes I was changed and out, we plonked our young Ronnie into the rear seat, then Marje and I got in and went to the nearest garage to ' tank up' . I filled her to the top which cost me about £5. (I think ' petrol was roughly seven shillings per gallon (35 pence) We then went on a trip around the Wirral in our 'new Rolls Royce'. As soon as we arrived back home Marj was outside with a bucket and leather to wash the journey's grime away.

Travelling to work was now an utter treat. It also proved a lot easier and ultimately cheaper than public transport. I was also home a lot earlier than I used to be. I was delighted with my investment'.

The months went by and now Christmas was approaching. During the run up to the festive season we were able to earn quite a lot of overtime by working what was known as the 'Turkey Trot'. these were extra foot patrols to protect the numerous food shops, butchers and poulterers premises in the division. We were protecting many thousands of pounds worth of stock. We would complete our afternoon shift at II pm, a quick cuppa in the canteen then again on patrol in twos until I am. The extra patrols were justified many times over by the amount of arrests made for attempts on the shops by the enterprising and unscrupulous ' low life' looking for easy pickings. Many kind shop keepers used to drop a bottle of whisky into the station for the Section, sometimes they would invite an officer into the back of the shop whilst on day duty, for 'a little drink'.

Each division held a children's party at Christmas. This was always a really enjoyable occasion. What parties they were. Every child, no matter what age received an excellent present. Every officer in the force paid into a fund in their respective divisions throughout the year. The fund also catered for our Christmas hampers. These were also very good and well stocked with almost every form of Christmas fayre, Turkey, sweets, nuts, stuffing, greens, and of course, a bottle of whisky, (or wine). There was always a wonderful atmosphere throughout the stations at Christmas time. We officers even used to extend the festive spirit to some of our 'clients' by taking some of then home in the jeep when they were drunk, even when some were 'boisterous'.

Those who were incarcerated over the Christmas eve/Christmas morning for 'over indulging' were often taken home when they had sobered up, instead of ,just being kicked out' onto the street. I've walked many a 'regular' to his house because it was Christmas instead of locking him up. There seemed to be some sort of mutual respect and understanding in those days. This has very largely disappeared now. One minute the beat man was the 'enemy' but the next, he was the absolute solution to all life's unpleasant problems (which were certainly very rarely answered via the text books. If Johnny was missing everyone looked to the beatman to be the saviour who would find him (or catch the villain who robbed granny of her handbag on her way home from 'tombola'). Many things the training manual did not cover. There was definitely no substitute whatsoever for experience on the streets. Many's the time I've had a large, cracked mug half full of whisky thrust at me by a grateful wife or mother when I've delivered her trouser soiled, sick stained, inebriate husband or son home when she was overjoyed to see that he was safe and no accident had befallen him to cause his late arrival. Mind you, sometimes the opposite happened when I would be slagged off for getting him back, when I was then asked angrily "Why didn't yer keep the bastard and throw away the key?"

I again attended Bruche, having been invited to 'Top the Bill' at one of their shows for Christmas, in December ('65). Again I stayed the night 'on the house'. It was just as well as, after being wined and dined, I was certainly in no fit state to get home to the Wirral from Warrington. I enjoyed taking part in such shows, the Esprit de corps' of the service invoked immense pride at being a part of it.

Christmas Eve I was on Night duty when I arrested two men on the roof of a large warehouse as they attempted to break in .

I arrested a driver so drunk that he actually fell out of his vehicle and into the road when I opened his door after he had stalled at a set of traffic lights. A busy Christmas.

On arriving home at 7-30am on Christmas morning, I didn't bother going to bed. Which father would, with an excited youngster already up and playing with his toys, and insisting, on my arrival that I looked at everything that Father Christmas had brought him. Christmas lunch time was the traditional time when myself, brother Tom and dad paraded for the traditional ritual of the 'Christmas dinner time pint' at our local, The Ring 'o' Bells, West Kirby, followed by Christmas dinner at Dad's in Saughall Massie. After dinner, before the afternoons nap, first, the Queen on the tele'. No Christmas is complete without watching the Queen's Broadcast to the Nation.

Marje, Ronnie and I returned home at tea time for a couple of hours before I was off again for night duty.

I was on parade for l0.45 pm. One or two of my colleagues, plus the Sergeants and Inspector, had, like myself, imbibed during the day (but some, most likely the evening also by their demeanour). The look of some of their eyes and the strong stink of 'Gold Spot' and strong mints (a dead give away) told all who was, and who was NOT, fit for duty.

Due to the demon drink, I dealt with a really bad traffic accident that night. Sadly, amongst those badly injured was a small girl. Her little teddy and new dolls were lying in the blood spattered wreckage of their car. All of the injured were taken to hospital by ambulance. The little girl was taken to Alder Hey. I accompanied the adults in another ambulance to the Northern Hospital (long since gone). What a sad and disturbing sight a hospital casualty department is at Christmas time. The treatment rooms and the nurses, adorned with tinsel and various decorations, the moaning and wailing of casualties, the frustrated crying of their loved ones, beside themselves with worry, unable to come to terms with the sight of their broken limbs and bodies. The nursing sister, trying to console a distraught relative on being told of the death of a loved one. Not a pleasant sight, but I was to experience this on more occasions that I would care to remember.

I managed to get out of an afternoon duty and substitute it for a Day duty when I had to take a urine sample to the Forensic Science Laboratory at Preston. Evidence for my Christmas Eve Drink/Driving case. It made a change going out of the City on a nice little journey. My visit to the laboratory was very interesting and informative. I was taken by Traffic Car (I had to take the evidence personally to ensure 'continuity') and needless to say, we didn't exactly rush ourselves to get back. After being deposited back at Rose Hill in the early afternoon, I sat down and attempted to catch up on my outstanding reports until going off duty at five o'clock. I wondered what the New Year would bring?

Author with pupil Sealand

I found that the time absolutely flew by.

My off duty hours were spent socialising, swimming, and indulging in my other weekend passion, flying. I qualified as a glider pilot, then went on to become a gliding instructor and eventually started to fly powered aircraft.

I spent many weekends and Summer leave periods flying at RAF Sealand. I found flying to be very invigorating and exhilarating.

I also spent time oil painting and |I liked to convey onto canvas the many 'air to ground' views I found interesting whilst flying, together with some of the aircraft that I flew. I had one large painting pictured with an accompanying article in the press. I also liked to do a spot of sea angling when the opportunity arose.

My second year at 'Spike Island' dawned and time marched on. One of my early 'claims to fame' was to come about due to nothing more than a piece of ' routine ' police duty! One very cold, wet night I was walking my beat along a deserted Dock Road in the pouring rain at 2am Saturday I9 March, I966. I thought I'd seek a few minute's refuge in one of the dock gate police huts, and there cadge a warm and a cup of tea from the gate 'bobby'.

As I trudged my wet and weary way along I saw the lights of a car approaching. As all had been so quiet and uneventful up to now, I decided to stop the car and check its occupants for 'something to do'!

Stepping into the road, I flashed my torch and signalled the vehicle to stop. The vehicle stopped and I went to the driver. 'Morning sir, Is this your car!' I asked the nervous looking driver. The young male driver informed me that the car was in fact a hired vehicle. I asked him when it was due to be returned and the young man then became agitated as he explained that he was about to return it to the hire firm later in the day! I again asked the young man when the vehicle was due to be returned. I was informed that it should have been returned a 'week or so' earlier. I asked the young man for his name and address. He duly obliged and produced his driving documents to confirm his identity.

It came to pass that he had originally hired the vehicle for a DAY, three weeks ago!. I asked him to get out of the vehicle as I didn't want him suddenly driving off into the night. I then inspected the vehicle and shone my torch into the vehicle's interior. I saw a lady's black glove on the front passenger seat. The seat appeared to be bloodstained and on the floor in front of the seat were a pair of lady's black calf length boots.

I asked the man, David Jessom, to account for the lady's glove and boots. He informed me that the items were the property of his girlfriend who had inadvertently left them in the car. 'What are those stains on the seat?" I asked. Jessom informed me that he had spilled some paint on the seat the preceding day. I once again asked him to confirm that. Technically, he was 'unlawfully' in possession of the vehicle. "I suppose you could say that" he replied. I told him that I was arresting him for the offence of 'Taking and driving away' a motor vehicle (as the offence then was).

Bramley Moore Dock Gate (scene of David Jessom's arrest)

76

The vehicle was secured and I took Jessom to the dock gate I was making for originally for my unofficial brew!. There, I telephoned for a 'Black Maria!' to come and collect my prisoner and I and convey us to Rose Hill. Whilst awaiting transport, I again asked Jessom to account for the stains on the seat, this time he either couldn't (or wouldn't) explain their presence.

The van eventually arrived and took us back to Rose Hill where I presented my 'car thief' before the Bridewell Sergeant, Sergeant Sankey. I stood before the Sergeant and outlined the circumstances of the arrest. I also mentioned the glove, boots and bloodstained seat. Sergeant Sankey had the car brought to Rose Hill immediately and the CID were summoned.

After Jessom being documented, fingerprinted and photographed, he was then seen and interviewed by detectives.

It so happened that the day previously, the naked body of a woman had been found dumped in a lay-by on the East Lancashire Road. At first nobody had attached any significance to the two incidents, but eventually, the subject of the murder was mentioned but Jessom completely denied any knowledge. However, once the murder had been mentioned, it was then decided to pursue this line and see if there was any connection. A more thorough examination of the car aroused further suspicion. Jessom's feeble explanation regarding the items of clothing belonging to his (fictitious) girlfriend was soon demolished and eventually after further lengthy questioning his attitude changed. Under the woman's body on the East Lancashire Road, was found a black glove. This was put to Jessom who then realised that the game was up. He admitted killing the woman, Ada Hogg, and dumping her naked body at the spot where she had been found. It was conclusively established that the glove under the body was the 'other' glove to the one found in Jessom's car. The boots were also established as having belonged to the murdered woman. Finally, the stains on the seat were established as being blood stains, Ada Hogg's bloodstains.

Jessom made a full and frank admission and duly appeared before a Judge and Jury at Liverpool Crown court on 3 May, 1966. He was eventually found guilty of Manslaughter, as it was established that Jessom had a long mental history. He was sent to Broadmoor Mental Hospital. I often wonder if Ada Hogg's killing would ever have been solved but for that wet and cold night's 'interception' ?.

I continued to enhance my experience via the wide variety of arrests, summonses and other incidents, accidents and calamities.

Life was a bit of a struggle financially and money was hard come by in those early days, however, Marje and I had started to save hard for a house of our own. Eventually we had saved enough for the deposit on a nice little semi situated in a small, quiet cul-de-sac in Hoylake. It was a lovely house. The neighbours were excellent, many of whom were known to us personally. Marje, being born in Hoylake had gone to school with our next door neighbour. We were almost on the main shopping street and the railway station was just round the corner.

One of Rose Hills stalwarts was a very jovial Constable of many years standing and quite portly in stature. He was known to all affectionately as 'The Vicar'. He was a very popular man and, when the occasion warranted, he was a very capable and efficient Police officer. . However, unfortunately, like many others in the force at that time, the 'Vicar' was a very prolific drinker; on duty. Indeed, he had been disciplined and reduced from Sergeant to constable on two occasions for being drunk on duty. He did however perform regularly as Acting Sergeant although it was highly unlikely that promotion would come his way again. His previous contraventions of the discipline code did not prevent him from his continuing 'indulgence' with the demon drink.

When the Vicar was in charge of the section on afternoon duty, he would 'select' a constable (who was partial to a pint) and they would make Licensed Premises' visits whilst out on foot (or mobile) patrol. Or, he would peg (visit) his men on their beat and then make licensed visits. the constable would normally be one of the men who had lengthy service, referred to by other members of the section as members of the 'Serious Drinking Squad.' It was always easy to tell who had accompanied the Sergeant on licensed premises visits (the majority of the Sergeants indulged in the 'occasional' glass from the benevolent licensee on such visits) as, on their arrival back at the station it was obvious that they had 'partaken'.

This type of thing was very prevalent on night duty. many of the bobbies had their own speck to go to and, on leaving the station, would make to their 'watering hole' at one of the many pubs hidden away on their respective beats, A tap on the side window then in through the side or rear door.

Once inside, helmet off, tunic undone, then down to some 'serious' drinking! Sometimes they wouldn't materialise until it was time to return to the station for their refreshments at 2 or 3 am, even when personal radios were introduced the routine went on. Again, the heavy aroma of strong mints or 'Gold Spot' reeked around the canteen and snooker room during the early hours.

Occasionally the word would be put about among certain officers (and sometimes the Sergeants) that a party was taking place at a certain premises, licensed or private, and off they would all go to partake of the happy juice.

One such incident occurred during a night shift in I966. I was down the cobbled side streets and dimly lit entries of the dock area checking the many warehouses that abounded the vicinity. Nearby was the large sugar refining factory complex of Tate and Lyle. It was a cold night and rain was falling in sheets, It was about 2 am, and all the ingredients were there for a good night's 'screwing' (breaking and entering). I was warily creeping along a narrow, cobbled street trying to be as quiet as possible and listening for any strange sounds that would indicate criminal activity.

As I rounded the corner of a large warehouse I came upon a parked motor car. The vehicle's engine was not running and it was not displaying its side lights. I could see by the dim light of a far away street lamp that there were two men sitting in the vehicle. At that time I was not as yet in possession of a radio, no handcuffs, just my wooden truncheon, torch and whistle. As I crept nearer to the vehicle I could see the two men, one was holding a cigarette cupped in his hand and every now and again, when he drew on it, part of his face projected an eerie and sinister glow. My heart was pounding, the nearest public telephone was nearly half a mile away at one of the police manned dock gates. Assistance was light years away. I retreated out of sight from the vehicle in case I was spotted by either of the vehicle's occupants. I made a note of the vehicle make, registration number, the venue, time and brief descriptions of the two men whom I could just about make out, in case harm should befall me. After pondering my next move, I decided that to leave the vicinity and summon help would take too long and thus possibly enable a large break in to take place. I therefore decided to go boldly to the vehicle and confront the two men.

As I approached the vehicle my nerves were as tight as a bow string and my heart was beating twenty to the dozen. I crept up to the driver's door and on my getting to the vehicle I could see that the ignition key was in position. I shone my torch into the eyes of the two men as I opened the driver's door. I did this to enable me to retrieve the ignition key before they had chance to drive off. As I reached into the vehicle, I was horrified to see that the two 'suspicious characters' sitting in the car were no less than my Chief Superintendent, Joe Bodger, in the front passenger seat, and in the driver's seat, Superintendent Tom Bradley.

After offering my apologies for startling the two of them, I told them that I thought that they were two men up to no good'. Both senior officers said they were very impressed by my actions and went on to explain that they, with other strategically positioned officers, were in fact keeping observations on a public house, the Goat.

I was then instructed to resume my beat and keep out of the immediate area of the Goat, but to 'be handy' in case I was needed, as the premises were ultimately to be raided. No other explanation was offered to me.

What I did not know (contrary to popular belief later), was that an 'after hours' party was in full swing, attended not only by various 'ladies of the night' and other unsavoury 'guests' but also near enough the whole night shift from Rose Hill together with officers (and Sergeants) from the neighbouring division, many in various states on inebriation and undress.

A short time later, under the leadership of Mr Bodger, the licensed premises were raided and a large number of officers were caught for a number of discipline offences, drinking on duty, improper behaviour and other equally serious matters. Some were fortunate enough to escape.

One constable, Cliff 'Hoppy' Hopkins, somehow managed to climb out onto the roof, then make his way along a wall before dropping down into a neighbouring street and making good his escape and resuming his beat as if nothing had happened. He was never connected to the incident and escaped scott free from investigation.

As the incident took place on my beat it was (wrongly) assumed that I was privy to the impending raid and one or two colleagues 'sent me to Coventry' over the matter. Even if I had have known that the boss was about that night, there was no way whatsoever that I could have warned anyone in time, anyway, I not only did not know the boss was there, I didn't know that a party was taking place at the Goat, let alone that most of my colleagues were inside the place.

The Goat Pub

'Hoppy' accepted that I knew nothing about the events of that night, and he and I remain close friends to this day and still see each other regularly.

Drinking on duty was not just confined to afternoon and night duty. One sunny weekday in the summer of '66, I was 'pegged' by my acting Sergeant, the 'vicar'. I was on Great Homer Street talking to Hannah Howard and Mary Dunn, the barrow women. Up strode the 'Vicar' removing his helmet. "Phew, it's bloody hot", he ' said as he mopped the perspiration from his brow with his handkerchief. The midday sun was very hot. "Good day girls" mused my acting Sergeant to Hannah and Mary. "E'yar lad, this'll quench yer thirst" said Hannah offering a nice juicy peach to the 'Vicar'.

"This bugger's already had two" interjected Mary pointing to me. "He always was a greedy sod" bantered the 'Vicar'. We thanked the ladies, for the fruit and resumed our foot patrol along the crowded 'Homer'.

I was known to most of the people of my 'parish' by now, to some, not as affectionately maybe as to others. "ey up, 'ere's 'andlebars" mothers would threaten their delinquent little mites when they misbehaved. I liked the majority of my 'flock', most of them were okay, the 'salt of the

80

earth'. Right Swas, we'll go and peg a few pubs" said my acting Sergeant. I knew that I was privileged! I also knew that I would be quenching my thirst other than via a couple of peaches!. As many people who remember, the old Great Homer Street and Scotland Road will recall, the area was well known for having a 'pub on every corner'- This in fact was near enough the truth. There were indeed pubs on near enough every street corner.

The Vicar and I visited every pub on 'the Homer', and to be sociable, the Vicar accepted the occasional glass of tipple from a friendly, benevolent landlord. "E're get that down yer" instructed the vicar as he pushed a pint, towards me.

We made our way eventually to Rose Hill and there, the Vicar commandeered the Inspector's white Anglia patrol supervision vehicle. The Inspector this day, was Inspector McKenzie (known to all as Dr Finley due to his resemblance to the Scottish doctor portrayed in the television series, Dr Finley's case book). "Riding's better than walking" commented the Vicar.

The Stingo Pub
(One of the 'Vicar's' favourite watering holes)

We drove to Roscommon Street and pegged the 'Rossie' (the Roscommon pub), then up to Netherfield Road where we visited the Vicar's favourite pub the "'Stingo' (just off our patch). By now the Vicar was slurring his speech "Don't you think you've had enough sarge? I nervously ventured. "Behave, you cheeky young pup" replied theVicar.

Between Netherfleld Road flats (The Braddocks) adjacent to the 'Stingo' and down to Great Homer Street were just the streets and pavements to where the rows of terraced houses once stood back to back before being demolished in the name of progress. Looking down from Netherfield Road the scene just resembled a map. Green grass now replacing the homes of communities past, the occasional street gas light, minus its top, stood up like a finger pointing to heaven. We started our journey down to Great Homer Street. At first we used the 'streets', but then the vicar decided, "Bugger this, we might as well cut straight across'". The Vicar was now quite sloshed.

We bumped across the streets, pavements, rubble, grass, running over a discarded mattress. "It's like the bloody dodgems" giggled my acting Sergeant, the arm band bearing his two acting Sergeant chevrons was loosely down by the wrist of his left arm, and the other on his right arm was just below his elbow, his helmet flung onto the back seat. What my inebriated chauffeur failed to notice were the regularly spaced metal coal holes in the pavements, most minus their cast iron grids (long since weighed in for scrap by local entrepreneurs). Suddenly, BANG !', we came to a dead stop. My face hit the windscreen.

"Christ Sarge" I exclaimed. "Fucking coal hole, didn't see that" slurred the Vicar. I got out of the vehicle, the Vicar sat there giggling. I expected the vehicle to be badly damaged. The Vicar got out and leaned against the side of the car and exploded into hysterical laughter. Fortunately there was not a person in sight. It was just as well we were in the middle of 'no man's land'.

On inspection it was revealed that the front nearside wheel had gone into an open coal hole. However, when the Vicar reversed the vehicle (he wouldn't let me drive the boss's car ') I managed to push the vehicle's wheel out of the hole. No doubt the coal holes were left specifically to trap any unwary acting Sergeant drunk enough to take his Inspector's car across the Division obstacle course.

After further inspecting the vehicle it looked okay. I gingerly got back into the vehicle. The Vicar restarted the engine after first stalling it. We moved off slowly. There was a scraping noise, a bang, then the engine roared like an angry lion. The exhaust was hanging off and we had flattened the silencer. "The boss'll have to use his own car tomorrow" giggled the Vicar, the anaesthetic of alcohol rendering him completely oblivious to the gravity of the situation.

We slowly and gently coaxed the car back to Rose Hill. By now it was time to go off duty. The Vicar attempted to sign the section off and we were dismissed, my acting Sergeant then slid off home leaving the afternoon Sergeant with a brief verbal account of a none existent chase of a motor cycle which had made good its escape after we hit a coal hole. By the time that the Vicar resumed duty the following day he was by then fully compos mentis' and able to furnish an elaborate report that would have done credit to Enid Blyton, in the guise of a Police traffic accident report. 'Would you believe it, his story was accepted (I wasn't mentioned) and he completely got away with it.

Three o clock one Sunday morning saw me walking up Richmond Row. I had just left Rose Hill after my refreshments and was resuming my night beat patrol. As I walked up the hill in the darkness I could see an

Austin Healey 3000 parked against its nearside kerb. The street lighting was reasonable, the vehicle was parked alongside a children's playground, opposite which was a piece of waste land.

Ahead was the traffic light controlled junction with St. Anne Street some 50 yards away. On reaching the car I walked round to the driver's door. There were no other persons about. The area was quiet. I approached the vehicle from the rear and on shining my torch into the interior of the vehicle, its soft top was up, I saw the driver leaning over indulging in oral sex with a man who was in the passenger seat.

I ordered the driver to get out of the vehicle. He turned and looked at me horrified. Although I didn't see who the passenger was I could however clearly see his erect penis. I saw that the driver was wearing full evening dress. He attempted to start the car. I leaned into the driver's open window and tried to snatch the ignition keys. By now the driver had started the car and accelerated away rapidly dragging me with him. My left arm was trapped and I continued to be dragged alongside the vehicle. The driver drove over the waste land and onto St Anne Street. He continued making violent manoeuvres in an effort to throw me off. My legs were burned as they were scraped along the road, the soles and heels of my (new) boots were burned and scraped from their uppers, I couldn't get free because of my trapped arm.

Fortunately for me, a knight in shining armour, in the guise of a naughty seventeen year old boy and his teenage mate, who had earlier taken his father's car from Upton on the Wirral (without his consent) were driving along St Anne Street at this time and saw me being dragged. The young lad had the presence of mind to chase the Healey and attempt to stop it. The Healey wouldn't stop so the enterprising youth decided to ram it. This damaged the Healey (on the side that I was trapped).

The Healey was forced to stop. I fell into the road and under my rescuer's car. The Healey however, calmly reversed over both of my feet then drove off, leaving me unconscious beneath the front of the youths' car, which by now had been reported stolen by the youth's father,

A police Landrover arrived and the crew, on seeing me underneath the car prone, and finding the vehicle was stolen, unceremoniously threw the two youths into the police vehicle. I was taken by ambulance to the City's Royal Infirmary. When I came to, my tearful wife Marje was at my bedside. Fortunately I had only suffered severe bruising, lacerations and burns to my lower legs and feet. No broken bones. My rescuers? Under the circumstances, the Chief Constable decided on a reprimand, followed by a letter of thanks for saving the life of one of his officers. The persons in the Healey?. The Austin Healey was found abandoned in Liverpool a short time later and the owner was eventually traced. The vehicle's owner lived in a large house close to one of Liverpools' cathedrals. He was interviewed at great length. After continually insisting that his vehicle had been stolen during the night of the incident, he finally, reluctantly admitted that a homosexual friend of his (he was also an admitted homosexual) 'sometimes' used his car.

The owner emphatically denied any knowledge of the incident

involving the injured policeman. His 'friend' was traced and also denied any knowledge on being interviewed.

Bearing in mind this incident involved attempted murder, gross indecency, dangerous driving, not to mention that of taking a driving away, as well as other ancillary traffic offences, and therefore should have been treated with the utmost seriousness I felt (and still do) that all was not as it should have been. I was never given the chance to see the person named by the owner on an identification parade and after attending our Criminal Records office (unofficially) I recognised the man named by the Healey's owner as being his 'friend' as that of the offending driver on the night. I confronted the investigating detective Sergeant, and told him of my' visit to Mercro (Merseyside Criminal Records Office). First, I was told off for 'not going through the channels' and then I was told, "No that's not him".

I insisted that it was him, and was told again, "Swasie, you want to get into the jacks (CID) don't you". I replied that I very much wanted the CID. "Right", said the Sergeant, "If you want CID bad enough, then he's not the man! Okay?" "No, it's bloody not OK" I retorted. "Right then, leave it with me" I was instructed. I was to learn soon afterwards that police text books were found in the Healey, and worse - the driver whom I had positively and vehemently identified was a close friend of a ranking Rose Hill CID officer who also associated with a number of senior divisional uniform and CID personnel. I also was made aware that he made frequent visits to Rose Hill (although not so much after the incident) CID office.

That could explain the close proximity to Rose Hill that the vehicle had been parked on the fateful night. Also, let us not forget that there was a serving member of Rose Hill CID staff who was known by his colleagues, (and many others) to be a homosexual. It appeared that due to this incident, I was starting to 'rock the boat' - 'again'.

The matter was never brought to a successful conclusion. Nobody was ever charged. OH! How I wish that I had been a bit more sure of my ground then, or knew then what I know now !

Even this "saga" didn't diminish my love of the job. The characters who lived in our division, indeed, the characters with whom I served, all added to the spice of life endured by a serving policeman. I wouldn't swap my career for any other, even bearing in mind that the financial reward for that of a Police Officer was not very high in my early days.

Another duty that many officers hated or considered to be boring or mundane was traffic point duty. One hardly ever sees an officer performing this duty for a whole shift. We all took our turn and were posted to point duty. This entailed being on your point for the full eight hour shift and being relieved for refreshments or the fall of night. Although there were overhead light during the hours of darkness. This duty was carried out with great skill, and to most, great pride in his (or her) individual skills whilst performing this tiring (both mentally and physically) but essential, form of police duty. Due to this duty, many friendships were formed with the local people, motorists and when engaged at school crossings, the local children. The kids, once they befriended me, would hold my hand and tell me their little secrets. Sometimes. I would have gifts of sweets or biscuits handed to me, or the occasional 'chewy' (chewing gum) to break the monotony of my routine. I treated my point duty and school crossings very seriously. Peak hour motorists eventually got to know me and waved as they made their way to or from work each day. I even made friends with many of the kids parents (and locked some of them up drunk, on a Saturday night).

It was surprising what an asset it was befriending little Johnny at his school crossing, as sometimes it was the same kid who would help me by defusing a very violent domestic I attended, thus possibly saving me violence or possible injury from one or both of his rowing parents, this type of thing was referred to by my Sergeant as "Swings and Roundabouts" or, " Bread and Butter stuff."

One such 'service' performed by one of the local 12 year olds was when I was walking along Soho Street in company with Constable 'Paddy' Elliott. This was not long after the notorious and sickening murder of three police officers in London when they were shot by the then well known despicable character Harry Roberts.

Paddy and I were passing a block of flats, On one of the top landings stood a lad of about 12 or so. Feelings were running very high regarding the policemens' murder amongst the police service and some of the local yobs used to try and provoke us by jeeringly referring to the murder. The young lad on the landing was no exception. "Harry Roberts Ha Ha Ha, Harry Roberts Ha Ha Ha" he mockingly taunted us. "I wish I could get my hands on the little bastard" Paddy muttered acidly.

Soho Street Liverpool

I saw a lad standing leaning against the wall of the flats. "Lo Sir" said the youngster. "Hello Son'" I replied. "'Ere I bet you can't fight him" I said, pointing to the still jeering kid up on the landing. "'Wha', I'd kill 'im" said the answer to a maiden's prayer. "I'll bet you half a crown (2/6d or 12-1/2p, a lot of money then) that you daren't go up there and smack him hard in the nose:", I gleefully challenged my little friend. Watch this then" replied the cocky little warrior. He vanished from our view as he ran up the concrete steps inside the flats, to appear a short time later on the same top landing as our still provocatively shouting little tyke continued his abuse.

The lad walked up to the jeering little chap, " "Harry Roberts Ha Ha Ha, Harry Ro____" Smack! Even from where we stood Paddy and I could see the blood come from the nose of the offending little brat. "Oh dear, the lad's hurt" I said, as I continued my beat. "What about the half crown?" Paddy asked. "What half crown?" said I displaying a deliriously happy grin. "You bastard" said Paddy.

Soho Street during the day appeared just like any other of the City's busy and bustling streets. One of the beat man's duties whilst patrolling his beat along Soho Street, was to take the Inspectors' detachable white uniform collars to the local Chinese laundry to be cleaned and starched. I was always given a bundle of these from my Inspector, Tommy Hogg, to take along there. Sometimes the bundle was quite substantial, as it would include a number of other Inspectors collars too.

We all had detachable collars but for some reason, only the Inspectors bothered to use the facilities of the local Chinese laundry.

A totally different picture was painted however, of Soho Street at night time. Usually we would patrol in pairs, especially towards weekends. There was a very real risk of the bobby being involved in some incident or other in Soho Street, and the incident nearly always resulted in the officer (or officers) being assaulted.

On Friday and Saturday nights, the shift would normally end at 11 pm, but there were always two volunteers required to stay on and work overtime until 1 am to cover the then notorious street. Similarly Scotland Road was covered in the same way. Each weekend the risk of afternoon and night shift patrols being assaulted was extremely high. However, there was never any shortage of volunteers for the overtime!

Chapter Seven - The Commandos

I had attended RAF Dishforth for my refresher course after my first twelve month's service and at the conclusion of my second year, I attended at RAF Leeming. I liked the latter as I managed to get some flying time in Chipmunks and also gliders.

My probationary period was now successfully concluded. Now I could concentrate of whatever it was I intended to try for. I favoured the CID. Still, I assumed that would be some time away as yet. I'd have to get some service in first.

Our Chief constable, Mr Balmer, had just introduced his 'Commando Squad'. This was to become well known internationally. He pioneered the use of strategically placed cameras throughout the city and his 'commandos' were dressed as various forms of down and outs, city gents, newspaper sellers, street sweepers and any other inconspicuous men and women that could be thought of. VIP visitors visited Liverpool to glean what they could for the benefit of their own police systems back home, such was the interest created by 'Bert Balmer's Commandos'.

This squad really aroused my interest. A spell in the squad would no doubt enhance my chances of entering the Criminal Investigation Department. I applied for the Commando Squad and was absolutely delighted to learn that my application had been favourably received and I was accepted.

I joined the elite squad and commenced my first duty there on Friday, 28 July 1967 I was paired off with another constable, Mike Bamford. During our first week, Mike and I arrested no fewer than five arrests for various forms of theft.

We recovered a stolen car radio, miscellaneous goods from large city stores, and wallets and purses from pickpockets. We were off to a fine start. I let my hair grow to quite a considerable length. Well down onto my shoulders, I also grew a beard. I dressed in old clothes and really looked a scruffy sight ambling round the City. Many was the time that my wife and I were asked if I had in fact left the Police force. Some of our friends and neighbours at first thought that I was employed on building sites.

Although most of the time we worked in pairs (for mutual protection) sometimes we did work 'solo' but always made sure that we were able to be contacted or contact the office or colleagues at certain times or places.

By now we had pocket radios but only in extreme cases or emergencies were these used. We went out of our way to ensure that nobody 'rumbled' us as being police officers. After arresting one 19 year old for theft of a car radio, the property of a 'person or persons at present unknown' the lad introduced me to his mother.

She was a well known prostitute and was privy to untold amounts of extremely valuable underworld information. Unofficially I struck a deal with her. She 'offered' to become very helpful to me in the future as a 'snout' (informant) and because of this, I decided to book her son's stolen radio in as 'found property' and I let him off with a verbal warning. He was not aware of my 'deal' with his mother.

Olive ,as I shall call her, certainly kept her side of the bargain. She was to put me on to many excellent 'detections' and subsequent recovery of stolen property. Some very valuable indeed. Due also to Olive's information, a lot of serious robberies were averted, burglaries and other major crimes detected and those responsible apprehended, together with large amounts of property from such crimes being recovered.

I received information from my 'snout' that a large amount of jewellery would be changing hands on Lime Street railway station one morning at 7am. The boss (the late Detective Inspector Johnny Ralphson) was informed and he gave his blessing for my partner and I go there the following morning and secrete ourselves and await the 'transaction'. The following morning my partner (Eric Fletcher) and I met as previously arranged at Lime street station, outside the gents' toilets, (there were always undesirables hanging around there). We were both in our usual scruffy 'garb'. Unfortunately, Eric had failed to leave his brief case at the office first. Consequently, after being given permission by the ticket collector to go onto the platform (after introducing ourselves) all was well until we spotted the vehicle that we were waiting for. I had secreted myself behind some hoardings, Eric behind some mail sacks. When it was time for us to leave our hiding places to make a dash to intercept the exchange of the jewellery we could see taking place, we ran along the platform and jumped over the ticket barrier.

Unfortunately, the ticket collector had failed to notify the uniformed British Transport Police constable nearby that we (two disguised police officers) were present. On seeing two 'ruffians', one carrying a leather brief case, the officer, courageously and correctly, attempted to tackle Eric after unsuccessfully shouting to him to stop. Eric made a magnificent side slip and managed to dodge the officer's outstretched arms, however, I was not so lucky. By now the constable had drawn his truncheon and as I too tried to dodge him I was felled by an almighty smack to the side of my head with his 'wooden protector'.

I was temporarily stunned. I felt myself being dragged to my feet in a vice like grip. I felt blood trickling down my face. "I'm a police officer" I managed to gasp. "And I'm J. Edgar Hoover" the bobby sarcastically replied. The previously 'brain dead' ticket collector on seeing this, suddenly realised that he had forgotten to inform the officer. He quickly rectified the situation and the officer let me go and together, he and I joined Eric at the vehicle. It so happened that, there was jewellery being clandestinely prepared to be taken over to the Isle of Man, jewellery from a large house burglary which had recently been committed on the outskirts of the city.

Two men were arrested and a large amount of stolen jewellery re-covered. Apart from a lump and a little cut, and a massive dent to my pride and dignity, I was otherwise Okay. The railway bobby explained that it was Eric's briefcase that had aroused his (the officers) suspicions.

Next time I'd make bloody sure that he left it before almost blowing what transpired to be a good job. Thanks again Olive. It was amazing how safe the streets of the city of Liverpool were becoming once the potential car thieves and robbers became aware of the cameras.

Although the whereabouts of the cameras were a well kept secret, they certainly had a very good deterrent effect on City centre crime.

The camera's didn't help me one sunny afternoon however, when I was on foot patrol in St Johns Lane in company with constable Joe Stubbs 'Joe Ninety'. As we neared the Mersey tunnel entrance I saw three men trying to snatch a purse from an old lady who had been crossing a piece of waste land. I ran across the street and onto the waste land. I grabbed the nearest attacker and shouted for help from passers by on the pavement thirty yards away. My pleas were ignored. Joe had made round the other side of a nearby building to cut off any escape route.

Although I managed to free the old lady's arm from her attackers, and recover her purse, the three then turned on me. One of the men picked up a large piece of concrete from the ground and struck me a violent blow to my face with it. This blow broke my nose and fractured my cheekbone, and also damaged my left eye. I fell to the floor and was repeatedly kicked about the head and body until I lost consciousness, the lady's purse still in my hand. Unknown to me, a Tunnel Police constable (now Superintendent in charge of the Mersey Tunnels Police) Bill Atkins and my colleague, Joe Ninety, arrived and managed to arrest two of the men, the third man escaped. The two would-be robbers were later given heavy sentences at Liverpool Crown court. After a spell off duty injured I subsequently recovered and returned to duty.

There were certainly 'perks' to serving in the Commando Squad. Sometimes, a female member of the squad and I would pretend to be a courting couple and sit canoodling on a seat whilst keeping observations on someone, or some premises. The girls in the squad were as plucky as their male counterparts and they themselves notched up many excellent arrests. I had cause to use the underground Gents' toilets in Victoria Street on one occasion and as I was standing at the urinal., a man came and stood in the next stall, winked at me ,and asked me "Would you like me to give you a wank?" He opened his fly and showed me his erect penis. "Let's go in here" he said, indicating a nearby open cubicle. At the same time I was also joined by my colleague . He was just in time to witness the man's request before I introduced myself to him and arrested him for importuning for immoral purposes. My prisoner bleated that it wasn't fair as he wouldn't have done it if he had known we were the Police. Sad! It just shows how things can happen unexpectedly. My partner and I were on our way in to go off duty when I decided to use the toilet!

Our squad benefited by the arrival of a woman Sergeant - Doreen Prisick. I liked working with Doreen. She was a bloody good copper. Doreen and I had very many successes in and around the City centre 'bus queues and large stores where we arrested many pick-pockets and petty thieves. On yet another occasion I was in company with constable Albert

Kirby (who now being Superintendent Kirby, recently led the successful operation when two children were arrested for the sickening murder of little James Bulger) when, keeping observations on premises where the front door was partly open at 2-I5 am, we arrested two males who were about to remove three typewriters worth £90 each. The typewriters were in the darkened doorway ready for placing into a nearby van.

My time in the Commando Squad was great. The comradeship was fantastic. Some of us would sometimes cover for our partners when they sneaked to the library to do some serious study with the intention of sitting their promotion exams. Some of us, after a decent lock up, would 'treat' ourselves to an hour or two in the cartoon cinema in Church Street, sometimes even getting involved in there, to the delight of the management. Reminiscences of incidents which occurred while serving in the Commandos would not be complete without reference to the 'Battle of the Beards'. There were three of us in the squad who had grown our hair long and cultivated long beards to add authenticity to our dishevelled appearances. This not only suited us perfectly, but also appeared to please the powers that be when foreign dignitaries were to visit, and see what degree of devotion to duty the men and women were prepared to offer.

During this era there were no serving uniformed police officers who were allowed to sport beards. To my knowledge, this applied throughout the country. It was the time when the Beatles took the City of Liverpool by storm on their official visit to their home town. The City was alive with thousands upon thousands of visitors, not only from all over the United Kingdom but from every corner of the globe. The City was absolutely saturated.

Consequently all Police leave and rest days were cancelled. It was obvious that every Police Officer would be required to perform duty during this time. The three of us sporting our beards, Constables Brian Hodgson, John Wiley and myself were therefore instructed to shave off our beards. This we refused to do, as when the city resumed back to normal, in a day or two, we would be returning to our commando duties. We couldn't grow our beards and hair long again, just like that (as the late Tommy Cooper would have said:) so we decided to stand fast on the issue.

There was a large parade held in the parade room at Hatton Garden. At first we were again ordered to remove our beards and long hair. Again we (very nervously and apprehensively) refused and stood fast. The Chief Superintendent then put in an appearance and ordered us to comply. Again, refusal! Finally, the Chief Constable himself attended and after listening to our side he sympathetically said, "Okay, but don't blame us if your'e dragged around by your precious bloody beards". We had won our stand. We were the talk of the wash house.

After all this unnecessary trouble and confrontation there were no incidents involving our beards or long hair. On that particular duty, we three were (I think) the first British bobbies in modern times to patrol the streets in uniform, wearing beards. Once this little lot was over we were 'back in harness' in our scruff. Eventually my relationship with 'Olive' turned sour and she set me up by arranging to meet me in a betting shop in Kensington. I turned up, she didn't. A lot of other unsavoury characters did however. I was certainly lined up for a beating. Fortunately I had my personal radio. I put out a 'Con requires assistance' call. These calls are absolutely guaranteed to bring colleagues running (from whatever it is they are doing) and I was duly rescued from the premises before I came to any harm. So ended Olive's and my honeymoon' period. Ah well, I hadn't done so badly out of our 'relationship'.

When I saw Olive again, she denied all knowledge of a 'set up' but when things turned 'iffy', and there was any doubt, it was time not to place oneself into a similar position again. I certainly gave Olive the 'sack' after that little scare.

After a lengthy period with the Commando Squad, I decided to apply for the CID as I considered that my past record would now benefit me considerably in this venture. I applied to become a detective and I was seconded to the CID as an aide. I was determined to make my career within the CID and now I was given the chance I was going to make the most of it.

My period as a CID aide was both enjoyable and interesting. I made a number of arrests and executed search warrants and recovered a fair amount of stolen property. The trouble was, the time passed so quickly that I was back in uniform before I knew where I was. I completed my first police driving course at the Old Swan Driving School. Unfortunately, one of my close colleagues, Paul Maguire, was sadly killed whilst out in North Wales on a simulated chase. I felt Paul's loss very deeply. I duly passed my course exams and test before being transferred to Westminster Road on uniformed mobile patrols. I enjoyed my time at Westminster Road, I was mainly engaged as the divisional Landrover driver. This vehicle was commonly referred to as the 'Battle Taxi'.

There was no doubting the deterrent effect that the appearance of the Landrover and it's crew had when called to various disturbances or other scenes of public disorder and domestic disputes. Although I was reasonably happy, I was impatiently awaiting the appearance of my name in the Chief Constable's orders to announce my permanent posting to the CID (I hoped).

Finally, my name appeared as I had hoped and prayed it would. I was to be Detective Constable 157 CID and posted to Lower Lane. I would still be covering Westminster Road, Anfield, Lower Lane and Bootle. I was absolutely overjoyed . At long last, I was now a real 'Detective'.

Chapter Eight - The New Detective Constable

Although I was posted in orders to Lower Lane, which was the Divisional Headquarters, I did in fact start my CID duties at Westminster Road, one of the satellite stations of the division.

My new Detective Inspector was Reg Exley and my sergeants were Frank Beardsmore and Jimmy Jenkinson. I soon settled down in my new environment and found my detective colleagues excellent to work with. Ironically, I was now working from the same office where my old friend, Detective Sergeant Charlie Povall used to compile the evidential files when I used to take my prisoners to him from the parks. By now, Charlie had moved on to pastures new, having retired.

'Wessie' Road CID Office first floor windows

My first Chief Inspector as a detective was Alec Williams (ex Birkenhead Borough) he summoned me to his office at Lower Lane during my first week to welcome me into the CID. He wished me well, then ordered me to "prune" my moustache a little. I promised him I would (but never managed to get round to complying with his request!).

I was now into stylish civvies so I thought I would enhance my image by growing my hair into the 'pageboy' style that was common at the time! What a poser I was! My hair style lasted for approximately 6 months before I decided to revert 'back to normal' and wear my hair in the conventional style.

One of my first 'solo' jobs as a detective, involved a particularly nasty wounding of an American sailor. An American warship was paying a visit to Liverpool and whilst here, members of her crew went ashore to visit the many bars, nightclubs and other equally enticing places of interest and entertainment in and around the city.

One young man from the ship, a young rating, was attacked and robbed in the City centre. He was taken to the David Lewis Northern Hospital, (one of my old 'tea specks') and treated for his injuries. As the detective in charge of the case I visited the casualty department and saw the young American. He had been beaten and stabbed. Fortunately, although the incident was serious, the victim's injuries were such that he would ultimately make a full (except for a small scar) recovery. The help and assistance I received from the medical staff at the Northern was excellent. The young casualty doctor, although very busy, didn't hesitate to give me all the assistance I required. I eventually apprehended the person responsible for the attack and he was later sentenced by the Liverpool Crown Court for an offence of robbery. The ship's captain made me very welcome aboard his ship and kindly presented me with a box of expensive cigars (which I duly passed on to my father as I am a non-smoker).

The long gone Northern Hospital

The young casualty doctor appeared with me as a witness in court, as his evidence was important with regard to the victim's injuries.

The 'young' doctor, was eventually to become my own General Practitioner, Dr Alan Price. I will always remember with gratitude, the assistance he gave me during that enquiry. Sadly, the Northern hospital is no more, but I still hold dear the memories of that fine old building and it's wonderful nurses and doctors.

Life as a Detective was to say the least varied. We were left to get on with the job as there was not the supervision that prevailed in the uniformed branch. Unfortunately this trust was (and still is) grossly abused by many members of the department.

Most members of the CID were, and are, very keen and dedicated officers, however, the opposite was quite often the case with many others. I found that in some cases to be a CID officer often manifests a certain amount of snobbery, and some "looked down" on their uniformed colleagues as though they were somewhat inferior. This snobbery was even more rife among CID wives who always insisted to lay people that their husbands had been "Promoted" to the rank of Detective. I can honestly say that although I had now become a member of the department, my utter respect and admiration for the uniformed man on the beat NEVER left me.

Many times I would stay on after my duty time was over and patiently sit with a young uniformed probationer constable and compile his arrest or prosecution file for him, just as Charlie Povall, (and he was a Detective Sergeant) had found time to do for me a long time before. I never allowed myself to forget that being a detective constable was no different whatsoever from being in Traffic, the Mounted or Dog section, or being a motor cyclist. ALL were of the same rank, Constable!. Sometimes this idiotic and childish snobbery did in fact cause animosity and resentment among the uniform fraternity, and rightly so. This persistent attitude is not good for the service and ultimately not good for the public to whom the service is answerable.

There were other things that I was soon to discover to my dislike. I found that most offices or sections contained their inevitable cliques. Grovelling and tittle tattle was often rife with some running to the boss with the latest gossip from the "serious rumour squad" which was sweeping the office concerning some poor individual or other. There were also the inevitable and monotonously regular visits to various watering holes, where the little gatherings would meet to prop up the bar for most of the evening when some would cadge free ale from the landlord who feared it wouldn't be in his best interests to refuse, and didn't have the courage to make those so inclined put their hands in their pockets and pay for their drinks. Mostly while they were so engaged, some other poor detective (probably the latest arrival onto the section) would be running round and taking on all of the jobs that were coming into the office.

I well remember one of my detective colleagues "booking out" to an enquiry in the office diary and asking one of his mates to 'Show him a call" in the same diary some two hours later from a certain place, when in actual fact he went to pick up his girlfriend, then drove over to West Kirby on the Wirral before walking out over the sands to Hilbre Island for an afternoon's sunbathing. He later returned to the office and resumed his "normal" duties some hours later, no one in authority being any the wiser!.

The same sort of thing occurred when some of the officers were "out on the pop", but officially carrying out their numerous enquiries.

Some landlords wouldn't play" but the majority of them did tolerate this form or behaviour, and so it went on (and still does to this day). It is of little wonder therefore that their uniformed colleagues felt frustrated when trying to contact the CID and being told that they "were engaged!" but knew damned well where most of them were, or at least what they were up to!

CID duty does indeed entail the frequenting of drinking dens of one sort or another, it is an essential part of being a detective to visit the haunts of known criminals and their associates. There is no doubt that enquiries into many serious offences were, and are, laboriously pursued with the utmost vigour via such establishments, and consequently a lot of these enquiries, due to such visits are eventually brought to a successful conclusion and their perpetrators brought to book. In every walk of life, there were some very hard working officers, there were also those perpetual 'hangers on' who lived off the success of their colleagues.

I was always very wary of becoming too friendly with pub landlords, as some enjoyed the fact that their premises were frequented by the 'Jacks' (CID officers) because this acted as a form of 'insurance' by discouraging the wrong element to patronise the pub.

However, there were the landlords who would willingly ply many officers with free drinks to ensure that they made regular visits. Fair enough! But whenever the landlord was subject to a 'walk through' by a uniformed sergeant and his constable during a licensed premises supervision visit, and was caught contravening some form of legislation, the landlord would often 'threaten' the uniformed officers by 'seeing his friends in the CID!" who may be senior in rank to the particular uniformed officer concerned. This sort of behaviour did not go down too well at all.

It was not unusual for a CID man to approach a uniformed colleague who had reported a landlord for a traffic offence or parking violation. The uniformed officer would be asked to 'Go easy' or even drop the matter completely, as 'the landlord's a mate of mine!'. Sometimes this tactic worked, most times it didn't however, and the detective would be given short shrift by the officer concerned.

I never consciously allowed myself to be compromised in any way by members of the licensing fraternity whenever I was in their company. That is not to say that I did not 'partake' myself in those places, but at least I always paid my way.

There were a lot of ambitious officers in the CID who went on to greater things by eventually being promoted to senior rank because of their integrity, ability and merit as they relentlessly carried out their duties in an honest and thorough manner.

Other procedures of which I did not approve (or partake) were the unfortunately too regular 'placing' of the occasional bottle of spirits or carton of cigarettes under certain bosses' desks from an overnight 'job'. This was to put a particular detective in good books of whichever boss was the recipient. Contrary to popular belief, this went on a lot! It would be untrue to say categorically that this sort of behaviour did not bear fruit, as it certainly gained reward in some manner or form for some of those who indulged in this unsavoury practice.

It was often intriguing to find that certain "plum" jobs, transfers or postings had been given to an officer who was not known for his good detection work or report writing. Some of these were known by their colleagues as downright "bad apples".

I once received information from an informant that a large consignment of cigarettes, cigars and pipe tobacco to the value of £20,000 was secreted inside an underground garage beneath a large block of flats in the City. I informed my superior officers and arrangements were made for the area to be "staked out". Eventually the villains arrived to collect their haul. There were four of them, all well known professional warehouse breakers of the underworld's "first division". They arrived in their vehicle and prepared to load their booty. As they started to load the cartons into their large transit van they were all arrested and the goods recovered.

Some of the senior detectives present had arrived in their own cars. This in itself was not unusual as we often, for convenience, would use our own car if the CID vehicles were all engaged. On this occasion however, after the villains were arrested and taken into custody, some of the tobacco and cigarettes found their way into the boots of some of those officers' cars. By the time that the Police van had arrived to collect the goods for removal to the Police station, the stock had somewhat diminished. A "slightly" depleted amount was eventually booked into the property book. Although it was originally my "job", it was taken over from me by an officer of senior rank. I heard later that a "back-hander" had been forthcoming from an insurance company regarding the matter, although to whom, I was never to discover. I saw many unsavoury incidents similar to those I had witnessed while serving at Rose Hill, but I always steered clear of those objectionable participants, whom I resented profusely.

I must emphasise that for every "bad apple" there was an orchard full of genuine officers whose integrity was of the highest standard and beyond reproach. It would however, be a brave man who attempted to "shop" those bad apples, as in some cases the seam ran right through the rock face of rank so who could one approach with certainty ?

At times my thoughts occasionally turned to the promotion side. Many times I had thought of sitting the sergeant's examination but at first I never did much about it.

To pass the exam warranted a great deal of devoted study, nothing less would suffice as law is a very complex subject. I suppose that like most of my colleagues (in and out of uniform) I preferred to be out on the streets, performing the practical side of the job at the sharp end, catching villains.

Towards the end of 1970 I attended the Metropolitan Police Detective Training School at Peel House, London. There I was to undergo a course of training and also at Scotland Yard (hopefully to make me into a better detective ?). I was billeted at a very fine, large detached house in Selbourne Gardens, Hendon. The gardens of this fine house backed onto the well known former airfield of RAF Hendon which included the RAF Museum. My landlady was a wonderful old lady, Mrs Dare. What a lovely lady she was. She was to look after me as if I were her own son.

My journey into London each day necessitated travelling by two separate underground tube trains each way. Each train was packed to capacity. I hated those daily journeys. I found that the commuters were by and large solely concerned only with themselves. I'm alright Jack, push the boat out, I'm aboard! It appeared to be every man for himself!

Travelling to work in London one morning, I was standing in the gangway of the train carriage holding onto the overhead strop, the inevitable confounded umbrella and briefcase stabbing me in the back and front, and choking to death on the despicably foul cigarette and pipe smoke that floated around lingering at head level, stinging my nostrils

As I stood there I saw an elderly, bowler hatted "city gent" dressed in the traditional dark blue pin striped suit with scarlet handkerchief protruding from his top breast pocket. He was reading the morning paper through a pair of gold rimmed half moon spectacles. In contrast, sitting next to him was a dirty young man in his early twenties wearing a leather jacket, jeans and his long unkempt hair hung over his dirty pimply face. Apparently the older man's arm was touching the arm of the youth and each was trying to keep his arm on the armrest between them. The next thing, as the train stopped at a station the young man got up from his seat shouting, "Here, have all the fucking seat" and punched the older man violently in the face cutting his lip and breaking his glasses. He then pushed through the carriage and vanished through the open door into the rush hour crowd . Nobody did a thing to help the poor distressed old man, who was very shocked. and left in a very distressed condition. I went to the to the old man and, removing his handkerchief from his top pocket dabbed his mouth and comforted him. I was the only person to assist the poor man. He declined to report the matter and when he regained his composure, unsteadily left the train, still very distressed, at his station further along the line. Not one person batted an eyelid. So much for helping a fellow man in distress. Certainly not on Londons' tubes anyway.

I spent my weekends walking around the various well known places and buildings of London. I also managed to accompany a Metropolitan Police colleague, (who was a member of the Met flying club) flying the club's Piper aircraft. Whilst walking in the City one day I met an ex Liverpool Police colleague in Piccadilly Circus. He had left the Police to become an airline pilot and was now flying for a commercial airline. He and I used to fly together back home in Liverpool. We went for a drink and arranged to meet the following day, my rest day. The next day, as he knew London far better than I, my friend conducted me on a guided tour of the Metropolis .

We visited Buckingham Palace, Madame Tussauds, Houses of Parliament, Tower of London and other equally interesting places. We even went into the House of Commons public gallery to witness the debacle of grown men trying to out shout each other in the name of Democracy . What an education that was. We had an excellent and very interesting day, although I must admit London is just not my scene.

With my pal being in the airlines, he kindly offered to arrange for me to fly home to Liverpool at weekends. This offer I gratefully accepted.

One Eleven jet from Heathrow to Liverpool, leaving London at 8 am Saturday morning and arriving at Liverpool Speke airport half an hour later. The fare? £1-9-0 return, (One pound and forty five pence). What it was to have friends in the right places! I returned on the Monday morning in time to be at the Yard for 9 am. On a couple of occasions Mrs Dare kindly allowed my son to stay at Selbourne Gardens for the weekend (at no cost). This gave me the chance to take him to see the Palace guards, the Horseguards and the Imperial War museum. He and I presented Mrs Dare with a bunch of flowers on the first occasion and a large box of chocolates the second.

One of my CID colleagues from Liverpool, Sergeant Jack Johnson also attended at Peel House and he and I sometimes used to travel home together in his car sharing the cost of the fuel.

I regularly attended at Post Mortem examinations whilst down there and was lectured by the very eminent and world famous Home Office Pathologist, Dr Charles St. Hill. I found this side of my duties very interesting and educationally beneficial. Forensic science was very important to a criminal investigator.

Eventually, I returned home to my family at the conclusion my period with the Met. I was glad to get back home and was looking forward to resuming my CID duties back in the 'fold'. Once I returned I continued my work as a (hopefully now much better) detective?

I dealt with many incidents, some unfortunately very tragic. I made many friends among the public (and many enemies among the villains) and always offered a sympathetic and understanding approach to the poor victims and casualties of such tragedies. Many of these friendships exist to this day. Court appearances consumed a large amount of a busy police officer's time. Obviously, the busier one was apprehending villains, the more one had to attend court. I certainly had my fair share of court appearances at both Magistrates and Crown Court.

Not every case of mine that went before the court resulted in the person being charged ultimately being convicted. It is surprising how some advocates tend to portray their clients to the court, and to juries in particular. It was equally surprising how they also portrayed each prosecution witness who gave evidence against their client.

One such case of mine involved a very serious indecent assault against a four year old boy. The case was before a judge and jury at Liverpool Crown Court.

The circumstances of the case are that the young boy was playing in a rear entry one day in the Anfield area of the City. The toddler was approached by a 23 year old man who started to talk to him and gave the boy a sweet. The man then tried to force the boy into committing an act of oral sex with him and in so doing injured the little boy's face. The frightened little lad then screamed with pain and his screams were heard by a woman engaged in cleaning her back yard step further along the entry. His screams were also heard by a man who was on a ladder cleaning windows nearby. Both of these people saw what was happening and rushed to the aid of the boy. The young man ran away on seeing them approach, and made good his escape. The boy was taken by his parents to hospital and treated for his (minor) injuries, which were slight bruising and scratches. The Police were summoned and Constable Griff Jones attended the scene in his patrol car. The officer noted details of the incident and searched the area in an effort to trace the offender without result. The CID were informed and I was the detective allocated to deal with the matter.

I commenced to make numerous enquiries in the area via informants and door to door visits to local residents.

After approximately two weeks, my enquiries eventually led me to a public house near to one of the major football grounds. I had received information that the man I was looking for in connection with the incident involving the little boy, was a barman at ——— public house. Further enquiries about the man referred to revealed that he was seen regularly in or near parks where children played and was also seen hanging around schools.

Armed with this information, I went to the public house after requesting discreet back up by uniformed colleagues in case of any 'breach of the peace'. Coincidentally, one of my back up colleagues was Constable Jones the officer who had originally dealt with the incident.

I entered the pub and there, behind the bar was my 'quarry'. After he had finished serving a customer I went to him and introduced myself, told him the nature of my enquiries and that I believed that he could help me with those enquiries. His face drained of colour. "How did you find out it was me" he gasped. I asked him to accompany me to Anfield CID office but he said that he couldn't leave the premises as there were no staff other himself on the premises. I told him that either he accompanied me to the station or I would be obliged to arrest him. He then instructed his customers to drink up and leave as 'due to circumstances beyond his control' he was closing the pub.

Constable Jones and a colleague conveyed my apprehensive barman to Anfield Police station while I followed in the CID car. I took him through to the CID office and there once again told him that I had reason to believe that he was the person responsible for an offence of indecent Assault and Gross Indecency on a four year old boy, naming the date, time and place of the offence disclosed. He was cautioned after which he said "I'm sorry, I don't know what came over me". He was asked if he wishes to make a statement regarding the matter and he elected to make a statement which I then, at his request, took down in writing at his dictation. In his statement, the man gave a full an frank admission regarding the offences with the young boy. At the end of the statement, he endorsed, in his own handwriting, certification of the fact that he had read the statement and he had been told that he could correct, alter or add anything he wished, and that the statement was true and made of his own free will. He then appended his signature.

This would quite clearly seem to have brought my enquiries with regard to this sordid affair to a successful conclusion.

The man was cautioned, and charged with indecent assault and gross indecency with the child. He was committed to the Crown Court after electing trial by jury at the Magistrates Court where he pleaded 'Not Guilty'? He was represented by a barrister with a formidable reputation amongst us bobbies. It amazes me, these 'persons in need of help and guidance' freely admit their heinous guilt but then decide after 'taking advice'! to elect trial by jury and deny the offence. Sometimes they are advised to elect trial at Crown Court, where they are then advised to plead 'Guilty'. Why couldn't they have pleaded the same at the lower court? The mind boggles. ; Let us not deceive ourselves. Going to the Crown Court after Magistrates Court incurs a greater fee then attending Magistrates Court alone.

During the trial (which was very distressing for the child and his family) all the witnesses gave their evidence for the Prosecution. They were then, in turn, cross examined by the accused's defence counsel. First, the woman who had witnessed the incident while cleaning her step. She was questioned at great length. It was put to her that she was mistaken and that it wasn't counsel's client that she saw on the day. She replied that she was certain it was the man in the dock that she saw committing the offences against the little boy. She was then asked what the weather was like on the day. Was it cloudy? What was the exact time? Who else was about? and many other memory taxing questions. As the lady was not certain as to what the weather was like, how could she be certain that the man she saw was the man in the dock? By the time the woman left the witness box she was quite confused, and angry that she was having her honest recollection of the incidents so categorically disputed. She left the court in tears. The next witness, the window cleaner, gave his evidence in a quiet voice "Will you speak up, we can't hear" snapped defence counsel. These strategic interruptions usually had the effect of unnerving some witnesses.

The window cleaner gave his evidence slowly, honestly deliberating before describing in detail what he had seen in the rear entry when the man in the dock was molesting the boy.

"Can you describe what the man was wearing at the time?" he was asked when defence cross examination commenced. "Er, I'm not too sure, Now, I think he had a dark anorak on and" ——"You think! You think!" he was rudely interrupted. "What d'you mean you think? I thought you were sure of what you saw?" he went on. The poor window cleaner was again knocked out of his stride at counsel's deliberate interruptions.

Counsel then asked the witness, "You are telling us the honest truth today aren't you Mr————?" The witness replied, "Of course I am. I don't tell lies". "Would you say that you are an honest man then?" put in counsel. "Yes I would" said the indignant witness, hurtfully looking to the judge for (unforthcoming) support.

"Once again, for the benefit of His Lordship and the members of the jury, I ask you, are you an honest person?" The witness was becoming a little cross at having his integrity questioned and snapped, "Of course I'm an honest person, I wouldn't be here now if I wasn't would I?" Counsel countered, "But is it not true that you have been convicted of offences of dishonesty in the past. Offences of theft?" By now the window cleaner was shuffling in the witness box uncomfortably. He didn't appear to know how to cope now. "Will you answer my question. Have you been convicted of offences of dishonesty in the past?"

The witness then muttered, "well, yes, but ——", "Mr —— will you speak up, we can't hear what your saying" smirked the delighted advocate looking toward the deadpan faces of the jurors. "Yes but that's not —" "thank you Mr ——, so your'e not an honest person then are you? That is all. No further questions m'lord" said the "Oscar seeking Rumpole of the Bailey", as he gathered his gown about him before depositing himself proudly down onto his seat.

The poor witness left the court dejectedly. his criminal past laid before the court for all to know. I momentarily forgot who it was that was on trial, the witness attending to give evidence as a public spirited citizen, or the smug piece of low life sneering in the dock.

Counsel went on to make good play of the fact that it would be wrong to give much credence to a self admitted dishonest person, asking the jury if they could rely on evidence from such a person whose dishonesty had been established.

I was then called into the witness box to give my evidence. I gave my evidence, slowly and precisely, taking my time to allow the judge, counsel and stenographer to write down what I was saying. I knew this barrister from previous altercations we had engaged in. When my turn came for his cross examination, I was prepared for any line of attack, in whatever form it came. I was cheekily asked by him at one stage to divulge my source of information and name my helpful informants. This I absolutely refused to do, under whatever penalty I may invoke or risk, (the same barrister had tried this before with me. He was not on).

During my evidence I had referred to the statement of admission that I had obtained from the accused. I now produced the statement and was asked if this was the actual document, the original. I confirmed that this was so. After I had concluded my answers to his very lengthy and deeply thorough cross examination, defence counsel stood, both hands gripping the front of his black gown while he looked at me for a period over the top of his gold rimmed half moon spectacles. He turned to the jury before returning his piercing gaze to me. This was the intimidating psyching ploy!. This certainly did work on some people. No way whatsoever did it have any effect on me. As far as I was concerned, he could go and get stuffed.

I looked him straight in the eyes. Eventually I stared him out. When he put his left arm down and leaning onto his bench, the other hand still clutching his gown, his yellowing wig atop of his head with some of his own brown hair protruding from under the sides, he asked me if his client really did give the statement 'voluntarily'? I confirmed that this was so.

Counsel then addressed me, "Officer, without wishing to be disrespectful to you, one can't help but notice your dark curling eyebrows and your very large handlebar moustache". (I though to myself, ey ey, what's next?) He went on, "As I say, there is no disrespect meant to you, but you do look very fierce. My client is somewhat backward and he says that he is terrified of you".

"He didn't seem very frighted when he drank the cup of tea I gave him during the interview" I countered. "Nevertheless officer, my client being backward and your looking so fierce had a frightening effect on him. He maintains that he made the statement admitting the offences because he was frightened of you".

"That isn't true" I replied. This line of attack went on for some time. The defence emphasised that they didn't dispute the contents of the document but maintained that it was obtained under intentional or unintentional duress, I vehemently refuted this but the barrister continued to pursue this routine, "to look at you standing there with your big shoulders and I emphasise, a fierce expression. why, you even frighten me" there were sniggers from the jury box. Well this is certainly a new line I thought.

Whereas to a layman, all this may be found to be very amusing, the outcome of the trial was not so amusing, especially to the parents of the child or the prosecution witnesses.

The Judge in his summing up at the conclusion of the trial made mention of the comments put forward by the defence in relation to the 'taking' of the statement of admission. He advised that if the jury thought that in fact the defendant had given the statement out of fear, because he was 'terrified of Mr Turner' then the statement would not have been freely given.

I don't know if this had any bearing on the outcome, but the accused was in fact acquitted of both charges and walked free.

To add insult to injury, he even grinned and gave a two fingered gesture to me as he left the court building. Let's just say I felt a 'little frustrated'. I even bore the brunt of acid comments from my two prosecution witnesses. Both stated that if that is what one goes through helping the police and courts, for nothing, it would be the last time either would help the police in future. There were, and are, many cases that end in a similarly and equally frustrating vein. No wonder that there are many who consider that the offender NOT the poor victims are those who need (and get) the help from all forms of society's 'Do Gooders". Perhaps one day, hopefully, the pendulum will start to swing the other way.

As in all walks of life there were and are many hard working and concientious members of the legal profession, many I am proud to call my friends, whose integrity is faultless, nevertheless, some bad apples prevail just as they do in the Police force !

Although I considered myself relentless in the apprehending and ultimate prosecution of society's deviants, I did sometimes accept that there were cases that should never be put before a court.

One such case, although trivial to some, was very serious to the defendant.

I was present at Liverpool City Magistrates' Court one morning waiting for one of my cases to come up before the 'beak' . I was sitting at the back of the court listening to those cases being heard before mine.

In actual fact, the case to which I refer was tried before the stipendiary magistrate. It was an offence of 'Angling without a licence' in one of the City's parks.

The middle aged man so charged had just been made redundant from his job after being employed for more than twenty years. Due to this he , quite naturally became very depressed and morose. His continued efforts to find himself new work failed to bear fruit.

His wife (whom he called as a witness) bought him a fishing rod and some ancillary angling kit, which, in the family's present financial situation, could not really be afforded.

One boring, depressing day, the man concerned took his wife's advice and went into the local park for a morning's quiet and pensive fishing. He had been there for approximately three hours and although he hadn't caught anything, he was enjoying the serenity and peace of his surroundings.

This enjoyable period was rudely interrupted by the pompous arrival of a Local Authority bailiff. Our unhappy, redundant, angler was asked if he had purchased a ticket permitting him to fish the park lake. Apparently, in his ignorance of such a requirement i.e to purchase an angling permit, our defendant did not have the required document for the Bailiff's inspection. However, the angler did volunteer to purchase a ticket there and then but this offer was refused by the Bailiff. The Bailiff was arrogant and completely lacked the initiative and discretion which could have been used to solve this minute problem. The man's repeated offer to purchase a permit was refused and he (the Bailiff) reported the angler to his authority, who in their tunnel visioned, red taped and bureaucratic wisdom, issued the poor unfortunate angler (who had NEVER suffered the indignity of a court appearance in his life) with a summons to appear before the City Magistrates Court. Not only was the man intimidated by having to sit amongst some of the City's 'riff raff' whilst awaiting his court appearance, but so was his equally law abiding wife, who came with him to give her support.

On hearing the case through, and hearing the sorrowful tale of woe from the defendant and his wife, the Stipendiary Magistrate nearly blew his top. He was completely at a loss as to why the City's resources and those of the Criminal Justice system were engaged in bringing a futile prosecution such as this Even hardened criminals sitting there in court were muttering their disapproval at such trivia being brought before the court.

As the man had pleaded guilty to the charge, the Stipendiary had absolutely no option whatsoever but to impose a penalty.

The man was fined £20 and the Local Authority were severely rebuked at bringing about such a prosecution and waste of court time. "You'll have to send me to jail, because I just can't afford to pay the fine" uttered the still very bewildered defendant. For the one and only time in my life, I stood up and went to the Clerk of the court and wrote out a cheque for twenty pounds and handed it to her. "The fine's been paid into court Sir" she informed the Magistrate. The defendant stood open mouthed. Once outside he and his wife (who was so overcome by the whole shoddy procedure that she wept uncontrollably) thanked me profusely and offered to pay me back the money as soon as he could. I wouldn't hear of it. I wished them both well and hoped his problems would eventually sort themselves out. I also hoped that the Bailiff concerned would receive his come - uppance one day !

Many sources of the detective's information were kept a closely guarded secret, known only to him or herself. These sources were come by, acquired, or 'earned' in many ways.

During our patrols or 'walkabouts', myself and some of my colleagues used to call into one or other of the local shops for a cuppa and a chat. One of my favourite haunts was a little second hand book shop in one of the side streets lying in the shadow of Anfield's famous football ground.

The owner of the shop was a tall grey haired 45 year old man who lived locally with his sister (I shall call him Andy) and sold second hand books, and other bits of bric a brac. Andy was a homosexual and was not very 'pro' police. I first met him when I attended his shop after the premises were broken into during one night.

It was obvious by Andy's demeanour and feminine behaviour that he was gay. Still, that's nothing to do with me thought I. Normally, when he requested the attendance of the police, he would be subject to adverse comments and even micky taking due to his tendencies. This I did not agree with and he was to receive the same attention as I would afford to others who required such.

Unusually for me, I actually felt sorry for Andy. Due to my enquiries regarding the break-in at his shop, I was to make further visits to his premises. As my visits and enquiries continued I must admit, I found Andy to be very polite and respectful, and even got to quite like the man. So long as he kept his gay lifestyle to himself and didn't encroach it onto others - what did I care. He never gave me any cause for criticism and I always found him to be pleasant. He was to behave differently to other officers however, because of the way he was treated by them.

Apparently, due to the manner in which I dealt with my enquiries at his shop (one which I never solved) Andy was impressed by my conduct and the sympathetic way in which I carried out my duty towards him. He obviously wasn't used to such attention. Why not? The old maxim applies - Live and let live!

As time went on and Andy was to get to know me better, he eventually came to trust me implicitly. If he ever needed the police, he would ring and ask for me when he was being harassed by local yobs, knowing that I would deal with the matter for him as best I could.

After a somewhat delicate matter which really amounted to Andy being subjected to blackmail (a very serious offence), I managed to deal with the matter without resorting to the big stick of prosecution and thus saving a lot of 'dirty linen' being embarrassingly washed in public. Due to my successful aversion of extreme unpleasantness, Andy now trusted me completely and as a gesture of his gratitude he became one of my best and most reliable informants. An extremely valuable asset to my 'detective's armoury'.

I myself, was subject to banter and the occasional ribald remarks from my colleagues because I refused to play their game and humiliate Andy by ridiculing him. He was regularly referred to as 'that bloody poof with the book shop' and any attention requested was 'reluctantly' given, or given without much enthusiasm.

However, it didn't alter the fact that his 'gay' leanings were his own business and he was entitled to the same degree of police attention as anyone else. It suited me to maintain contact anyway as it meant that I was regularly clearing up crime and that is what I was paid to do.

There were the occasional times when Andy was to become a pain, like the occasion when I walked into his shop from the street in company with a colleague. I asked if all was well and Andy then pulled out his handkerchief and started to cry because the yobs had given him a bad time. "Christ Andy, I'm not your bloody minder" I reminded him, "Sort them out yourself can't you?" Andy quickly turned his head away and minced into the back of the shop sobbing, "I was going to make you a coffee, but I'm not now, so there!"

On occasions such as this, I would walk out of the shop "See you Andy, Byeee!" "Christ, must be the time of the month" grinned my sarcastic colleague.

Neither Joe Public or any of my colleagues even knew the degree of important information that Andy supplied to me and subsequently enabled me to clear up many unsolved crimes in the area, recover stolen property and put a few villains where they belonged, behind bars.

Sadly, tragedy was to befall Andy. A tiff with a male friend had led to a violent argument culminating in Andy receiving a knife wound which subsequently proved fatal, my source of regular information, and a friendship, were brought to an untimely end.

The man who inflicted the wound was charged and convicted of Andy's manslaughter. Irrespective of what others thought of my 'gay' friend, I liked the man and was very sorry to learn of his demise.

My new mode of transport now took the form of a more modern four door Ford Anglia after 'part-exing' my old 'Pop'.

Like most of my colleagues serving at Westminster Road, I used to park my vehicle alongside the station in Rockley Street. Our station at Westminster Road also incorporated in the building complex, Liverpool's Westminster Road fire Station, the entrance and exit for their fire engines also being in Rockley Street.

Our CID office windows overlooked the street where our vehicles were parked which enabled us to keep a constant eye on them.

One morning, whilst our office was a hive of activity, some of us typing out reports, completing files and preparing evidence for court, we suddenly heard a loud bang.

After the crew of a fire engine next door had completed one of their regular mornings' fire and hose drill (which always left their engine house floor and part of the cobbled street outside wet with pools of water from the fire hoses) a fire engine had been driven out of the engine house and

105

skidded. The machine then crashed into the rear vehicle forming the line of our parked cars. On hearing the crunch and the sound of breaking glass, we all rushed to the window. Looking down into the street below we were horrified at the sight that greeted us.

The fire engine, having embedded itself into the vehicle at the end of the line, had then pushed that vehicle into the next, which in turn had been catapulted into the next and so on. The whole line of vehicles were quite badly damaged. Fortunately there were no injuries, there were however, many unprintable expletives uttered from myself and my mortified colleagues.

Some of us were luckier than others, one or two of the vehicles suffered very serious damage. My 'new' Anglia suffered a bent front bumper and a crumpled rear bumper and boot lid. The Fire Brigade instructed us to forward our damage estimates and told us that these would be settled. True to their word, the damage bills were settled within a matter of a few weeks or so.

Whilst serving at Westminster Road, I was to have another, far more embarrassing dealing with my fire brigade colleagues next door.

Early one morning, my sergeant, Frank Beardsmore, and I were up with the lark and out on observations in County Road. We were watching a nearby newsagents shop as Frank had information that a youth he was after for a number of burglaries would be meeting a friend at this particular shop before they both left in the friend's car for London.

After an hour's wait, our suspect arrived at 6am and went into the shop, returning a short time later with a newspaper. He stood outside the shop reading his paper awaiting the arrival of his friend.

Frank and I went to the youth and Frank introduced himself to him. Suddenly, the youth pushed Frank in the chest and ran off like a scalded cat. I gave chase and we ran along back entries, over walls and across front gardens before I finally managed to bring him down with a rugby tackle near Everton Football Ground, some distance from where we had started. There was a violent struggle, during which I eventually overpowered him. For some reason, Liverpool Police, unlike neighbouring County forces, did not issue handcuffs to its officers. However, many of us took it upon ourselves to acquire this important and useful item by purchasing our own. Handcuffs were not part of the standard issue as Liverpool lagged far behind in this department,. Indeed, it was not long since the uniformed branch had started to be issued with pocketed shirts and epaulettes. Having and using one's own handcuffs was frowned upon (by those in authority who had probably never seen an angry man, let alone been confronted by one!).

I had been carrying and using handcuffs since my entry into the Commando Squad, having purchased these via an advertisement in Police Review.

To prevent my prisoner offering more violence, and to make sure that he didn't escape, I snapped my handcuffs onto his wrist and then onto my own. He was now staying with me whatever!

My abusive young thug and I walked back to where we had

originally left Frank, a distance of nearly a mile. Frank greeted me with "Good lad Swasie, I'd never have caught him, that's for sure", I felt quite proud of my physical prowess as an Olympic candidate for the marathon! We walked to our CID car parked nearby and my (Frank's) prisoner and I seated ourselves in the back. Frank drove us back to Westminster Road Station.

On arrival at the station, my sergeant instructed me to remove the handcuffs from the youth and deposit him upstairs into the CID sergeant's office. As I walked through the front office of the building, my heart missed a beat when I suddenly remembered that this morning I had travelled to work by train, having left my car outside a garage in Hoylake for it to undergo a service.

The key to the handcuffs was on the same ring as my ignition keys ....in Hoylake. I then remembered that one of my colleagues, Derek Whalley, (now Detective Inspector) had a set of handcuffs of his own and I had noticed that his car was parked outside as I entered the building. I was saved? Derek would put matters right and release us, or so I thought!

As I entered our office I saw Derek sitting at his desk typing. I went to him, and as there were other persons present, I discreetly whispered in his ear, "Hey Degs, could you undo these, I've left my keys at home".

Detective Sergeant Frank Beardsmore (reclining with pipe)

As yet, Sergeant Beardsmore was not aware of my 'faux pas'.

Derek stood up and produced his key, it was obvious that it wouldn't open my 'cuffs as his were of a different make.

I was now becoming quite apprehensive. It is always the way that

107

when things run smoothly nothing is said and a 'blind eye' is turned. However, if there are any 'ripples' things are quite different.Now I would have to explain my being handcuffed to a prisoner when we didn't have handcuffs in our force. I wasn't so much worried about my sergeant, Frank, but if the detective inspector Reg Exley was to become aware of the situation, I might have problems. I had no alternative but to go through to the sergeants office dragging the protesting prisoner and 'cough' to Frank, in front of the other sergeants, AND the prisoner. Frank didn't hesitate to let all and sundry know that I had dropped an almighty clanger. The prisoner then joined in by complaining that the 'cuffs were hurting him and he was going to make a complaint. All I needed now was the inspector to make an appearance and make my day.

"We'll have to get the Fire Brigade" mused Frank to the delight of all those present. When I realised that he was not joking, I senselessly asked him, "Do we have to Sarge?" "Well how the hell do we free you both then?" was his angry response.

As he was not prepared to let me go discreetly next door to the Fire Station to have ourselves freed (as he considered, quite rightly I suppose, that this would be a security risk) he requested the attendance of the Fire Service at the Police Station. There was no way that I was going downstairs to present myself to everybody and his dog as the Village idiot, so I awaited the arrival of the firemen in the CID office.

A short time later the Fire Brigade arrived in the form of two burly firemen, one of them a Sub officer. His colleague was 'armed' with a large, sinister looking pair of bolt croppers. I stood there and had the most humiliating experience of having to watch while my handcuffs were sliced through like a knife through butter and ruined beyond repair. First the prisoner was released, then as the fireman was about to release me, one office smart Alec jibed, "Don't bother with him, it'll teach him a lesson. Leave 'em on!" Christ I felt like melting and disappearing into the floor.

My highly successful chase culminating in the capture of the escaping prisoner ended in utter humiliation with the added indignity of a severe roasting from my detective inspector (somebody just couldn't resist letting him know) for my use of 'unofficial' equipment, not to mention the fact that my handcuffs were now cut into four separate pieces and were fit only for the bin.

Roasting or not, I purchased a new pair within the following week. I ensured however, that I would always, have a spare key to hand in future. "Swings and roundabouts" as my old sergeant, Sergeant Sankey used to say - "Swings and roundabouts".

Another sergeant whom I liked working with at Westminster Road and Anfield, was Alan Griffiths. Alan was always willing to go out and look for jobs even though he always had enough to be getting on with After sitting and bashing away at the typewriter for an hour or two he would turn to me and say "Come on Swas, let's go out and see what's doing". He nearly always preferred to use his own car, a large luxurious two tone grey Austin Westminster with deep leather upholstered seats. Many were the times we used to 'patrol' our patch in that beautiful vehicle. We were out on one such 'patrol' during which we visited local scrap yards inspecting and endorsing their 'record of transactions' book whilst the nervous scrap dealer looked on, hoping we wouldn't find anything untoward in his scriptures. Alan decided to drive up a narrow entry which led off Netherfield Road into a little cul-de-sac. A red brick, derelict looking building caught his eye. Although weeds and grass grew near the walls of the building, none grew alongside the old rotted looking wooden doors.

As the saying goes 'grass doesn't grow on a busy street!' We decided to stop and see if we could look inside the premises. There was a crack in one of the heavily padlocked doors, but we found that a large panel of plywood had been strategically placed to deny prying eyes to see what was inside.

Our suspicions were now aroused and we decided to try to gain access to the premises. As it was so securely locked, we couldn't get in. I looked around and found a length of wood thin enough to push in the crack in the door.

I manipulated the plywood panel away from the crack to enable us to see inside. There, stacked in rows were a large number of brand new lorry tyres, each tyre probably worth eighty to one hundred pounds or so. Such a valuable commodity would surely not be left in such a derelict and vulnerable place legitimately. They must be stolen.

Alan and I made exhaustive enquiries to establish who owned (or possibly rented) the old building. We drew a blank, as the whole of that area was soon to be demolished as redevelopment was to take place. We decided to secrete ourselves nearby in another derelict building overnight hoping to catch any 'visitors' to the site.

Our persevering initiative paid off. During the early hours we heard a vehicle approach and looking out from our place of concealment, we saw a large van arrive and stop outside the building we were watching.

The vehicles lights and engine were switched off and a man alighted from the vehicle. He went to the rear of the van and opened the van doors. He then unlocked and removed the large padlock from the doors of the building. We waited and saw the man reappear rolling one of the large tyres which he then struggled to place into the back of the van.

At this point Alan and I went to the man and confronted him. We introduced ourselves to him and asked him to account for the presence of the tyres and also his strange nocturnal behaviour. At first the man tried to insult our intelligence with some ridiculous tale of 'doing a good turn for a mate, whose name temporarily escaped him, but they drank together'. He went on to say that he was only collecting some of the tyres for this 'mate'.

He was informed that it didn't matter if he couldn't remember anything as he would have all the time in the world while he sat in a cell if he didn't come up with the right answer to our questions.

Finally, he admitted that the tyres were from a large warehouse break in Birmingham a couple of days earlier and he was 'minding them'.

He would not reveal the identity of the 'breakers(s)' but readily admitted having 'received' stolen property. He was subsequently

Anfield Bridewell

arrested and charged with the offence of 'receiving'. (Handling as it is now) and due to the value of the items recovered (£8,000) plus his previous record and that fact that the 'breakers' were not identified, he was sent to prison for a lengthy term.

After my tours of duty at Westminster Road and also Anfield, I was posted to the divisional headquarters, CID Lower Lane.

This area took in Croxteth, Fazakerley, Walton, Orrell and included part of Bootle, Lower Lane was a busy office to work from. Alan also joined me at Lower Lane. Soon after my arrival I dealt with a break in at one of the lodges at a nearby cemetery and forged a new friendship with the cemetery's superintendent. We were talking about firearms and shooting in general and I happened to say that I was a keen shooting enthusiast and possessed a couple of shotguns. I was informed that the parks and cemeteries were inundated with rabbits and other pests and invited to wander around the various cemeteries and parks after closing with a view to eliminating such pests. I knew that my colleague, Alan Griffiths, my sergeant, was also a keen member of the 'huntin', shootin' and fishin' fraternity and asked if he could also be included in the invitation and accompany me on such excursions. This was granted and Alan and I received authorisation in writing from the local authority to enable us in our spare time to pursue our shooting hobby.

Many were the occasions that I filled the freezer with skinned rabbits and plucked wood pigeons ready for the pot, care of the City of Liverpool Cemeteries and Parks department.

I still pursued my other hobby when time allowed. Sea fishing. I was now in possession of a small boat which I had purchased from a friend of mine, a local Hoylake fisherman. This small craft enabled me to get

110

out from Hoylake for a relaxing few hours into the wide blue yonder!

I had been fishing, shrimping and cockling since I was a toddler and was very familiar with the local waters and beaches. On many occasions I would be accompanied by one or two of my equally enthusiastic angling colleagues (of all ranks).

I was just beginning to get myself established on my new patch and becoming conversant with all the 'goings on' and familiarising myself with the local tearaways and members of the criminal fraternity when disaster befell me.

I received an accidental injury to my right hand whilst off duty when a large Alsatian dog caused me to fall down a flight of concrete steps. I broke a number of bones in my right hand which, although having been reset, did not heal properly and my hand became gangrenous. Eventually , due to this it was necessary to amputate two of my fingers and part of my hand. I became absolutely inconsolable. The most important thing, my job, and what about my painting, drawing, writing and all the other things that I had not yet thought of ? I was devastated as I was right-handed.

I clearly remember the day after the operation. My bed was completely surrounded by friends and relatives, all very concerned and wishing me well. I could not get the worry of the almost certain fact that I would have to leave my beloved career out of my troubled mind. This acute depression did nothing to enhance my recovery. So bad did the depression become that the medical and nursing staff were becoming quite worried. I confided in the ward sister - Sister Ogilvy, that the cause of my worry was the uncertainty of my future with the police force.

Unknown to me, the sister informed the matron of my plight and she took it upon herself to contact my superiors.

My Chief inspector, Mr Kellet and Detective Sergeant Tommy Hall came to the hospital to see the Matron.

I was lying in my bed dozing when the Matron appeared with my two bosses. "I've got some visitors for you Mr Turner" Matron informed me. What a pleasant surprise it was to see Tommy and the boss.

"Hello sir, thank you for coming to see me" I said with sincere gratitude. They made themselves comfortable, Tommy depositing himself into my bedside chair, Mr Kellet sitting on the edge of my bed. The Chief Inspector took hold of my left hand and said reassuringly, "Now then Swasie, what's all this worry I've been hearing about?"

My emotions got the better of me. At first I had to bite my lip as I filled up. Tommy said "It's okay Swas, we understand". The tears just flowed uncontrollably. I absolutely sobbed my heart out. Perhaps it was the after-effects of the anaesthetic (and my self pity) combined. I just could not control myself.

I will never forget that visit. The boss, (who sometimes could be a right bastard) was the epitome of understanding, reassurance and kindness itself. He said "If it's the job, don't worry, you'll be alright". Unfortunately, due to the severity of my injury and the inevitable predicament it would leave me in, I found this difficult to accept. Tommy tried a different approach in an effort to bring my tears to a halt and a smile to my lips by saying "if you don't do something about it, you'll finish up swimming around in circles!" It worked, "Fuck off Tom" I managed to counter and even grinned at his bloody cheek.

"That's better" said Mr Kellet, adding "That's more like the Swasie I know". The two of them spent well over two hours at my bed and by the time it came for them to leave, promising that one or other (or both of them together) would continue to visit me regularly, I felt a lot better. Indeed, visits by the police were so regular that the sister had to call a halt and 'thin down' my visitors as it was starting to over-tire me. "I'm beginning to think I'm working in a police station there's that many bobbies about" the sister wryly remarked. The doctors and nurses were absolutely fantastic. Mind you, the relationship between the police and hospital staff have always been very close.

I then received visits from the Force Welfare Department - Jim Bentley (later to received the British Empire Medal for his selfless and untiring work in this field) and his colleague Barbara Gall maintained regular visits to ensure that my family and I wanted for nothing.

After consulting the doctors on my leaving hospital, Jim suggested that I might like to take advantage of the facilities offered by the Police Seaside Convalescent Home at Hove, near Brighton.

I took his advice and after the paper formalities were speedily completed, I travelled down to London. I was met at Euston station by

The Matron, Miss Samuals, Police Convalescent Home, Hove.

112

an officer from the City of London police who then conveyed me across the Metropolis to catch the Brighton train at Victoria station.

He carried my case and saw me onto the train. On my arrival at Brighton, I was met by a member of the convalescent Home staff and taken to my destination by the home's mini-bus. The beautiful, impressive building stood out prominently on the Hove sea front, my home for the next three weeks.

As we arrived, my driver carried my case up the stone steps, and at the top of these stood the Matron, Miss Samuels, a very stern looking woman, but looks deceived, she was a wonderful lady with a heart of gold. Matron summoned a porter to take my case from the driver and instructed him to take me and my case to my room on the fifth floor (room 519). The porter and I took the lift and deposited the case in my splendid room with a wonderful panoramic view of the sea from Brighton in the East to Worthing Pier in the West. I was then given a conducted tour of the fifth floor and shown the facilities afforded there, toilets, showers, washing and ironing etc.

Sister attended my room and assisted me to wash and change after which I went down to the lounge to await the bell which would summon us for our evening meal. Before I was allowed out, I had to see the doctor, after which my time was my own and I could do as I pleased.

The home was nicely placed across the road from the sea on the Hove sea front overlooking the pebbled beach, flowered gardens and tennis courts. Inside the gardens a strategically placed pub - 'The Marine' bar was situated. It certainly was a wonderful 'God's little Acre'.

A long line of beach huts fringed the top of the beach, one of which belonged to the home for the sole use of the patients.

As we entered the dining hall, I was politely ushered to my allocated place at one of the highly polished mahogany tables. At the top table sat the matron and her staff.

After saying grace, we sat down and were waited on by a team of very friendly, hard working and efficient, smart white jacketed stewards. At the conclusion of our excellent meal (the food was always of the very highest quality and quantity) the 'President', who was one of the patients elected by his fellows, stood up and read out any items of note or announcements from the staff, before asking me to stand and introduce myself to all, he then requested two other new arrivals to do the same.

Once this informal 'ice breaking' was completed we were given a few do's and don'ts before leaving the dining hall.

I made many friends during my stay and was to realise how true it is that there is always someone worse off than yourself. Limbless, blind, or terminally ill colleagues of all ages paled one's own problems into insignificance. One man I befriended, whose friendship was to become permanent, was an officer from the Staffordshire force, Ted Highfield. Ted was to succumb to severe stress after discovering the mutilated body of a murdered teenage girl who was the same age as his own daughter.

Ted and I got on really well, Each brought the other out of the morose and depressing periods that we each suffered. At first I was a bit quiet but I soon got to know everybody, especially with Ted's help and soon settled into the routine of the establishment.

I spent most of my time on the beach. It was summer and the weather was very hot. Long days of sunshine, topless girls sunbathing, ice cream and nothing to do but laze around, life didn't seem that bad after all.

Although I was a keen and proficient swimmer, due to my still needing constant regular dressings on my hand I was forbidden to go into the water. This frustrated me, sitting there watching the others splashing about while I sweated in a deckchair.

Although I was quite tanned, I was not as deeply tanned as Ted. He was almost black. Ted and I used to fool about during our lighter moods and used to speak to each other as though we were members of an ethnic minority , as we were both so brown.

On one such occasion, Ted was in the water and the beach was packed with people, many of the holiday-makers. He swam to the shore pretending to be exhausted and as he staggered through the surf and up the beach, his dark brown body emphasised by his vivid deep yellow satin trunks, he shouted in a 'caribbean' accent , "Is dis England. Where is de national Assistance Office?" We all fell about laughing at his highly amusing antics. "I want de dole" he went on, much to the amusement of the local gathering.

Ted then joined the others back in the water after his 'act' was concluded.

I was itching to get into the water. I saw my chance when an effeminate looking young man who I had been watching, mincing up and down alongside the waters edge, posing in his pink flowered shorts and sun-glasses with a black strap round his head, carrying a large surf board, decided to settle on the beach to sunbathe. He spread his towel ever so carefully, like a waitress laying a table cloth. He then lay on his back alongside his surf board, closed his eyes, hands by his sides, and proceeded to top up his already adequate sun tan.

I gave it a minute or two and signalled to Ted, pointing to the prone young man and his board. Creeping up to the sun-worshipper I gently pushed his board away from him with my foot. Ted joined me and, picking up the board, carried it to the water and held it whilst I sat astride. Then, holding my right hand aloft and out of harm's way, I paddled with my left hand and stooged about with the gang in the water. It was great. Ted stayed with me to ensure my safety.

Suddenly the young man discovered his board missing. On looking around he spotted me on my 'stolen vehicle'! enjoying my little self. Obviously knowing where I was from, he screamed at me in a high pitched voice, "hey you, give me my board or I'll report you to the home". Ted (wrongly) advised him to 'visit the Foreign Office' forthwith, I tried to tell the hapless young man that I would return his board and not to panic. He did no more than storm up the beach and over to the Home.

A short time later he returned with the Matron resembling Hatti

Jacques and the sister. What a sight, The three of them marching down the beach like a scene from a 'Carry On' film. Miss Samuels frantically gesticulating to me to get over to he 'pronto'. They stood at the water's edge and Miss Samuels blew on her 'referee's' whistle hanging on a cord around her neck. "come here this minute" she shouted to me. Ted and I gingerly made our way to the beach with the board. The indignant young man was whining, "That's him Matron, he won't give me my board" the matron roared, "Give him his board back at once and come with me". Ted said, "I think Matron's cross with you Swas" and half grinned. She turned to him and stormed "That'll do from you". Ted jumped two paces backward. I abandoned the board to the whinging wimp (who I learned was a relative of a resident who lived next door to the home) and went back to Matron's office with her and Sister.

The Police Seaside Convalescent Home, Hove, East Sussex.

On entering her office, minus Sister, Matron plonked herself down behind her desk and donned her really official angry Matron's head' and spat out "Shut the door". As she sat in her high chair, I stood before her large desk like a delinquent schoolboy who had been caught scrumping apples.

Matron gave me a lengthy lecture on how she ran, and intended to continue running, a happy home for broken bobbies and didn't need the likes of me creating ripples by upsetting the local populace. She asked me what the hell did I think I was playing at? "You know damn well your'e not supposed to go into the water don't you?" she continued to scold. "Ted Highfield made me do it" I whimpered like the one who reported me, wearing my 'don't shout at me 'cos I've got a sore hand' look.

115

"Oh go on, get out" she snapped, "Don't you dare take that man's board again or you'll be sent home" she added. I'm almost certain that I saw traces of a grin form around her eyes as I left her office, muttering "Sorry Ma'am". I was to learn later from the Sister that Matron had indeed found the incident highly amusing and had even remarked at my initiative in getting myself into the water. Actually, while I was there, one patient, an officer from the Met. was indeed sent home. He broke the strict rule that patients must be in by 10pm when he arrived back after an evenings drinking at 11.45pm causing the worried night sister to unlock the doors and let him in.

My stay at Hove was very beneficial, the staff were so kind, they even allowed my wife Marje to come down and stay for a couple of days to assist my recovery. Such were the great lengths to which the service would aspire in their endeavours to assist officers and facilitate their ultimate return to good health, and hopefully, duty.

As we sat outside the beach hut, many of the local residents would stop and chat as they went about their constitutional or when out exercising their dogs. The majority of them expressed their gratitude at the way we performed such hazardous duties whilst protecting them, and their real concern for the injuries we maintained whilst performing such duties.

As Ted and I sat outside our hut one day, there were quite a number of us enjoying the sunshine, one or two happily dozing, lying back in our deck chairs. A middle aged lady approached me and began to strike up a conversation. She was obviously not a local lady as she asked me where we had all come from and why were all sitting there. Were we from a club or some organisation she asked. Before I told her who and what we all were, I made Ted, her and myself a cup of tea in the hut. As we sat and started to chat the lady produced a bible and proceeded to inform Ted and I of all the advantages of becoming a born again Christian. Oh dear, that's all we needed. As she was obviously looking for a convert I told her that we were all here because we had been sent from the courts as being in need of help and guidance. I told her that we were all deviants of some form or another. One of our colleagues, a Superintendent from Kent, who was renowned for his acute lack of humour and considered himself far above the rest of us, was sleeping nearby in a deck chair. He was recovering from a gall stone operation. I indicated him to our new lady friend, "See him" I said, "He's really been naughty". Our potential bible thumper looked really concerned, "Oh ! dear, what has he done?" she asked. Those nearby pricked up their ears and awaited what was coming next, Ted put his head in his hands and said " Oh no". "Well he's got an acute sexual problem" I said. I went on "When he gets close to a woman he just can't stop himself putting his hands down the inside of their blouses". I lied mischievously. I told her that I was sure that as he was also religious he would no doubt benefit from her ministerings. "Do you think so" the lady keenly asked. "I certainly do" I replied as Ted and a number of others got up out of their deck chairs saying something about going for an ice cream or some other urgently required purchase.

The lady went to our self opinionated, permanently aloof 'needer of her help' and tapped him gently, bringing him abruptly out of his fantasy land of nod. "Hello, would you like to see if I can help you regarding your naughty sexual urges?" she asked in all her naivety. I went back inside the hut before the inevitable explosion that was sure to follow. "How dare you madam, Who the hell are you may I ask?" I then left the scene and joined the others further along the sea front, all of whom were falling about like drunks. "I don't know how you do it" said a police woman from one of the Southern forces. "Your'e one bastard" joined Ted. I must admit, I nearly wet myself, I didn't think she'd fall for that. We dare not look around. We later returned but neither the lady nor the Super were anywhere to be seen. In fact, neither 'paraded' outside the beach hut again. Anyway, thankfully, 'Happy Jack' the super, left at the end of the week after his three week stay. Good riddance! Some people just can't take a joke. I would have liked to have seen the lady again to see what in fact was the result of her attempted 'crusade' with 'Mr Happy".

After spending three wonderful and beneficially therapeutic weeks at Hove, I returned home to continue my recovery with the necessary and regular physiotherapy.

Chief Inspector Kellet and the lads made regular visits to my home but I was still very apprehensive about my job.

I finally plucked up the courage to ask the boss straight what he thought of my chances at being accepted back on duty. "I'll sort something out" he promised optimistically. Monitoring my progress were my two wonderful GP's, Doctors Rigby and Price from West Kirby. They were both absolutely marvellous, they certainly could not be bettered.

They continued my treatment, and encouraged me gradually to use my injured hand as often as possible. Mr Kellet eventually suggested that I resume work and remain in the office, even if I were only to answer the telephone. Doctor Price agreed and I was signed off and allowed to return to work. Officially there was no such thing as 'light duties' so either I was fully fit, or not fit for duty, in the eyes of the service, one or the other.

However, the boss took it upon himself to 'hide me away' from officialdom by sitting me at a desk in a small office at Lower Lane, away from prying eyes.

My 'duties' included answering the telephone, making tea or running the occasional errand for someone or other. At least I was back on duty. How the boss managed it I'll never know, preventing the powers that be knowing how bad my injury was. I was kept away from the force doctor and I used to 'slide away' to my physio sessions, nobody but the boss being any the wiser.

After I had been back a month or so, Mr Kellet had a new idea. He decided that it would now be a good thing if I were to get out of the office into the fresh air. I was to be put in charge of all cycle theft enquiries throughout the whole of the division. "Just visit the complainants and reassure them that we are doing our best" suggested the boss. He considered that this idea had two advantages, first it would release other detectives from these minor enquiries and second, it would start to get me 'out and about' again. You may even clear a few of the offences up he added hopefully.

I was absolutely delighted with this turn of events. I put my efforts into this new venture wholeheartedly. Not only did I successfully detect many of these offences, but I also recovered a few of the stolen cycles, much to the delight of their owners, and also the boss, whose crime detection figures showed a sharp rise. I even managed to get a number of cycle thieves before the Juvenile and Magistrates' courts. Things were looking good, I was back on course again.

I figured that it the Force ever were to consider my injury so serious that it was a disability, there wouldn't be much that they could do if my successful detections were maintained and time were to elapse.

My hand was eventually fitted with a brace to protect it (as it was considerably weaker and smaller by half) and assist my grip. Once I became used to this piece of 'ironmongery' on the end of my arm, things were to become easier. At first, I was a little self conscious and continually wore a glove to hide my embarrassment, however, as time went by I eventually shed this to expose the brace.

After what seemed an eternity I gradually began to be given other more serious offences to deal with until finally I was 'back in the fold' and integrated into the old routine, taking my fair share of all jobs allocated.

Off duty, I started to get out in the boat again, as soon as the season, and weather, permitted. My colleagues now began to call me 'Swas the Spaz' due to my injury. I received this in the manner it was intended, a term of light hearted endearment, and found it quite amusing. I also interpreted this as proof that I was accepted by them as being 'back to normal' again. As my work necessitated, by its very nature, a lot of report writing and typing, to overcome my difficulties, I became very proficient at writing (and typing) left handed. This was to be quite a struggle at first but my determination paid off and I became totally ambidextrous.

There is no doubt that without the subterfuge and solo initiative of Chief Inspector Kellet in 'working the oracle' getting me back to work, a force medical would have ensued, resulting in the certainty of my being medically cast from the job with a disability pension. Thank you Mister Kellet sir, I am permanently indebted to you for having undoubtedly saved my career.

Having become totally 'back in the frame' I now took my turn as the Night Jack. Each division had a (solo) night detective who attended all jobs requiring the involvement or attendance of the CID. He would then give the incident 'first aid' during the night watch until a morning duty officer would be allocated to deal with the incident in its entirety. Being the 'Night CID' really tested one's capabilities. During the normal daytime duty periods help and assistance in the form of senior detectives and other CID colleagues were readily to hand, during the night however, the detective was left to his own initiative and capability (unless he had to call out CID assistance from an officer's home) although there was a night superintendent who covered the whole force area.

I enjoyed my night duty spells. Some nights were quiet when the lucky detective could endorse his night report at the end of the duty watch with a 'nil return' but most nights saw the all too regular offences of burglary, theft, stolen vehicles and the inevitable array of serious assaults when the clubs and shabeens emptied out.

When I was able, I always attended calls with my uniform colleagues, one never knew what would greet the officer's arrival, however minor the incident at first appeared to be. Many times my arrival was justified when a domestic incident suddenly got out of hand and resorted in violence towards the officer.

Situated on Lower Lane's patch was the well known golf driving range, the Jack Sharp Golf Centre, in Higher Lane, Fazakerley. During one of my duties as Night Jack, I was directed to the centre at the request of a uniformed patrol officer who had discovered the alarm ringing and on investigating, found that the premises had been forcibly entered.

On my arrival I was greeted by my colleague who was sitting in his panda car with its door open awaiting my arrival. The premises had been forcibly entered via the front door. A provisional search failed to reveal any person on the premises but there were various rooms to which we could not gain access.

The keyholder, (the Club Steward) was summoned and attended some twenty minutes later. The Keyholder deactivated the alarm whilst my colleague and I, armed with the stewards keys, carried out a more thorough search of the building to ensure that there were no unauthorised persons still present. Whilst my colleague and I were so engaged, the steward poured out three pints of lager, one for each of us present, and having done so took money from his pocket and placed it into the till. At the conclusion of our search the steward then invited the bobby and I to join him in a drink as it was such a warm night.

Thanking him I took a long swig from my glass, pure, refreshing nectar!, reaching parts that other's couldn't, as it was said! The steward did the same. The uniformed bobby was busily making up his note book and entering details of the break for his form 52 (crime form) the third full pint glass remained as yet untouched since being placed on the counter by the steward.

Suddenly, in walked the bobby's Inspector. This man was a particularly nasty individual well known for his continual attempts to catch his men doing anything they shouldn't, however trivial and minor. Due to his regular blunders he was known as a walking disaster (and even named after one). "Caught you!" said the inspector to the astonished young constable. The inspector then picked up the full pint of untouched lager from the counter and instructed the bobby to follow him outside. The constable did as he was instructed and I also followed to see what going on. I saw the inspector throw the contents of the glass away and he then told the (by now mesmerised) young constable to follow him back to Lower Lane. The officer was told that he would be reported for drinking on duty and that he would be subject to discipline proceedings. The glass, went on the inspector, would be retained for fingerprint examination.

The young officer was to say the least duly alarmed and worried by the inspector's venom as he (the constable) was comparatively young in service.

I decided to interrupt proceedings, "Excuse me Sir, but are you serious about this?" I asked. Turning to me the Inspector (who was obviously overjoyed at having caught one of his subordinates at last) spat out "I'm doing Constable ..... for drinking on duty" and stood there, the thumb of one hand tucked into his top left tunic pocket, the other holding the now empty pint glass. He then got into his car, closed the door and started the engine. As he was about to drive off I tapped on his window. The window was lowered six inches, "Yes?" said the inspector. "In that case sir, I'll have to take a statement from the steward for my crime report" I bluffed. The inspector switched off his engine and got out of his vehicle. "What crime report? The constable is seeing to that" said the smarmy self-opinionated and pompous two-pipped pillock. I went on "I mean the theft of the pint of lager crime report Sir". We had now been joined by the steward who had heard the conversation between the inspector and I. "Explain yourself Constable Turner" said the inspector 'Smartarse' wondering what I was up to.

I told the inspector that the young constable had declined any drink saying that he was not allowed to drink on duty, to which the steward remarked that he would drink two pints himself anyway. Therefore, having paid for the drinks, and the inspector in taking one of them and throwing it away, the inspector had technically 'permanently deprived the steward of it' (part of the definition of theft) and as the constable was to be reported for discipline proceedings I was therefore obliged to make the whole of the circumstances subject of a comprehensive report contained in a crime file, namely the theft of a pint of lager, the property of the steward. I had no alternative, I said. "The detective's right. The drink you threw away was mine" said the steward obviously catching the drift, and adding for good measure, "The bobby wouldn't have one."

Inspector 'Smartarse' spluttered, coughed and stammered "Well this time I'll overlook it" hoping to save face he continued, "I'll show you a visit and sign your book whilst I'm here." Giving the bobby a 'peg' possibly made him feel that he was impressing us all by his 'efficiency'. He then got into his vehicle, started the engine and drove off into the night, his wheels throwing up gravel and sand as he did so.

The young bobby turned to the steward and uttered a sigh, "If you don't mind I will have that pint now if I may" he asked with a cheeky grin, and looking at me said "Nice one Swas!" We then helped to secure the premises and resumed our respective duties for the rest of the night watch. I never saw eye to eye with that particular inspector again. More of him later!

Whenever a sudden death occurred, the CID were informed and nearly always attended initially in case there were suspicious circumstances. As in most cases, there were not, the uniformed officer would deal with the matter. I dealt with one tragic death involving a young 15 year old boy who had not long started his first job at a local container base after having recently left school. The lad soon became very popular with his workmates and due to his reputation for always being early to work, one of them suggested that as he was always first in of a morning, he should open up and have the tea made for the arrival of the rest of the gang. The young lad performed this task with relish, much to the delight of his workmates. An early morning cuppa was thus assured as they all arrived for work each day.

The young man and his mates worked from a 'hut or cabin' as it was referred to. In actual fact it was a container from the base which, as well as storing equipment such as paints, strippers, drums of grease, timber and oxy-acetylene welding bottles, also doubled as the mens' canteen. A table and cabinet together with a propane gas powered light and cooker enabled it to be used for the latter.

After booking on at 7 am one morning as 'early Jack' I left the office to do some of the jobs that had been committed during the night. I was driving the CID car along Southport Road with my driver's window open, not thinking about anything in particular when all of a sudden I heard a loud bang and at the same time the early morning dark grey sky was illuminated by an orange flash from the direction in which I was heading. It came from the nearby container base and I made haste to see what had caused the bang. On my arrival I saw that a number of people were running about the yard of the premises. Strewn about the yard were pieces of concrete, trailers parked at crazy angles and what was left of a container which had completely disintegrated to every part of the yard. Nearby a railway signal box had lost all of its windows. The six foot steel mesh fence and many of its concrete fence posts were down and scattered about.

I got out of my car and went to the obvious seat of the explosion. I saw the badly burned body of a young man lying on the concrete. He was barely alive. As I knelt beside him and covered him with my coat, I was joined by the Fire Brigade and Ambulance service. The young man was taken to Walton Hospital but unfortunately died before he arrived.

I caused the studio to attend and the scene was photographed in detail. As I was the CID officer on the scene, enquires into the tragic incident were to be my responsibility. I painstakingly drew a plan in which I indicated every piece of wreckage and other items I deemed to be of equal significance, measured and indicated the distance they were from the seat of the explosion, as this would be crucial for the coroner and his jury should there be an inquest. I made extensive enquiries over the ensuing days throughout members of the staff and others who were in the proximity at the time, including the signalman stationed at the nearby signal box. All of their statements would be crucial in helping me to compile the file which, hopefully, would establish the cause of the tragedy.

It transpired that the fatal explosion which had so tragically cost the new boy his young life was literally brought about inadvertently by the boy's enthusiasm to be the 'early bird'.

At the conclusion of each day's work the men would return their working gear, paint, tools etc. to the hut and finally the oxy-acetylene bottles used for welding, would be wheeled inside on their trolley and placed behind the doors which would then be locked until they were opened the following morning prior to the day's work.

The day of the accident dawned and the boy duly arrived for work early as usual. After opening the large doors to the 'cabin', the lad then went to the lamp, struck a match to light it and there was a massive explosion. Unknown to anyone, the oxy-acetylene bottles had only been shut down at the torch and not at the bottles themselves. This apparently was not an uncommon practice among some welders. However it appeared that such was the power from the high pressure bottles that seepage via the torch could not be prevented and consequently a lethal, highly volatile cocktail of gas and oxygen built up overnight inside the container. Once the doors were opened and fresh air (More oxygen) was allowed in, adding this extra ingredient, making it explosively complete, the igniting of the match set off one tremendously powerful explosion. That, together with the paint, thinners and other combustible materials caused heat of severe magnitude. The poor boy never stood a chance and was almost incinerated on the spot.

It was very distressing for me trying to comfort the young man's heartbroken parents when I sadly had to explain the tragic cause of their sons premature demise. By far, one of the worst duties a police officer has to perform is one of informing relatives of the death of a loved one. These messages NEVER become any easier to deliver, however many times one had to perform such a sad task.

The oxy-welding equipment should of course have been closed tightly at the bottles as well as at the torch, and the poor colleague of the deceased who neglected to perform this routine, albeit probably inadvertently, will no doubt live with this knowledge for ever. However, the explosion was obviously accidental and no blame was apportioned.

Tragedies occur in many unforeseen ways. There was the case of a young man who, after spending an evening drinking and socialising with his friends eventually made his way home to his flat. One the way home he purchased a take away meal for his supper. Once home, as it was a cold night, he lit his gas fire, closed the door and placed a rolled up rug against the bottom of the door to prevent a draught. After consuming most of his meal, the man then lay on the settee and settled down to watch television intending to eventually retire for the night.

However, probably due to the drink consumed earlier, the man nodded off into a deep sleep. The following morning, the old lady living in the flat below awoke and detected a strong smell of gas. On checking that all of her own gas appliances were switched off correctly, she realised that the gas must be escaping from the flat above. The young man's flat. She went upstairs and knocked loudly on the young man's door. The smell of gas was now very strong. She could hear the hissing of the television indicating that it had not been switched off. Her knocking still drew no response so she tried the door. It was not locked. The old lady opened the door with a push and noticed the rug behind the door. The smell of gas was overpowering. She fortunately had the sense to turn the gas of at the unlit fire and also turned the television off. After managing to open the windows and covering her face with a tea towel she unsuccessfully tried to rouse the figure lying prone on the settee. She was then forced to make her way downstairs and out into the open for some fresh air. The Police, Fire and Ambulance services were summoned and I, together with uniformed colleagues attended the scene.

The old lady was very distraught on our arrival and hastily described the circumstances leading to our being summoned. On entering the house there was still a strong smell of gas present. A colleague and I, together with the Ambulance crew went to the upstairs room where the man lay. It was obvious that he was beyond even the skilled help of the medics. The police surgeon attended and requested the attendance of the Gas Bard to check all gas appliances in the building.

The man lay on the settee, his head on a cushion, his partly consumed meal on the floor nearby in its plastic container. It was obvious that he had succumbed to the fumes. It was equally obvious what had caused the unfortunate man's death .

Once he had lit the gas fire after closing the door and sealing the room by placing the rug against it, not only preventing the draught coming in but in doing so starved the room of oxygen. As he went to sleep the fire continued to burn and consume the room's oxygen. Finally, after burning up all of the oxygen, the fire, being starved, burned itself out. The gas however, still continued to flow from the appliance into the room. As the gas finally totally filled the room the poor sleeping man suffocated.

How easy it is for tragedies to occur through innocent carelessness. Another waste of life due to a completely preventable accident.

Another incident involving gas occurred when I was summoned to attend a large semi detached house in Aintree. A crowd of inquisitive neighbours and nosey bystanders were gathered outside the house when I arrived. A police car and an Ambulance were already at the scene. I was met at the door by a uniformed colleague who took me through to a rear downstairs room where I was greeted by another tragic sight.

Again, there was a horrible smell of gas. As I entered the room I saw a middle aged man sitting in a large easy chair in front of a marble fireplace containing an unlit gas fire, obviously very dead. The man's head was slumped forward onto his chest, and his head was totally enveloped inside a large white shopping bag, This was sealed at his neck by a ligature ,tightly tied. Leading from the gas fire was a black rubber tube. This tube led up and into the plastic bag. Just then a woman and a small boy came into the room, the former sobbing uncontrollably (the man's wife and son). My colleague and I quickly escorted them gently into the front room and sat them both down. My colleague and I were to gently unfold the tragic circumstances leading to the man's self-induced gassing in the next room.

We were joined by a policewoman who I immediately requested to remove the boy from the house and take to a neighbour or relative.

My male colleague made a cup of strong tea for the deceased's wife and after a while she was able to regain some of her composure and started to enlighten me as to a tragic story of matrimonial and domestic upheaval.

She admitted to having an affair with another man and her husband had found out. She told her husband she would cease to see the other man but this she did not do. Again the husband found out and became unbalanced and distraught about the adulterous relationship and just could not accept it.

She left him to go to work earlier in the day, it was then that he had deliberately taken his own life as he could not bear to carry on under such circumstances. It was a sad and conclusive case of suicide without doubt.

To make matters worse, whilst I was sitting talking to the lady, a man came into the room and put his arm around the widow's shoulders. I asked him who he was and I ascertained that he was in fact the woman's lover. What a bloody cheek! The deceased wasn't even cold yet, and in his own house at that, then in walks a contributory factor to the sordid and tragic affair having the audacity to attend the scene.

Although the moral side of the saga was no business of mine, I couldn't help but feel for the poor young boy who had witnessed such a traumatic sight, that of his dead father after having killed himself in the family home. I doubt if the memory would ever leave him. I took the tactless individual outside and gave him some very appropriate 'off the cuff' advice! I later learned that he was in fact a colleague from another force, another 'asset' to the service!

The 'bread and butter' jobs of the CID are mainly concerned with various degrees of theft. Some thefts are carried out with the utmost vigour after meticulous preparation. Such is the audacity of some of the criminals involved that large sums of money are netted if their operations prove successful.

One such raid took place at a large timber yard in Regent road adjacent to the City's dockland area. During one night, the yard was unlawfully entered by forcing the steel gates to the premises, and a large amount of timber and hundreds of expensive sheets of 10 x 6 marine plywood were removed by lorry to vanish into the night. The weight of the stock taken was considerable which indicated that a large vehicle, possibly an articulated lorry must have been used to accommodate such a load.

It befell me, as the investigating officer, to try to trace the missing loot, and those responsible for its theft. I visited the yard, interviewing staff and had the gates and other items forensically examined and photographed in the hope of acquiring a lead. I had very little to go on as the perpetrators were obviously very professional and had ensured that their tracks were efficiently covered.

However, my enquiries did reveal that a large articulated lorry had been seen in the area during the fateful night. It was seen parked near to the attacked premises by a crew member of a tug boat, but as it was not unusual for lorries to park in the area overnight, the man thought no more of it and could not furnish any useful description of the vehicle.

I checked to see if there were any vehicles similar to that of the parked artic. that had recently been reported stolen, but this line of enquiry bore no fruit.

My enquiries continued and I visited building sites, timber yards, and other likely places of disposal in an effort to trace the missing timber, but my efforts continued to prove negative. Even my usual informants could not, or would not help. Weeks passed and the trail went completely cold. I was of course carrying out numerous other investigations at the same time, as is the norm for all operational CID officers when pre-occupied with multiple investigations.

One quiet Sunday morning, some weeks after the timber-yard job, my detective sergeant, George Robinson (the Acid Drop Kid!) and I decided to leave our steaming typewriters and go out on mobile patrol for a breath of fresh air. George was driving the CID car at a slow and leisurely pace around a local housing estate in Bootle, meandering up and down the side roads staring at nothing in particular. As we turned the corner from one road into another, one house in particular caught my eye. "Turn around and go back again George" I requested. "Why? what's up Swas?" he asked. "I don't know, it's just something I saw", I said not knowing exactly what it was. We turned around and drove slowly back to the corner. I turned to George and said, "Take a look at that semi on the corner". George did as he was asked and said "Yes, what about it?"

The house was an end, corner semi-detached dwelling with long, wide, overgrown and untidy front and side gardens, which were littered with debris and other rubbish. A child's rusty tricycle was in the porch in front of the dirty, almost paintless front door which had a broken glass panel at the top and a cracked glass panel alongside held together with a piece of plastic adhesive tape. The house in general was in a poor state, and needed a lot of maintenance. The window frames, as well as the front door were also in dire need of a protective and cosmetic coat of paint.

What drew my attention to the place was that built onto the side of the house was a large extension including wide spacious windows. The structure was built entirely of plywood sheeting and had been recently painted. "What do you thing of the extension George?" I asked. "Hmmm, something doesn't look right I must admit" said my sergeant. "I'll be interested to know where the wood came from for that" I mused.

We parked the car and went to the house and knocked on the door. We heard the ferocious sound of a large dog barking from within, followed by a woman's shouts of "shut that bloody dog in while I go to the door". The door was opened by a middle aged woman clad in the proverbial pinafore, her head covered in curlers, a cigarette hanging from her lips. George introduced us and asked if the man of the house was at home. "My husband's out. Why? What d'yer want 'im for?" she asked in a not too friendly manner. George replied, "We'd just like a quick word with him" but we were greeted with the woman slamming the door in our faces. Although it was just a shot in the dark, I thought there may be a good chance that it could be a breakthrough into my plywood job. I was now worried in case the material might be disposed of before we had chance to establish this.

As we left to walk down the cracked, and rubble strewn concrete path I shouted "Tell him we'll be back." I decided to enlist the aid of the studio and have the extension photographed in detail as I didn't intend to leave anything to chance.

After arranging to meet the force photographer at the scene, George and I returned to the house a short time later. This time I had by now armed myself with the file concerning the break in at the timber yard which contained all I needed to know about the stolen plywood and timber.

This time our knock was answered by a six foot, heavily built man, clad in dirty vest, and trousers supported by a thick leather belt. He had obviously forgotten to shave due to the amount of stubble on his face. "What the fuck do you want?" he asked ,aggressively leaning towards us in a threatening posture. We introduced ourselves to him and I told him that I was making enquiries into the multi-thousand pound theft of a quantity of plywood from a timber yard by the docks. I pointed to the extension built onto his house and asked if he minded the structure being photographed. He became more abusive and threatened to damage any camera produced to carry out this task.

This time I decided to resort to threats. I told the unco-operative house holder that if he interfered in any way or damaged any equipment I would not hesitate to arrest him for obstructing us in the execution of our duty, and also for damage to any item we used to pursue our enquiries. I signalled the photographer to join us as he was still sitting in his vehicle.

I again asked our angry man to allow us inside to see the extension and have it photographed. The reluctant man still refused ,telling us that we could not enter without a warrant to do so. He was immediately informed hat such a warrant could be furnished within minutes.

I asked him where he had obtained the timber for the extension. Realising that we were not going to go away and that it would be futile to obstruct us further, he started to mellow when the gravity of the situation started to dawn on him. "The wood's bought and paid for" he said. I asked him for the name of the firm or persons that had sold and delivered the timber to his address. "I bought the wood off a bloke in the pub" came the well used and standard reply of a cornered thief. Knowing that I now had him on the ropes, I again asked him for the name and address of his supplier and was greeted with what I wanted to hear. "I only know him as Dougie, I have a drink with him now and then".

We entered the house and went inside the wooden structure. I inspected every panel and support and George and I were able to detect (and have meticulously photographed) the tell tale signs of the trade-marked sheets of timber which were still partly visible despite frantic efforts to secrete them by scraping and painting over them.

Our previously aggressive and violence threatening householder was now becoming very co-operative as the thought of taking the blame for the full offence of breaking and entering obviously frightened him considerably. He even turned on his wife who thought she was giving him her moral support by joining him and subjecting us to abuse.

Although he adamantly protested his innocence with regard to the actual break in at the yard, he did finally acknowledge that he had bought the timber having 'had an idea' that it had been stolen.

I asked him who had delivered the timber and he told me that it was "dropped off while I was out" thus eliminating the prospects of my tracing the lorry and or the driver concerned. I told him that I was not satisfied with his explanation and was arresting him for the offence of breaking and entering the timber yard and stealing the timber. This produced the instant reply "I didn't screw the yard, I only bought a few sheets and some wood off this bloke." Giving the quivering individual one more opportunity to do himself a bit of good, I again asked him for the name of the man concerned. I was told "I don't know, you don't ask questions when you buy bent stuff". He was arrested amidst wails of protest by his wife who insisted in continuing her profanities and constant shouts of 'police brutality' to the deaf ears of myself and those of my colleagues.

It was established beyond doubt that the timber was from the attacked yard when it was later identified as such by the complainant firm. The structure was then demolished and retrieved by the rightful owners.

Due to this development those responsible for the break were eventually traced and brought to justice, although unfortunately no other timber or sheets were recovered.

Months later, I was to investigate another break in at premises in the same area. This time the premises concerned housed a boat building firm, makers of luxury motor cruisers (the internationally renowned firm of Stewart Stevens.) This firm manufactured very expensive vessels which were exported all over the world, many of their customers being rich Arab sheiks from the Emirates.

I attended the scene of the break-in on the morning of the incident and ascertained what had been taken. The thieves again using a vehicle, had made off with various expensive fittings and a number of high powered top of the range inboard and outboard engines, their haul being of very substantial value.

After pursuing various lines of enquiry vigorously, I found that my own knowledge of boats and nautical terminology assisted me greatly. Eventually, after receiving a tip off from an informant, I traced and recovered two of the outboard engines from a flat in Kirkby on the outskirts of Liverpool. Sadly I was only able to instigate a successful prosecution for the offence of receiving stolen property, as again, the engines had been purchased from that proverbial and well travelled 'unknown man in the pub'! I never managed to bring those particular raiders to book, nor recover any more of the missing property. Never mind, I had recovered some of the booty, which was better than nothing.

The firm's proprietors were very impressed with the efforts of the police and the recovery of the two expensive engines.

Due to my keen interest in boats I became a frequent visitor to the firm's premises and watched with interest the manufacture of their superb vessels. Stewart Stevens became a permanent 'tea speck' and I was able to purchase items for my own boat from there.

I became curious as to why there were a number of boat hulls lined up outside in the yard, as there never appeared to be any work carried out on them. They just lay there, upside down, those that were the right way up were gathering the seasons rains and contained other debris awaiting disposal. On asking, I was told that these hulls were in fact rejects (seconds) and were to be ultimately destroyed. As the firm only allowed their completed vessels to leave the premises in a flawless and top class condition, anything that fell short of these standards was classed as a reject, no matter how slight the defect. It certainly emphasised the high standard of manufacture that was insisted upon by the makers.

The hulls were made of moulded glass fibre and were of various individual lengths. A hull would be considered a reject if it had nothing more than a blemish which was visible or perhaps a small mark or scratch which could not be erased or eliminated.

Although I could understand this, it seemed such a terrible waste of what seemed perfectly good hulls for them to be classed as defective due to nothing more than such a minor blemish or discolouration in the otherwise smooth glassed hull.

Whilst enjoying a cuppa with the managerial staff during one of my visits, I casually brought up the subject of these sub standard hulls which were gathering the rain outside, and cheekily asked the firm's proprietor what were the chances of a 'hard working but underpaid' detective constable being able to purchase one of those discarded seconds? Everyone looked at each other as I spoke of the unthinkable! There was a lot of humming and hahring and numerous sighs. I was again told that the sub standard items were not for sale as they were for destruction.

I persisted with my audacity and assured all present that if I were allowed the privilege of acquiring a hull, it would be for my own use only!. Eventually Mr Stevens himself condescended to allow me to obtain a hull after being convinced of my honourable intentions. He insisted that it should never be used or identified in any way as a 'Stewart Stevens' vessel. This request was instantly and faithfully promised.

I was later taken outside by the firm's manager to look at eight of the rejected hulls. I eventually selected a 21ft hull that to me, looked perfect. Mind you, they all did. I asked the reason why this particular hull was a reject and the boss, to my astonishment pointed out a small ripple on the outside of the otherwise smooth hull on the port (left) side near to the stern. I couldn't even notice such a minor fault.

The manager and I returned to the office where he conferred with his colleagues deciding the hull's worth.

They decided to ask the princely sum of £150! and even added that they would transport the hull on one of their lorries to my home. The hull was duly delivered by lorry and deposited onto my front lawn, causing me to make frantic promises to my wife that it would remain there for a very short period only !

I made numerous drawings as to how I wanted the vessel to eventually look when the hull was built into a sea going boat. I enlisted the aid of a close friend, a very able, competent and professional joiner, John McCoy. We finally decided on a design and during the next twelve months! (not quite the short period I had promised my wife !), the hull was transformed by John's miracle woodwork as I purchased the materials required for the building programme.

My boat 'Cocklelily', C/o Stuart Stevens

Eventually John brought my drawings to life and after adding the portholes and windows, the final touches were added by a Hoylake boat builder, Alan Tolley, when he installed the 100E Ford engine, the rudder and steering mechanism. The new boat was then taken and placed on her moorings at Hoylake, My friends and colleagues were to enjoy many trips in the "Cockellily" during the ensuing years. I sold my former, smaller boat to off-set the costs of the 'new' vessel.

Life in the CID went on and we were all kept busy by the numerous deviants and felons of our sick society.

Back home in Hoylake lived a man who, although I did not know him, always used to speak to me when we met in the street. I often used to wonder why, he would always go out of his way to speak, sometimes even crossing the road to do so. There was something about this man that I did not like. I asked one or two mates in my local if they knew this particular character. I was informed that he was well liked in the area as he spent a lot of time with the local children and ran children's football teams. Even my wife used to say what a nice man he appeared to be when he used to let on to us. I was repeatedly scolded by my wife for ignoring him when he used to greet us in passing. I couldn't help but show my dislike for him.

One day my wife and I were out shopping in Hoylake's main street when we were greeted by our 'friend'. "That man has just said hello to you" said my wife after I had ignored him. I replied, "I know, I heard him". My wife told me not to be so damned ignorant when people spoke to me!. Although I did not know why, I did not like him and that was that.

One Sunday morning Marje and I took our young son to nearby Hoylake football ground where a local fete had been organised. I had plenty of time as I wasn't going on duty until later, after lunch. Marje and I were walking around the various tents and stalls when I stopped to buy some ice cream for the three of us. Just as we were leaving the ice cream stall our attention was drawn to a nearby 'Bonny Baby' contest. Standing there judging the entries was my 'friend', who, by now, I had learned was a Mr Day. As we stood there amid a number of children who were playing and rolling about on the grass, and parents of the little contestants anxiously waiting to see if their particular offspring would be judged the winner, I heard a little boy who was standing near me say to his little friend, "See that man on the stage" (indicating Mr Day, who was holding a microphone and requesting silence while he announced the winners) "He gives you money and sweets if you put your hand in his pockets." I knew this particular boy's father as he was a personal friend of mine. I decided to have a word with him and his lad later, before I went to work!.

As I left for work after lunch, I called at my friend's house after having spoken to him by 'phone. I had quite a lengthy chat and voiced my sentiments and fears with regard to Mr Day. I was informed that his little boy played football in one of Day's teams. My friend called his boy into the room and asked him to tell us all about Mr Day and he also asked him about Day giving sweets and money away. The little boy was at first understandably apprehensive and reluctant to discuss the subject, but after gentle coaxing and reassurances the little boy enlightened his father and I as to the activities of our Mr Day. He unfolded an alarming tale.

Day ran three sets of children's football teams, whose teams ages were six to eight years, nine to ten years, and eleven and twelve year olds, junior, intermediate and senior teams. Day himself provided the strip for each team and organised fixtures.

After the conclusion of a match, when played locally, Day would-invite two or three of 'his' youngsters back to his ground floor flat for pop, crisps, and 'games'? Ironically, Day's flat was situate almost opposite the local Police station!.

Some of these 'games' did involve the little boys placing their hands into Day's trouser pockets, when they would be invited to rummage inside his pocket to see what they could find. He would then give each one money or sweets. The boy went on to describe other 'games' which involved masturbation and other forms of indecency, and indecent exposure by the adult. My friend was starting to have difficulty with his self control as by now it was obvious that matters were extremely serious.

The boy went on to inform us that a pair of his friend's underpants were on the top of a wardrobe in Day's bedroom, (this snippet of information proved crucial!). Due to the gravity of developments, I sought the permission of my friend to involve the local (Cheshire) Police. As it was obvious that I was going to be late for duty, I telephoned my boss (Detective Inspector Tony Frost) informing him of the situation. He instructed me to stay over in Hoylake and assist the local police if required. I then rang a friend who was a uniformed Constable in Hoylake Bob Kesteven at his home as it was his day off. Fortunately by coincidence, the detective on duty happened to be there at the time having a cup of tea. Bob and the duty detective, Detective Constable Tom Parry told me to remain where I was as they would attend immediately. The two officers duly arrived fifteen minutes later. The young boy was now officially (but very gently) interviewed in the presence of myself and both of his parents, who constantly reassured the youngster that he had nothing to fear.

Although the boy was of tender years, his recollection of events and detailed description of Day's flat and its contents, including numerous hiding places of some of his chums' clothing were later to be proved 'spot on'. The investigation brought to light more instances of varying degrees of indecency performed with 'named' boys.

All those named were traced and interviewed and statements taken. Subsequently Day was visited the following evening at his flat by CID officers. At first Day denied all knowledge of anything untoward relating to children. He insisted that no child had ever been inside his flat, and accused those who stated otherwise of being blatant liars.

The officers let him rant on with his denials and counter accusations before requesting to search the flat. Ignoring Day's protestations, the flat was searched and, hey presto! a pair of child's underpants was recovered from the top of the wardrobe in Day's bedroom, together with other items of clothing secreted, as described in the boy's statement!. Foolishly, Day denied any knowledge as to how the clothing came to be in his flat and insisted that he knew nothing about them. This was very incriminating behaviour indeed.

Day was taken across the road to the Police station and interviewed at length. His flat was subject to a rigorous and meticulous forensic scrutiny. Eventually Day, realising the futility of his continual denials, finally admitted to a string of offences against the boys. These offences included indecent assault, gross indecency and buggery.

He subsequently appeared before Chester Crown Court where he thankfully pleaded 'guilty' to all of the offences with which he had been charged, thus eliminating the necessity of the children to appear and give evidence. It was revealed in court that Day had committed similar offences on young boys when he ran children's football teams in Southend on Sea some years before, where he had received 6 months imprisonment. On this occasion at Chester Crown Court, Day was sent to prison for three years. My original assessment of the man was right. It was just as well that I allowed my wife's chastisement to go over my head!.

The Day incident not only received wide press publicity but became the talk of Hoylake for a long time. I was congratulated by many local residents for my speed in getting the sordid little man locked away as soon as my early suspicions were confirmed.

Off duty, I used to enjoy a pint with the lads. My local pub in Hoylake, the Ship Inn, was but a short walk from my home. It was situated on the main street through the centre of the town. Most of the patrons of the Ship Inn bar had allotments down the fields over the railway lines. Each Sunday lunchtime, especially in the summer, a number of us would take items of produce from our plots up to the pub to give to the old folk in the bar. We also had a committee in being for a local (registered) charity that we had all formed to which we all regularly subscribed cash to its fund. This fund was used to purchase food and coal for the local old age pensioners during the winter, and also for the purchase of Christmas presents for those of them who were old or lived alone.

Each Saturday night, a draw was held to swell the fund's coffers All went well for a number of years and the little charity's aims were achieved and fulfilled. As time went on I was disturbed to hear bits of tittle tattle filtering back to me down at the allotments or in the bar of the Ship, concerning dissension with regard to the charity. A new treasurer had been appointed, and this particular man was a person who I personally would be loathe to trust with other peoples' money. He certainly was not revered by some in the district due to his reputation as a 'loafer'. However, I was not always about due to my various shifts and duties and hadn't had a chance to voice my sentiments prior to his appointment.

The dissension and undertone continued and one or two were so frustrated that they started to confide in me and voice their fears with regard to the charity's cash. I decided to don my 'detective's head' I and see what I could unearth. I knew the treasurer reasonably well as I occasionally played darts or conversed with him in the bar over a pint. Although I didn't have all that much time for him I decided to keep his company and socialise with him whilst at the Ship and see what I could learn.

Our treasurer also had an allotment so it was easy to see him regularly during my off duty periods.

I learned from him and others that he had started an association with a young girl who was only half his age. I was told that he was lavishing his new girlfriend with gifts of one sort or another. These gifts eventually took the form of expensive jewellery.

The man himself was of extremely modest means, and was well known as not having worked since before Robert Peel was a cadet!!. It was therefore intriguing to know where the money was coming from to maintain his continual supply of such gifts to secure the maintenance of his romance?.

It became obvious that his source of revenue for such items must be our charity fund. I instructed one of the committee to go and make an official complaint outlining the committees' fears to the local police, again my Cheshire colleagues became officially involved. Their subsequent enquiries soon led to those fears being substantiated. The treasurer, was arrested and after being interviewed made a lengthy statement of admission regarding his continual dipping into the pensioners' charity fund until it became exhausted and the charity's bank account was empty.

He appeared before the court and pleaded guilty to the theft of the charity fund's cash and was given a suspended prison sentence and ordered to repay all of the money he had stolen. It would be a long time, if ever, that he would be accepted by the local people of Hoylake again. I was very pleased to have been instrumental in bringing this man to justice.

I often wondered if some of the thieving which I investigated actually involved human beings? as such were the depths of depravity that some unscrupulous people would stoop to enable themselves to make a 'quick buck'!.

A particular case involving such 'low life' came to light when I was sent to investigate what was first thought to be a case of criminal damage to a burial vault in Anfield Cemetery. The vault was a fine marble and stone structure which was well over a hundred years old. It must have cost a fortune to erect, even in those days. I saw that, sadly, some of the ornamental masonry had been damaged and pieces of broken stone and marble littered the immediate area. Closer examination of the structure revealed that all was not as at first thought. I saw that there was a hole at the base of the structure and although it was daylight I went to the car and retrieved my torch to make a closer examination of the interior of the hole. On shining my torch into the aperture I saw stone steps leading down into the darkness. I pulled the stone at the side until there was enough space for me to enter the vault. With the aid of my torch I descended down into the depths of the tomb. I reached the bottom of the steps and saw a number of coffins. One of them had been forcibly opened and the lid removed revealing the almost perfectly preserved body of a little girl. The coffin must have been well sealed, possibly air tight, as the body and its covering were almost intact and in a good, preserved state. I noticed that other coffins had been damaged. It was quite obvious that the thief or thieves were after whatever they could get from the interior of the vault. I was concerned to see that the little girl's face bore what appeared to be large spots or pimples. Wondering if she had died of some horrendous disease I beat a hasty retreat. I soon had the vault resealed by the authorities, (the family grave was so old that there were no traceable relatives) I never did solve that particularly vile crime, the desecration of a grave to see what could be stolen from the dead, and all they finished up with was a couple of pounds worth of lead!. What a pity the thief or thieves hadn't caught something nasty in the way of disease from the poor little mite's body. It goes to show just what kind of slime there is living amongst us, the mind boggles! I suffered no ill effects from my gruesome discovery, apart from the need of having my suit cleaned after climbing in and out of the vault.

Equally distasteful and unpleasant, was an investigation into a series of thefts from patients at a large old peoples home. Allegations had been made by a relative that her elderly aunt had died and a lot of her property was missing. I spent many days at the home and made extensive enquiries into the serious allegation. I interviewed all members of the staff, from the Matron downwards. The Matron afforded me the utmost assistance into the unsavoury matter and it was not long before I started to find that not only was the particular allegation which I was investigating true, but it was widespread among some of the staff. One nurse tearfully admitted to having taken items of jewellery from one of the patients who had been suffering severe senility before eventually dying. The nurse informed me that. "There's a few of us at it'". Sadly, she was telling the truth. There were indeed others 'at it'. I uncovered a small network of such thefts from elderly patients by some members of the staff. During the ensuing three days I arrested those nurses responsible and they duly appeared before the court. Each was heavily fined and dismissed from their posts. This was the type of enquiry that was most distasteful and unpleasant to carry out, but equally distasteful was the type of person that I was dealing with. Still that was part of the job and it must be carried out thoroughly.

On my rest days I went on the occasional 'safari' out to my colleague's pony trekking farm in Llanrhaeadr on the outskirts of Oswestry. I found it very relaxing when I went there and made my way up into the mountains after hares and rabbits. Occasionally I would take one of the horses and spend the day on a pleasant ride along the narrow tracks. I really loved the utter solitude and peace of those mountains.

If nothing else, those days were certainly therapeutic in clearing away the cobwebs of the inner City and the smell of criminal investigations. The only drawback was the inevitable return at the end of the day to 'normality'!.

One day I was approached by my Chief Inspector, who, thinking of a days nautical recreation, asked if there was any chance of a day out fishing in the boat. As this was the least that I could so for my 'Saviour' who had saved my career earlier, I readily agreed. "CERTAINLY SIR" I enthused and promptly arranged for us both to go out in the boat on the next rest day that the tide (and hopefully the weather) was right for us to do so.

Eventually such a day materialised, I was to meet my chief Inspector at Hoylake beach when we would walk out to the boat and await the incoming tide to float us off to sea for some well earned recreational fishing. The boat was not yet one hundred per cent complete with regard to interior fittings to the inner deck area and could only take three persons with a degree of comfort. However, there being only the boss and I going out that day I decided to take my young son along and he enthusiastically carried the day's food and drink in his back pack. I carried the bait and the fishing rods.

My son and I were at our beach rendezvous early so we walked out to the boat and placed the gear aboard and prepared the vessel for ' take off'. At the appointed time I heard a whistle and shout from the slipway. I saw the boss standing there and with him was a young boy? I went across and realised that the boss had brought along, uninvited, his own son. This had thrown a spanner in the works as there was absolutely no room in the boat for four. As both had travelled a long distance from the other side of Liverpool I had no alternative but to sadly (and angrily) cancel my son's eagerly awaited day's outing. I was very annoyed indeed watching him walk sadly and dejectedly along the promenade to catch his but back home. That was just not on I thought, it made me feel a right heel.

"That was a bit naughty boss" I said, "Why didn't you say there would be two of you, I've had to send my lad home now". All I received in the form of a reply was ' Sorry Swas, I didn't realise".

We made our way over to the boat and I wondered just how long we were supposed to be going out for. They had rods, boxes, holdalls, cases "Christ boss, why didn't you just get Pickfords to bring your gear over" I exclaimed with frustration. All we needed now was the proverbial kitchen sink, (and a periscope) judging by the amount we were going to carry !

As we awaited the flood tides arrival leaning against the boat and loosening the mooring rope,' the youngster decided to pretend that the boat was an obstacle course and started climbing onto the gunwales and jumping down into the boat, climbing out and doing the same thing again, (perhaps he thought it was a floating trampoline). I could see that his lovely son and I were really going to get on! "Don't do that son, you might spring the planking" I said frightened that he might cause some damage by his jumping about on the vessel. "I'm not doing any harm" he cheekily replied. "Do as you're bloody told" I quickly and angrily countered. The boss didn't say a word. I thought at first a mist had descended, but realised that it was in fact steam coming out of my ears as I contained my anger with considerable difficulty.

Eventually the water arrived and once we were afloat and able to make off, we let go and the little engine putt putted us down the channel and out to sea where we later dropped anchor at the 'Ridge' buoys, 3 miles out off Hoylake.

We settled down to a day's angling but this was frequently interrupted by the boy's misbehaviour, climbing about, standing up, sitting down and fidgeting about in general.

Finally I could stand it no longer. I threw down my fishing rod and told the boy that if he didn't behave himself I would abort the day's activities and go back home forthwith. I said to the boss, "I'm sorry boss, but I'm not putting up with this". This outburst had the' desired effect for a while, but eventually the lad became bored and started off again. I did no more than start the engine, told the boss to reel in his line and made for the shore telling the boss, "Right, that's it for today, we're going home". I was completely brassed off. We made our return journey in utter silence, the atmosphere could have been cut with a knife. I took the boat into the shallows almost to the end of the slipway, anchored it secure and we all walked ashore to our vehicles parked nearby. Without a further word being spoken each of us departed and I drove home (spitting feathers) but wondering if this episode would manifest itself at some future date at work.

I didn't have to wait long to find out. From the following day onwards work became very 'strained' when the boss and I were in the office or in each others company. I then started to get files returned for various obscure reasons or files of colleagues instructing me to 'take them over'. I would receive my files endorsed in large red inked handwriting saying that I'd missed this or hadn't mentioned that, or large red rings encircling an occasional spelling mistake or incorrect punctuation. These things had always 'gone through' on previous occasions and been successfully submitted to the appropriate departments or authorities. Things that had previously been accepted were now becoming magnified and whatever had caused the boss's displeasure would be written in red across my typing, ensuring that the whole page have to be retyped.

As time went on things became worse. The boss would completely ignore me when we passed in the corridors. When there would be a conference held in the general office any comments I made would be completely ignored or dismissed out of hand and the agenda would move on. Weeks went by and the situation became ludicrous. I was transferred across the division to Anfield but the situation with regard to elasticated bouncing files continued. Things were becoming absolutely intolerable. Although I was working my fingers to the bone, unfortunately whatever I did, it just didn't please 'sir' !.

Things went on and on from bad to worse until even my sergeants were asking me what I had done to the boss to have upset him so, it was that obvious. Eventually after one of my files had been submitted (after minute scrutiny from my sergeant and Inspector) to the Chief Inspector, it was returned from him with large red letters across the top page, S.M. (see me), other similar requests to colleagues were in small letters at the base of the page P.S.M. (Please see me). I rang Lower Lane and was informed by the Chief Inspector's secretary that I was to attend his office two days later, at 10 o'clock on Saturday morning.

At 10 am on the dot I presented myself outside the closed door of the boss's office and nervously tapped seeking admittance. Hearing the curt command "Come In", I opened the door and walked in. The boss was sitting at his desk scrutinising paperwork which was littering his desk top, "Shut the door" he said without looking up. I closed the door and stood there in front of his desk. Although there two empty chairs at hand I stood there wondering if I would be offered the courtesy of being told to sit down. I wasn't! After standing there waiting for what was to come, I started to watch fascinated a large bluebottle whizzing round the office practising take offs and landings on any suitable landing strip it deemed appropriate. The boss finally condescended to look up, eyeing what had walked in as though I was something he had scraped from his shoe. After what seemed to have been an eternity the boss said, "D'you know why you are here?", his face was completely devoid of any form of friendly expression. "I'm afraid not sir" I answered in all honesty.

The boss went on to inform me, "I'm not happy with your work, it's as simple as that" he grunted. "May I ask why sir?" I enquired, wondering what this question would produce. "I don't have to explain anything to you Swasie, Suffice to say I'm not happy with you being on the staff", he said sharply.

On the staff!, not on the 'section', on the 'staff'! this was starting to look serious for me. Surely he, who once performed a miracle and saved my job so brilliantly, was not going to get me kicked out of the CID, or 'Off the Staff' as he looked to be indicating.

"With respect sir, things haven't been the same since that day in the boat" I bleated like a wimp. "It's got bugger all to do with the day in the boat, I'm just not happy with you" said my angry chief. ——"But surely——" I went on, but was rudely interrupted by the boss's quick counter, "Look Swasie, I think the CID is too much for you with that hand of yours". Oh, this is a new tack now I thought, it's certainly taken him a very long time to realise this. Sod it, in for a penny in for a pound as the saying goes. I argued, "My work is no worse than anyone else's and you know it" I snapped, adding as an afterthought, "What's up? Don't I come up with the goodies?" We both knew what that cutting remark meant. "I'll pretend didn't hear that" the boss said slowly and stared at me with a look that could kill. "I consider that I work as hard and efficiently as any other member of the office staff" I said. The boss snapped, "Look, I'm not arguing with you, I've made my mind up. I"m sending this report (indicating a typewritten report he held up in his hand) and you to 'Taffy' Davies (the Chief Superintendent and overall boss of the CID) on Monday morning. Mr Davies had the ultimate power to hire or fire officers into or from the department. He was also renowned for his lack of compassion and could be quite ruthless.

I asked the boss if I could read the report referred to which he was holding in his hand. He refused to allow my request.

My last instruction was to attend Mr Davies' office at Force Headquarters on Monday morning at ten o clock. My 'interview' had ended. Before I left I asked the boss once more if he would kindly reconsider his decision before sending me to the certainty of being posted out of the CID, for which I had worked so hard. My request fell on deaf ears, he was determined to get me 'defrocked'. All because of that bloody day's incident in the boat. First the boss works wonders and keeps me in the job, then because he gets upset, due to what I considered to be no fault of mine, he decides to get me the chop for daring to cross him. I knew beyond doubt that there was no hope of my being able to persuade the Chief Super CID to go against the boss's recommendation. I'd just have to sweat over the weekend.

I left the boss's office feeling very dejected. I was bitter when I thought of others on the section who were quite frankly either bone idle or just plain incompetent, but for one reason or another were tolerated by he who was now giving me the 'bums rush'. I'd no sooner told my sergeant (in confidence) of the developments, when all the dogs throughout the division (and possibly the force) were barking the fact that Swasie was being kicked out of the 'Jacks'. Perhaps I should have learned the art of acute grovelling after all ! I would be spending a restless weekend giving a lot of thought to the inevitable consequences of being turfed out of the CID, not least the big drop in finances. I awaited Monday morning with trepidation.

That Saturday night I decided to go out for a few drinks to drown my sorrows.

I met a mate in the Ship Inn, Hoylake, Jimmy Hunter. Jim had been the youngest man in the Merchant Navy to qualify for his 'Master' certificate and had travelled the oceans of the world, many times solo. He owned and worked his own trawler, the 'Margareta' which operated out of Fleetwood. Jim was a powerful and strong man in his late forties. He was like his equally tough brother Roy (now deceased) an ex-prize fighter of some repute. Jim and I quaffed a few ales and mixed some banter with the Ship's licensee, Bill Royden before embarking on a tour of the local pubs around Hoylake.

After the pubs closed we moved on to visit a club or two in New Brighton. We visited 'Billy Blues', the 'Late Extra' and one or two more before we decided to make our way home in the early hours. As Jim was driving, he sensibly remained on pints of orange and soda after his initial couple of pints in Hoylake. As we drove along Seabank Road Jim turned into a side road assuming it would be a short cut that would get us home sooner.

We continued along the road and I saw two men wheeling a motor cycle. On the petrol tank of the machine was a large cardboard box. I could see bottles and packages protruding out of the top. "Stop a minute Jim" I said, I wanted to see what they were up to. We stopped the car and Jim and I went to the two. I introduced myself to them and asked them what they had in the box. One of the two, a six foot, slim man of twenty five or so (Lofty) replied, "Just some drinks for a party". I looked into the box and saw a number of large bottles of whisky and sealed cartons of cigarettes. "Where are these from?" I asked. The man accompanying Lofty was holding the handlebars of the motor cycle and he said "Run for it" as he left hold of the machine and was about to run, but was grabbed by Jim in a vice like hold. Lofty punched me in the face and he also was about to run but I replied with a punch to his face and managed to hold on to him. Lofty was bleeding from his nose and said "Okay mate, I give in. We've screwed a shop". Jim and I placed the two in the car and put the box of whisky and cigarettes into the boot We then drove to the shop indicated to us by Lofty as the one that they had broken into a short time earlier, before our chance interception. "That's it there" said 'Lofty indicating a large self service shop - 225 Seabank Road. Jim stopped and I popped out and saw that the shop's front door had been forced.

I got back into Jim's car and said, "Manor Road, Jim", (Manor Road was just around the corner and there was the local Police Station) On arrival at the station I went inside, introduced myself and sought assistance to remove the two and the stolen goods into the building. We were assisted in this task by the night detective and a number of his uniformed colleagues, (one of whom was to become my inspector when I was to serve at Manor Road nearly twenty years later) who carried in the 'goodies'.

Once inside, I again formally introduced myself to the station sergeant in the presence of the two prisoners and a couple of Manor Road officers. "What's happened to you?" the sergeant asked; 'Lofty' as he dabbed at his bloody nose with his handkerchief. Pointing to me, Lofty snarled "Flying Officer Kite here snotted me one!" meaning I suppose that I had hit him. I quickly corrected his version by telling the sergeant, "His head caught the car as he was getting in!". The sergeant gave me a knowing look which said "Yes I'm sure it did" as he proceeded to make a note of the property recovered.

The night detective went round to visit the shop and the proprietor was woken to verify that the goods recovered were from his shop. This was duly confirmed and both men responsible for the break were formally cautioned and charged with the offence of shopbreaking, after each making a written statement in which both admitted their guilt in the joint enterprise. Both were later bailed to appear before the Wallasey Magistrates Court at a later date, (On their subsequent appearance before the court when both pleaded 'Guilty" to the offence, each was fined the sum of £40). Jim and I later left the station and made our way home. Although I was happy with such a detection, Monday morning still hung over me and my happiness was short lived.

Like many other officers, I did not like having to visit Headquarters down town. The place was crawling with top brass, not to mention their numerous lap dogs and those members of the 'chairbourne infantry' who, never having seen an angry man, had secured themselves a nice little niche somewhere in the building where they could remain well out of harm's way and far away from the sharp end. It was surprising the faces one saw appearing out of the woodwork when one visited the 'big house'.

On arriving at Force Headquarters, I gingerly walked up the stairs and along the passage until I reached the Chief Super's office. The door was closed. I took a deep breath and knocked. There was no sound from within so I knocked again, this time a little louder."WAIT !" came a loud bellow from the other side of the door. Christ that's a fine start, I've upset him already . After a lengthy wait the door finally opened and out walked two very senior officers, followed to the door by the massive frame of CID's Chief Super from the valleys, who was shortly (if he had not already done so) to decide my future with the department. He looked me up and down as I stood there, and nodding for me to follow him, retraced his steps back inside, He went back behind his desk and slumped his large form into the big comfortable chair which uttered creaking protests as he did so.

"SHUT THE DOOR." he growled as he directed me with his finger to stand in front of his desk. He looked down at a report in front of him, which I instantly recognised as being the one from my Chief Inspector. Picking it up he gave it a long, careful scrutiny. Finally, looking up at me, report in one hand and stroking his double chins with his other he said in his deep Welsh accent "I've read your Chief Inspector's report and I'm putting you back into uniform as from tomorrow".

Although I knew that this was coming, I couldn't believe that my years of being a detective were coming to an undignified end. With no disrespect whatsoever to the uniformed branch of the job, I wanted to remain in the CID as it was the chosen area which I (vainly perhaps) considered to be my vocation. I tried one more plea, "This is my career, can't I appeal to your better nature sir?" I asked with what degree of dignity I could muster in such futile circumstances. "Uniform tomorrow" said the unmoved Taff. I asked if I could read the report from my Chief Inspector.

It was as though I had lighted a blue touch paper of an explosive firework. The Chief Super bellowed " Don't argue with me, where d'you want to be posted?" as a deeply generous concession. It was obvious that my nautical saga had brought about the demise of my service in the CID, and it was equally obvious, even to an idiot, that further attempts to salvage it would be akin to spitting into the wind. "Can I stay in the same division sir?" I asked. I didn't fancy starting all over again somewhere else. "Right, you'll stay in 'B' division at Lower Lane. Get your uniform sorted out and I'll inform your Chief Superintendent".

He then proceeded to make formal arrangements over the telephone which resulted in my being instructed to parade at Lower Lane in full uniform for morning duty at 7 am the day after next. Tomorrow would be spent in my being kitted out into uniform again.

That day my friend Jimmy Hunter and I made the pages of the Liverpool Echo under the headline "Off duty City detective engaged in Wallasey arrest" and went on to outline my and Jim's public spirited saga in Wallasey two nights earlier. We were also to make the Birkenhead and Wallasey News later in the week.

At least I went out in a 'blaze of glory'. However, it didn't assist my present dilemma.

Chapter Nine - Return to the Cloth

Thursday, 1 February 1973, saw me at the stores in Kent Street to be re-issued with my new Policeman's set!. I returned home and promptly ironed my tunic and trousers to razor sharp creases ready for the following morning's 'audience' with Mr Grant, the Chief Superintendent.

The next morning I drove into Lower Lane car park, this time I parked at the far end of the building near to the canteen, instead of parking near to the CID office at the other end.

I wandered into the canteen for a cup of tea as I was twenty minutes early, I was to see God at nine o'clock sharp. On seeing the boss, I felt as welcome as a cat in a bird cage, (and was made to feel just as popular!). Mr Grant was a man of few words, and even fewer smiles, today was no exception. My 'welcoming' interview lasted no more than ten minutes, during which time I was given the usual do's and don'ts before learning that I was to work from Anfield Police Station almost opposite the famous football ground. My new Sergeants at Anfield were to be John Hewer (later to become a Chief Superintendent and ultimately the Commandant of the Police Training centre at Bruche) and Fred Tomlinson (sadly now deceased) both of these were excellent men to work under.

As it was now getting on towards refreshment time for the morning shift (10 o'clock), Mr Grant told me to get myself a cup of tea before making my way over to my new station, 3 miles away to meet my new section and Sergeants.

I arrived at the Bridewell and after parking my car in a side street I entered the station to be greeted by Jock Stewart, the enquiry office constable (who was known by his colleagues as 'The Slug" "Welcome to the fold Swasie" he said and added Sergeant Hewer will be here in a minute, he's just gone out for some milk for the tea". I could see that my new Sergeant had at least got his priorities right!.

Jock and I were joined by the Sergeant with his important ingredient for the forthcoming brew. A short time later, at ten o'clock the troops arrived for their refreshments, it was scoff time'!. I did not need any introduction to the lads, and was looking forward to working with them. I spent many happy months working the Anfield section and during that time I dealt with many incidents and arrests. One particular incident occurred one lunch time when I had cause to attend the Salisbury Public House to deal with an allegation of theft. I went to the scene and parked my Police vehicle outside the premises. My colleague, Griff Jones and I went inside to deal with the matter. When our task was completed 15 minutes later Griff and I were leaving the pub to resume our patrol. As we went outside I was mortified to discover that my patrol vehicle was missing! I was baffled as I distinctly remembered securing the vehicle before leaving it. I wondered if one of my colleagues had removed it as a joke (and sincerely hoped that this was in fact the case). If the vehicle had been stolen, not only would I be acutely embarrassed but I was going to have some serious explaining to do, and I wasn't exactly the Chief Super's most popular Constable!. I had the added indignity of being asked by the pub staff where my vehicle was. I hastily replied that one of my colleagues had taken it to carry out an enquiry. Griff and I had to walk back to Anfield Bridewell and I felt sick at the prospect of having to report my police vehicle stolen. There was no way I was going to use my radio to check if all was well so I decided to await my return to the station before planning my next move.

Half an hour later Griff and I arrived back our station. There outside, parked neatly against the kerb was my vehicle, fully locked and secured. As we entered the building we saw a number of colleagues leaning against the counter, each wearing a wide grin. "Did you find your vehicle?" asked Jock to the laughter of all present. One of the lads, Vic Manders, informed me that he casually tried the lock as he and a colleague were passing and saw the vehicle outside the pub. They thought we were "having a sly pint", what! and park a Police patrol vehicle outside as we did so? I thanked Vic for his absolutely amusing jape and informed him that I was highly amused!!.

After completing my spell at Anfield I was then transferred to Lower Lane Section under the command of Inspector Jock Ward (now deceased) and Sergeant Bill Roberts.

The day came for me to parade for duty at the new venue. Again I was to start my term on a morning shift. At 6-30 am on my first morning, I wandered into the parade room and joined my new comrades. All those present shook my hand and welcomed me to their midst. All were discreet enough not to mention my previous departure from the 'Jacks' when I was last at Lower Lane. Apparently I was privileged, as I was one of the few CID men that the members of the section had time for due to the fact that I had always unhesitatingly helped my uniformed brethren whenever I could, and this was now paying dividends.

I was to become very happy on the section to which I had been posted. They were a great bunch, Jed "Sockless" Consett, Robbie Riddel, Jack O'Reilly, Trish McCoy, Barbara Cutting and many others whose names escape me. I could not possibly have selected a better section of colleagues personally.

During the parade I was 'officially' welcomed by Inspector Ward and Sergeant Roberts, two of the best supervisors anyone could wish to have as their guides and mentors.

When parade was over we were allowed to visit the canteen for a quick cuppa before venturing out onto the damp and cold morning streets. I was to accompany "Sockless" on mobile patrol for the next few days to 'get the feel' of my new uniformed patch The lads were kindness itself and did not hesitate to reintroduce me to one or two procedures that they thought I may have forgotten or which had been introduced before my return to Lower Lane.

Since my departure from the CID my ultimate transfer back into uniform went smoothly and I quickly adapted accordingly, (I had no option!). Balls to the CID!.

There was one fly in the ointment at Lower Lane, who I had cause to dislike a long time ago during my early CID days.

He was a uniformed officer who posed in the guise of Collator. This post was a very important position if it was handled correctly. The collator was supposed to be ultimately responsible for the gathering and storing of intelligence regarding the activities of criminals and their associates. This entailed the filing of easy accessible documentation for the convenience of those officers requiring such important data to assist them. Any officer with useful information regarding criminal activity would supply the collator with said information, which would then be stored to be drawn upon when necessary.

No doubt this was done by the officer concerned. However, what annoyed me was the sight of him donning his civilian jacket over his uniform and going walkies allegedly to the bank or other similar important places. I used to see him regularly walking around the shopping areas carrying a plastic carrier bag as he idled his time instead of performing the duties for which he was being paid. These 'outings' of his included the running of errands for the Chief Super and his cronies.

He would never be in his office when he was wanted due to these regular 'outings' when he was performing his vanishing act !

This was another day job, every evening and weekend off !(unless there was the occasional football match, when he would be paid overtime for such duty, whereas we, the shift men were not and of course, having a day job eliminated the risk of being confronted by 'angry men!.

Soon after arriving at Lower Lane, I was very sad to learn of the sudden death of one of our forces most popular young Inspectors, Eric Leach. I class myself as being very privileged to have served under such a wonderful man as Eric. An illustration of his popularity was indicated when Eric's funeral took place at Priory Road church. The whole area was completely saturated with people blocking all roads. It seemed that everyone was there to pay their last respects to such a wonderful person. Every single colleague, male and female who had the opportunity of serving with him was devastated at his sudden and unexpected demise. Eric's brother John, another gentleman, was also a serving Inspector in the force. (John later qualified as a barrister and continued to grace the courts with his presence as both an efficient prosecutor and advocate).

My collator 'friend' and I never managed to see eye to eye and whenever we met I couldn't resist showing my contempt for him in one way or another (I must admit in hindsight, it was not conduct becoming of a Police Officer), as I was never to have much respect for those I considered only as Uniform Carriers !.

Unfortunately like many others of a similar ilk who secure themselves similar day posts, some are only in these particular positions in name only. I could not help but show my resentment for this particular snivelling individual. He really relished his position as the Chief Super's 'lap dog', and snout (informer). Due to my attitude towards him and the like, I was not to endear myself to some of the 'powers' upstairs.

One of the advantages of having served for so long in the CID was the fact that I was extremely familiar with the movements of many of the division's perpetrators of crime and their associates, and could offer valuable assistance to my colleagues in this sphere.

During the course of my duties I started to have dealings with the proprietor of a sweets and tobacconist shop which also served the area as a newsagents. The owner of this shop was a well known local councillor. This man considered himself to be the patron saint of citizens of his local council estate. Frequently when I arrested anyone in the area they would threaten to report me to Councillor _____. Occasionally when they did this, our defender of the parish would visit Lower Lane and take up their 'gripe' with his friend the Chief Super. In fact this state of affairs was to occur frequently and the particular councillor concerned eventually seemed to have instigated some sort of vendetta or crusade against me whenever I dared to summons or arrest someone near his premises.

On more that one occasion I was summoned upstairs to see my Superintendent Mr Grant (later to become Chief Superintendent). I was not asked for my account of whatever it was that had invoked the councillor's displeasure, but instead told to 'stop harassing the public'.

Due to this constant misbehaviour of mine, I was not to become one of Mr Grant's (or his successor's) favourite constables. On more than one occasion I was to be threatened with being posted elsewhere if I did not stop upsetting Councillor _____. My Super told me that he was becoming very concerned with 'my manner with the public', all because I was carrying out my duties in the manner I considered were correct and impartial. There was no mention of my consistent arrest, summons rate, or prosecutions of offenders.

My local knowledge paid off when I was patrolling the streets early one dark morning in my patrol car. As I was 'diligently sleuthing' in the Norris Green area, my headlights picked out a youth (who was known to me) standing beneath the foliage of a large unruly privet hedge which bordered a garden. I stopped my vehicle and wound the window down. "What are you doing up so early Gary?" I asked the nineteen year old. "Gary" informed me that he was waiting for a mate! (at four o'clock in the morning!) I wasn't happy with his reply and got out of my vehicle. "Come on, we can do better than that" I said. I told him to empty his pockets. He did so and produced a penknife and a screwdriver. I asked him why he was carrying such items as, unless he had a good excuse, I could take him in for 'possessing housebreaking implements". "They were just in my pockets" he said. I knew Gary well. Our paths had crossed one or twice before! As the youth didn't live far away, I decided to take him home. I asked him if there was any 'swag' in his house. "No, I'm going straight now boss" said the innocent victim of circumstances. Although Gary was of tender years, he was a veteran thief and breaker. "Let's have a little look in the house then eh?" I suggested. At first he became quite indignant and quickly informed me that his mum an dad were in bed, and anyway, I would need a warrant he authoritatively informed me. "Okay, I'll get a warrant then" I bluffed and added that if anything was found I would arrest his father as head of the household. "Alright Mr Turner, there's just a bike I took outside the shops yesterday" Gary volunteered. We went to the house and I recovered an expensive gent's racing cycle, almost new.

As I placed Gary into my car and summoned a van to retrieve the cycle, I turned to Gary and said sarcastically, "there, don't you feel better now you've got that off your chest?' Gary, thinking I was being my 'welfare orientated self' just nodded. I do hope the councillor doesn't mind someone getting their stolen property back! I arrested the youth and took him to Lower Lane where he was charged with the theft of the cycle. He made a statement under caution in which he admitted the offence. The owner was eventually traced and he was reunited with his proud and expensive possession.

One of the drawbacks, or risks a working bobby has to face, are complaints from the public who wish to make them in an official capacity. I was not to be denied this form of action by irate members of the public who considered my upholding of the law to be in many cases an infringement of their liberty.

If a person decides to make such an official complaint against an officer of any rank, a rigid set of procedures are then instigated. It has been said by many that it is not right that the police should investigate themselves, as those performing such duties could be considered biased when investigating allegations against their colleagues.

Let me categorically state that this is not so. Officers of the force's complains and discipline department (the 'Rubber Heel Squad") are very carefully considered before selection. There are NO volunteers into the department. Many officers posted to the squad are not ever aware of such postings until being told immediately prior to their transfer. Consequently these officers selected never shirked their responsibilities when carrying out their duties, however unpleasant they may be. Indeed, many wrongs were put right and many 'bad apples' were weeded out, and if necessary prosecuted due to this branch of the force's activities.

Suffice to say then that when a person makes an official complaint to a Sergeant or Inspector concerning the conduct of an officer, this will then be recorded and documented.

Arrangements are then made for the aggrieved person to be interviewed and a statement obtained by the Discipline Department. Once this is done, the wheels are then set in motion. It could be said that an innocent officer therefore would have nothing to worry about. Not at all! So thorough would be the investigation by the Discipline Department that the officer could only breathe a sigh of relief when (and if) he is cleared of any allegations or it is decided that the allegation has not been substantiated and 'no further action' is contemplated.

When an officer was eventually cleared it was very rare, if ever that he or she would be given any redress, or a malicious complainant prosecuted.

Some complaints against myself were indeed subject to my being served with the appropriate papers by 'Complaints and discipline".

Sometimes there were just too ridiculous to believe, but they were still investigated!!

One pathetic attempt to discredit me occurred after I had cause to admonish three young members of the public for their anti-social behaviour outside a public house the three men had just left. Unknown to me the trio then went to a nearby Police Station to complain about my conduct. I was fully interviewed by a Superintendent allocated by the C & D Department who then served me with the notorious form 156B (Discipline form), after which I was cautioned and asked if I wished to make any reply, which he would then take down in writing. The printed wording of this particular form is as follows: (verbatim),

"It appears that an offence may have been committed against discipline, it being alleged :-About 9.45pm, on the above date whilst you were on duty in Stanley Road, Bootle, outside the Royal Hotel, in company with another constable, you made the remark "There's some baddies" in the presence of the complainant, Mr .... as the complainant walked past you with his two friends. The remark annoyed the complainant as he believed the remark was directed at himself and his friends"

This was then followed by the printed official caution after which I could make a reply.

Could the Complaints and Discipline department of such a large police force have really consumed such valuable time and resources (and appointed a Superintendent no less) to serve me with a piece of paper containing such utter drivel that it would surely have been put to better use hanging from a wooden roller on the wall of a toilet.

The answer was 'yes'! It goes without saying that I did not even dignify the proceedings with a reply. The matter was eventually concluded having gone absolutely nowhere. One thing it would tend to illustrate however, the fact that 'Joe Public's' gripes, however legitimate or malicious, major or trivial, all are fully investigated and enquired into. As time went on, I was to receive more of these forms! as we shall see.

A hard working, regular 'thief taker' is bound to invoke malice and hostility among some of his 'clients' and many complaints are made purely for reasons of pique. Those employed in their various nine to five hideaways would never, ever know what a discipline form looked like.

Like all good bobbies, I continued to harass and persecute the baddies. I was building quite a reputation throughout the areas I patrolled. I had been given the name 'Iron Hand' by those that must have caught sight of my brace. Such a name could be quite beneficial to me I thought.

Bill Roberts and Jock Ward decided to allow one or two of us to patrol on foot in plain clothes on occasions to give additional protection to the local residents. This proved to be a good idea and a few local 'bucks' were netted who would otherwise have got away with their sins had we been in uniform.

Walking along Stopgate Lane in company with a policewoman one morning, both of us dressed in tee-shirt and jeans, we had occasion to stop a man who was carrying a large polythene wrapped parcel under his arm.

My colleague and I went to him and introduced ourselves, showing him our warrant cards. He was asked what it was he was carrying in the parcel. "Just some tiles" was his reply. On inspecting the contents of his parcel we saw that there were a number of brand new plastic floor tiles. He was asked to account for his possession of the tiles and he admitted having taken them from his place of work at a large car manufacturers on the outskirts of the City from where he was making his way home after completing his night shift. He went on after further questioning to admit that he had taken the items without permission. He was cautioned and told he would be arrested and a vehicle was summoned to convey the three of us to Lower Lane.

It transpired that the offender was the brother of a famous footballer who was currently playing for one of the City's first division teams. The financially solvent brother immediately engaged counsel to defend the erring member of his family.

At his trial before the Liverpool Magistrates court, the defending barrister attacked my colleague and I, basing his attack on the 'way we were dressed!!!' "Is it not true that you were both dressed up to resemble the well known Disney character Mickey Mouse?" each of us was asked with the utmost cynicism and contempt. This brought guffaws from those present in the court. Counsel went on to suggest that at first we were 'acting silly in the street and making fun of his client', at 7.30 in the morning whilst the two of us were engaged in the serious business of a crime patrol? The mind boggles.

A mobile shop in the form of a very large van operated around the roads of one of the local council estates in the division. At the end of the day's trading the vehicle would be parked in the road outside the house of the owner's relatives. This particular road was quite narrow and the vehicle took up a large proportion of the carriageway. Due to this I repeatedly had cause to admonish those responsible for the vehicle which caused them to resent me personally and become hostile towards me.

I was driving my Police Landrover in the early hours of one morning in company with a female colleague, W/P Barbara Cutting. I saw the mobile shop again parked in the narrow roadway and noticed that it was not displaying its obligatory lights, although the latter is a widespread misdemeanour, no doubt committed by us all at some time or another.

I stopped the Landrover and my colleagues and I went to the van and looked it over. Shining my torch onto the vehicle's tax disc (the excise licence) I saw that although it was a current licence, something about it appeared to be amiss, though what it was I just could not establish. As I was not happy with the item I decided to confiscate the disc but the vehicle was locked up and secured. The nearside louvre window was devoid of glass but had a piece of steel mesh secured over the opening and screwed in place on the inside. I pondered for a while and asked my colleague if she could find anything wrong with the disc. She inspected it thoroughly but was satisfied that it was current and correct. I was still convinced that there was something untoward appertaining to the disc however.

Finally , I made up my mind, I was going to confiscate the disc and make further enquiries as to its authenticity, although what was wrong with it I had still not fathomed out, even though it was openly displayed for all to see. As I couldn't gain access to the vehicle, I forced the steel mesh covering the window with the Landrover's wheelbrace. In my endeavours to gain entry to the vehicle the noise of my activities awoke the vehicle owner's household.

An upstairs window was opened and the owner's father leaned out and shouted down to us 'I saw you break into the van and take some stuff out' I corrected him and explained that I was about to take the vehicle's excise licence for the purpose of enquiring into its origin and told him that nothing had been removed from the vehicle at this stage.

The irate father then shouted that he was going to report me as he actually saw me remove groceries from the van and place these into the Landrover. By now he was joined by his equally incensed wife who also started to scream abuse, in doing so causing lights to go on in many of the houses in the vicinity. Due to the gravity of the allegations now being made, I decided to play this saga exactly 'by the book'. I immediately requested the attendance of my Sergeant and Inspector and both of these officers arrived in minutes. By the time they both arrived the angry man and his wife, including some of the local residents, were standing by the 'attacked' van baying for my blood, clad in their night attire with coats around their shoulders.

The van owner's parents maintained their tirade of abuse against me and the father insisted to Sergeant Roberts and Inspector Ward that he was adamant that he saw me take groceries from the van and place them into the (empty) Landrover. As my malicious accuser would not rescind his allegations against me, nor would his wife, Inspector Ward ordered my colleague and I to return to Lower Lane in the Sergeant's car forthwith. The Landrover would remain at the scene. The local populace seemed to be enjoying the developments, especially as they had heard that I had been caught stealing from the van and would now be for it! I was not the most popular bobby on the estate to say the least. Apparently it mattered not that there was no property in the van to be found other than the recovered tax disc which I had handed to the Inspector. The pair were adamant however, in pursuing their malicious allegations against me.

The Inspector summoned the night CID, the night Superintendent and also the studio to attend the scene. He intended that the van should be fingerprinted and photographed, together with the Landrover as he and the Sergeant intended to pursue the matter to the bitter end, no matter whose head would roll.

I 'pig-headedly' returned to Lower Lane as instructed and awaited the return of my Sergeant and Inspector. I could still not ascertain what it was that had aroused my suspicions, but, although I was now beside myself with apprehension, I knew that there was certainly something that would eventually justify my actions (or so I hoped!), and eliminate the predicament I had placed myself in. Poor Barbara, even she thought I had overstepped the mark this time! and there was nothing she could do to help me. No doubt the father and his overjoyed audience thought that they would shortly be 'dancing on my grave'.

Eventually, after what seemed an eternity, Sergeant Roberts and Inspector Ward returned to Lower Lane. I was summoned to Mr. Ward's office. The Inspector asked me to account for my actions which had resulted in the attendance of half of the police force and half of the estate? and added, 'Christ Swasie, you'd better have some justification for your sake'.

I completed the night watch and remained on duty. I heard no more about the matter for a couple of days. I was then seen by a Chief Inspector from C & D who informed me that he was making enquiries into an allegation of theft. So the family were still pressing on with their dirty little campaign to 'throw me to the lions'.

A week or so later Sergeant Roberts was briefing the section during morning parade and brought us all to attention as Inspector Ward entered the Parade room. Finally, as the parade was about to be dismissed Inspector Ward asked me to attend his office with Sergeant Roberts immediately after parade. I saw that the Inspector was in possession of a large official looking envelope, I wondered what fate awaited me!

Sergeant Roberts and I entered the Inspector's office and I looked at the boss's face to see if it indicated what was to come. The Inspector sat behind his desk expressionless, he was giving nothing away. On his desk in from of him lay the 'official looking' envelope, alongside which lay an equally important looking report. 'Sit down gentlemen' offered Jock courteously. By now my heart was pounding. My personal radio crackled into life noisily, making me jump as one of my colleagues tested his set as he was leaving the building. 'Turn that bloody thing off' said Jock as he picked up the typewritten report. I did as I was told and sat forward in my chair. The Inspector took a deep sigh, then leaned towards me and handed me the report, 'Right Swasie, read that' he instructed, and unbeknown to me, winked at Sergeant Roberts.

The report commenced with 'With reference to the incident on ......', and went on to state that enquiries into the issue and authenticity of the confiscated vehicle excise licence number ...... recovered from motor car goods, registered number ...., have revealed that this particular licence had not in fact been issued. The document is one of a number that were stolen during an armed Post Office robbery which had recently taken place in Wednesbury, near Wolverhampton ....., I was right!!, my actions were justified, I was exonerated! I stood up gasping with relief (and joy). The rest of the report remained unread as I replaced it onto the smiling Inspector's desk. I still couldn't say what it was that had caused me to suspect something was wrong (if I had continued reading the report all would have been revealed), so the Inspector obliged and explained how I had unconsciously detected a breach of the law.

The explanation was so simple: On being issued, the details of an excise licence are either written in longhand, in ink, by the issuing counter clerk, or, typed by the issuing authority. This particular licence was completed in type, BUT ... on a portable typewriter; the letters of which are different from the standard office typewriter in that they have 'tops and tails' to their letters, the latter machines do not.

'Bloody well done Swasie' said the Inspector. He then said that I could now go and arrest the owner of the vehicle provisionally for 'armed robbery' and bring him in, adding as an afterthought to Sergeant Roberts, 'Go with him Bill, I want him brought here in one piece.' I was absolutely elated. I drove Bill and I in the Landrover to a discreet spot from where we could see the mobile shop and awaited the arrival of it's owner to commence his day's trading.

As I sat behind the wheel with my Sergeant alongside of me, I turned to him and confided, 'I'm going to relish this Bill, after what they tried to put me through'. 'I don't blame you', replied Bill.

Eventually the owner of the van and his wife made an appearance and went to the van. I waited until they had unlocked and entered the vehicle before I drove up to the front of the van to prevent it from being driven away. My Sergeant and I got out of the Landrover and went to the driver who was now sitting in the driving seat, his wife sat alongside him. 'Good morning Mr .....,' I said, 'Are you the registered owner of this vehicle?' The driver looked at me with utter contempt and growled menacingly, 'Piss of handlebars, you know bloody well it's mine'. I stood there and throwing out my chest I said (with glee), 'In that case I'm arresting you for an offence of armed robbery at.... Post Office in Wednesbury on ......' and pulled him from his vehicle unceremoniously. He shouted to his wife to go and fetch his father, shouting, 'Tell him Turner's got me' My sergeant and I bundled the hapless man into the back of the Landrover and locked the door as his hysterical wife ran to alert the family.

As we drove off, the family and an entourage of neighbours ran alongside banging the side of our vehicle. There were promised shouts that they would follow us to Lower Lane.

While we were en route to the station I thought that I would add to my prisoner's fear and discomfort by telling him that I intended to 'throw the book at him' to make sure that he got what he deserved. His ego was now well deflated and long gone. There was no sign of cockiness in his voice now as he bleated to my 'deaf' ears. 'Honest Mr Turner, I don't know anything about no Post Office job', and held his head in his hands as he started to sob. Oh dear, he was getting upset because he was in trouble, how sad!

On our arrival at the Police Station, Sergeant Roberts and I took my dejected prisoner through to the charge office where I presented him to the Bridewell Sergeant, Sergeant Hitchmo, another one of nature's gentlemen. and one of a dying breed.

We were joined by some of the Bridewell staff and Inspector Ward also put in an appearance. Not to let an opportunity slip by, I played to the gallery. "Good morning Sergeant. I have arrested this man for an offence of armed robbery. the circumstances are ....." and I went on to tell the sergeant my version of Hans Christian Andersen which was to lead to my unfortunate prisoner's incarceration. By now my frightened prisoner realised the gravity of the situation he was in and readily admitted having bought the licence from an unknown man in the 'Crown' (a pub on the East Lancashire Road) knowing it was stolen. Personally, I believed him as, knowing him as I did, I knew that his pedigree didn't include violence or robbery, he was just a petty thief and I didn't think that he would have the 'bottle' to involve himself in such a serious offence. Still, let him sweat!

After lengthy interviews by the CID it was indeed accepted that he had nothing to do with any robbery but he was however charged with 'receiving' stolen property. He was dealt with by the City magistrates and fined. There was no doubt that this 'near miss' had brought him and his family down to earth with a bang.

The complaint against me? It died a sudden death, and I didn't receive any redress which appeared to be 'par for the course'.

I still continued to receive more than my share of 'hassle' via our local miscreants 'welfare orientated' Councillor.

Whenever he was to become aware that I had summoned or chastised somebody in the locality he would be on the telephone to his friend the Chief Super, demanding to know details of my latest persecution of the public. On many occasions he even called at the station in person and made his complaint over coffee with the boss. Sometimes, after such calls or visits I would be summoned upstairs to explain why I had upset Mr. ..... again. Other times I even had to answer in writing in the form of a report.

I was patrolling my area one day near to this man's shop when I saw two little girls walking along the pavement. One was carrying a loaf and the other was carrying a bottle of sterilised milk. What a pretty little sight they both were. Each resplendent in their colourful little dresses and ribbons in their hair. As they walked along I saw with horror that the youngster carrying the bottle of milk had a cigarette dangling from he lips. I went to them and asked the little girl where on earth she had obtained the cigarette from. The cigarette was not lit and the girl said that they had both been to Mr. .....'s shop nearby and bought the milk, bread and some 'loosies' for her mum. I asked her how much the 'loosies' were and she told me that she had paid ten pence, two pence each, as she opened he other hand and revealed another four 'loosies' (individually sold cigarettes) a common practice in the area, but not to children! The little girls informed me that 'all the kids get them from .....'s shop. My favourite Councillor was being naughty. I retrieved the cigarettes and told the girls to tell their parents that they must not be sent for cigarettes and that I was returning these particular 'loosies' back to the shop.

I returned the items to the shop and gave the proprietor one hell of a rocket, telling him that if such a sale were to occur again, I would summons him and have him before the court. His indignant and blasphemous reply was to the effect that my Chief Superintendent would be made fully aware of my threats to him. Oh dear, not another visit upstairs? Lo and behold, before I went off duty that day I was required to grace the Chief Superintendent's office with my presence yet again. I was not asked for any explanation this time, but just told in no uncertain terms to 'lay off Mr. ....' and dismissed without further ado. There was no way whatsoever that Mr .... was going to receive preferential treatment from me. He would be treated exactly the same as anyone else who 'broke the rules' - of that I was adamant. Councillor or no Councillor, friend of the boss or no, if I ever caught him selling cigarettes to any child under age again, I would report him for summons and see what happened.

Even my sergeant was beginning to get fed up with my continual dealings with the erring councillor. He (Bill Roberts) was beginning to believe that there was something of a 'vendetta' between us. This was absolutely untrue. I was performing my duties in a totally impartial capacity and I was not prepared to close my eyes to certain blatant acts of law breaking, irrespective of whether they were minor or not and the fact that the perpetrator was a councillor. It is true that I did keep a regular check to see if he was 'still at it' after my warnings, but surely I was entitled if I were to uphold the law. Other shopkeepers had been successfully prosecuted for similar misdemeanours, so why should he consider himself immune due to his status.

Sergeant Roberts was accompanying me whilst I was driving my Landrover on mobile patrol one day when the same thing happened again. This time it was a girl of about twelve years of age who I saw walking along carrying a packet of cigarettes. She had just left the councillor's shop. Bill had not observed this and he wondered why I stopped alongside her. I asked the girl where she had obtained the cigarettes from and she confirmed that she had just been sold the items by Mr. ..... I alighted from my vehicle and asked the girl to accompany me back to the shop. There, I asked her to again tell me, in the presence of the councillor, who had sold her the packet of twenty cigarettes. She indicated Mr. ..... and said, "Him, I always get my mum and dad's ciggies off him." I then asked the girl to take me to her parents and warned the shopkeeper that I would be returning to him shortly to pursue the matter further with him after I had obtained a statement from the little girl in the presence of her parents.

I once again reminded him of the offence regarding the sale of cigarettes to a person under sixteen years. There were other customers present in the shop at this time and I ensured that my manners and attitude were impeccable and beyond reproach. The irate shopkeeper stormed "Right, you've gone too far this time, I'll get my coat". The little girl and I left the shop to walk the few hundred yards to her nearby home. I retained the cigarettes. As I passed the Landrover, I explained to my sergeant who was still sitting in the front passenger seat "I won't be a minute Bill, I'm just going for a statement". Bill's head went back, he eyes rolled upwards, wishing he wasn't where he was! We walked down the path to the house and the girl whet ahead and pushed the partly open front door before disappearing from my view, she returned seconds later with her mother, a middle aged matronly woman wearing the proverbial 'pinnie' and headscarf tied in a knot above her forehead. The lady was very pleasant but somewhat apprehensive at my presence.

"What on earth's the matter, officer?" she asked as her offspring huddled against her, her little face buried in her mothers hip.

"I'm sorry to disturb you Love," I said, and went on to explain my reason for being there and drew her attention to the fact that by sending her young child to purchase cigarettes she was committing an offence, namely aiding and abetting the purchase of cigarettes by a child under age (I ascertained that the child was in fact 11 years old). The lady apologised and appeared to be genuinely contrite, assuring me that no such thing would occur again.

I told her that I accepted this but I would like both her and her daughter to furnish me with a statement as I intended to prosecute the shopkeeper who had sold the cigarettes after repeated warnings to him regarding such sales. She agreed to comply with my request. As I was about to enter the house my attention was drawn to a group of people who had arrived outside the gate, one of whom was the shopkeeper. Sergeant Roberts had got out of the Police vehicle and was talking to the group. The shopkeeper had brushed past the sergeant and strode down the path towards me and the two females. Gesticulating at me with his finger, the irate shopkeeper shouted, 'I'm going to have you' and proceeded to entice his little gathering to support him. Sergeant Roberts joined us and told the councillor to be quiet and assist matters by returning to his shop. The councillor continued to shout about police harassment and told the lady and the girl to 'say nothing' as he was going to make a complaint against me to the Chief Constable.

He continued to prod my chest with his finger shouting how he was going to make sure that I would be moved from the area. I told him that if he did not cease prodding me, I would arrest him for 'assaulting a police officer'.

He either must have been drunk with his own power or thought that I was bluffing, because whatever the reason, the silly man continued to poke me in the chest and said; 'go on then, try it, arrest me'. Priding myself on always doing as I was told, I 'obeyed the last order'.

I grabbed his lapels and propelled him backwards swiftly up the path, through the gate and out to the Landrover. I began to open the rear door prior to putting him inside but my sergeant decided to intervene and pour oil on troubled waters by trying to reason with him. My dishevelled 'friend of the Chief Super' continued his threats to me. My sergeant managed to calm the man down and in actual fact, 'pulled rank' on me by rescuing the man from my grasp and told him to behave himself and go home. He agreed to leave the scene and return to his shop, but not before uttering further threats to 'have me before the Chief Constable,' these threats being made to 'save face' in front of his little gathering. I returned to the house and obtained the two statements to 'start the ball rolling' and as we were making our way, having resumed patrol, I even received a rollicking from Bill for creating an 'international incident' over a few fags.

The matter certainly did not end there, not only was I to make the Chief Superintendent's carpet more threadbare by having to walk on it AGAIN, but I was also to be served with the inevitable discipline form (156B) (which, at the conclusion of the C & D's enquiries, a 'No further Action' was decided).

Author with Landrover, Moblie Patrol.

There was one most unusual outcome to the affair.The Chief Superintendent issued an official 'Chief Super's Order' stating the Constable Turner was NOT to patrol ....Road (where the councillor's shop was situated) unless absolutely necessary. This precedent had never before, or since, been set! All because of one councillor who I kept 'upsetting; because HE broke the law.

As I considered this stupid instruction to have no legal substance I deemed it an 'unlawful order' and chose to ignore it. With regard to my attempt to summons the man for under age selling of cigarettes, this also did not go anywhere! As there were double yellow lines running along the roadside outside this particular shop whose proprietor seemed to treat the law with utter contempt, I then decided to enforce the 'No Parking' legislation. This no doubt resulted in mobile customers purchasing their morning papers and tobacco elsewhere. As Sergeant Sankey said 'Swings and Roundabouts'!

Duty went on with monotonous regularity, every now and again punctuated by one incident or another.

One day, a 13 year old school boy arrived home from school for his lunch break before returning for his afternoon lessons. After putting his meal in the oven to warm at his neat little home in the secluded area of Hartley Village, where the world famous jams are produced and bottled, the boy went out into the rear yard taking a quantity of sugar. The lad had been having science lessons during the morning and whilst awaiting his lunch decided to put into practice what he had learned during the morning. Going into a brick outhouse, he placed a pair of steel bicycle handlebars into a vice on the bench and tightened one end of the bars securely closed. He then poured into the other open end, a quantity of weed-killer, (sodium chlorate) and sugar. Having done this, he then took a lump hammer to hammer the open end closed, sealing inside the weed-killer and sugar. Raising the hammer he made his strike. There was a violent explosion which could be heard half a mile away. Part of the roof of the outhouse was blown away and tools and bits of masonry littered the yard.

The emergency services were summoned and I was directed to attend the scene. The Fire Brigade, Ambulance and myself arrived at the same time. The boy was lying in the yard, part of his right arm blown off. He was placed into the ambulance and rushed to Walton Hospital for immediate surgery. Shortly after, we were joined by the boy's devoted parents who were in a bad state of shock. I took them both to the hospital and then returned to the scene. After establishing that there was no major structural damage to nearby buildings, and no risk of fire, the Fire Brigade left the area.

A colleague and I carried out a detailed inspection of the scene, mainly the interior of the outhouse and I requested that the photographic studio attend. I recovered various items to assist my enquiries and also for forensic examination. I recovered parts of the arm and hand which I placed in a plastic bag together with ice cubes from the kitchen fridge, and leaving my colleague to interview neighbours, I raced to Walton Hospital although I was certain that the items I had retrieved would be of little use to the surgeons as they were so badly mutilated. The items were of no use and the boy's arm was amputated below the elbow. I returned to the scene to continue my investigations. I had only briefly spoken to the boy's parents to inform them of the tragedy's possible cause. They were both understandably very shocked and devastated by the incident which resulted in such appalling injuries to their son. I made further enquires via neighbours and also at his school. I established that the boy was a very intelligent, well-behaved and popular pupil at the school, and a very keen student.

I would leave the boy and his parents for the time being until all were fit enough to be interviewed. I did however monitor the boy's progress. I called at the hospital during that night to see how he was and I called in to see him on my way to work the following morning. Although he was deeply sedated, I did manage to strike up a rapport with him. I told him that I too was an amputee and to hopefully comfort him I lied that my injury too was due to 'messing around with chemicals' as I removed my brace and showed him my scarred half hand. This apparently had the desired effect and although he was frightened that he would get into trouble for what he had done, we struck up a friendship and trust that was to last for ever. I reassured him that all would be well and nothing would happen to him regarding the police and his school.

Due to his honesty and that of his family, I was able to bring the matter to a speedy conclusion. Technically, there had been an offence committed under the 'Explosive Substances Act', however, I recommended that no action be taken by the authorities and successfully suggested that the matter be treated as that of a tragic accident. This indeed was the eventual outcome. I visited the boy (I shall call him Phil) every day whilst he was in hospital, whether I was on or off duty. I continued my visits to him and his family at his home after his eventual discharge. As my own son was exactly the same age as Phil, I took him along and introduced him to the family, Due to this Phil and my son were to become firm and everlasting friends.

As time went on, Phil grew stronger and was eventually fitted with an artificial arm. Due to his determined perseverance he gradually became more adept in the use of the limb. As he progressed I started to take him and my son on various outings to Hoylake foreshore to gather cockles and as his confidence grew we finally started going out in the boat fishing. He could by now do almost anything with his artificial limb. He subsequently returned and ultimately completed his scholastic education. (Phil is now fully employed and happily married). I maintain contact with him and his charming family to the present day.

At 9 o'clock one wet, windy and miserable morning, I entered the canteen at Lower Lane looking forward to my beans, egg and bacon, having been out braving the elements since 7 o'clock. I joined a small queue of equally wet and cold colleagues who were also eagerly awaiting breakfast. The canteen lady who would not be rushed left her mouth watering sizzling pans to pour out some tea and hot water before handing all on a tray together with marmalade and toast to the collator who had just walked in and to the head of the queue to collect. My old 'friend' the collator! He had just arrived to start his day's 'work' but not until he had his cuppa and taken the Chief Superintendent his also. He paid for the tray full of tea and toast (out of his own pocket, as usual) and made for the closed doors of the canteen taking his tray of endearing little goodies to the boss. Leaving the queue, I made for the doors and held one open for him. As he was about to go through the door it 'slipped' out of my hand, swung to and struck the tray knocking it to the ground with a loud clatter, spilling tea, sugar, milk water and toast and marmalade all over the recently polished floor tiles. "Oh dear, my hand slipped" I said as I returned to the counter for my breakfast leaving the collator in his normal position, kneeling on the floor! retrieving the items from his tray. The lads in the queue found this highly amusing. Erna, the lady behind the counter, did not.

The collator returned to the counter (behind us) to re-order. He poked me with his finger "you did that deliberately" he hissed. "Don't be silly" I replied. As we sat eating our breakfast, we watched the hapless collator take the replenished tray up to the Chief Super's office. Some minutes later the canteen 'phone rang. A policewoman answered, then shouted to me; "Swasie, the Chief Super wants you, Now!" I finished my breakfast and made my way up to the boss's office. My knock was greeted with a grunted "come in". I entered and saw the Chief Super, cheeks bulging as he ate his toast, cup of tea in hand. the tray was on the boss's desk in front of him. sitting in another chair was the collator. His cup and saucer on the edge of the desk.

The Chief Superintendent waited until he had emptied his mouth of toast before washing it down with a mouthful of tea.

Finally, he looked at me, his face bright red. "What did you knock the tray out of ....'s hand for?" he asked angrily. I put on a very sad look and replied, "I feel awful sir, I just can't get used to having half a hand" emphasising my pained and depressed expression.

The boss's mood changed dramatically, "Oh, I'm so sorry. I forgot about your hand" he said appearing to be genuinely concerned. He then added, "Alright Swasie, you can go, I didn't realise." I left the room looking very hurt and forlorn. After closing the door I listened and heard the boss say "I felt a right bloody fool, you know he's got a bad hand". I returned downstairs. That'll teach the creeping sod to go telling tales, I thought. I never saw the collator queue jump again, he always took his turn after that as far as I knew. As they say, there are many ways to skin a cat!

Shifts went on, mornings, afternoons, nights, each with their own type of occurrences and incidents.

Morning shifts comprised mainly of dealing with the night before burglaries, school crossing duties, traffic accidents and truants. There were also shop-lifters, summonses to deliver and court appearances.

Afternoon shifts 3pm to 11pm. The first half of the shift was usually akin to those of mornings, shop-lifters, school crossings etc. the latter half became busier later on with drunks, drink driving, assaults, missing children and stolen cars.

Night shifts were usually the busiest earlier in the shift. Drunks, burglaries, assaults, woundings, car thefts and drunk drivers, and of course the inevitable traffic accidents.

My favourite shift was 7am to 3 pm. This was because once 3 pm came, the shift ended and the rest of the day and evening was your own. I didn't mind nights as they were always busy with plenty to do. The shift I never liked at all was the 3 pm to 11pm afternoon shift. I found that when on this shift, one's morning time was spent preparing for work in the afternoon, and consequently curtailed most other activities.

Most unpopular with the shift personnel were the 'short changes'. These occurred when, after completing a week on night duty, one would go off duty at 7am on the Monday morning, only to have to return for afternoon duty at 3pm the same day. Similarly, when completing a week of afternoon duties and going home at 11pm, one would have to return for morning duty at 6.45 am the following morning. I doubt if these 'short changes would have been tolerated within industry.

After being 'fell out' at the conclusion of one night duty parade, I and my Landrover crew were directed to a house near to the East Lancashire Road where, we were informed, a large scale disturbance was taking place. At 11.30pm we arrived at the address given but all appeared to be quiet on arrival. The family at this particular address were known to me as I had dealings with the three sons on previous occasions. I decided to check that all was well and knocked on the door. I was greeted by one of the three brothers, a twenty year old with a chip on his shoulder and an ardent dislike of the 'cloth'. "What d'you want?" he grunted unpleasantly. I informed him of the reason for my visit and was told that there was no disturbance and even if the police had been sent for "we wouldn't want scum like you" I was told. The door was then firmly slammed in my face. Just then, the youth's parents arrived home, both of whom were the worse for drink. The father, whilst having difficulty trying to insert the Yale key into the front door lock slurred "wash goin' on 'ere?" I tried to explain but was rudely interrupted by the father who was equally as anti-police as his sons and said "Fuck off Turner, we don't want you 'ere". His wife quickly advised him; "Shut up dad, 'e'll 'have yer in the back of the truck as sure as look at yer, ". being her inebriated comment. Finally the front door was opened and they both disappeared into the dark interior of the hall and again the door was slammed. I rejoined by colleagues in the Landrover and we resumed our nocturnal patrol of the division.

Later on, at about 2.30 am my attention was drawn to a high powered car, with three youths aboard in Stopgate Lane, approximately two hundred yards ahead of me, having just overtaken me at speed and then slowed down.

I closed on the vehicle and asked my observer to check the registered owner of the vehicle. The check revealed that the vehicle was in fact stolen, having been taken from outside a public house nearby a short time earlier.

I signalled the driver by flashing my headlights and activating my blue strobe light. All attempts to get the vehicle to stop failed and the vehicle then accelerated through a red light at the junction of the East Lancashire Road. I followed, checking that it was safe to continue over the junction after him. It was obvious that a Landrover had no chance of keeping up with a high powered car and we radioed for assistance. Although the vehicle was starting to pull away from me, I knew that further along the road there was a tight bend. I also knew that if the stolen vehicle maintained his speed, there would be no chance of negotiating the bend successfully. I was to be proved right with disastrous consequences. I saw the vehicle mount the pavement and career across a grassed area before it slammed head on into a tree whilst still under power. The car appeared to burst in a cloud of steam and debris which was clearly illuminated by the sodium street lighting.

I would be very surprised indeed if anyone were to survive such an impact, I said to my observer. Before coming to a stop we had requested the fire and Ambulance services, as there was absolutely no doubt that both would be needed.

I stopped the Landrover and went to the mangled wreckage of the vehicle. The only sound was the click of hot metal cooling and the slight hissing of air as it slowly escaped from a deflating tyre whose rim had been buckled on impact with the kerb. There was a low moaning sound coming from the back of the car via the glassless window. I shone my torch into the vehicle and saw that the two males in the front seats were beyond any mortal help, and the youth trapped in the rear seat looked as though he also would soon be meeting his maker before he could be released by no persons other than the Fire Brigade.

My observer was physically sick at the sight of the carnage. The Fire Brigade had to cut all three youths from the wreckage. All were dead when they were released. Fate had decided that these three would be not stealing anybody else's vehicle in the future.

The bodies were removed and the area measured and photographed by the studio, and cleared of wreckage and debris. The uneviable task of informing the relatives of the dead would be undertaken as soon as possible.

I became involved in another 'off duty' arrest when, whilst enjoying a quiet drive with my wife through the suburban lanes and by-ways of the Wirral I saw two youths riding a motor cycle. They were very unsteady and did not appear to be familiar with the machine, plus the fact that neither were wearing any appropriate motor cycling clothing. I then noticed that the rider was holding the accelerator control which was detached from the machine's handlebars, but attached to the engine by a cable. Things were not right! I caused the machine to eventually stop in a secluded road in Caldy. I went to the two youths and introduced myself showing them my police warrant card. Both youths were 17 years of age and appeared to come from respectable families. After first attempting to convince me that all was legal with regard to the ownership of the machine, I insisted that I was not impressed and they both admitted having taken it from a driveway a couple of miles away 'for a laugh'.

At my request, my wife reluctantly went to a nearby house and asked the occupier to dial 999 after explaining the circumstances. A short time later three mobile patrols arrived from Hoylake. After I again introduced myself, I explained the circumstances of the youths' detention and both youths again admitted having taken the motor cycle without the owner's permission. Both were arrested and they, and the machine, were taken to Hoylake police station. I also attended and gave the necessary details to facilitate the ultimately successful prosecution.

During a night duty, another violent explosion occurred. This time it happened in a well known and popular night club, 'Ozzie' Wades, which lies in the shadow of the famous Everton football club ground.

After the death of the owner, 'Ozzie', the club continued to carry on with his widow, Ada at the helm. The club was very popular with officers of all ranks and departments and Ada was a well liked and respected old lady and very pro-police, (Ada was to run the club efficiently until her death when she was almost 90 years of age). There was hardly any reason for an official police visit to Ada's as she always ensured that there

159

was never trouble on the premises. When, very rarely, there was anything unsavoury, Ada nearly always successfully dealt with the matter herself, such was the respect she commanded, even though she had an efficient and well disciplined door staff.

Every Christmas, I was always rooted out by Ada and invited to join her at the Club for a drink, although she herself did not drink alcohol. Wherever I was stationed, Ada always managed to find me.

This particular night, the club was full of revellers when all of a sudden the explosion occurred. Many people, mostly women, were injured by broken glass and torn metal. Fourteen people were taken to hospital by a fleet of ambulances. My Landrover and crew were the first of the emergency services to arrive. As my colleagues and I entered the club and went down stairs, the place was in complete darkness. We illuminated the scene with our torches which revealed broken glass, glasses and heavy iron tables strewn across the floors of each room including the dance floor.

Many of the casualties were bleeding profusely from their wounds. Some were hysterical. It was very frightening. Water was everywhere and I was worried about electric cables and wires near the water. My colleagues and I individually carried out a number of the women to the fresh air above where they were then placed into the newly arrived ambulances. We were then ably assisted by our fir brigade colleagues. Ada, was calmness itself. she was fearful that it was the work of the IRA as she said that a relative of hers was serving in Northern Ireland in the Security forces. This fear was quickly dispelled. What had in fact caused such a devastating explosion was found to be a large stainless steel hot water boiler. This had been allowed to boil its contents almost devoid of water thus building high pressure via steam. Eventually the whole thing blew up with disastrous results. My Inspector, Jock Ward arrived and took charge. The fire brigade checked the premises thoroughly to ensure that there were no further risks.

I removed the bits of heater that were left for further examination to enable a fully comprehensive report to be compiled explaining the exact cause of the explosion.

There were incidents that had their humorous side (to some!). Sergeant bill Roberts and I were directed to a domestic dispute between a man and his wife one afternoon. We were greeted at the house by a woman (Mrs Chambers) sporting a black eye. she was crying and told my Sergeant and I that her husband had hit her and was breaking the crockery. We went in and followed the sound of the breaking items. We entered a large room and there was her husband, systematically smashing anything that he could lay his hands on. We tried to calm him down and he told us that he was depressed and had consumed a large number of Distalgesic tablets. His wife told us to ignore this as there never were any tablets of any kind in the house. Not taking any chances, I went into the kitchen and filled a glass with water and added the total contents of a salt cellar and stirred it until it resembled a glass of milk. Bill saw me doing this and grinned. I went to Mr Chambers and advised him to drink 'this glass of milk' all in one gulp as it will neutralise the tablets'.

Thinking it was a glass of milk, the man took one almighty gulp and swallowed almost the whole of the glass' contents. As soon as he had done so he retched the whole lot up again and covered my hapless sergeant with the contents of his heaving stomach from head to toe.

Bill hurriedly retreated to the bathroom to seek the assistance of a cloth and towel, almost being sick himself in the process.

When my sergeant reappeared, we pacified the couple and they seemed to make up their differences. My sergeant and I then left to resume our patrol. No further action - advice given! Although Bill was not very amused, I was nearly wetting myself and giggling like a little schoolgirl.

Whilst driving my patrol car one day behind a large heavy goods vehicle which was belching out clouds of acrid black smoke, I decided to stop the vehicle for a routine check. I drew alongside and signalled the driver to stop.

As I went to the driver, little did I realise that I was about to reveal a case of many unusual and amusing features. The driver, a man of 6ft, in his late thirties with a thick mop a dark brown hair and a dirty, oil stained face leaned out from the cab of his lorry and asked me in a well spoken and cultured voice, "Is anything wrong officer ?" I asked him to get out of the vehicle and he duly obliged after first switching off the engine. I asked him to whom did the vehicle belong and he told me that his hobby was "tinkering" with engines and that he was testing the vehicle after eventually getting the engine to start. I again asked him for the name and address of the vehicle's registered owner. He stood there in his dirty blue overalls and wiped his equally dirty hands with a cloth. "It belongs to a chap who leaves it in a scrap yard in the Dingle" (the South end of the City) he said. I started to become impatient and again asked him for the owners name. The well spoken driver replied, "Gosh, there's no need to shout, I don't know his name, I only know him by sight". I appeared to be getting nowhere fast. I then asked him if he had the owner s permission to have the lorry out on the road. I received an equally evasive answer to this simple question. "Well, he knows I'm trying to get it going for him" voiced the "Oxford don". I saw that the vehicle, a 5 ton Ford flat back lorry of some vintage was not displaying a current excise licence. "Is the vehicle taxed ?" I asked. "Oh, I don't know about that", the driver replied. I told the driver that I was not satisfied with his explanation and was arresting him on suspicion of having taken the lorry without the consent of the owner or other lawful authority. The driver replied, "When you check, you'll find he " said I could take it". He retrieved his jacket from the vehicle, secured it and I took possession of the keys.

As I placed my hapless "prisoner" into the back of my Police car he said, "You'll be sorry, you're making a big mistake". I then took him to Lower Lane Police Station and there presented him to the Bridewell Sergeant, none other than Bill Roberts. I addressed the Sergeant, "I have arrested this man for unauthorised taking of a motor vehicle.......", I was rudely interrupted by the well spoken "felon", Don't be so damned silly" he said indignantly. "QUIET" barked the Sergeant, adding "Carry on officer" as he instructed me to continue, I went on to outline the circumstances of the arrest and the man's subsequent arrival at Lower Lane. After I had finished the Sergeant asked my detainee if he had heard and understood what had been said. He replied, "You'll all be blinking sorry for this". In accordance with procedure I told him to empty his pockets. As he was doing so I just happened to remark, "Christ, It's warm.' to which my prisoner replied angrily, "Don't you dare take the Lord's name in vain". I replied, "Why?, are you a vicar or something ?" He replied sharply, "Yes, as a matter of fact I am", showing my Sergeant and I proof of this as he emptied his pockets of various documents. One of these documents certified that he had in fact recently returned to this country from a missionary tour of one of the third world countries. I suppose you have a full blown heavy goods licence as well do you ?, I asked sarcastically. "I do indeed" he said, handing same to the Sergeant. I just couldn't resist, "I suppose your'e a bloody bush pilot as well are you?' I asked with a sneer. After further rummaging in his jacket pocket he produced more documentation and handed it to the by now very amused Sergeant. "I think you'll find my pilot's licence in order Sergeant", he said by now obviously enjoying his more than adequate batting innings against my more inadequate maiden over of sarcasm. I must admit, he was making more of a chump out of me than I was trying to make of him. Serves me right for trying to be smart at the expense of someone who was smarter. I then added "You'll tell us next you've got an Oxford degree'. "No, I received my degree at Leeds University actually" he more than happily informed me. Bill turned to me and instructed me to pack in my abortive attempts to belittle someone who was obviously a man of undeniable intellect.

After being fingerprinted, photographed and documented he was led away to a cell while arrangements were made to establish the true owner of the vehicle and also to have the lorry brought into the Lower Lane vehicle compound. It did in fact transpire that our man was a fully qualified minister of religion and had indeed just returned from a third world country after a tour of missionary work. It was also true that he was a fully qualified heavy goods driver and a qualified aircraft pilot also. His hobbies included train spotting and vehicle engine maintenance. Further checks revealed that he was a regular visitor to a local scrap yard in the South end of the City when he would "mess about" with the engines of scrap vehicles in the hope of getting them operational again. The owner of the lorry was eventually traced and although he said he allowed our man to "see to" the engine, he obviously realised the implications of "allowing" a person to take an untaxed and uninsured vehicle onto the road. He therefore, sensibly, confirmed that he did not, nor would not, give permission for the vehicle to taken from the yard and onto the road. A written statement was reluctantly given to this effect and the "Vicar", who he only knew by his first name, was additionally charged with ancillary traffic offences

These offences included, using the vehicle without a current vehicle excise licence, using whilst uninsured, using with bald tyres, excessive smoke emission, using a vehicle in an unroadworthy condition, and others. Later in the day when all had been established my indignant prisoner was bailed to appear before the Liverpool City Magistrates court in Dale Street. On his first appearance he pleaded "Not Guilty" and elected trial before the Magistrates court and this was subsequently arranged for a later date.

On the appointed day I arrived at court for the trial before the Stipendiary Magistrate. I sat in court and eventually after the defendant's name was called, in walked the Minister dressed in his "Dog collar', in his hand he held a copy of the Holy Bible. He entered the dock to the amazed stare of those in court, especially the Stipendiary Magistrate. The defendant's solicitor was asked if his client would prefer to sit behind his advocate (he obviously didn't think it looked right, a Minister of the church standing in the dock). The defendant, on hearing the question from the bench replied, "No, I shall remain here thank you". I must admit, it was a most unusual sight when I entered the witness box and looked across at the "Vicar" standing there in full "uniform", bible in hand, where many extremely bad men had stood previously.

After giving my evidence I was then cross examined by the defence solicitor. During this the defendant had to be admonished by the Magistrate. The defendant's advocate had put a question to me and as I was in the course of answering, I was interrupted by the defendant who shouted across the court to me "You're lying officer, may you roast in hell for this". Not very 'Vicarlike' I thought. The trial was eventually concluded after most of the defendant's and my recollection of events differed considerably. This no doubt presented the Stipendiary with quite a dilemma as to whom he should believe, a Vicar or a Police officer.

Eventually, after much deliberation, the Magistrate decided that there was an "element" of doubt as to that day's circumstances and therefore he would dismiss the case of "Taking the vehicle without consent" as this involved dishonesty, however the ancillary traffic offences he found proved.

As the defendant thought that permission would have been granted if sought, that eliminated any dishonest intent to take the lorry. The defendant was penalised for the traffic offences by means of monetary fines. I was satisfied with the outcome, but it just goes to show what a varied set of events can ensue from a simple thing like a vehicle belching smoke. After the trial I was the subject of many jokes and innuendos; both Sergeant Roberts (who never let me forget that my Mickey taking backfired on me in no uncertain terms on that day) AND my colleagues who thought it hilarious that I should lock up a Vicar for"pinching" a lorry !

Every time a Police officer had cause to stop a vehicle for some reason or other it did not necessarily follow that the "offender" would end up in court. In the majority of instances a friendly ticking off or a bit of advice would not only normally suffice but would also enhance police and public relations by the invoking of a little initiative on the part of the officer.

One such occasion occurred when I was on mobile patrol, driving along Southport Road. I was travelling at the maximum permissible speed of thirty miles per hour. I saw a Grey and Blue Rolls Royce approach me from behind and then cheekily overtake me. I paced him for a short distance and noted that his speed was 38 miles per hour. I decided to give the erring driver a chance to explain his audacity in overtaking a police vehicle whilst having to exceed the speed limit to enable him to do so. I caused the vehicle to stop and went to the very apologetic driver. I asked the driver, an elderly man (who I immediately recognised as one of the City of Liverpool"s most ardent benefactors) if he was aware that he had just contravened the speed limit along that particular stretch of road and he said that he was unaware that he had, but accepted without question that he had done so and again apologised as he should have been aware of his speed had he concentrated more.

I knew the man to be a thorough gentlemen and I was therefore prepared to overlook his temporary lapse and give him an admonishment for his misdemeanour. I accepted his apology but warned him that I would report him the next time I caught him committing such a contravention. After inspecting his driving documents I allowed the Rolls Royce to glide silently on its way into the City, no doubt to the John Moores building, HIS building. what a kind and thorough gentleman was Sir John Moores .

Not far from where Mr Moores and I had our little "chat" the Queens Drive swimming baths are situated. During the early hours of one Sunday morning the swimming pool premises were forcibly entered and the office ransacked. Straight after the morning parade on this day, Constable Robbie Riddell and I were dispatched to the scene of the break. On our arrival we were met by the keyholder, the pool attendant. He showed us both into the premises and indicated where the attack on his premises had taken place and made us a cup of tea while we inspected the damage and sought any clues which may have been left by those responsible.

In the pool happily swimming about were three dolphins which were there being housed for display purposes to entertain the fee-paying public. As I ventured to the side of the pool for a closer look at these fascinating animals the three of them swam to the side and popped their heads up to greet me with their enthusiastic and friendly greeting in the form of a loud clicking noise. I asked the attendant if they were as friendly as they seemed to be. "Well they are with their trainer" he replied. I asked him if it would be alright if I were to go into the pool and swim with them while my colleague completed his paperwork. I was reliably informed that no other persons would be present for some time yet, so with that, I stripped naked and dived into the pool with my new found friends, with, I must admit, a little apprehension. The dolphins were friendly enough and two of them nuzzled up to me and started to play about. I held on to one of them and was immediately taken for a tour of the pool. The third member of the trio followed the other two but he kept nipping my thighs and naked bottom.

I enjoyed myself with the three for ten minutes or so before Robbie informed me that it was time to go. I left the pool and my new friends and, borrowing a towel dried myself, and donned my uniform, "I enjoyed that little saga" I said and thanked the attendant. Pointing to the biggest of the three dolphins, who bore an ugly scar across the top of his head, I said "He doesn't seem to play much does he?'. The attendant informed me that the particular animal to which I was referring was named "Nipper" because he occasionally bites. "Thanks for telling me" I said as we parted.

The following evening (Monday) the Liverpool Echo ran a big article about the City's aquatic visitors who were to show their prowess to the City's population and illustrated the article with a photograph of the three dolphins with their trainer. I wonder what the trainer would have said had he known of his charges' unauthorised playmate being in with them the previous day and more to the point, I wonder what my dear Chief Superintendent would have made of it ?

As before, when weather and tides permitted my colleagues on the section and I regularly went out in my boat for a day's fishing. The section's main matelots were Robbie Riddell and 'Sockless' Consett. Such was the good weather that the three of us having completed a night duty, decided to go out in the boat after getting changed and making over to my house. I rang the Coastguard for a Met report and they confirmed that the forecast was ideal for a day out on the sea. Sockless said that as he was tired he would have a sleep once he was aboard the vessel, and leave the fishing to Robbie and I. After collecting one or two items from my home we were on our way out to sea from Hoylake by 8-30 am, after finishing duty an hour and a half earlier. Off we went and eventually reached our fishing "speck" and dropped the anchor to bob about and do some angling for four or five hours. I sat and patiently fished while Robbie also decided to join Sockless and get some sleep. The two of them lay back on their life-jackets and dozed. I had a pack of sandwiches and a flask of tea, Eventually Robbie woke up and joined me in a welcome cup of tea. Sockless woke up some time later complaining of feeling very sick. Perhaps it was the rocking of the boat?. The time wore on Sockless's facial colouring gradually turned more green by the minute. He groaned and groaned.

As Robbie and I started to suffer pangs of hunger I decided to open the pack of sandwiches. We gratefully devoured the sandwiches which bore a colourful spread of Mayonnaise, then followed a cup of tea to wash them down. I offered a sandwich to Sockless who, on seeing the contents promptly requested me to insert my remaining sandwiches into one of the orifices of my lower abdomen. I realised that he didn't want a sandwich as he didn't appear to be hungry! I again showed him the spread on the bread and told him that he would feel better if he ate something. This time he advised me to call at the Foreign Office with my bread and was promptly sick over the side. Eventually the colouring returned to my sick colleague's cheeks and he started to look normal again, After a cup of hot tea he felt better. Although I personally have never suffered sea sickness, I am aware that there is apparently no feeling of comparison by those who have!

The tide eventually turned and we concluded our day's fishing and returned to shore with our catch of a dozen "flatties"! (Dabs and flounders). Although all three of us had enjoyed a splendid day we were very tired when we paraded for duty at II o clock that night.

Off duty times became regularly occupied by Bill (my Sergeant) and I shrimping and cockling as well as going out fishing in the boat. Eventually it became so well known by all that Bill and I regularly had fish or shell fish that we were being asked for these crustaceans by all and sundry from all ranks. Bill and I started to go out whenever we had the time to cater for the demand from our colleagues, It certainly paid my petrol and tunnel fares.

A most unusual set of events occurred after a shopkeeper was robbed and murdered in the Division. During the intense activity that ensued after the crime was discovered, meticulous examination of the scene was carried out and exhaustive enquiries commenced. Items were removed from the scene (the shop premises) for eventual fingerprint examination and analysis. Included in this potential "evidence" were a number of empty lemonade bottles. They were gathered and subsequently stored at Westminster Road and dusted with fingerprint powder for examination.

Westminster Road Police Station had somewhat of an eccentric Janitor. He would often adorn his thin wisps of hair with fat from the frying pan that the lads had just used to cook their meals, as he made himself ready for a night on the town after his days work. He was also often seen cleaning his few teeth with his finger after first dipping it into a tub of VIM !! The enterprising Janitor spotted the cell full of lemonade bottles as he went about his chores. Nobody had thought to mention to him to leave the bottles well alone!

Seeing the opportunity of making a few bob, he decided to use his initiative and duly wiped the bottles clean before taking them all round to a local shop to collect the coppers on each "returned" bottle !!

Needless to say, the investigation team were really pleased and impressed with the Janitors entrepreneurial initiative ?

Fortunately for the enquiry this incident did not impede the eventual successful outcome , and the person responsible for the murder was caught and convicted of his heinous crime. The Janitor was obviously senior officer material! The mind boggles yet again.

Bill Roberts and I became ardent and addicted shell fishermen and were down on the shore at every opportunity at all hours of the day and night when off duty times permitted. I was still regularly maintaining my training as a firearms officer which I relished.

One of the most important ancillary jobs to Police work is that performed by the school crossing patrols. When these patrols are not available for one reason or another the job is carried out by a Police officer. Police officers, when performing this duty rarely encounter any difficulty from the motorist, but unfortunately this is not always the case with the regular school crossing patrols. These people are mainly of pensionable age and their powers are very limited whilst engaged in this task.

However, common sense does not always prevail and some of these patrols don't have their work made easy by a sometimes impatient and arrogant public. These unsung heroes who religiously perform their duties guiding the nations children safely to and fro, four times daily in all weathers across our busy roads, are not afforded the respect of their office on many occasions.

Possibly their job is not made any easier due to their age and what some may (wrongly) consider as a menial job. I have had to deal with the occasional incident involving abuse and even assault on these important members of our society. I personally have, without exception, found these people to be very friendly, dutiful and mindful of their charges when looking after their safety. However, there are some motorists who, for one reason or another, do not always agree with my sentiments, I witnessed one blatant contravention one morning when my colleague Constable Robbie Riddell and I were in our Landrover when we were waiting in a line of traffic which had been stopped by a crossing patrol to allow a number of children to cross the busy A59, (Scotland Road). Traffic was also stationary travelling towards the City in the opposite direction. The patrol called the children across and as he was doing so an irate and impatient motorist who was at the front of the line of traffic on the opposite side of the road kept revving his engine and moving slowly forward as he did so. This frightened the children and the crossing patrol, and elderly man in his sixties, shouted at the motorist to behave and wait until the children had reached safety. The patrol was greeted with a torrent of abuse from the driver. He had obviously not seen our clearly marked Police vehicle or surely he would not have behaved in such a way. Such was the irate motorist's patience however, that he again revved the engine of his vehicle and, not waiting to be allowed to move drove off, completely ignoring the shouts of the crossing patrol. The patrol was dressed as required by the regulations, i.e. he wore a black cap, sparkling white full length coat and held upright the standard "Lollypop" (sign, highly visible bearing the words, STOP CHILDREN, inside a red circle). The crossing patrol, bravely (and foolishly) tried to stop the offending vehicle from driving away. In his attempt to do so the man was struck. The children scattered in panic but all fortunately made it safely to the pavement. I switched on my blue light and did a U turn made possible by the courtesy of every motorist at the scene, after asking the patrol if he needed an ambulance, which he refused. I gave chase and after a short distance managed to intercept and stop the vehicle which so narrowly missed causing a major incident.

Robbie and I went to the driver, a bespectacled man wearing a blue pin-striped suit in his fifties. Robbie could hardly contain his acute anger at the man's gross misconduct that so nearly ended in tragedy. I thought Robbie was going to rip the door from the vehicle. He opened the door and dragged the man from his car and unceremoniously frogmarched him to our vehicle and dumped him into the back. Robbie didn't mince his words when he informed the motorist what we had seen, and asked him to account for his atrocious behaviour. We were greeted with a most amazing reply from the pompous individual. "I'm half an hour late for work", said the brainless moron. Robbie asked him if he had seen the crossing patrol and his flock and we were again given an unbelievable reply, "Yes, but iitold you, I'm late for work". I thought by the colour of my colleague's face that he was having difficulty controlling his temper, as indeed I was myself. The driver said that he was not aware that he had struck anyone with his vehicle, but he was duly cautioned by Robbie and informed that by the time he (Robbie) had completed his report into the incident the unfortunate man would be summoned for as many offences as could be compiled and to put before the court.

By the time we had finished with him, I think the man was fully aware that he had made we two officers very cross indeed. After checking his documents and completing the formalities prior to the preparation of a prosecution file Robbie and I left the by now very frightened man and returned to the scene. One or two public spirited motorists and pedestrians who had witnessed the incident had kindly given their names and addresses to the patrol and assured him of their willingness to support him in court should they be needed. Although the old man had declined my original offer of an ambulance, I saw that he was holding his arm and I therefore insisted that he allow Robbie and I to convey him to the nearby Walton Hospital for a routine check, plus the fact that Robbie and I wanted all the incriminating evidence that we could muster to throw at this particular defendant.

We delivered our 67 year old charge to the casualty department and after arranging to see him later at his home I returned to the station to enable Robbie to commence his paperwork preparatory to getting our dangerously impatient motorist before the court. Our subsequent visit to the home of our injured crossing patrol revealed that he had suffered a badly bruised elbow. He was absent from his post for a week, to the concern of the local children and their anxious parents. The motorist later appeared before the City Magistrates court where his licence was endorsed and he was heavily fined, and quite deservedly so.

After an equally nasty incident I was very glad to oblige a neighbour when she called at my home when I was off duty. She too had witnessed an unsavoury incident involving an elderly school crossing patrol and although she didn't wish to be involved with the Police officially she wondered what she could do about the incident that she had seen earlier that morning.

After taking her offspring to nearby Warwick Road Primary School she stood and watched as the children were being ushered across the road by the school crossing patrol after he had stopped the traffic to enable him to do so. At the front of the traffic queue was a large heavy lorry. The lorry driver, for reasons best known to himself suddenly jumped down from his cab and grabbed hold of the crossing patrol and threatened him with violence in very frightening and abusive terms for having caused him to stop his lorry. Some of the children became very frightened and started to cry. The crossing patrol himself was obviously shocked and frightened by the younger man's threats to do him harm. The driver then got back into his lorry and again in this incident, drove off before being directed to do so by the crossing patrol. The lady noted the vehicle's registration number and also the Liverpool address of the lorry's owners which was clearly displayed on the side of the vehicle. The lady knew I was a Police officer serving in Liverpool and wondered if I could do anything about the matter in an unofficial vein.

I did in fact make overtures to the management of the firm but after tracing the driver concerned he adamantly denied any knowledge of the incident. I informed my neighbour that she was an inferred liar and this had the desired effect by infuriating her so much at being so labelled, that she willingly allowed me to involve the local Police (which was a different force to that of my own) with a view to instigating official enquiries into the matter which would hopefully result in the successful prosecution of the offending driver.

I arranged for my Wirral (Cheshire County) colleagues to interview the neighbour with the result that ultimately the driver of the lorry concerned eventually appeared before the Magistrates and received his just deserts. I was more than happy to oblige in assisting justice to be administered to one of Society' selfish deviants.

Our Police club at Fairfield held regular functions, dances and parties and our section often took our wives to one or other of these to give us all a chance to socialise. There was always a good 'do' on a Saturday evening and there were always top class acts to entertain. Unfortunately as we attended more of these social evenings, we were to learn that no matter how early one arrived in an attempt to secure a good seat near to the stage we were always beaten by various members of the civilian staff or traffic wardens who somehow managed to get inside before the doors were officially opened and secure a seat for themselves and their little cliques. Due to this one or two of the members of the section abstained from visiting the club's social activities unless it was something of specific significance which warranted our attendance.

When I did visit the Police club for the occasional pint I never ceased to be amazed at the sight of well built six foot men degrading themselves by their utter, unashamed and ceaseless grovelling to any senior officer who they happened to encounter.

One particular Saturday afternoon I decided to call in at the club for a pint after delivering some cockles I had spent the morning gathering, to a friend who resided near the club. As I entered the bar dressed in my fishing cap and smock I saw a number of colleagues gathered around one of my Superintendents, Mr Hoole. All were obviously engaged in the regular ritual of grovelling round the Super. None of my colleagues acknowledged my presence as they were too busy vying for a suitable position to enable them to buy the boss's next drink, and anyway, one doesn't speak to Swasie when he's dressed like that! I hastily add that Basil Hoole, being the thorough gentleman that he is, saw me and greeted me heartily. He looked at me and smiled, "Hello Swasie, have you been out fishing?" he asked in his usual friendly manner. I confirmed that this was so and the Super added, "well always remember me when you have any fish to spare". Once it was obvious that my demeanour and attire were not offensive and it was safe to speak, the lads also started to speak.

It was always the same when there were any senior officers or dignitaries about, the snivellers abounded. I conversed with Mr Hoole on the subject of his intended future fish and shellfish acquisitions but when we were joined by those who shortly before did not wish to know me until the boss spoke, I couldn't be bothered to reciprocate. Mr Hoole asked me if I could supply him with some shrimps and I informed him that I would have some for him when I next went on duty the following Monday afternoon.

To the dismay of the grovel brigade the Super bought me a nice cool pint of bitter. What a decent man he is. I stayed for half an hour or so chatting with the boss while the others now vied for my affection by asking me how the boat was doing and how was the fishing ?. What a load of wimps some men are! It eventually became almost the norm for me to be requested to ring the homes of some senior officers when I had fish or cockles, even on Sunday mornings. My mate Bill Roberts and I soon became known for our fish.

I was continually trying to make inroads among those whom I thought may be able to assist my possible return to the ranks of the CID.

Although I was occasionally made various promises, none of these were ever to bear fruit. Things did change for a time however on the arrival of a new Chief Inspector (who ultimately became a Superintendent). His name was Brian O'Connor. He was definitely a man's man. He always got things moving when others of similar rank could not make a decision and dithered about while thinking what to do.

I was to get on well with Mr O'Connor and he became very impressed with my Thief Taking capabilities. Due to this he rewarded my efforts by transferring me to the plain clothes Vice squad.

Chapter Ten - Plain Clothes Vice Squad

I joined the ranks of my plain clothes colleagues and soon found the work very interesting (and educational!) and I devoted my time and efforts relentlessly to the squad. Some of the work was really eye opening to say the least.

Much of my work involved the official (and sometimes unofficial) attendance at many of the numerous night clubs which abound in and around any large city. Sometimes I would be accompanied by a female colleague when we would visit some clubs which on many occasions were little more than shabeens. We would then report back our findings as to the conduct of the management or the way in which the premises were being conducted. Anything untoward would then be duly acted upon and possible raids contemplated and arranged. On some of these visits, what we saw was nothing short of utter filth and degradation. It is amazing what some deviant people are willing to pay to see such dirt. The Dirty Mac brigade used to frequent those places in great numbers, no doubt to fantasize and hopefully fulfil their lustful urges.

I soon got to know those of the City's prostitutes whom I had not previously encountered during my service. I found a lot of these girls to be quite friendly and many of them genuinely believed that they were just earning a living and didn't consider themselves to be doing anything other than a service. Maybe they had a point. Perhaps if, as some suggest, society were to legalise prostitution ,then the far too many cases of sexual assault and rape could possibly be reduced or eliminated if there were properly and clinically organised premises where these services could be legally obtained. I found that when these girls were treated properly and fairly they sometimes reciprocated by becoming useful informants.

When one is involved with the seedier side of life it is inevitable that the officer has to mix (and be nice) with all sorts of society's low life. There are some very evil people among us. Some people who are thought of as the epitome of virtue by those whom they live and work amongst are in actual fact living a double life, as some of them are nothing more than the dregs of humanity. It was amazing how some of those occupying positions in various professions, i.e.; doctors, priests, lawyers, accountants etc., were sometimes detected as being sexual deviants and paedophiles, whilst enjoying their lucrative status. It took much hard work and strenuous effort to weed out these perverts and bring them to book. Once detected, they would not hesitate to use any trick they could think of to evade the consequence of their actions even trying to bring individual officers who were carrying out the investigation into disrepute by maligning their integrity by any means possible.

After keeping observations from our vehicle discreetly parked near to the public toilets situated outside Walton Hospital, a colleague and I entered the premises and caught two men committing an act of buggery inside one of the cubicles. One of these men was a local itinerant, a tramp. The other man was a practising barrister.

Upon the two men being arrested ,the tramp admitted his part in the act but the lawyer blubbered and bleated for another chance as the adverse publicity which would ensue could ruin him. He had no concern whatsoever for his partner in crime with whom he had been engaging in anal intercourse.

The lawyer informed us that his wife was a grammar school teacher and his two teenage sons were away at a well known boarding school. I told him that he should have thought of that before allowing himself to succumb to his illegal and disgusting desires. Both men were arrested and charged with the offence and subsequently dealt with by the courts. How on earth such educated people were prepared to risk all in their pursuance of such activities always completely amazed me, especially those in the very profession that prosecuted such offenders. I have also had the unpleasant task of arresting ministers of religion and scout masters for similar types of unlawful sexual activity against youngsters. In matters of this nature I always carried out my duties with the utmost vigour.

I continued to secretly hope that my work would be noticed and appreciated to such an extent that I would eventually be returned to the CID. I kept dropping subtle hints to those who could assist in that direction but it was not to be. There was no doubt that I had well and truly blotted my copy book on that score. Eventually, after eight months or so my period with the Plain Clothes Vice Squad came to an end and I finished my tour with the department. I had enjoyed every minute and considered the experience as invaluable.

I was to return to my uniform duties, this time however, I was to return to my old stamping ground, Westminster Road accompanied by one or two others from Lower Lane. Before resuming my uniform duties I took my annual leave and spent a couple of weeks with my family in a caravan at friend's site on the outskirts of Barmouth.

What a beautiful neck of the woods it is down there. The weather was warm and sunny and my son and I spent endless hours swimming in the warm clear waters of the local bays and fished the hidden coves, and numerous pools for prawns and crabs.

We also spent some time on nearby Shell Island lazing about and watching the aircraft taking off and landing from the local airfield.

As all good things come to an end, our very relaxing holiday came to the inevitable close and we returned home to come back down to earth and prepare for our resumption of the rat race.

Chapter Eleven - Back with the Troops

Fully rejuvenated I resumed uniformed duties and got to know the new 'members' of the team who had arrived before me that I did not know. I very soon got back into the swing of things and felt back at home behind the wheel of the divisional Landrover (my favourite Battle Taxi). I now had two new Sergeants, Bob Dillon and Albie Worthington, (sadly Albie was to tragically succumb to cancer a short time later at the young age of 4I years). My two Sergeants were a pleasure to work with, both being very able and conscientious officers to whom we could always go for help of any kind. The section of men and women at Westminster Road were as good as those of my previous section at Lower Lane. We all worked hard and occasionally socialised by means of get togethers at various venues. Soon after my arrival on the new section my wife and I enjoyed a very pleasant evening with the lads and their wives at a place called Toad Hall, a club and restaurant situated amongst the sandhills of Formby beach area.

On our arrival this night however, I was amazed to see one of our notorious, 'shady' Inspectors, acting as the club's doorman in full evening dress, (I was more amazed still when I later learned that he was supposed to be on duty) I didn't like this particular individual, whose integrity was held in utter contempt by most officers who knew him. Most of those officers would have liked nothing more than for the job to discover this man's other activities, both on and off duty! Especially if they were to discover him acting as a paid bouncer out of his force area when he should have been in uniform working in the City. How tempting to drop him in it, but I decided to leave well alone. This particular officer was eventually dismissed from the force and was later incarcerated for offences of dishonesty.

A particularly unpleasant and heart rending task that most police officers may well all too frequently have to perform is that of having to inform people of the death one of their loved ones. At 5-I5pm, one very wet and dark winter's evening a young man had telephoned his wife who lived some four miles away to tell her that he was just about to set off home after his day's work at his factory. As he was driving home some ten minutes later his car was struck head on by a stolen vehicle being driven at a fast speed in the opposite direction. The poor man was killed instantly and as is nearly always the case, the offending driver escaped injury. I was instructed to go to the home of the deceased man and inform his wife of the tragedy. A short time later I knocked on the front door of the smart semi on the outskirts of the City and was greeted by a cheerful, heavily pregnant woman whose facial expression turned from cheerfulness to one of concern when she saw my uniform and realised that it was not the expected arrival of her husband for his tea, which she was about to remove from the cooker and place onto the table.

I confirmed the name and address of the household and asked if I could step inside. She asked me in and offered me a cup of tea whilst she prepared to put her husband's meal out, informing me that he was due in at any moment.

Now was the time to don my firm, but very diplomatic head. I cheekily asked if there was any whisky in the house and she replied by retrieving a three quarters full bottle of the spirit from a nearby cabinet and proceeded to pour me out a glass. I gently pushed the hand holding the glass back towards her and told her to prepare for some very bad news. I sat her down and quietly told her of the tragic loss of her eagerly awaited husband. At first she stared unbelievably at me then suddenly she burst into uncontrollable tears and screamed hysterically. I left her for a brief moment while I went to summon a female neighbour, who, fortunately was also a personal friend of hers. The poor expectant mother was completely inconsolable. Looking at her I couldn't help but think that the bastard responsible should be dragged here to see what his thieving activities had left in their wake. How dearly I wished that person could take the place of the poor victim of his crime. I left the broken woman and her neighbour, both of whom were crying bitterly, and resumed my patrol having performed another one of life's dirty jobs, which unfortunately, I would have to repeat many times again in the future.

A much lighter side of events occurred whilst I was driving my Landrover around the division with my crew whilst on night duty some time later, during the hours of one Friday night and Saturday morning.

A local resident had telephoned the Police to complain of a noisy party being held in one of the pubs after they had closed. The pub concerned was situated less that 500 yards from the Police Station! (and was the haunt of one or two officers). I went to the premises and even as we approached we could hear the noise. "Christ, no wonder someone rang in" said one of the lads from the darkness at the rear of the vehicle. I discreetly parked the Landrover at the rear of the pub and walked round to the side door which led to the living quarters. After numerous long rings of the bell, the door was eventually opened by the bleary eyed wife of the licensee. "Hiya Swashie" she slurred before stepping aside to allow me in. The noise coming from the upstairs living accommodation was deafening, especially as it was now half past midnight. The inebriated woman, half full glass of spirits in hand, slowly and with difficulty, made her way upstairs, signalling me to follow her. As we entered the large and very spacious lounge of the flat I saw that there were a large number of people in various states of intoxication. I recognised a number of male and female colleagues, many of them in various states of uniform dress, this was obviously a Police "do'. Eventually the licensee himself spotted me and came over. I saw an almost naked woman gyrating around on a small dais swirling a piece of purple chiffon above her head. She appeared to be attempting to keep in time with the loud music. A very drunk man (a colleague) was stripped down to his vest and trousers (which were open) and he was making a futile attempt to grab the singer/

stripper to the amusement and loud encouragement from all those present. The landlord asked me if I would like a drink, being quite oblivious to my deliberate expression of concern over the permitted and distasteful behaviour of all those present. I refused his compromising offer and told him in no uncertain terms to sort the place out and return proceedings to some form of normality. The reason for the party was that it was a young officer's stag night. The very officer who was to tie the knot the following afternoon was none other than the potential groper. I was then approached by another drunk colleague who slurred, "ere Swas, get this down yer" as he held out a full pint of beer, spilling some over the carpet as he did so. I dutifully refused his offer and again instructed the landlord to get his house in order as there were complaints from nearby residents which were more than justified, and which were the initial cause for my official attendance.

The landlord turned the music down to a more acceptable and reasonable amount of decibels to the groans and abuse from some whose brains were very obviously out of gear. I advised him to start clearing his premises. The young A Division bobby would be in enough of a state for his forthcoming betrothal as it was.

There was still a plentiful amount of food adorning two tables and still a large amount of unconsumed drink. I was again offered a drink by the landlord's wife, but I was dammed if I was going to compromise myself by being seen supping a pint of grog. As I was leaving, I warned the landlord that if I had cause to attend his premises again within the near future he would find himself in trouble with the licensing authorities. I also reminded those colleagues who I knew, and those who were sober enough ,to remember that they were Police officers and to behave as such.

Although I do not consider myself to be in any form a saint, at least I had to appear to be so as I was there in an official capacity. I received a few boos and hisses as I threatened to wield the big stick. My threats were necessary as I didn't want any of my colleagues to find themselves on the wrong side of the Complaints & Discipline department just for the sake of an off duty party. I returned to the station and informed my Sergeant that all was okay as it was just another party that had been a little boisterous and that suitable advice had been given. .

I was to learn that one idiot had let the side down by getting himself arrested by officers of the Lancashire Constabulary due to his driving home from the party drunk. Some of my pals had listened and accepted my advice in the spirit that it was intended, some however, had obviously not.

Things turned out differently the following night. My crew and I were meandering slowly along Scotland Road in the early hours of a by now quiet Sunday morning while most of the city slumbered peacefully. I drove slowly along to enable my observer to check the shop doorways by illuminating their dark recesses with his torch. As we were checking that all was well with our ratepayers properties my attention was drawn to a young man who was walking along the opposite pavement in the same direction as our own. I saw that he was carrying a large white carrier bag which appeared to be heavy and bulky.

Curiosity getting the better of me, I decided to go over and check him out. I drove over to the other side of the road and drew alongside our early morning pedestrian. "Good morning, we're out early aren't we?" I said as I greeted him. The man appeared nervous at my approach. "I'm not doing any harm," he replied tensely. I noticed that he had a strong Lancashire accent indicating that he was not a local. I asked him where he was from and he said nervously, "Why? I haven't done anything". I wondered why he was being so evasive. I asked him what he had in the bag. "Why do you want to know?" he answered. I was beginning to wonder about this man's apprehension at my questioning, which I felt was quite justified at such an early hour on a Sunday morning. I was asking these questions in a friendly manner and wondered why it was that he was being so evasive with his answers. Adopting a more assertive attitude I again asked him firmly, "I'm asking for your name and address!, The young man, in his mid twenties, then informed me that he lived, "near Southport !". "That's not good enough" I countered angrily at his continued evasiveness. I again asked him what it was he was carrying in the carrier bag. This question produced an even more nervous reaction. "Just a couple of towels", he said becoming more agitated as he tried to hide the bag behind his back. I alighted from my vehicle and went to him. I was joined by a colleague from the rear of the Landrover. "Let me see that bag" I demanded. It was by now obvious that something was not quite right with this man. The man now appeared to be very frightened. He meekly handed the bag to me saying, "It's not like you think officer". I was puzzled by this remark but was very soon startled to find out its significance. I took hold of the bag which felt heavy for just containing towels. I opened the bag and felt inside. I felt the soft, thick material of towelling but underneath I discovered to my horror a point three eight calibre Smith and Wesson revolver, fortunately, devoid of its ammunition.

Without further ado I told my colleague to grab him and give him a thorough search. The young man was made to lean against the side of the vehicle with his arms outstretched and his legs spread wide. He was thoroughly searched for further weapons and or ammunition. None was revealed and the man was placed into the rear of the Landrover.

I drove to Westminster Road to enable further enquiries to be carried out in the security and safety of the Police Station. When we arrived at the station, our man was taken straight through the building to the charge office.

The charge office Sergeant greeted our arrival by asking the nature of the young man's detention. The Sergeant then recognised the new visitor and asked him, "What the hell are you doing here Gary?" It was obvious that the Sergeant, a recent transferee from Lancashire Constabulary, knew our new guest personally. Gary commenced by explaining that although he had no criticism of the Police for bringing him to the station, he could fully explain, hopefully to everyone's satisfaction, his possession of the firearm that led to his rapid deployment to the Police

Station. The man was in fact a neighbour of the Sergeant and was the legitimate holder of a firearm certificate as he was a current member of a Lancashire gun club. However, he did confess that although he had attended at his club on the Saturday night he had then gone to his mother in law's house in the City. While there a domestic altercation had broken out and he took the gun out of its leather case hoping to frighten her by the sight of it. This confession was therefore very incriminating and a blatant infringement of both the firearms act and the regulations governing the safe keeping of such a lethal weapon. I was prepared to throw the book at this individual but was asked to step into an adjoining room to speak to the Sergeant.

I was asked politely by the Sergeant if I would accept the man's explanation and would I be prepared to deal with the matter unofficially by means of a very severe 'rollocking' as the Sergeant was prepared to guarantee that the man was a very decent citizen and that it was very obvious to him personally that it was a 'one off' infringement that although it was inexcusable, it was one that he felt sure would never be repeated as he would point out to his neighbour the error of his ways and the gravity of such irresponsible conduct. Although I was not happy at the thought of letting such an unusual and good job go, after some thought and further persuasion from my genuinely concerned Sergeant, I allowed my better judgement to be overruled and, after locking away the weapon and insisting that the offender returned to collect the weapon with its leather case , later in the day I severely scolded the idiot and left the office to allow the Sergeant to deliver his chastisement.

A couple of weeks later I was asked by a colleague, Jack O Reilly if I would rendezvous with him one afternoon at the bottom of Sleepers Hill as he intended to arrest a deserter from one of the Guards regiments and he would require the services of the Landrover should he do so. I met him at the appointed time and place and we proceeded to a run down row of terraced houses on the main road. These houses opened directly onto the pavement. Jack and I arrived and Jack duly knocked on the heavily scratched and sparsely painted dark green door. The door was opened by a very well built woman wearing a pinafore and her hair hidden beneath a hundred plastic hair rollers which were in turn covered by a flowered headscarf. She was munching a mouthful of bread by the look of the half eaten thick jam sandwich that she held in her hand. Clutching at her bosom was a screaming, nappyless child who had obviously just decided to relieve itself by urinating down the front of her clothes. I heard a dog barking from within. Jack told her the nature of his visit and although the woman vehemently denied that any such deserter was in her house, nevertheless, Jack insisted on a quick check of the premises. We were invited in by the woman and we entered the house and side stepped the various pools of water and dog excreta that adorned the threadbare carpet and mats on the floors. On entering the rear downstairs room I saw three more infants of both sexes in equally similar states of nakedness as the one held by our hostess. We established that no such deserter was secreted at the house and Jack started to enter the details of the house's occupier in his notebook for his report. As he was doing so the woman asked us if we would like a cup of tea. The thought nauseated me to think of drinking out of cups which I could clearly see about the room which were heavily stained with tea and what appeared to be egg on some. We were also joined by the house's pet mongrel, a skinny, scraggy necked, brown and white bitch bearing sores and exposing skin where patches of long gone hair once grew. The little hound insisted on jumping up at Jack and I and depositing more of its meagre remains of knotted hair on our trousers. Jack very rapidly refused the lady's offer of refreshment as politely as he could without offending, insisting that he didn't have the time or he would have thankfully accepted! (what a liar !). I interrupted proceedings and said, "it's okay Jack, I'll do your next enquiry and come back for you in twenty minutes, you have your tea!'?. I then left the house at a fast rate of knots and told my crew what I had done. As I drove off we were hardly able to control ourselves due to our hilarious laughter.

On my return some twenty minutes later my knock was greeted by my colleague's almost instant answering of the door, the woman quickly followed him to the door saying "Officer, you haven't finished your tea". Jack entered the rear of the Landrover almost before the door was fully open. I'm sure that he could easily have entered by doing a limbo under it, such was his eagerness to get away from that house. As I politely thanked the lady for her hospitality and got back into the vehicle, Jack threatened that if I ever were to pull such a stunt again he would punch my lights out. That's gratitude I thought as I drove off.

Not all of our duties involved the apprehension of various forms of the City's criminal fraternity, other equally important jobs manifested themselves in various ways, but all required equal devotion to the task involved. One evening a poor 40 year old lady was found wandering about the streets near to Everton football ground in a state of acute distress. She was completely stripped to the waist and only wore a flimsy cotton skirt. Robbie Riddell and I arrived in the Landrover and saw the poor lady being subject to ridicule and mickey taking by the local youths, many of them young girls. We placed the lady into the rear of our vehicle took her straight to Walton Hospital. She was unable to give us any details as to her identity and although she did not appear to be physically injured, due to her being very disorientated, it appeared that she might be suffering from some mental disorder. We took her to the casualty department where, after examination, she was seen by a psychiatrist. It was decided that she should be admitted to Rainhill Mental hospital and Robbie and I were requested to convey the lady there for further, residential treatment via a certificated medical order under the Mental Health Act. After verification from our Sergeant that we could oblige, Robbie and I together with a nurse, conveyed the unfortunate and sick woman to Rainhill. On our arrival were met by nursing staff who had been informed of our journey by Walton Hospital. The patient and our nurse were taken to the appropriate part of the building complex while Robbie and I were taken to a room to await the return of our nurse. We were told to sit down and make ourselves at home by our charming female escort, a nursing sister from one of the wards. As we sat there a white coated gentleman, wearing horn rimmed spectacles and sporting a stethoscope which was hanging down his front entered the room and asked us both if we would like a cup of tea and a biscuit. We both gratefully accepted his offer and thanked the doctor for his hospitality. The doctor returned a short time later with two plastic mugs of tea, but no biscuits Robbie and I started to sip our tea and the doctor asked Robbie how long he had been a Police officer. As Robbie was answering, the door to our room again opened and in walked the nursing sister carrying a tray of tea and biscuits. "Mr Baxter, what the hell are you doing in here?, and where did you get the coat and stethoscope from?' she asked angrily. She was very annoyed with our host . "Take those off and give them to me, and get back to your ward" she snapped. As the man left us the sister remarked, "I'm sorry about that, he's harmless really". In actual fact our 'Doctor' was a patient himself !. Eventually our nurse returned and we left and took her back to Walton Hospital before concluding our duty for the day, sincerely hoping that all would end well for the poor woman, and that she would soon be returned to her home and reunited with her family.

Equally sad are those jobs which involve children. A report was received by the Police from a concerned neighbour regarding four children living next door to her who's ages ranged from 5 months to 5 years. Policewoman Maltberg and I attended the scene at 8am one morning and although we could hear the children's movements inside we could not get any of them to answer the door to admit us. Finally, my colleague and I broke into the house by forcing the rear door. The place was in a state of utter filth and smelled of stale urine and excreta, which littered the ground and upper floors, human excreta! On seeing us the three eldest children started to cry for their parents. All three children were wet and cold. Upstairs in a cot in the front bedroom the 5 month old baby girl lay in her soaking wet cot, next to which was an electric fire. This fire was not now lit as the coin in the pre - payment meter had dropped and the electricity supply had expired. This was just as well as the fire was only inches from the baby's cot, the wet mattress of which was already singed due to the fire's close proximity when lit. The infant was crying also. My colleague picked her up and removed her soaking wet and heavily soiled nappy to reveal her very sore little bottom. Wrapping the children in borrowed blankets from neighbours we removed them to the Police Station and arranged for the Social Services to collect and house them into their care. We then attempted to contact the children's parents. It was two days before the parents could be found. The father had not been home for the last three days, and the mother had not been there for the last five days. Both had originally set off on separate drinking sprees to various parts of the City and were only found on their subsequent return to the house. I had the studio attend on our initial attendance and photographs were taken of the children and the atrocious state of the house in which they had been left. The only food the children utilised as sustenance was mouldy fat in a long abandoned and dirty chip pan, which bore the pitiful little fingermarks of those who had scraped out handfuls to relieve their acute hunger. Needless to say those totally irresponsible and criminally negligent parents were successfully prosecuted and the children were taken from them and placed into care. I personally received threats and much abuse from them for causing such developments. I would unhesitatingly do the same again.

Another sad incident involving a small child occurred on Christmas Eve 1974, when my observer and I were requested to attend at a large supermarket where a store detective had detained an elderly man and woman, together with their small grandchild. The store detective had witnessed the old man take a sachet of bacon from a shelf and pass it to his wife. The old lady then placed the sachet into one of her pockets. The detective followed the trio around the store and saw them go to the check-out and pay for the contents of the basket the lady was carrying, but not for the bacon secreted in her pocket. All three then left the store followed by the lady store detective out into the street where they were intercepted. They were told the reason for their being stopped and asked to accompany the detective back to the shop. They were taken to the store's security office and detained pending the arrival of ourselves.

On our arrival at the store I parked the Landrover outside the crowded main entrance. Leaving my colleague in the vehicle I made my way through the store to the security office. I was met by the store's manager and the store detective, who was known to me and my colleagues as somewhat of a body snatcher! (one who has an insatiable appetite for arresting persons, however minor their indiscretion). Also in the room were the two elderly detainees, a man and his wife who were both in their seventies, together with their six year old grandson who had just arrived from his home in Wales to stay with his grandparents over the Christmas period. The child was obviously very frightened at the detention of the old people and was crying. His fear was intensified when he saw the uniformed figure of myself arrive. I was informed by the store detective that the old lady had been seen to take a sachet of bacon which she had been given by her husband and secrete this item into one of her pockets for she then made no attempt to pay before leaving the store. The old lady looked at me as she held her tiny grandson to her. Her lips quivered as she said quietly, "I didn't pinch it son, I didn't realise I'd put it in my pocket by mistake. The old man butted in, "as soon as we realised what she'd done we offered to pay for it but she (the detective) didn't want to know". I must admit, I certainly felt sorry for the old couple. Perhaps they were genuine and the lady may well have not realised what she had inadvertently done due to her possible senility. I thought there was certainly an element of doubt and that there were grounds for compassion to be afforded to the couple, especially as it was Christmas. I took the store detective outside the room and asked her if she was absolutely happy that what she had witnessed could not have been an inadvertent act. She was adamant that the two should be arrested for theft. I, however, did not agree. I was not satisfied that we were dealing with a couple of geriatric criminals. I could not persuade the detective to give the couple the benefit of the doubt on this occasion and we returned to the office. I asked the couple if they had both understood the gravity of the offence of theft but each was emphatic that it was a genuine mistake. I was prepared to accept this and again looked towards the store detective who shook her head negatively. The detective turned to the couple and told them they were to be conveyed to Westminster Road Police Station where they would be charged with the theft of the bacon.

She looked at me and told me she would complete a statement of evidence and send it on to the Police Station. The infant screamed at us pitifully, "Please don't take my gan gans away" the poor lad was beside himself with the thought of his beloved grandparents being taken away by the police and locked up for the duration of the festive period. I looked at the detective and whispered,"The three of them are bloody terrified!" but she would not be steered from her intended course of action. She again nodded non-acceptance of my dissension and said, "No, I'm doing them" I turned on her sharply, "In that case, never mind sending the statement. Get your bloody arse in the jeep and take them into the Sergeant yourself and present your case to him". The detective was convinced that she was right and insisted that she write her statement and send it down to the station later (which was almost always the case, with which I did not agree) I again informed her in most direct terms, "You certainly will not. If you want them arrested you'll come with them to the station, Now". In most cases it was accepted as the norm for the detaining detective to "send" the Prisoner(s) with the bobby where he would give evidence of the arrest to the Bridewell Sergeant while the store detective remained behind and completed the statement which was then forwarded to the station - and not necessarily by the store detective concerned. I was not running round after any store detective for such a disputed incident as this.

Due to her insistence I had to convey the old couple to the station. The child was crying uncontrollably as we placed his grandparents into the back of the Landrover, followed by the store detective. We placed the child in the front between my observer and myself hoping to bribe him to lose his fear by allowing him to sit with us and listen to the radio but our feeble attempts to gain his confidence proved futile. We were taking away his Gan Gans and therefore we were the 'enemy'!. I couldn't blame him at all for thinking such. I will never forget those pitiful cries from the little lad begging us not to take the old couple away.

As we were helping to place the couple into the rear of our vehicle it was my colleague and I, not the store detective, who received torrents of abuse from sympathetic passers by at the couples dilemma.

After depositing our passengers at the station I did not hesitate to illustrate my utter contempt for the proceedings that caused our arrival to the station Sergeant. To my great satisfaction, and also that of my colleague, the Sergeant sensibly refused the charge as he was of the same opinion as myself, there appeared to be the possibility of a genuine mistake and therefore the benefit must be accorded to the pensioners.

Swasie in His Landrover

Without further distress to the three, they were released and allowed to leave the station. The store detective was absolutely fuming with rage, (perhaps she had lost a bit of 'commission' by losing a body!"

Although I agree whole heartedly with the apprehension of 'felons', one must be completely sure of the grounds for detention, and satisfied as to the intent of the person concerned before 'striking' . I must confess that being an enthusiastic and fanatical 'seeker' of villains, I was never inclined to agree with the nation's "do gooders brigade" when it came to worrying about the welfare of those responsible for their crimes. As far as I am concerned (and will always remain so) my only concern is for the poor victims of those louts, I have never had any time whatsoever for any perpetrators of offences against their fellow citizens or their property. As a consequence of this attitude it can be reasonably assumed that I did not (and do not) see eye to eye with some members of the Probation service. I ardently considered it my job to try and prevent crime and protect the law abiding members of society and their property, and apprehend those amongst us who don't wish to abide by the rules. I have always believed that the punishment should fit the crime and in no way do I lend myself to any form of sympathy towards the criminal fraternity.

I have been accused of having an attitude where things are either black or white, there not being any grey. I accept this criticism. I hear howls of condemnation from those who are more inclined to believe that the criminal needs help for having committed his crime and are therefore more sympathetically orientated towards him. I would suggest that those of such ilk would do more good by directing their misguided sympathies and soft option attitudes in the direction of those who have been wronged. In the past I have been many times the subject of complaint from various probation officers for my 'hard' attitude when I had cause to apprehend or deal with some of their 'clients. I was accused of insensitivity by not being prepared to possibly overlook or deal more sympathetically with some and that I did not help their efforts to reform or repent by showing a little mercy or understanding when I caught them yet again slipping off life's rails of conformity onto the trackside of wickedness.

If I caught them committing offences, especially whilst on bail or probation, they were to receive no quarter and were subsequently arrested or summoned to place them once again before the court. One particular probation officer and myself did not get on at all well. I did not enhance my popularity with this man when I had to deal with an incident involving him one busy morning when he was driving through the peak hour rush in a particularly traffic congested and busy area of the city. I was driving my police Landrover behind a red Renault car and was accompanied by my Sergeant, Bill Roberts. We were travelling along County Road towards Aintree. As we approached a notorious junction, governed by traffic lights, which were showing green in our favour, I saw a double decker bus approaching from the opposite direction. As the bus and the Renault converged, the car suddenly turned right without indicating, drove across the path of the bus and entered the side road. The bus driver had to swerve and brake violently to avoid a collision. The Renault continued along the road it had entered and parked in a lay-by some distance down the road. We could clearly hear the curses coming from the cab of the bus as the driver blasphemed the idiot who caused him to make such a violent manoeuvre. After the Sergeant and I had ascertained that none of the passengers or the driver where injured, we satisfactorily pacified the bus driver by our assurances that the offending driver would well and truly be spoken to. I obtained the drivers details and those of the bus company in case the matter were to be taken further, and allowed him to continue on his route. I drove down to the Renault and saw the male driver lock his car and walk away accompanied by his female passenger. After parking my vehicle the Sergeant and I went over to them. I recognised the man as one of the City's probation officers, one with whom I did not get on!. "Good morning sir" I said politely and continued, "Are you aware that you very nearly caused a serious accident?" He looked down his nose at me and replied, "Behave yourself, I had plenty of time to get across", spitting crumbs of a pie he was eating onto the front of my tunic as he spoke. He held a half consumed pie in his hand and continued to eat it as I was addressing him. I told him not to be so arrogant and informed him that his driving was to say the least 'Careless'. I requested him to be courteous enough to empty his mouth before he spoke to me. No doubt to impress his female companion he said, "I'll have you know that I'm a senior probation officer", causing Bill and I to wish we had an umbrella handy as more half eaten crumbs were propelled in our direction from the mouth of the ignorant man. Oh dear, after hearing of his elevated position in life I really was most intimidated and impressed! I brushed the front of my tunic to remove the unwelcome debris, took the man's lapel and pulled him to me and whispered into his ear, "I don't give a monkey's who or what you are, empty your mouth before you speak to me you ignorant sod". It was as though he had been struck by lightning, he pushed me away and shouted to his lady friend, "Did you hear that?, He's just threatened me!" The lady made no reply. "I'll see your superintendent about you two" the irate man from the probation service threatened. Sergeant Roberts asked the indignant man for his driving licence. This added to the man's fury, especially when took my time writing out a form for the production of the man's driving documents after being told not to waste his time, as he and his lady friend (a colleague from the probation service) were in a hurry and that their time was valuable. After duly completing the form, and after ascertaining the man's name and address, I proceeded to caution him and then went on to add a verbal N.I.P. (notice of intended prosecution) which was a necessary procedure for those offences I contemplated reporting him for, namely those of Driving without due care and attention and or Driving without consideration for other road users, both of these offences carried an additional penalty of licence endorsement. After informing him of these facts I asked him if he wished to say anything in answer to the allegations regarding his driving. He replied, "Your'e talking rubbish. I'll see you in court". The following day I visited the Aintree bus depot and obtained a full witness statement from the bus driver concerned in the incident.

Within a couple of days I was to receive a not unexpected visit from a senior officer of the Complaints and Discipline department regarding a number of complaints concerning my alleged bad behaviour toward my potential defendant. His complaints were never substantiated and he was eventually summoned to appear before the City Magistrates Court. On his subsequent appearance before the court he pleaded 'Not Guilty' but after hearing all the evidence the bench found the case proved and the offender, as well as being fined, also suffered the added indignity of having his licence endorsed. This little 'saga' did little to improve my popularity with the City's Probation staff, which didn't cause me any tears.

My habit of continuing to stop some people at random continued to pay dividends. One incident worthy of note occurred as I was driving my Landrover along the Dock Road, in company with my old mate Constable Robbie Riddell. It was the evening peak hour and as the dockers made their weary way home in the drizzle I noticed one man as I slowly cruised along who appeared nervous as I slowly drove past him. I stopped and as he approached my vehicle I bid him good evening and asked him where he had been. "I'm on me way home from work" he said, adding, "I work on the docks". It was unusual that he was not carrying a bag as most dockers usually have a haversack for their caddy and sandwiches. "Have you got anything in your pockets to tell me who you are?" I asked. The man said "No". I asked him if he had anything in his pockets, the man now appeared more nervous. "No not really," he said, a strange remark I thought. "Well what have you got in your pockets then" I persisted. "Just a few peanuts" he replied. I asked him to show me and he produced a handful of peanuts from his mac pocket. I asked him where he got the nuts from. "I got them off the floor in the dock shed, there's loads of them" he said. "Oh so you've stolen some nuts off the dock estate?" I said pointedly. "Ar 'ay boss, there's loads all over the floor from burst sacks" said my dejected informant. "Get in the back and we'll sort it out" I instructed. I placed the man in the rear of the vehicle, and as I got back into the driving seat Robbie said, "Fuckin Hell Swasie, your'e not locking him up for a handful of nuts surely?" "He might have a ton of them at home" I replied.

We made our way to Westminster Road to howls of protest from my vehemently protesting 'prisoner' at being arrested for a pitiful amount of what he considered to be a 'perk of the job'. During the journey I asked our indignant docker if there was any other property from the docks in his house which should not be there. "There's fuck all in our 'ouse" he eloquently informed me.

On our arrival at the station, Robbie informed me he wished to distance himself from involvement in the matter and promptly did a 'limbo dance' under a closed cupboard door to illustrate his lack of enthusiasm.

I presented my prisoner before the desk sergeant and gave the details of the arrest. "Good afternoon Sergeant, I have arrested this man for an offence of theft from the docks" I announced. I went on to elaborate how the man had 'feloniously' removed a quantity of peanuts from the docks. At the conclusion of my tale the Sergeant then asked, "Right then Swasie, where's the evidence?" I then instructed the prisoner to empty the contents of his pockets onto the Station counter. Seeing the handful of peanuts the Sergeant looked at me and again asked "Where's the evidence Swasie?" On being informed that this was the evidence, the Sergeant very nearly miscarried on the spot. "Are you telling me you've brought this man here for stealing an amount of peanuts that wouldn't even fill a bird feeder?" he snarled. "Yes Sergeant" I replied. Just then, the Inspector entered the room - none other than my old friend who had been nick-named after a disaster. "What's the problem Sergeant" asked the Inspector. The Sergeant took the Inspector by the arm, " A quiet word Sir," and both left the charge office. The Inspector returned a short time later and took me to one side. He expressed his and the Sergeant's acute disdain at my pathetic arrest for such trivia and told me to put the man back in the Landrover and to convey him to his home after interrupting his journey, post haste. "I was wanting to search his home" I bleated in an attempt to justify my actions. "Search nothing" snapped the Inspector, "Get him home now and let's hope he doesn't make a complaint".

As I drove the man home in the Landrover I winked at my colleague sitting in the front seat and turned to the docker (who was not aware of my being rebuked and instructed to just take him home) and said, "I've got to search your house. Is there anything there that shouldn't be?. It's better if you tell me now, it will save a prolonged search of the premises"!. The docker sighed, "Okay boss, there's a load of gear in the bedroom". We arrived at his house and he took my colleague and I

185

up to a back bedroom where we recovered a large quantity of brand new jeans, approximately £900 worth!. We loaded our vehicle with the stolen goods and I 're' arrested the docker. We then returned to Westminster Road with the prisoner and the stolen goods. After being charged and processed the prisoner was placed in a cell. Instead of being complimented by the Inspector for my persistence and initiative, resulting in a good arrest and subsequent recovery of a substantial amount of stolen property, I received a rocket from him for my 'disobedience'!!, as I had been instructed ONLY to return the man to his home?!.

Another unusual incident occurred one Sunday morning as I patrolled the quiet streets of Kirkdale as the City began to awake from it's slumbers. My attention was drawn to a vehicle being driven by a young man, and because of the manner in which it was being driven I wondered if in fact he was a qualified driver. I decided to stop the vehicle. I drew alongside and asked my observer, Ronnie Saxon to signal the young man to stop. The young man ignored my observer's signals and increased his speed.

A radio check failed to reveal that the vehicle was stolen, nevertheless, due to the behaviour of the mini's driver, and his evasive manoeuvres I was convinced that something was wrong, enough for me to pursue and apprehend the driver and enable me to carry out a more thorough check on him and the vehicle, and establish the reasons for the driver's reluctance to stop for the Police. We drove up and down the narrow side streets of the area, narrowly missing the cars of local residents, which were parked on each side of the carriageways. Eventually the mini stopped on waste land behind Scotland Road, and the young fair haired driver left his vehicle and ran into a nearby block of flats.

Ron and I then gave chase on foot, and on entering the flats we heard a door slam somewhere on one of the upper floors above us. We ran up the stairs and on reaching the second landing I saw a door that was slightly ajar. I could hear noises coming from within. I knocked and the door opened further as my hand made contact. I listened intently. All was quiet except for the sound of heavy panting from behind a door along the hall of the flat. I knocked again and asked, "Is anyone there?". My question was greeted with silence but for the sound of the laborious breathing. I crept along the hallway and stood by the door behind which the heavy breathing emanated. I gently pushed the door of the room open and saw the fair hair of the mini driver's head resting on the pillow. The young man was in bed and covered by his blankets and appeared to be fast asleep. I ventured over to the bed and lifted the blanket. Just as I expected. There was my youth, fully clothed in his bomber jacket and jeans. He suddenly became wide awake and said, "I haven't done anything". I pulled him out of the bed and took him down to our Landrover and placed him into the back. I asked him to whom did the mini belong and he informed me that the vehicle belonged to him. A subsequent check revealed that all details which he supplied regarding him and his ownership of the mini were correct. I then asked him to account for his behaviour and he informed Ron and I that as he had never had any dealings with the Police before he just panicked!.

At this moment we were joined by a middle aged man and woman. The woman looked into the Landrover and on seeing the young man inside quickly informed me that our "detainee" was her son and demanded to know the reason for his being in our vehicle. I explained the reason for the young man's detention, informing her of the circumstances leading up to this. The lady was not satisfied with my conduct, as unknown to me, she and her husband, had been woken from their sleep in an adjacent room of the flat when their son was taken from the premises, and she intended to complain about the manner in which their son was detained.

As there had been no offence of such degree to warrant further detention of the young man, he was allowed to go. I still felt justified by my actions as I did not see why he should have been so determined to evade me. Another form I56B from the Complaints and Discipline department ?.

I was again interviewed by the Complaints department regarding this latest incident and was surprised to learn that my "suspected felon" was in fact a student who was shortly to be ordained as a fully fledged priest. It was however, accepted that his behaviour had certainly been a contributory factor to his subsequent apprehension, and no further action was taken against me.

When burglars set out to commit their despicable and contemptible crimes, many do so armed with an array of 'tools' to facilitate their foul deeds. Many arm themselves with any weapon that they can bring to hand. Others purposely carry weapons on them for protection. One such burglar had his dog with him when he broke into the rear of a shop in County Road during one night's thieving expedition.

A member of the public who lived near to the attacked shop, rang the Police to complain that she could hear noises coming from the rear yard of a chemist's shop at the top of her street. It was 3 am and my colleague, Dave Hay and I were directed to the scene. As we neared the shop I free wheeled my vehicle to eliminate the noise of our approach. I parked the Landrover against the high wall of the rear yard, climbed onto the bonnet, up and over the wall, and down into the pitch black darkness of the yard. As I shone my torch, its powerful beam cut through the ink black darkness like a knife.

I saw a man with a pickaxe crouching near a large hole in the brickwork of the rear of the shop. More sinister and frightening, was the large Alsatian dog by his side, its red eyes reflected menacingly the light from my torch. The man said "Get him Shane, and the dog snarled and sprang at me. It gripped my right leg in its jaws and snarled ferociously. I raised my right hand high then brought it down rapidly with a sickening thud as my metal brace hit it in the centre of its head just above its eyes knocking it cold. To make sure it stayed down I stamped on its head with my foot. I lunged at the man and grabbed his shirt with both hands, my head accidentally striking him in the face. I wasn't going to give him the chance to use the pickaxe on me!. Dave jumped over to assist me in overpowering the struggling shopbreaker. We subdued him and after releasing the bolt on the inside of the yard door we put our prisoner into the Landrover and conveyed him to Westminster Road Bridewell without further ado.

It transpired that the burglar lived above the shop with his family and the fierce dog. This would explain why the yard door was bolted from the inside. Our man was charged with burglary of the shop, for which he was subsequently sentenced by the Crown Court to three months imprisonment and for a more serious offence of 'wounding' me (with the dog) he was given a further nine months, twelve months in all.

After the initial arrest I had to attend Walton Hospital to have stitches inserted to my dog bite wound. This particular case made some of the National press and due to this I received a lot of banter from my colleagues, and friends at my local pub for my 'act of cruelty' to an animal!. In actual fact I was genuinely sorry for the dog as I love all animals, having always had Alsatians in the family as pets, but it was purely a matter of self defence.

A more amusing (and embarrassing) incident occurred one morning as I drove along Westminster Road on mobile patrol. My attention was drawn to another police vehicle which was parked in what was a derelict street of houses. I saw the uniformed officer standing by his vehicle surrounded by a group of people. There were other vehicles parked nearby. I wondered what had happened as I had not heard of any incident over my radio. I decided to see if my 'colleague' required assistance. I turned off the main road and drove down the narrow cobbled street and parked my vehicle near to my 'colleague's' patrol car. 'That's odd', I thought, I don't recognise the officer, I wondered if he was from another division?. I alighted from my vehicle, "What's up offs?" I asked, wondering if I could be off assistance. I heard angry shouts of "CUT!, CUT!", from a portly man sporting long unkempt hair and a bushy beard, wearing thick horn rimmed spectacles. As he approached me I saw that he held a large megaphone in his hand. Is everything alright?", I asked. My question was abruptly answered with, "No, everything's not alright. Surely you know who we are?". I admitted to total ignorance, "No sir, I've not the faintest idea who you are" I replied in all innocence. "Well you bloody well should know, this has been arranged with your Chief Constable for more than three weeks now", my bearded informant went on indignantly. I realised now that the people standing near the 'police' car were in fact members of a film crew!. "Oh dear", I offered, "have I interrupted something?". The bearded gentleman (presumably the film's director or producer) was quick to inform me, "Yes, you've just ruined a scene from Z cars (a weekly TV series) which will now have to be completely re-shot"!. I offered my apologies to the angry man and embarrassingly made my way back to my vehicle with my tail between my legs. I drove away to resume my patrol ! Leaving the cast having to start all over again due to my untimely and unwelcome interruption.

A later scrutinous delve into standing orders revealed that an order was in fact published a couple of weeks earlier informing us of the impending visit of the film crew. My 'faux pas was undoubtedly due to my having missed that particular page in orders!. I decided that I would keep that little incident to myself, if that were to get out I'd no doubt receive a lot of stick from my colleagues. That would teach me to be more observant when reading orders. I hoped that the irate film director wouldn't decide to do something silly such as complain to the Chief Constable, or seek recompense for the loss of his original scene due to my neglect by not reading orders?.

Fortunately nothing further was heard and I managed to keep my 'clanger' a secret. Every time I watched Z cars I was reminded of that day and cringed with embarrassment!. To my knowledge, none of my colleagues ever found out about the matter.

Due to a most disturbing incident during another night shift I was eventually to lose a colleague (who was also a close friend) from the section.

An audible alarm had activated above a jewellers shop not a stone's throw from the previous incident and a mobile patrol attended which comprised of three officers, one of whom was my friend. I also made for the scene and attended a short time after the first patrol. An inspection of the premises revealed that all appeared to be correct as there were no traces of a break or unlawful entry. Due to this, I left my three colleagues to it and resumed my patrol.

During our meal break an hour or so later, I was taken to one side by my friend who appeared to be very agitated. What he told me brought back memories of Rose Hill!. My friend insisted on my complete and utter confidentiality, swearing me to complete secrecy. After assuring him of this he went on to inform me what he had witnessed after my departure from the jeweller's shop earlier.

As there was no sign of a break in, and the alarm bell continued to ring, one of the officers commented that seeing that the alarm was already ringing it wouldn't make any difference if he broke one of the side display windows. This he then did, and after doing so, reached in and removed two expensive watches giving one to his colleague (not my friend) . I suggested that my mate should report the two concerned, but in view of my own experiences, who to ?.

Later, the window breaker actually boasted to some members of the section about the features and capabilities of his and his colleague's 'new' watches.

My friend was so disturbed and frightened by what he had seen he eventually went on sick leave. He subsequently transferred away from the section. The two 'bent' coppers responsible for the theft continued serve and the matter was never revealed.

I and my section were frequently engaged on football duty. We regularly worked at both Anfield (Liverpool Football Club's ground) and Goodison Park (Everton's ground). I thoroughly enjoyed these duties as we saw some good first division matches.

As these matches required a large Police attendance, each match day brought all sorts of previously unseen bobbies out of the hidie holes of their respective day jobs, when they would don their uniforms to grab their rich overtime pickings. To make matters more annoying to us shift working officers, certain of these 'day men' were always strategically placed at some 'cushy' spot out of harms way, ie; the Director's box, players' entrance or some other equally safe venue.

During one match which drew a capacity crowd at Anfield, my colleagues and I were told that a bobby had been dragged into the famous 'Kop' and badly beaten by the crowd. At the half time interval we were visited by our Chief Superintendent Mr Grant. I asked him how our colleague was after his beating in the Kop. Mr Grant huffed and puffed before uncomfortably muttering that he was alright and not badly hurt. Reassured we all went about our various duties during the second half. In fact, we learned that no such attack had taken place, our original information was as a result of a rumour. I was subsequently hauled before Mr Grant and given a severe dressing down for trying to extract the Michael from him and telling 'falsehoods'(another disciplinary offence) If it was untrue, or the boss didn't know, or wasn't aware of such incident, why the hell couldn't he say so ?, instead of standing there with his air of superiority making out he knew all. He was never one to spend much time with his 'minnows', let alone converse with them at a football match!

After another Liverpool game, one of our Policewomen was assaulted. Although she was not badly hurt the lads were annoyed to think that some 'buck' had punched one of our female colleagues in the mouth. It was deemed bad enough if it were a male colleague. We arrested the man responsible, a thirty year old Scandinavian seaman. A regular visitor to our shores. We took him to Westminster Road in our Landrover. The bullying hardcase was a regular spectator at Anfield and would attend whenever his nautical trips would allow so that he could watch his idols . During our journey to the station he emphatically insisted that the alleged assault was in fact an accident and went to great lengths to convince us of his acute contrition over the affair.

On this particular day, the Sergeant on duty in the charge office was a particularly volatile chap, who, when very busy or under pressure, was renowned for his 'short fuse'. As we were almost at the station I suggested to our prisoner that he should apologise to the Sergeant but, under no circumstances make light of his surname as the Sergeant was of Polish extraction. I told him the Sergeant's name was, Sergeant Yurracunt!. Unseen by our prisoner, behind their hands, my colleagues were trying hard to subdue their giggles as they foresaw the possible results of my advice being followed?

We arrived at the station and, being a match day, ours was not the only prisoner to be taken before the busy Sergeant!.

As the Sergeant was already dealing with a prisoner, I leaned towards my own charge and whispered into his ear, "Just say Sergeant Yurracunt, I'm sorry"!. The Sergeant was then interrupted by our very apologetic policewoman beater. "Sergeant Yurrancunt" he said loudly. On hearing this, the Sergeant looked up in utter amazement. He threw down his pen, leaned forward and grabbed the unsuspecting sailor by his shirt and pulled him across the counter in front of all hands. "What did you call me" growled the Sergeant slowly and menacingly. The man again uttered, "Sergeant Yurracunt, I would like........", he was flung backwards as the Sergeant shouted, "how dare you swear at me" Seeing the Sergeant's face, we dragged our prisoner back out of harm's way.

Eventually as his turn came to be dealt with, our man was by then a gibbering, frightened and homesick Scandinavian, no doubt preferring to be in the hands of his own country's policemen. Perhaps he will be a little more reluctant to assault the cloth in future. The saga of Sergeant 'Yurracunt' is now well known throughout the Merseyside force on both sides of the Mersey, another little 'gem' of the force's 'folklore'.

During my CID days I regularly attended a local Chinese take-away on Warbreck Moor. This establishment was well known for its excellent oriental cuisine. My favourite meal from there was curried king prawns and rice. Whenever I could, since being back in uniform, I would go along there for my favourite "nosh"!.

Just after midnight during a night shift at Westminster Road I felt pangs of hunger as I drove along the city's streets in company with Fred Owen my observer. As 'scoff time' was some three hours away and it would not be closing time at the take-away, I asked Fred if he fancied some curry and rice. "WHY NOT ?" he replied, I decided to chance going off our patch to my favourite 'scoff house' some three and a half miles away. I drove along County Road, Rice Lane, past Walton Hospital, on past Hornby Road (where Walton Prison lies) then past the well known Black Bull pub and eventually arrived outside the take-away and stopped on the opposite side of the road facing out of the city towards Aintree. As there were still a couple of customers in the shop I decided to wait until the shop emptied.

Although there were only two people in the shop, they were so long getting served that I wondered if they were waiting for some exotic dish to be brought from the Orient itself!. They seemed to be ages, in actual fact it was nearly half an hour before they finally left the shop,

I didn't like being away from my patch for so long, even though things were quiet. I didn't relish the idea of a patrolling Sergeant or Inspector catching us on their 'manor' as we were not authorised to be there. Still, the yearning for curried king prawns and rice outweighed our apprehension as we waited a little longer to make sure the shop was empty before I ventured in with our 'order'!.

Now that the shop was clear I went in to see Chan the proprietor, "Hiya Chan" I said as I entered the shop, "Everything okay ?" I added, trying to give the impression that I was only popping in to check that all was well. "Hokay Mr Turner, said Chan. "You wah summah ooeat" he asked as he gesticulated to his cook in the back of the shop, (who was in fact his wife)."Oh, go on then, two curried king prawn and rice" I said. I saw three little yellow faces, framed with shiny black hair peering round the door-frame which led to the kitchen, one on top of the other, all three staring at the uniform, fascinated.

Chan turned towards the open doorway and shouted through to his wife, "Cullay ha hue". There was the sound of a wok being banged about and the hiss of its contents cooking and sizzling over the flame. The appetizing aroma drifted through, making my stomach rumble with enthusiasm as it anticipated its forthcoming replenishment. Chan's wife summoned him into the kitchen and he took two cartons and disappeared, soon to return with the cartons; full of the desired fare for Fred and I.

"Thanks Chan" I said gratefully taking the plastic carrier bag containing the two meals. "What do I owe you?", I asked. "No, you no pay Mr Turner"he insisted pushing my outstretched hand (and my fiver!) away. I wasn't going to argue, "Thanks Chan" I said as I left the shop and returned to the Landrover.

No sooner had I started the engine when a White Ford Anglia drew alongside. I saw the dreaded two silver pips as an arm reached across and wound down the passengers window, and the silver braided peak of the Inspector's cap as he looked up at me and asked, "What are you doing in Warbreck Moor Swasie ?". It was my old friend, the Inspector who was nicknamed after a disaster, the very one with whom I had to threaten with submitting a crime report over a pint of lager a long time before! I thought bloody hell, he's got me over a barrel now!

On my way to the chip shop earlier, I remembered seeing an army Landrover in front of me. I quickly replied "I've just followed a military Landrover as I thought it was unusual to see one this late!' The Inspector looked at me and said - "Yes, go on, I'm listening." I went on to say that I spoke to the driver, a Lance Corporal, who told me that he was from the nearby Daysbrook Lane Barracks and he had just slipped out for some chips. My explanation seemed to satisfy the Inspector who fortunately didn't get out of his vehicle as he would have smelled our supper and known that I was lying, 'Telling a Falsehood!", (another offence against discipline!). The Inspector abruptly instructed me to get back into my own sub division post haste, and as he was about to drive off Fred shouted across me. "Do you want to sign our books before you go sir?" I could have stuffed him, 'Thanks Fred, Nice one" I grunted, as my note book had not been made up since my last tour of duty, (yet another breach of the discipline code!). "No you just get back to your own patch' denying himself the big chance to have thrown the book at me for the heinous offences I had committed, just for a take-away supper! THAT was a near miss !!.

During the following night's shift I ventured into the casualty department at Walton Hospital hoping for a cuppa with the staff in the Sister's office. The staff were all busy patching up various degrees of 'walking wounded' so I decided to call later when things were hopefully more quiet.

As I was about to leave I saw a drunken man staggering about in one of the corridors of the unit. The Sister informed me that she and her staff had been receiving threats and torrents of abuse from this man since he had arrived an hour earlier. On his arrival he was treated for a cut to his forehead which had required stitching. The drunk informed the staff that he had fallen and banged his head. To be on the safe side in case of concussion, the doctor had decided to admit the patient overnight and he was bedded in a side ward. Not only did he then become abusive and threatening to the young nurses and staff but was sick all over the floor and his bed before he then crouched down and defecated onto the polished floor. When Sister went to him she also was threatened with violence.

Sister didn't think that there was anything wrong with the man except that he was drunk. I asked her for a mop and bucket and on her providing me with these items I went to the drunken bully (who was still fully dressed) and told him to get back and clean up his mess or I would lock him up for being drunk and disorderly. It was surprising how quickly the drunk sobered up as he realised that I meant what I had said!. Although he was still drunk he managed to slur, "Okay Bosh, fair enough!" and took the mop and bucket from me and returned to clean up his mess. Sister grinned at me and said, "You do have a way with people don't you Swasie ?" as she and I escorted the mumbling drunk to the soiled side ward. I stood by as he cleaned the smelly mess from the floor. He certainly didn't appear to be as drunk (or as threatening) now!.

As he finished his task I escorted him to the toilet with his mop and bucket before returning with him to the Sister. On seeing her, he then apologised to her and her nurses for his behaviour and he then insisted on leaving the hospital to go home as he now felt 'okay'. The staff didn't argue as they were glad to see the back of him. This particular individual, they informed me, regularly came in drunk at weekends complaining of some slight injury or illness, in the hope of getting a nice warm bed for the night before returning home to his hovel the following morning.   My colleagues and I more than willingly threw out similar characters who abused and threatened the busy, hard-working staff and diverted their important skills from more needy cases by having to waste their time on them. Unfortunately all hospital casualty units are subject to these drunken weekend time wasters, and we in the Police service were always monitoring the situation.

At the beginning of 1973 my family and I moved from Hoylake back to near the spot where we had started our married life. We bought a detached bungalow not far from dad's house and were able to see him more often. I was also posted to the Task Force (the forerunner of the Operational Support Division as it now is) and was to spend six happy months with this department. My tour with the Task Force involved various arrests, a whole spectrum of offences including those that were drug related. I also performed observation roles at various (and sometimes unusual) venues. It was also during this tour that I successfully completed my second (Class I) driving course.

At the conclusion of my tour I returned to join my old section at Lower Lane, which was still being led by Sergeant Roberts. I decided to try for the Sergeant's exam which was being held in November.

Off duty I was still managing to get myself involved with the apprehension of villains.

Lower Lane Bridewell

After arriving home from work in the early hours of one morning , I should have finished duty at ll pm but was delayed due to making an arrest, I took my large German Shepherd dog, which was fully trained for his walk around the block. As we walked along the quiet and deserted streets I suddenly heard noises coming from the direction of a neighbour's house. I shone my torch and saw a youth crouched against the front door of the house. He appeared to be tampering with the door lock. I asked him what he was up to and the youth then jumped over the garden fence and ran into nearby woods. I released the dog and ordered him after the youth. I soon heard crashing and snarling in the undergrowth, followed by screams for help from the youth. I made for the cries and found the youth cowering on the ground, my dog sat there growling and in its mouth he had a piece of the youth's blue woollen jersey. The youth pleaded with me to call the dog off, which I (reluctantly) did.

After introducing myself to the youth as a Police officer and asking him to account for his behaviour at the house, the youth admitted attempting to forcibly enter the house to 'see what he could get'. We all then set off along the road to a telephone kiosk where I dialled 999 for the police to come and collect my burglar. As I was making the call my dog sat outside guarding the youth, Oh how I hoped that the youth would make a run for it again!. The elbow of his jersey and the seat of his trousers were already shredded evidence of my dog's capabilities.

A short time later I was joined by my Cheshire Constabulary colleagues, their Inspector also arrived. After I had outlined the circumstances of the youth's detention the youth himself again admitted his despicable nocturnal intentions and complained bitterly at being bitten by my dog, (I sincerely hoped that my dog would not suffer gangrene of his gums!). The poor deprived 16 year old little mite was conveyed to the Local Police Station where he was later charged with attempted burglary of a dwelling. Really!, I suppose it was the householder's fault for having something that the poor deprived young man wanted!!. The youth was duly dealt with by the Juvenile Court, and my dog happily suffered no contamination after biting him!

It is often said, "New house, new baby!" and this appeared to be true. After being in our new home for less than a year, Marje gave birth to our daughter Jo at St Catherines Hospital, Birkenhead on the 12th of December 1974. Little Jo was the apple of my eye and as soon as she was able, she accompanied me down on the shore fishing, shrimping and cockling. She became such a well known little figure among the fishing fraternity and the Lifeboat crew, they christened her "Cocklelily". The same name as my boat.

Our off duty socialising with colleagues was greatly enhanced with the attending of Christmas parties again at Fairfield, this time with little Jo. (Our son Ron was now 15 years old and too heavy to sit on Santa's knee).

Back at work I was now performing the occasional role of 'Acting Sergeant'. I was fortunate in this as usually this duty is only performed by those who have passed the exam and are qualified to aspire to the elevated rank of Sergeant. Although my last dismal attempt at the exam ended in failure I did intend to try again ?. Although my heart was willing and I was full of good intentions, I could never get down to the devoted study required. As the time approached to sit the exam I would start to read up on various aspects of the law and procedure, but the inevitable result ensued at these dismal and futile efforts. Perhaps one day I really would make a determined effort to gain the elusive prize ?. November would come and I would attend at Mather Avenue Training school to waste everyone's time, including my own. With me were the usual aspiring (but equally pessimistic) candidates for the annual ritualistic 'day out'

After sitting the exam and knowing that the outcome was a foregone conclusion, I would make my way home assuring myself that next year I was DEFINITELY going to make a determined try!. I could never see me overcoming such an insurmountable hurdle and actually becoming a fully fledged Sergeant. That was just 'pie in the sky'.

Eventually the exam results were published in Chief Constable's Orders and I was enviable of those who had made it. It was amazing how many of us used to make adverse comments when the names of those successful officers appeared in orders having been promoted. Some would say"Bloody hell!, have you seen who's just been made?" or "Fancy making an idiot like him!". These comments were always made by the likes of those who had not taken the exam or those who had, but had failed miserably, (like myself!). I have to admit that these utterances were made out of nothing more than jealousy or pure pique. I must admit to having been one of the biggest offenders. The obvious answer to such biased critisism was, "How can you comment when you haven't even sat (or passed) the exam?!".

Shifts, shifts and more shifts at Lower Lane. Whilst patrolling with my crew in the Landrover in the early hours of one morning I was driving along the East Lancashire Road. We were shortly to head in to the station for our 'scoff' (refreshments). My attention was drawn to a large animal in the centre of the road. I switched my headlights to full beam and they immediately picked out a large brown hare. As I approached, the animal started to run along the road in front of me but due to the powerful glare of my headlights he didn't alter direction and stayed directly in front of me. I accelerated and eventually overhauled him, my wheels passing each side of him as I did so. The differential box on one of my axles struck and stunned the animal as I passed over him. I stopped my vehicle and one of the lads and myself went back to the unconscious hare. I picked it up by its hind legs and quickly dispatched it with a blow of my right hand. Returning to Lower Lane I placed the hare into the boot of my car. I would prepare to hang and 'jug' it later on my return home from duty.

As I entered the station and walked past the enquiry desk en route to wash my hands before making to the canteen for my meal, I saw Sergeant Roberts and the night Superintendent, Mr Whitfield. I stopped to greet them both and I heard the Superintendent uttering his concern over one of the prisoners who was in custody in one of the cells. Unknown to me a man had been arrested for assaulting a colleague earlier and had been arrested and brought into the station. On the prisoners arrival it was seen that his face was somewhat bloodied. This was the subject of the Super's concern. Also hearing the Super's comments was the radio operator, Constable Dave Stoba, who was sitting nearby in his little cubicle. Dave sarcastically said (in pure good natured banter) "Swasie hit him with his iron hand sir!". The Super turned to me and commented in no uncertain terms that he sincerely hoped that I hadn't. I innocently asked the Superintendent to explain himself. He again told me that he hoped that I hadn't hit the prisoner who was in the cell with a bloody face. I denied any knowledge of any prisoner as I had only just entered the station. "Let me see your hand" said Mr Whitfield. I duly exposed both hands for the Super's inspection (completely forgetting about my despatching of the hare). There for all to see, was my bloodstained right hand. The Super asked me to explain, adding that my excuse had better be 'a dammed good one'. "Well, there was this hare on the East Lancs Road sir......" I went on. There was no way that the Super would accept my tale. Even after Sergeant Roberts's reassurances that I had not even seen the injured prisoner, plus my showing the Super the dead hare in my car boot, was he totally convinced!. "That bloody hand's going to get you into trouble one day" he warned. I gave Dave Stoba a rollocking for dropping me in it, but I knew that Dave was only joking and was totally unaware of my bloodstained hand.

Mr Whitfield remained sceptical about the affair ever after!.

On one occasion we used the Landrover as an ambulance when we were stopped by a very distressed woman near the Black Bull shopping centre. The poor woman was cradling her 13 month old baby daughter in her arms. The baby was very pale and although wrapped in a woollen shawl, appeared to be cold to the touch. The young mother tearfully explained that a passer by had accidentally bumped into her minutes earlier causing her to drop the baby onto the pavement. The little infant landed on its head. Without hesitation we placed the mother and her infant into our vehicle and, Blue light flashing, tore through the streets at a fast rate of knots to Walton Hospital. There, their baby was thoroughly examined by the hospitals very able medical staff (as it happened, the hospital houses one of the country's most advanced head injuries unit). Fortunately, the woman's fears were eventually alleviated by the news that her baby would suffer no permanent damage by the mishap, and all ended well.

The young mother later not only took the trouble to write to the Chief Constable thanking my crew and I for our speedy attention, but also called into the station to thank us all personally. Little gestures such as that were very much appreciated.

One would normally consider a Doctor's surgery as a place of sanctuary, and certainly not the place where it would be necessary to arrest a person who was drunk and disorderly at 9 o'clock in the morning!.

However it was at such a time I was directed to such a surgery in Norris Green one morning. I had just completed duty at a school crossing and was told to make haste to the surgery as a man there was threatening staff and patients.

As I entered the premises I could hear shouting and swearing from within. The receptionist directed me through to the doctor's waiting room. There were a number of patients waiting to see the doctor, amongst them were pregnant women and a number of frightened children who were crying. In the centre of the waiting room was a man with his fists raised shouting obscenities and threatening to fight anyone who went near him. It was obvious by his demeanour that he was the worse for drink. On seeing me he turned his threats and venom onto me, describing the police (and me in particular) in various derogatory terms. As I approached the man he attempted to strike me but I quickly removed him from the premises and placed him into the rear of my vehicle. I took him to Lower Lane and there presented my drunk and disorderly prisoner to the Station Sergeant. None other than Bill Roberts. My prisoner was instantly recognised by the Sergeant as the man who a long time before, had emptied the contents of his stomach all over the front of his uniform. I'm sure Sergeant Roberts appreciated such a wonderful reunion!, This time however, the Sergeant managed to remain dry when dealing with him. The prisoner, (whose name was Chambers) was kept in custody to appear before the City Magistrates court later in the day. Chambers was not amused as we made to his cell when I couldn't resist telling him that he should behave himself as he was obviously 'potty'!.

I later attended a Chinese take-away to deal with an allegation of theft. When I arrived at the shop I was taken through to the back of the premises where I obtained details of the theft from the proprietor's English wife.

Whilst there I saw that the place was absolutely filthy, sacks of rice that had burst and were spewing their contents about the floor. I saw mouse droppings in and near food containers. Cooked chickens lay on the floor next to a soiled cat litter and soiled nappies also littered the floor. The stench was overpowering. I contacted Lower Lane by radio and requested that the Environmental Health Inspector attend as soon as possible. I concluded my enquiries regarding the theft allegation and added that I was now awaiting the Health Inspector and was myself going to furnish a full and comprehensive report concerning the filthy conditions that prevailed in the premises.

A short time later the Health Inspector arrived and without hesitation condemned the premises forthwith. A Local Authority order was placed on display in the window of the premises preventing the premises opening to business and explaining the reasons for the closure. Considering the amount of profits made by fish and chip shops, and the fact that their sole 'bread and butter' depends on the maintenance of hygiene and cleanliness, I have no regrets whatsoever in causing the establishment the loss of its business. The proprietor was successfully prosecuted by the local council via the Environmental Health Inspector.

Whenever I was out on patrol and saw anyone carrying a parcel, I nearly always stopped to check them. Due to this habit I detected many thefts, especially from places of employment, and recovered a large amount of property. This "habit" rubbed off onto many of my colleagues as very often, the parcels were found to contain property which had been acquired illegally in one way or another. It was surprising what could ensue by stopping a person on their way home from work with a parcel!.

One man I intercepted was making his way home from his place of work at Bemrose's Printing works at the end of the day. I politely asked him what it was that he had in his parcel. He informed me that it was 'just some cotton wool' for his daughter who was ill. I ascertained that the cotton wool was in fact from his works and he admitted that he had not received permission to remove it from the premises. I have experienced in the past that quite often, when such detections are made, it is not the first time that the offender has taken property from work. I inevitably recovered more property from previous 'takings' from their home. This occasion was to be no exception!.

I arrested the man for stealing the cotton wool and a subsequent search of his home revealed more of Bemrose's property. We recovered more rolls of cotton wool in their sealed wrappers, 15 gallons of white spirit, 15 gallons of paraffin, a number of new 5 gallon containers, new copper sheeting and a long length of new chain

All from his place of work !

Similarly, when I had occasion to stop and speak to motorists, I sometimes requested to see inside their boot. Many times due to this, I recovered stolen property. One taxi that I stopped due to him displaying only one rear light and requested the driver to open his boot was met with hostility. I insisted however that he open his boot. He duly obliged and there inside, still in its cardboard case was a brand new industrial sewing machine. A very expensive piece of machinery. After further questioning, the driver finally admitted that the sewing machine was stolen. He was arrested and two similar new machines were recovered from his home. They had been stolen from an imported consignment at the docks.

Time went on with monotonous regularity and I continued dealing with the various crises and incidents which were the lot of the hard working copper. The occasional nurses 'do' at Walton or Fazakerley hospitals came when invitations were handed into Lower Lane for the lads and girls of the sections. Most of the gang on our section would attend. We sometimes took along a 'civvy' mate to make up the numbers. These 'do's' were great fun. Plenty of booze and grub, (and nurses!).

I rigorously maintained my firearms training at Fairfield and Altcar army ranges.

In 1975, Liverpool saw the first activity of the IRA. An incident occurred in a Manchester restaurant when a shot was fired. Three men fled to Liverpool. These three men were members of a very dangerous IRA cell. As they entered the City of Liverpool they were stopped by an alert Police Constable who was about to check them and their vehicle when one of the three produced a gun and fired at the officer, thankfully missing him. The sound of the shot caused an officer in nearby Hope Street Police Station (Nick Doran) to come out of the station to investigate the bang. A shot was again fired which hit the railings near to where Nick was standing and a fragment of metal hit him wounding him in the chin. The three men then drove off and holed up in the City.

This incident and its subsequent follow up made national press and television coverage by the media. Eventually the cell left the City and were captured at a flat in Waterloo, but not before another colleague, Detective Sergeant Tommy Davies (Later to become Superintendent) was shot and seriously injured.

During this period I performed 'active' armed duties in various parts of the city. We gave a couple of residents a scare one night when myself and (the late) Sergeant Harry Tranter were on armed foot patrol near to Walton Prison (due to an incident inside the prison involving a 'device'). As we were walking along we spotted a small fire in a garden shed to one of the houses. Harry and I knocked on the door and were greeted by a very astonished householder when she saw the guns on the belts of two armed Police Officers at her door. We told her the reason for our call and she took us through the house to the equal astonishment of her family who were watching television, and out into the rear garden. Harry and I soon extinguished the fire which had been caused by smouldering rubbish near to the shed. We were thanked by the puzzled lady and resumed our patrol, leaving the grateful (and fascinated) lady at her front gate staring in disbelief at having her evening's television viewing interrupted by armed police!

The following night whilst in the City centre area (still armed) I was summoned by a uniformed beat constable to check out a couple in a parked car near to a Police Station which was holding members of an IRA cell. The Constable was suspicious of a vehicle being parked in such a 'sensitive' area and in view of two of his colleagues having already been shot at, quite rightly requested an armed officer to attend.

On my arrival I saw that the car was discreetly parked in the shadows and was not displaying any lights. It was obvious that the two occupants (a male and a female) did not wish their presence to be known. As the nearby station was holding a hardened IRA killer I approached the vehicle carefully, gun in hand!. The look of sheer horror from the couple was paramount as I checked them out at the point of a gun. The poor, frightened couple it transpired, were nothing more than a pair of lovers who were trying to do a bit of private courting. However, better safe than sorry. The couple were moved on and away from the 'sensitive' area without being given the true reason for the fact that it was an armed Policeman who had spoken to them. I explained that it was just a routine security check due to recent terrorist activity in the area. My armed colleagues and I continued our duties for some time until the IRA crises were over.

I resumed 'normal' duties again and started patrolling in plain clothes on occasions with a new Sergeant, Bill Dugdale (a recent 'import' and newly promoted, from Lancs County). The two of us were patrolling in plain clothes one late afternoon when we intercepted a man making his way home from work. He was carrying a large parcel under his arm. Bill and I decided to stop him and check what it was he was carrying.

The young man worked as a shelf stacker at the nearby Kwiksave superstore. A check of his parcel revealed that it contained two bags of sugar which the man readily admitted having taken from work a short time earlier to 'flog in the pub'. Bill and I summoned a police vehicle and we all went to the home of the arrested man. There, we recovered more stolen items from the store, namely 3 cartons of bagged sugar, cartons of tinned salmon, trays of eggs and other foodstuffs. The young man, although admitting his part in the thefts from his employers, was reluctant to shoulder all blame and named other employees who were also 'at it'!. Subsequently Sergeant Dugdale and I arrested other members of staff and recovered a large amount of foodstuffs, the property of the supermarket.

Eventually, with each person arrested naming others equally involved, we finally arrested the assistant manager of the store. From the garage at his home in Aintree we recovered a substantial amount of property which had been stockpiled over a long period.

The assistant manager and his staff appeared before the court and were all heavily fined for various offences of theft. We also arrested others (non-employees) and charged them with 'receiving' stolen goods. Quite a substantial coup from a routine 'stop and search'.

A 'minor' theft had serious repercussions for one enterprising thief who thought that money would solve his problems when his dishonest endeavour was discovered. He was stopped as he was leaving a pub at closing time. Whilst on mobile patrol I spotted him leaving a local pub and under his arm was a cardboard carton. I went to him and asked him what he was carrying under his arm. He informed me nervously that it was "some tiles I bought in town this afternoon"!. A closer inspection revealed that the cardboard box was not labelled and was dirty and dusty. There were bits of straw protruding from under the lid and the box bore scuff marks on its corners and sides.

I decided to bluff my way through my chat with him. "They're from a building site, I've seen those boxes before I lied. The man, Thompson, finally admitted having taken them from his place of work, a building site in the city, during the day. He admitted having taken the box of tiles from the site stores as he was tiling his kitchen at home. I told him that I was arresting him for the offence of theft disclosed and he then pulled out a wad of banknotes and thrust a £20 pound note into the breast pocket of my tunic. I retrieved the note and asked him for an explanation. Thompson then thrust another £20 note into my hand and told me I could have more 'If forty quid wasn't enough to drop the charge ?' I called Lower Lane on my radio and asked the operator to log my call and make a note of the serial numbers of the two banknotes that I had just been offered as a bribe.

Coincidentally, at the time of my transmission Superintendent Hoole happened to be in the radio room. His voice came back to me over the air waves confirming that not only had my call been logged as requested (I could use this evidence in court if required), but that he had heard all of my transmission and would attend court as a witness if required to do so in the event of a trial.

Thompson was arrested and eventually charged with the offence of theft together with the more heinous offence of attempting to bribe a police officer. As the latter offence could only be dealt with by a Crown Court, Thompson appeared before a judge and jury for both matters to be heard. He was sentenced to six months imprisonment for the theft and eighteen months imprisonment for the attempted bribery, two years in all. The judge remarked that the bribery sentence was intended to illustrate the gravity of that particular offence, and act as a deterrent to others.

Life at Lower Lane continued with various degrees of excitement. I received a wound to my right arm which required stitching when a youth I was arresting attempted to jab a broken bottle into my face. As I put my arm up to protect my face the bottle lacerated my arm.

After resuming duty after this incident I was again injured when attending a house fire in City Road near to the Everton ground. I was told that children were trapped in the house and forced an entry by punching one of the downstairs windows in. In doing this I sustained a cut to my hand as I gained access. Unknown to me there were in fact no persons in the house and as I searched upstairs I was overcome by smoke and fumes from the burning furniture. I was eventually taken to Walton Hospital and treated for smoke inhalation and stitches were inserted into my cut hand.

I was beginning to feel the need for some form of change and again made a (futile) attempt at passing the Sergeants exam. Although I was more than happy working with my colleagues, I had started to become restless and felt like same sort of change. I would still like to return to the CID but that avenue was now closed. Promotion? that seemed a dream away. "One day"! I did intend to do something about it, but when? and what? was another matter!. Again I was envious of those who managed to discipline themselves and really get down to serious study. Like most others however, I liked my pint, and I liked being out catching criminals. The only way to do anything about taking the Sergeant's exam seriously would be to make sacrifices. This appeared to be easier said than done!.

Although we were given support by our Sergeants and Inspectors, I found that when the 'chips were down' and decisions had to be taken by those more senior, some were extremely weak and hesitant if there was any risk of 'come back' by making the wrong decision.

Such an example of weakness was illustrated when a local woman was dismissed from her job as a shop assistant. Apparently the woman's employer considered that there were 'financial irregularities' and dispensed with her services. The woman became very abusive and threatening and was ejected from the premises of her former employ, (a busy off licence on a council estate), by the management.

The following morning the woman returned with her son, an ex soldier. Both blockaded the entrance to the shop and stood holding placards bearing the word 'PICKET' and persisted in trying to dissuade shoppers patronising the premises. This had an obvious effect on business and the management requested the attendance of the Police to remove the two from outside the shop and eliminate the physical obstruction to their customers.

As the press had become aware of the situation they also were at the scene. I was instructed to attend the incident but ONLY in an 'Advisory' capacity. This instruction had come from no less than the Chief Superintendent himself. I attended the scene with a colleague and on our arrival saw that a large crowd had gathered, completely obstructing the pavement thus preventing entry to the shop concerned and also making normal use of the footwalk impossible. At the centre of the crowd were the mother and son with their placards. I threaded my way through the crowd to the two and told them to move on as they were committing an offence by obstructing the free passage of the highway. I was told in no uncertain terms by the woman (who was obviously playing to the press and the delighted crowd) that she and her son were (lawful) pickets and were 'peacefully encouraging' people to refrain from using the shop. I noticed that the crowd appeared to be in sympathy with the couples' efforts. I again pointed out the fact that they were causing a 'wilful' obstruction and instructed them to move on. Again the two refused, informing me that they knew the law better than I regarding picketing! and informed me that there was nothing I could do about it as they were 'lawfully' picketing the site of an 'industrial dispute'.

I once more told them, for the last time, to move. "Or what ?" said the barrack room lawyer defending his mother's stance. "OR you will both be arrested" I countered. As they both refused yet again to clear the doorway of the shop I grabbed the ex-soldier first and after a difficult struggle eventually managed to get him into our Police vehicle. My colleague and I had similar trouble getting the woman into the vehicle to join her son, but eventually we were successful in our endeavours.

Once they were both safely inside our vehicle the crowd started to disperse. The couple were quite confident that they had both been arrested unlawfully and intended taking the matter 'as far as they could'!. I was amazed to find that our arrival at Lower Lane was greeted by members of the press. Once we were inside the station I saw senior officers milling about in typical panic!.

I deposited my two prisoners in front of the station Sergeant (Bill Roberts), and after outlining the circumstances of the arrest he accepted the charge.

As the documentation and administrative procedures were taking place I was summoned to see the Chief Superintendent, Mr Carol. After entering his office and being told to close the door, I was given a right dressing down for 'acting against instructions!' I was only to 'Monitor' the situation he ranted. I was informed that I had left the Police service open to proceedings for 'wrongful arrest'. It was clearly pointed out that as the Chief Constable bore vicarious liability for the action of his officers, he could be sued and compensation sought from him. Instead of the Chief Super listening to my side I was shouted down and told that I had certainly 'bitten off more than I could chew' this time!. I had obviously really endeared myself to the boss over this, of that there was no doubt!. What the hell did he expect me to do when half the street was blocked under the watchful gaze of the press? A good dose of 'bottle' would work wonders if prescribed to those who were frightened to stand by their men, instead of worrying about confounded 'ripples' being made.

From the day of that arrest I seemed to be writing reports on the matter for an eternity. Each report submitted was returned for some petty little added question to be answered.

The two defendants appeared before the City Magistrates court and each engaged counsel. The court was told (again in the presence of the press) that the matter was going to be a fight all the way, if necessary to the highest court in the land!.

The first hearing was adjourned and the matter went on and on. After a number of further adjournments, the defendants' original counsel withdrew from the case (perhaps they could see the futility of their continuing representation ?). It was now April 1976. The case was still unheard and had been ongoing since the back end of 1975. Again the case was remanded to July. July came and the case was AGAIN put off until an afternoon in September. This was becoming a nonsense. The September hearing was again put off for an afternoon hearing in October !.

On 26 October 1976, the case was PART HEARD ! in the afternoon before being again remanded for final ? hearing to a November morning.

On the next hearing, again a remand, this time to FEBRUARY 1977!

On the final day of this mammoth case involving nothing more than a summary offence (which by now had lost its media attraction, although the defendants still retained (a different) counsel, the late Mr Howe) the case was heard and finally concluded. The two defendants were found guilty of the offence 'Wilful Obstruction'. The punishment handed out by the court? Each defendant was fined the sum of £5 and each was allowed seven days to pay! I shudder to think what their legal costs would be? After the case was over I was seen by Mr Carol (in passing) and told, "Well done, all that cost for such a job"! He obviously failed to remember that the incident had scared the daylights out of him at the time! I wondered if he could manage to sleep alright now that the 'little' case was finally over? If that was an example of 'life at the top', I'd be happy if I made Sergeant, and stayed there!. After that job, I formed a new collective noun for the dictionary. Added to, a 'flock' of sheep, a 'herd' of cows, a 'crowd' of people, was a 'PANIC' of Chief Supers! Thank goodness the Chief Constable's "vicarious" wallet remained intact!

As well as my 'picket' file, I had many other more important occurrences occupying my time . One such incident involved the frightening assault on a new young Constable, who was seriously injured by a gang on his first tour of night duty.

Sergeant Tranter and I were directed to a "Con Requires" (an urgent call from a Constable requiring assistance, when everything else takes second priority). As we arrived at the scene in Landford Avenue, near to the East Lancashire Road, we saw a large crowd of youths. The youths ran away in all directions on seeing the approach of our Landrover. We were approached by a local resident who informed us that he had summoned an ambulance for the young officer (Constable Julian Pickles) who was lying unconscious in his house after he and his family had rescued the officer from his attackers and carried him into the safety of their home. What a sickening sight to see a badly injured and bleeding colleague lying there. He was just a lad, brand new, straight out of the box! What an introduction to the job for him, his first tour of nights. The young officer's unconscious body was taken by ambulance to Walton Hospital. Feelings were running high throughout the section and none of us had our refreshment period that night as we were all hell bent on catching those responsible for the attack on our colleague.

At 5 am the same morning, a 'phone call was received by the Police from a resident living near the scene of the young bobby's assault. The resident requested the police as she had just seen one of the officer's attackers walking past her house. A number of officers made for the venue, Sergeant Tranter and I being the first to arrive. The lady kindly volunteered to accompany us in our vehicle to point out the attacker. A short time later the lady exclaimed, "There he is, that's him" indicating a long haired yob meandering along as though he was about to attend his theological college to address a class in the virtues of benevolence and kindness. I drove my vehicle over to the youth of 20 or so and stopped alongside him. Sergeant Tranter and I detained the youth and asked the lady to repeat her allegations to us in the presence of the youth. The lady bravely alighted from our vehicle and confronted the youth. She then positively identified him as being one of those who she had seen earlier attacking the young policeman. She stated that she saw him personally kicking the officer in the head as he lay on the ground. What a brave and courageous lady. It is a pity that society does not have more of her kind. The youth replied to her with a tirade of abuse and threatened to attack her also. The lady was placed into another police vehicle that had arrived and taken to Lower Lane for a statement to be taken from her. Sergeant Tranter searched the youth before placing him into our Landrover. As the youth was being searched he spat into the Sergeant's face. This didn't please Sergeant Tranter. The enraged Sergeant threw a punch at the youth who promptly ducked. Sergeant Tranter's punch struck me full in the face completely closing and eventually blackening my left eye. The youth was unceremoniously placed into the back of the vehicle and conveyed post haste to Lower Lane. He was charged with the initial Grievous bodily harm to the young constable and the added assault on Sergeant Tranter (Spitting in his face). It was eventually dealt with by the Crown Court and the judge awarded financial rewards to the householder and members of his family and also to the lady who accompanied us to identify the youth. It was nearly a fortnight before my left eye returned to normal. Harry certainly packed one hell of a punch.

Duties continued and I dealt with the usual every day incidents, including assisting in the delivery of two babies and I also sadly had to deal with a couple of 'cot deaths' which were extremely distressing for all concerned. I also continued with the mundane, regular mobile and foot patrols. The time continued to roll on by and I was becoming more and more restless and yearned for a move to something different. I scrutinised Chief Constable's orders and when different posts were advertised I relentlessly applied for those that interested me. Although I applied for many, my applications never bore fruit. I saw an advertisement in the Police Review requesting applications from experienced CID officers who were interested, to apply to the Royal Ulster Constabulary for service in Belfast. I decided to apply, thinking that if I were to complete a tour over there it might open the gates for me to get back into the CID in my own force on my return. I applied and was informed that I could not be considered as only 'serving' CID officers need apply, and secondly, my application should have been made 'VIA' my own Chief Constable. Never mind, I considered it worth a try!.

I was still upsetting some members of the public by carrying out my duties and again received one or two complaints for my pains along the way. It seemed that the only times that I went to see my senior officers was for the proverbial 'rollocking'!. A vacancy occurred in the 'Crown Court Section' so I decided to give it a try and submitted my application. To my surprise my application was successful and I was accepted and posted to St Georges Hall, the Liverpool Crown Court.

Chapter Twelve - Crown Court Officer

I arrived at the Crown Court and went underground to meet my new Sergeant, 'Dickie' Duncliffe and his section, my new section! What a character 'Dickie' was. He was able to make light of any situation whatsoever. His wisecracks and sarcasm knew no bounds and he never allowed any degree of pomp and ceremony to overawe him. He, like his section, were all 'old timers'. They (as well as myself) felt that I was too young to be among their ranks. I felt that the section, its officers and the procedures were all locked in a time warp! The day's duties revolved around (certain officers) escorting the judges from their cars to the courts and back at lunch time and at the end of the day. Other 'duties' were being present in the courts, perfecting the art of 'hiding' for most of the day, and improving one's skills at cards. I served with the section for six months and although I did actually enjoy most of my stay, I found to my dismay that it was certainly non-productive as far as my job prospects were concerned and in short, just was not my 'cup of tea'!

Although I witnessed many interesting trials, I found that the work there was utterly mundane and uninteresting in general. I certainly did not consider myself an 'active' Police Officer.

I found that some of the judges were utter gentlemen and ambassadors to their profession. However, I found others to be very arrogant, obnoxious and very self-opinionated. These revelled in the unashamed and embarrassing grovelling afforded them by some of my colleagues. I found that some barristers, both male and female, strutted about the building with their noses in the air as if there was a continual pungent smell about. They also seemed so full of their own importance and treated those outside their profession as something akin to dirt, such was their arrogance.

I often requested anyone entering the court building from outside to allow me to inspect their baggage or cases. Nearly always my request was granted with polite assistance and understanding. One supercilious Crown Court clerk, however, resented a mere Constable stopping him as he was about to enter St Georges Hall for the day's hearings. I politely asked him what was in his bulky black leather brief case. He curtly replied, "Documents, d'you mind moving aside and allowing me to pass?" and attempted to brush past me. I stood firm and again asked him, "Do you mind if I have a look please sir?" He snapped, "Yes, I do mind" and again tried to push past me. I was having none of this. I took hold of his arm and again requested to inspect the contents of his briefcase. I informed him that I was carrying out my duties and that it was in everybody's interests of safety and security. It made not the slightest difference to him. I was promptly informed that I was a "bloody idiot" and he then stormed off to another entrance.

I made my way through the building to intercept him at the next entrance. As he entered I stepped into his path and requested to inspect the contents of his case yet again. This time, the pompous clerk blew a fuse. Turning to two of my colleagues standing nearby he proceeded to threaten to have me put before one of the judges for impeding him. He also ranted that he intended to complain to the Chief Constable! He shouted to one of the officers, Constable Jim Farquar, to "call me off"! Jim had served at the Crown Court for many years and asked me what the problem was. We were interrupted by the now near hysterical clerk shouting, "I'm a Crown Court official, for God's sake." I again quietly and politely requested to see into his case or he would not be allowed in.

The situation was now becoming nonsensical as neither he nor I would back down. He was obviously distressed at young girl clerks seeing him, the high and mighty, being stopped. I insisted on seeing the contents of the case, he insisted that I wasn't going to! Finally, an embarrassed Jim asked me to allow him through as he could personally 'vouch' for the gentleman. I reluctantly agreed and was promptly informed by the irate (and by now somewhat late) clerk that I would be hearing more about the episode in due course. I reciprocated by again demanding to see the contents of his case! He wrenched open the case in temper spluttering "There, idiot, documents! Satisfied?" Unfortunately his documents spilled all over the floor as he shook the case in front of me. His face changed colour from red to purple as quickly as an octopus changes its camouflage. "Thank you very much sir, you may enter," I said and walked away, leaving him retrieving his documents from the floor (assisted by my two colleagues). The man was in such a temper that he fell as he ran up the stone steps inside the building, adding to his indignity. Although I fully expected repercussions over the incident, I heard nothing more, except at the dinner table later when a highly amused Sergeant Duncliffe told me that he wished that he had been present and witnessed the incident, as the person concerned was "one arrogant bastard".

Liverpool Crown Court, St. Georges Hall

As the work there involved the escorting of judges (by the selected few!) and occasionally assisting prison officers with an unruly prisoner and spending a lot of my time watching my colleagues playing cards, I tried to utilise my time there by attempting to study for the forthcoming Sergeant's exam. I obviously didn't utilise it efficiently enough, as again I was to fail miserably.

At the conclusion of a six month 'tour' (everyone else on the section had been there for years) I was posted back to Lower Lane and returned to my old section, thus enhancing the premature approach of senility to the long-suffering Sergeant Roberts! I had obviously been a square peg in a round hole on the Crown Court section! Anyway, I couldn't stand the sight of some of those 'fat cats' lawyers as they strutted about egotistically preening themselves.

I have already referred to to fact that there is good and bad in all walks of life and all professions . It could be argued that I am tarring all of the legal profession with the same brush. This is not the position as many of the cases I was involved with were only sucessful thanks to the skills and integrity of the advocates. However, it has been my lot to have had to deal with some of the more unscrupulous members of that profession , whose actions can obviously blemish the whole.

Chapter Thirteen - Once more into the breach

Returning to 'proper' Police work after having such an easy (and lazy) time in my 'day' job I found shift work and being back at the 'sharp end' quite a contrast. I even missed my 'cushy number' at first.

However, being back with the real coppers soon brought back my enthusiasm. I still intended getting stuck into the studying, but how? How the hell did those lads study so profusely without letting the every day matters distract them? I wish I knew the answer! 'Sockless' (Ged Consett) and Robbie Riddel had no such 'delusions of grandeur'. The three of us (known as the three musketeers) were very close friends both on and off duty. Perhaps I unconsciously didn't want to set a precedent by being the 'odd one out' and getting down to studying? I don't know. I gradually settled down again but at the back of my mind I still had the feeling of being 'tied down' at Lower Lane, and continued to scrutinise orders in the hope of finding something interesting.

After spending nearly a year at Lower Lane I was again posted to Westminster Road. Same Division, same routine, different section. I made the most of my time there at 'Wessie' again, and my Sergeant, Derek Hough, and I made regular nocturnal, after duty visits to the Elm Tree pub and nearby Lulu's to 'rekindle' old friendships.

After another lengthy period my frustration grew again and my yearning for another move became paramount.

After taking a prisoner down to the Main Bridewell one night, one of the Bridewell officers, Peter Phillips, tipped me off that a vacancy was soon to occur there, at the Main. I decided to give the matter some thought. I was a little apprehensive as I wasn't sure what the duties there entailed. Working from Westminster Road was okay and my colleagues were fine, but I was certainly restless and was definitely in need of a move.

Finally, I decided to take the bull by the horns and apply for a position at the infamous Main Bridewell, in Liverpool's Cheapside. Eventually I was sent for by Superintendent Townsend. Although outwardly Mr Townsend appeared to be very surly, he was noted for being scrupulously fair and straight. I received a lengthy lecture from Mr Townsend as to my 'well known pedigree' and was informed that if I did manage to get into the Main Bridewell to work there, I would have to 'behave' myself!

I felt as though I was an errant schoolboy being chastised by his teacher! My interview with Superintendent Townsend proved successful and eventually my name appeared in Chief Constable's orders alongside my posting to the Main Bridewell.

Chapter Fourteen - The Main Bridewell

My first day there in mid-1978 started by being taken upstairs to see the 'Governor'. Liverpool Main Bridewell's Governor is the only British Police Officer to officially hold that rank, as the building itself is classified as a Prison as well as a Police station. The Governor at that time was Chief Inspector George Savage, who I remembered from my days at Bruche, when he was an Instructor. The boss welcomed me into the fold and explained the nature of my duties there, pointing out various possible pitfalls which I may encounter, and certain people to watch! He then gave me a complete tour of the building complex showing me the various secret passages and historic things of interest. What a fascinating history that building has, what stories it could tell, and what many secrets it held. I found my 'tour' very interesting and informative, it was certainly strongly recommended! I wondered if the ghost of 'Black Jack' Gribbin , still loitered about haunting the many corridors and passages of the notorious old building?

I very soon got to know who was who at the Main. If I thought that I had already encountered the 'Serious Drinking Squad' at Rose Hill, then here were stationed the 'VERY Serious Drinking Squad'! Being new, I was regularly asked to 'cover' an afternoon court for a colleague while he 'went to the bank' at two o'clock. It was not uncommon for me to still be there two hours later when my somewhat inebriated colleague returned (from the Bank!) He would arrive reeking of ale, glazed of eye and reluctant to have to speak because of slurred speech. The 'Bank' had been moved to the Rose and Crown, opposite the Main Bridewell, or round the corner to the 'Vernon' in Dale Street!

At first I really liked it at the Main and enjoyed the work there. It is absolutely amazing what a variety of important jobs are carried out in that building complex. It is in fact a purpose-built prison and is used as a top priority holding station for very serious offenders. When I started there I worked in the 'front' office, at the Bridewell counter. Here we dealt with the reception and charging of every prisoner, male or female, that was brought into custody.

Prisoners were brought in by bobbies on the beat from other parts of the country, from the courts (prior to transportation to prison) and by officers from the Warrant Department (fines, defaulters, maintenance arrears etc.) and prisoners considered too dangerous to be housed at 'normal' Police Stations. Even in the comparative 'safety' of the building, we were still not immune from the occasional assault from violent prisoners. The Bridewell Constable would search the prisoner and assist the Sergeant or Inspector to look after the prisoner's property, and complete the administrative requirements. The officer would take the prisoners to their cells and assist the Matron and her staff to feed the inmates (male and female).

The exceptionally busy times were at the beginning and end of the working day. Prior to the courts commencing every day (except Sundays), the Bridewell staff had to ensure that all court registers were up to date and also to make sure that all outstanding matters (unpaid fines or 'live' warrants) were duly endorsed on those registers for the information of the bench. As this was being laboriously done, remand prisoners in custody would arrive from Risley to be dealt with, their property checked, and then they would be housed underground prior to their appearance before the courts. This increased activity would add to the mayhem, and the place seemed in utter chaos until these jobs were completed (not a place for Superintendents!). Once all prisoners were safely underground having had their property checked (in each individual's presence) the administrative procedures continued until court commenced. Lunch time during the mid-day break was also a busy period, when meals were distributed and the documentation process would begin again to cater for the afternoon courts.

The morning shift men (although officially 7 a.m. to 3 pm.) managed to get away half an hour or so early depending on how benevolently early his afternoon relief would be. It was the norm for front office staff to arrive for duty half an hour or so early to allow their colleague on the previous shift to get away.

The Main Bridewell certainly dealt with some of the dregs of society. Sometimes the more horrendous the crime, the more 'unscrupulous' members of the legal profession, in the main solicitors, would crawl out of the woodwork to vie for their chance to represent the perpetrators of such crimes. Most solicitors were known by most of us staff and many were referred to by their first names. By and large, we enjoyed a happy relationship with most of the advocates, but there were, however, some who didn't 'play the game'. Those individuals were not only well known to us at the Main, but were also not liked by us and even some of their own colleagues. It was not uncommon to witness two lawyers squabbling over who should represent whom, or one accusing another of 'pinching' his client. Yet others would not represent someone because the a Legal Aid certificate had not been granted (what price justice?) It was certainly an education being there on such occasions.

Those lawyers who deserved it certainly received courtesy and assistance from the Bridewell staff. Others , however ,who were not greatly endowed with integrity would slip a dozen business cards into a crowded cell (touting as it was referred to); this behaviour was just not on.

I was soon to learn that certain officers would go missing for lengthy periods while others covered for them. These officers were, of course, imbibing in the Rose and Crown, or the Vernon. At the end of the hearings those prisoners returning to Risley, or those committed to Walton Prison, would be returned to cells to await the afternoon 'call out'. This was the period when the regulating Sergeant mustered all available officers to assist him in placing the prisoners into their transport for their journey to Risley or Walton. Again, one or two would miss this 'ritual' as they were still 'engaged' across the road! Once the transport had left the complex, those officers who were on 9 to 5 duty would then go home. The earlier that call out was finished, the earlier they could get away.

Most times this enabled an 'early dart' for those concerned.

Very often, as the courts were our responsibility, Bridewell officers would be called up into court to assist with an unruly defendant or one who who had been remanded into custody, but didn't want to go.

The Rose and Crown, Cheapside.

On one such occasion I was called to the Magistrates' Court Fines Office in Dale Street to eject an abusive 'customer'. As I arrived at the office I saw an old man who was shouting threats to the young female counter staff. He was repeatedly banging his heavy wooden walking stick on the counter to loudly reinforce his threats to the terrified young women. As the man would not cease his disorderly behaviour I took hold of him and dragged him out into Dale Street and told him to behave himself and go home before he landed himself into serious trouble. The old man was unconcerned at my veiled threat. He took hold of the ferrule end of his stick with both hands and adopted the stance of a golfer about to strike the ball and send it down the fairway. I noticed a number of people who had stopped to stare at the amazing spectacle of a frail old man (in his seventies) threatening a Police officer in broad daylight in the heart of the City. I recognised a number of advocates also standing there gawping. I told the man not to be so silly and make his way home.

To my utter disbelief, the nasty old geriatric swung his stick the full arc, striking me a terrific blow to the side of my face with the handle of the stick. The blow was of such ferocity that it completely dislocated my jaw. I felt blood trickle down my face and saw the drips starting to stain my shirt and tie. Although I was temporarily stunned, I managed to maintain my feet and grabbed the old man. I couldn't speak but I snatched his stick, broke it over my knee and grabbed the old man by the

212

scruff of his neck. I don't think his feet touched the ground as I took him round to the Bridewell, running the gauntlet of the amazed onlookers. Had it not been so serious, the whole spectacle could have resembled something out of the "Keystone Cops".

The pain in my face was excruciating but not one person saw fit to assist me. Even though I was physically superior in size (and age) it must have been obvious to all that I had sustained a bad injury. I made a mental note of those solicitors present, as they might need a favour one day!

I took the old man (minus his two pieces of broken stick, these were handed in later by an enterprising member of the public) and placed him before the Inspector at the Bridewell counter. I painfully and slowly managed to get across to him, to his amusement and disbelief, that the geriatric prisoner was responsible for my injury.

The Bridewell surgeon, Dr 'Morrie' Kirwan was summoned, and a short time later attended to treat my injury. A subsequent X-ray confirmed a dislocation of my jaw and cuts to the inside of my mouth. It goes without saying how embarrassing it was for me, a strapping six-footer weighing fifteen stone, being subjected to such a painful injury from such a decrepit old man of 74 years!

This man, who had already achieved notoriety in the press by attempting to sue the late (legendary) Bill Shankly (Manager of Liverpool Football Club) for some nondescript matter that didn't get anywhere, except to cause distress to Mr Shankly and his family by his persistence in pursuing such a lost imaginary and vindictive cause. It was more embarrassing still when I attended Birkenhead Crown Court. At the conclusion of the case the old man, Joseph Howard, was found guilty of assault occasioning actual bodily harm. He was sent to prison for 28 days. The lads certainly subjected me to a lot of mickey-taking over the incident for a long time after.

Whilst on day shift, just prior to 2 p.m. one afternoon, I was asked by a colleague (from the exclusive 'squad') if I would look after his afternoon court (Number 1 Court, the Stipendiary's) for "a few minutes", while he attended to some business. I duly obliged and sat in court and read the records of the defendants, escorted those from and into custody, leaving my own duties to do this. My colleague's "couple of minutes" lasted for nearly two hours. When he eventually turned up he was quite the worse for drink and he was panicking. We were housing some PTA (Prevention of Terrorism Act) prisoners at the time, and as he had been making his way back to court to relieve me (from the Rose and Crown) he had lost his keys to the Bridewell and its cells, somewhere en route. When the court concluded a short time later I went with him and retraced his steps in the hope of finding the keys.

If those keys were not recovered there would be such a hue and cry that it would pale the Dr Crippin murders into insignificance. On the ring were the key to the main door of the Bridewell, all cell keys and keys to 'sensitive' offices. The tremendous significance of such a loss need not be emphasised. We retraced his journey from the pub to the discreet side entrance to the courts but our search proved fruitless. My colleague was sobering up pretty fast now as the gravity of the situation was beginning to thread through his alcoholically numbed brain. I decided to try a shot in the dark. There was an iron grid in the gutter near to the Rose and Crown and I thought that it may be just possible that my colleague may have strayed a little to his left as he fumbled for his keys ready to admit himself into the court entrance and he just may have dropped them down into the murky slime at the bottom of the drain. My colleague insisted that he hadn't gone anywhere near the grid as it was 'off course' from his route to the court door. "Nevertheless, there's just a chance you may have dropped them into the grid," I said. The particular officer concerned was noted for his aggression when having consumed alcohol. This time was no exception. Normally I would have let him get on with his problem, but the loss of these keys would cause so much trouble for everyone at the Main, including the boss, that I decided that finding the keys far outweighed my falling out with him. It was imperative that the keys were found, irrespective of who had lost them. I discreetly escorted my colleague back into the building using my own key and returned to the grid, with a window pole.

What a spectacle I must have been. A Police officer, in shirt sleeve order, minus cap, out in the street standing there, my hands covered in thick black sludge as I rifled through the city's sewage. No doubt my hands were rummaging amongst dirt which included many customers' excess alcohol consumption (and rejection) from the Rose and Crown! After a number of 'feelings' amongst the debris I decided to make one more stomach churning try with the pole. It was by now getting uncomfortably close to 'call out' time when I would be missed. How the hell I was going to explain my appearance to those inside on my return? I would have to ponder that one later!

I once again probed the window pole into the murky depths. "Clink!" I saw a slight glint from below! Could this be the elusive keys? I probed again. "Clink!" There it was again. I got down on my knees and reached down into the grid. The stink was unbearable. I rummaged through the filth and slime and finally, to my joy, there were the keys, I had found them! I had saved my undeserving colleague's neck, but so serious was the breach of security, no-one would ever have to know. I tried to make my way back into the Main as furtively as possible, hoping that no-one in authority would discover my dirty and unkempt form as I did so.

After a thorough scrub I returned to my section. Although my shirt was reasonably clean, it was very wet! "Where the bloody hell have you been?" snarled the regulating Sergeant (the late Don Palin). He and I didn't get on all that well as it was. He would make an absolute meal of it if he knew where I had been and why! I told him that I had been asked to attend at the Magistrates' Courts office to which Don replied, looking at my shirt, "Was it raining in there? He wasn't an old codger was he?" (referring to my assault the last time I attended there). The Sergeant was no doubt pleased with his sarcastic quip and decided to let the matter rest at my intended humiliation in front of those present.

Just before we all went off duty I decided to finally put my careless (and selfish) colleague out of his misery. I returned his keys to him. He thanked me profusely (at the time) and then made his way off duty, back into the Rose and Crown! Although he was genuinely grateful now the crisis was over, I knew the matter would be completely forgotten in a couple of hours' time when he would succumb to further inebriation.

Occasionally, Marje would meet me in the Rose and Crown at 5.30 p.m. when we would have a few drinks with the lads before making our way home. (Marje was now working at a shop in nearby Lord Street.)

At the Main Bridewell there was always an incident occurring which was worthy of note. I once wrote out a card which was placed above the Bridewell counter, intended purely to amuse. The card, bearing large printed letters, read, "Please do not ask for bail, as a refusal often offends". All who saw the notice - staff, visitors, dignitaries and prisoners alike - thought the card amusing. However, our old friend the solicitor who used to scatter his cards among the cell prisoners, decided (after the card had been on display for almost a year) to make an issue of it in court. Consequently the card was ordered to be removed. The incident, or the solicitor involved, are not worthy of further comment.

One Saturday morning, at about 11.30, I admitted a solicitor's "runner" (office dogsbody) into the building. The "runner" was in fact an ex-colleague. The very man who was the doorman at the club we visited years before. The Inspector who should have been on duty in the city instead of being on the door at Toad Hall.

I admitted him and said to Inspector Taylor, "Mr .... sir, to see the prisoner Benson". Ronnie Taylor, the Inspector, was dealing with some paperwork on the counter and the ex-colleague leaned against the counter and started to peruse the pages of the Bridewell Memo (Incident) Book. I slammed the book shut. "That's a confidential Police document", I said icily, hardly containing my contempt for the man. Quite unconcerned at my behaviour the ex-colleague turned to the Inspector and said, "I've come to see my client, Ron. Can I go through?" Inspector Taylor instructed me to escort the visitor to the cell to see his "client". I unlocked the cell door and the visitor went inside and sat on the bench alongside the prisoner. I stood outside in the corridor, the cell door was ajar. My ex-colleague suddenly shouted, "Officer, do you mind pulling the door to; this is a 'privileged' conversation, not for your ears". I'm sure his 'client' was very impressed. I replied, "Certainly, SIR" and slammed the cell door closed and turned the key. A short time later I was given the opportunity to get away early. This opportunity was taken with gratitude and I went off duty. My shift went off duty an hour or two later at 2.30 p.m. It was rest day the following day (Sunday) and I didn't return to duty until 8.45 a.m. on Monday morning.

As I breezed into the building fresh and sprightly on the Monday morning I was greeted by those behind the counter with, "You're in the shit, Swasie, the boss wants you in his office!" I made my way up the stone stairs to the first floor landing and knocked apprehensively on the Governor's door. I knew damned well why he wanted to see me! The door was opened by the Matron who had just taken the boss his tea and toast. "Swasie to see you, sir", she said as she opened the door wider to admit me. I was directed to close the door as the Matron left.

I closed the door and saluted the Governor. "Good morning sir. I believe you wish to see me" I politely snivelled. The Governor (now Chief Inspector Beattie) replied coldly, "I don't WANT to see you, but I bloody well have to". I pretended to be surprised and naive. "Is anything wrong, sir?" I asked. "You know bloody well there's something wrong. I've just had the Chief Constable on the 'phone bending my ear about your little stunt on Saturday", he said. "Saturday?" I said, looking puzzled. The boss was not entering into the spirit of things at all. His face reddened. Leaning over his desk he growled slowly and quietly. "Don't come it with me Turner. What happened when you locked a solicitor in the cell and went home on Saturday?" "Oh, you mean that Saturday?" I said.

It was obvious by the boss's expression that his patience was now being sorely tested. I explained all about my escorting the visitor to the cell to see the prisoner. I went on to tell him about the abrupt demand that the door be closed. "Right", interjected Mr Beattie, "Well why didn't you tell someone so that he could be let out later?" "I did tell someone sir," I said. The boss snarled, "Who did you tell?" I looked at him and said, "Well, erm, it was erm, hmmn, I can't remember, er . . ." I was again interrupted by the now irate boss, "No you can't, because you just buggered off without telling anyone. I know you Swasie. Get out of my sight before I do something I'll regret." I stood to attention, saluted, left the boss's office and made my way downstairs. I remember thinking "I really must do something about my failing memory." (It had been nearly three hours before the "runner" was discovered and released from the smelly cell!)

When drunks were brought in, some, due to their advanced state of inebriation, could not be identified at the time. They would be searched to prevent them from harming themselves. We would remove penknives, ties, belts and anything else that could inflict injury. They would then be placed into a 'safety' cell for the night to sleep off their intoxication.

The 'safety' cell consisted of a raised, hard bed in the centre of the floor so that the drunk could be easily observed through a peep hole while he slept. These cells could accommodate four persons. If they could not be named at the time of their admission they would be referred to by an item of their clothing, i.e. "Cell No 3 'Blue jeans' or 'Red jumper'" etc.

As I arrived for duty one morning, I relieved my night duty colleague and set out to check the cell state and make a body count. I checked the number of prisoners and their names to ensure that the numbers tallied with those on my 'bedding board'. All was well until I reached the drunks' cell. I checked my list. The occupants of the cell's names were entered on my board "Brown, O'Coat and Devlin". I leaned against the door and shouted to those inside, "Right, answer yer names! Brown", there was no answer. "BROWN!" I shouted, louder this time. Again, no answer. "O'coat!" Again, no answer. I was starting to get annoyed now. "O'COAT!" I bellowed, "answer your bloody names in there!" Still utter silence. "Devlin?" "Here, Boss" came the reply. I unlocked the door and went inside to see what they were playing at. I saw the scruffy figure of a man lying on the hard wooden bed. "What's your name lad?" I asked the bleary-eyed figure. "Devlin, Boss", he politely replied. I marked a tick against his name which was below the names of the other two, Brown and O'coat. "Where's the other two, Brown and O'coat?" I asked. Devlin informed me that he had been alone in the cell throughout his overnight stay.

I thought that he was being like most prisoners - unco-operative and telling me lies. The bedding board said that there should be three inmates in cell number three, so where were the other two? I told Devlin not to be so smart, but he still persisted that he had not had any company. As I was getting myself nowhere fast, I slammed the cell door closed and reported to my morning Inspector, Don Calkley. "There's two prisoners unaccounted for, sir," I informed him. The Inspector instructed me to make another head count to make sure. Once again, I did the rounds of the building and checked the names and number of inmates with the overnight bedding board. The result was the same.

"Two short sir," I again confirmed to the Inspector. He and I then dug out every custody sheet and laboriously went through every arrest brought in during the previous two shifts, a mammoth task. At the conclusion of our major search we could find no trace of the two prisoners, Brown and O'coat. "We'll have to ring the night shift lads and get them out of bed." said the Inspector. I telephoned the previous night's Inspector, Bill Formby. He was the epitome of utter delight at having his day's hibernation so rudely disturbed. No, he wasn't aware of Brown or O'Coat's overnight detention. I then rang Constable George Emmerson, waking him from his slumbers also. George listened to my concerned reason for telephoning him and in a short time he very thoroughly revealed all, angrily punctuating his explanation with fully descriptive adjectives as to my competency (and sanity).

George explained that a young bobby had brought in a completely incapable male drunk from the City centre in the early hours of the morning. The prisoner was in such a state of intoxication, that because of his drunken stupor he could not even reveal his own name. He was duly searched and then placed into a safety cell (number three) and allowed to sleep it off. As he was wearing a brown overcoat, he was entered onto the bedding board, being referred to as "Brown O'coat". As it read on the board, Brown, then underneath, O'coat. Finally, when the man sobered up enough to reveal his name, Devlin, "Devlin" was then entered onto the board underneath the other two names. From top to bottom, the board thus read "Brown, O'coat, Devlin" one underneath the other, giving the impression of three separate names. Once the name Devlin had been ascertained, Brown O'coat should have been crossed out! As it was not, I ultimately misinterpreted the bedding board and this caused my most embarrassing faux pas. All concerned were definitely not amused. It was a very, very long time before I was allowed to try and forget the unfortunate (and inexcusable) mistake.

During a quiet spell in the small hours of one morning, I sat doodling with my pen. First I drew the Liver bird. Looking at my drawing, this gave me an idea. I decided to design a "Main Bridewell" tie, to be worn exclusively by those who had served, or were serving, at the well known venue. After much doodling, I finally settled for a design which consisted of the Crown, representing the Police service, under which was the Liver bird (Liverpool) and instead of the 'sprig' in its beak I placed a key, bearing the letters M at one end and B at the handle end (Main Bridewell). Finally, underneath all, a Portcullis (representing a place of incarceration). As the Main Bridewell in Liverpool boasted the only British Police rank of 'Governor' I incorporated a capital letter G to signify that rank, intending just a few of the ties to bear that letter.

Having done this and coloured it in, intending it to be displayed on a navy blue tie, I canvassed my colleagues and ex-colleagues who had served there, including the Governor and some of his predecessors. All were very enthusiastic and encouraging, and stated that they would be very willing to purchase and wear such an exclusive tie.

I contacted a tie manufacturer in Macclesfield, Cheshire, who advised me to send them a copy of my design. Eventually, they sent me a woven 'proof'. It was beautiful. Taking a chance, I went ahead and ordered the firm to make the ties (the minimum ordered had to be fifty!) I hoped my optimism would prove to be justified. On my subsequent receipt of the items I contacted all those who had enthusiastically encouraged me with my venture and all the ties were snapped up immediately on sight, including eight bearing the letter G. The latter eight went to the Governor, six of his predecessors and the then Home Secretary, Mr Willie Whitelaw, when he visited the premises. It was with immense pride that I saw Mr Whitelaw on television, wearing the tie!

Such was the ensuing demand for the tie that a further 150 were ordered and even they could not satisfy the demand. (Recently I have been informed that more again have been manufactured.) These well-known ties are very much sought after by serving (and ex-serving) members of the Bridewell staff.

After the success of that tie, I went on to design another tie, the A of J tie (Administration of Justice Department). This design proved equally popular with those serving in the department, which included a large number of civilian staff. The tie was maroon, and bore the gold letters A J, between which was a white quill. Those who purchased and wore this tie include members of the Probation Service, Court Clerks and even one or two of the Magistrates.

One weekend I went off into the wilds of Llanrhaeadr, and up into the mountains beyond the little town of Oswestry. There I regularly went on a shoot for rabbits and hares. On this occasion, I was accompanied by two friends. The land was part of a pony trekking station on a farm owned by the family of a colleague. We spent a pleasant day up in the mountains and eventually returned with our 'bag' for the day. As we were returning to my colleague's farm, we passed a neighbour of his, who was engaged in breaking in one of his horses in one of the adjacent fields. We watched the antics of the horse as it clearly indicated its disapproval of having someone on its back. During my youth I was a keen horse rider, and I asked if I could try and mount the handsome beast. I was encouraged by its owner to try my luck and see if I could. The horse was a fine big chestnut which stood at sixteen hands. I was almost on his back when he suddenly decided he didn't want me on board! He reared up. Then, stamping his forelegs firmly onto the ground, he kicked up his hind legs and threw me unceremoniously over his head. I landed with a heavy thud, which completely winded me. I felt a stab of pain in my right shoulder and lay there for a few seconds trying to get my breath back. Fortunately, once the animal had rid himself of me he just stood there (presumably grinning to himself). With the help of my amused friends I regained my feet and we resumed our journey back to my colleague's farm. I felt pain in my right shoulder as I carried my shotgun, its sling over the tender area. All three of us called for a pint into the quaint little pub down in the village. As I sat at the bar, the friendly landlady, Olwen, asked me "Are you alright? You look very pale." One of my friends informed her of my fruitless attempt to mount the horse, much to everybody's amusement. Although I was in some discomfort, I also could see the funny side of things and joined in the banter. The pain in my shoulder persisted and I thought that I must have bruised it as I fell.

That night, and through to Monday morning, there was no let up in the pain. I hoped it would wear off as time went by. As I paraded for duty on the Monday morning, the Governor called me over. "What's up, Swasie? You look as though you've seen a ghost!" I told him about my being thrown from the horse two days earlier and he remarked that I appeared to be holding my arm at a peculiar angle. "It is a bit sore," I confirmed. "I think we'll call Morrie (the Police Bridewell surgeon) out and get him to have a look at you," said the Governor, most concerned. Dr Kirwan was summoned and I was taken into his surgery for him to look at me. After he examined my shoulder and it was established that I could not perform one or two simple manipulations, Dr Kirwan sent me to the Royal Teaching Hospital for an X-Ray as he feared that I may have a broken shoulder. Subsequent X-Rays at the hospital confirmed Morrie's findings. I had, in fact, broken my collar bone away from my breast bone. No wonder my right arm was "hanging funny"! Due to this little outing into the mountains I had to go off duty for three weeks and even after my ultimate return I had to perform 'menial' jobs and keep well out of the way of prisoners to eliminate any prospects of further injury. I must remember not to mount strange horses in future!

I did, however, relish my periodic visits to the farm. I had been going there since I was first invited by my colleague, Bob Williams, when we were both recruits at Rose Hill back in the early sixties. Bob took me and introduced me to his parents (sadly both now deceased) and his brothers. I was made very welcome amongst them all and have been a regular visitor to their farm ever since. Indeed, I now consider myself as almost one of their family. Being up there in the mountains, in the cold, crisp air, more than compensates for the rigours and traumas of life as a Policeman in a large, bustling city. Near the farm are the well-known waterfalls of 'Pistyll Rhaeadr', reputed to be one of the 'seven wonders' of Wales. The beautiful panoramic views of such a hidden part of the world are well worth the journey to see. I often wondered whatever possessed Bob to leave such a little paradise to join the Police in far away Liverpool.

The amount of drinking that went on in and at the Bridewell was phenomenal. If you were a member of one or two particular shifts and were not a heavy drinker, you weren't in the "gang". However, those who did partake were quick to enlist the 'services' of the non-drinkers, to cover for them. Due to this, I began to dislike one or two of my colleagues there whose sole aim in life appeared to revolve around the 'altar' of alcohol, interspersed with the occasional inconvenient bout of Police duty. Governors came and went. Some were a pleasure and a privilege to work under, some were definitely not! The female civilian staff consisted of the Matron (who we referred to as "Mother Hen") and her wardresses (most of whom appeared to be related to her).

My interest in my work eventually began to wane and deteriorate, mainly due to the obsessive drinking (and unchecked drunkenness) of some of my colleagues. My section was joined by a 'new' acquisition, Inspector Tommy Hall, one of my ex-Detective Sergeants. Tom is a fantastic fellow. I like him very much. He was a very efficient (and very amusing) officer. I was pleased for him that he had been promoted, and certainly pleased that he had come to serve with us at the Main.

Tom had dealt with an incident out in Huyton prior to him being posted to us. He had attended at a house fire on a local estate. The fire had consumed most of a garage adjacent to the house and on the opposite side of the road, a crowd of onlookers, including many children, had gathered to watch the fire-fighters. One of the children in the crowd was a little boy, Liam Cookson. Suddenly, there was a tremendous explosion. The intense heat had caused a large propane gas cylinder inside the burning garage to explode. The explosion sent splinters of metal shrapnel in all directions. Young Liam was struck and cut down by the flying metal and received horrific injuries to his face, and part of his right arm was severed just below the elbow. Tom (like myself with young Phil Batemen some years earlier) had accompanied young Liam to the hospital and, as he was dealing with the incident, took a personal interest in the boy's welfare (typical Tom).

As the young boy slowly, painfully and courageously fought his adversity, Tom started sitting on Liam's bed (like he did when I had lost half my hand) and telling him (grossly exaggerated) stories about one of his bobbies (me) who had fought back from a bad injury and resumed flying and boating, as well as resuming his Police career. Little Liam was filled with all sorts of 'feats' which I was supposed to have accomplished in the face of adversity.

Tom informed me that Liam would very much like to meet me. I was extremely honoured and was more than willing to oblige the little lad. Tom took me out to the boy's home on his discharge from hospital and introduced me to him and his very charming parents, Pop and Julie. What a wonderful and courageous lad Liam was. Although he was obviously still racked with pain from his appalling and disfiguring injuries, he still managed a smile for me and even thanked me for going out to see him. I felt humbled at being in his presence. I promised him I would take him out in the boat and show him the aircraft at Sealand as soon as he was fit enough and of course, subject to mum and dad's approval.

The family were delighted at my offer and between then and the time that such an outing was to come about, Marje and I went over to Huyton to visit Liam regularly. During the days following my sad but very impressive visit to Liam's home I concentrated on what I could do for the poor little boy. I approached his mother and father and asked them if they thought he would like a tour of the Main Bridewell complex, including the cells and courts etc. I thought that the sight of the walls bearing the restraining rings and the underground passageways would surely fascinate and interest the lad, being of such an inquisitive and impressionable age.

Liam's parents were very enthusiastic at my suggestion so I set about "doing the honours". I made an approach to the (latest) Governor, Chief Inspector Mothers, and sought permission for my suggested venture. Like many others of his rank, he ummed and arrhed before finally making a decision. Eventually I managed to get his permission for young Liam and his parents to tour the Bridewell complex (however, not without reservations). I would have to arrange and conduct the visit in my own time (no problem) and the visit (understandably) would have to be made on a Sunday.

My request for Liam to ride in a Police car was refused. This would not be possible as he "wouldn't be covered by insurance!" Yet another example of senior officers' initiative, discretion and decision-making! Fair enough, I could understand the Sunday morning, and being in my own time logic, but a ride in a patrol car? I'd soon sort that one out myself!

Cartoon of the Main Bridewell Govenor, 'The Hatchet Man'
(Not Appreciated !)

At the rear of the Bridewell, across a yard, is the Liverpool Fire Brigade Control Room. Access is easily obtained by unlocking the iron 'cage' door at the end of the underground cell passageway, a short walk across the yard, and you're there. Many times some of us nipped through when all was quiet and had a cuppa with the girls in the control room. My own colleagues were looking forward to the impending visit by Liam and his family and many donated cash to buy him sweets and little presents.

I rang an 'A' Division mate who was on mobile patrol on the day and without any hesitation he agreed to take young Liam for a ride in his patrol car (balls to the Governor!) Whilst chatting to the girls in the Fire Control Room I mentioned in passing the forthcoming visit by young Liam. The girls remembered the incident only too well. They were most interested and overjoyed that the lad was making progress with his recovery. They emphatically insisted that I bring the boy through to them on the day and this I promised to do. Unknown to me, the girls set about arranging their own form of welcome for Liam. Those wonderful girls and their male firefighting colleagues of the Merseyside Fire Service completely outshone the efforts of my colleagues and myself in the Police service.

When the day arrived I donned my uniform and 'paraded' at the Main Bridewell to await the arrival of my charges. As it was my weekend off, and it was Sunday, I had satisfied the boss's criteria. I had requested he also attend to illustrate the importance of the occasion by his rank - he did not attend. Liam and his parents arrived at 10 a.m. sharp as arranged. My colleagues and I greeted them and the lads presented Liam with sweets, a pen and some badges. I gave him a polished helmet plate which I pinned to his jumper. He stood there proudly displaying the badge to all as though he was the new 'Sheriff of Cheapside'. His poor badly scarred face lit up with joy and gratitude. The sight of him stood there with his armless sleeve hanging limply at his side brought lumps to the throats of all those present.

Liam enthusiastically inspected the cells and wanted to 'see some murderers'! I took him to the fingerprint room and took the fingerprints of his left hand and gave him the prints on the official form. I told him I only needed one form (stealing Tommy Hall's crack that he made to me years before). It worked again too and Liam laughed at my little 'funny'. We went up to the courts and Liam insisted in sitting in the 'Judge's' (Magistrate's) chair. After this, my colleague from "A" Division arrived and took the boy for a ride in his patrol car and allowed him to listen to the vehicle's radio. (Such a small thing to us, but a fantastic treat to someone like Liam; I hope the boss didn't see him!) After his little ride and having seen all that there was to be seen I took my little party through to the Fire Control room to see the girls as I had promised.

As we entered the Control Room one of the lady officers stepped forward and presented Liam with a massive box of chocolates. Then, the Chief of the Merseyside Fire Brigade himself and Chief Fire Officer of the New York Fire Department (who was over here on a course) stepped forward and presented Liam with a brass collage displaying a vintage fire engine. He received a large, coloured, shoulder patch of the New York

Fire Department from the American officer. The Control Room consoles were shown and explained, then Liam was permitted (to his sheer delight) to make a radio call to a fire engine. After this we were all taken outside into the yard. There, with its full crew, was the fire engine that Liam had just called. It had arrived specifically to convey young Liam on a tour of the City. Also present were the press. The Brigade certainly did the occasion proud and undoubtedly made Liam's day. Obviously, the Chief

Swasie with Liam Cookson, Mum Julie, New York Fire Chief and Liverpool Chief Fire Officer

Fire Officer had consumed his prescription of 'Bottle' by ensuring such a wonderful day for the boy!

As well as the boy and his family, I myself was overwhelmed by the treatment and generosity afforded by the Fire Service. They had certainly put my dismal effort to shame. Tommy Hall and I monitored the young boy's progress from then on. Young Liam became well known by press coverage as he was to become a pioneering guinea pig by testing a new Russian artificial arm that had been invented and manufactured in the Soviet Union.

The limb was a wonderful invention and Liam was very soon able to become proficient in its use. As he became more expert in using the new limb so he resumed his normal, boisterous self, and was to be seen riding his bicycle around the area of his home regularly. He went on to ride motor cycles on nearby waste land and soon became a very efficient young motor cyclist (even though he was many years from getting his licence).

It wasn't long before the arm succumbed to such rough treatment and a replacement had to be sent from Mother Russia! I am more than proud and privileged to be able to include such a brave and courageous young person and his family among my friends. I took Liam out fishing and shrimping many times and we also visited RAF Sealand to see the gliders.

The Main Bridewell had its 'regulars', all of whom were characters in their own right. Many of the regular drunks were addressed by the Christian or nicknames. The majority of these men (and some women) were harmless, although sometimes were a nuisance. Their only misdeeds were nothing more than drinking themselves into an alcoholic stupor, not unlike some colleagues, come to think of it!

One of these regulars, the late 'Tucker' Murphy, was often brought in drunk with his little faithful mongrel 'Scruffy' (very apt) tied to his wrist by a length of string. We let 'Scruffy' in with him sometimes if we knew that he would be later bailed. Tragically, poor Tucker's home (which wasn't much) was torched by some persons unknown and little Scruffy perished in the fire. Although old Tucker was once a very 'hard case' and had partaken in many a bar room brawl in his younger days, the loss of little Scruffy affected him considerably.

Tucker, like so many other of the City's 'winos' was eventually to succumb to sclerosis of the liver and was found dead in a derelict building one wet and windy night. We all liked Tucker, and those of the lads who were smokers used to keep him in cigarettes during his regular 'stays' with us.

When prisoners were taken underground to facilitate their appearance before the Court, they were placed into a large, communal cell. A separate cell was for female prisoners, and yet other cells were allocated for the detention of juveniles and those prisoners who had to be kept apart from the others for one reason or another.

One busy morning, all such cells were occupied and pandemonium reigned supreme below the courts. A large number of remand prisoners had arrived from Risley Remand Centre and as there were so many, these were allocated the large, communal cell, other prisoners being placed into the adjacent cells.

One male prisoner, whose surname was also a female's Christian name (I shall use another similar but incorrect name) was brought to us from the 'front office' having just been arrested on an outstanding warrant for non-payment of a fine. I shall refer to him as Mr 'Joyce'. This particular prisoner was listed (and indeed was) a male. Joyce however, lived, partly dressed and preferred to be referred to, as a female. He was shortly to undergo surgery for a 'sex change' operation. He spoke very effeminately and 'minced' along, dangling his limp wrist at waist level as he walked. He wore a thin layer of make up and although he wore trousers, on this day he wore a white blouse under his coat instead of a shirt. After being arrested Mr Joyce had been documented and processed before being brought underground to us prior to his appearance before the court. Mr Joyce certainly presented those of us in authority underground that morning with quite a dilemma.

As the Bridewell officer brought Joyce underground, together with the appropriate paperwork authorising his custody, Joyce's demeanour and appearance brought titters and giggles from various officers and prison officers present. He presented a problem which was not so amusing, however. Officially, he was listed as a male, but he was also 'partly' female (he was already starting to sprout breasts due to his taking of medication in the form of hormone treatment). He was also certainly 'geared up' mentally for his forthcoming change to being a full female. All cell accommodation was full, including the females' cell. Where on earth then did we put Joyce?

One of the officers thought the problem was easy to solve. He took Joyce to the communal cell, opened the door and placed him inside, saying "You're listed as male, so you can go in with the males." The cell was full of lecherous (no doubt some of them sex-starved) prisoners and many of them had been in custody for some time. As soon as Joyce was pushed inside, his frightened protests ignored, the cell fell silent. As the door was being slammed shut there was uproar from within. Inside the cell there was chaos! We opened the door again within seconds and retrieved the by now almost naked Joyce. There is no doubt that he would have been 'gang raped' within a very short time, but for his timely rescue. The officer who had placed him into the cell was subject to a complaint for a serious breach of his duties. An official complaint was lodged by Joyce (and rightly so) against the officer concerned.

Joyce could not be placed into the females' cell because he was a male. Alternatively, he couldn't be placed into a males' cell amongst a lot of sex-hungry prisoners. A compromise was reached. Joyce's clothing was recovered and he was allowed to sit in the underground reception area with us officers until he made his appearance before the court.

He subsequently appeared before the bench and the Magistrates were informed of his earlier 'near miss'. The kind members of the bench showed their sympathy and understanding of his problems by not imposing a custodial penalty, but instead, allowed him yet again time to pay his outstanding fines, thus eliminating further risk to himself had he been kept in custody. The gravity of such a situation should need no explanation.

I took my turn performing duties in the courts as 'Dock Officer'. This involved reading prisoners' records to the court, collecting court sheets and warrants from the bench and general court security. During trials I would sit in the dock with the defendant and would give the impression that I was deeply engrossed in my court 'administrative' work. In actual fact I used to draw caricatures of members of the bench or the various advocates, even some of the defendants. Eventually, my secret cartoon 'portrait' drawing was discovered and once it became known, I was sometimes asked by those I had portrayed on paper if they could have the drawing. I was more than happy to oblige.

Two of the region's most outstanding and prolific members of the legal profession's advocacy were Liverpool's Rex Makin and Birkenhead's (now deceased) 'Barney' Berkson. The more that I saw of these particular two, the more they were to command my utter admiration and total respect. Each would defend his client with the utmost vigour and tenacity and would move heaven and earth to establish the innocence of those who had enlisted their aid. I, myself, have 'crossed swords' with both of these very clever advocates, during which time I was subject to the most ardent and scrupulous cross-examination where no quarter was given. I was, however, treated with courtesy and fairness during such questioning. Both of these men were not only extremely able and competent advocates, but were also gentlemen of impeccable fortitude who pursued their client's goal relentlessly. I was to get to know each of these gentlemen personally and have engaged Mr Makin's services on more than one occasion. He became our family solicitor and he has acted on our behalf with the utmost efficiency.

My family now contained yet another member of the Police fraternity. My son Ron successfully applied to become a Constable in the Mersey Tunnel Police, the force's youngest recruit ever. I was very pleased to see that 'like father, like son' he was to immerse himself fully into his duties.

Mersey Tunnels Police Constable Ron Turner (Authors Son)

It was strange at first, seeing my own son bringing prisoners into the Main Bridewell. He also arrested many for various offences (many, other than traffic related) and started to earn a name for himself amongst his own colleagues and was soon well-known amongst my own as he continued to bring his 'felons' before the Bridewell counter.

Another off duty incident manifested itself when a young man, who was employed at a local garage where I purchased my petrol, knocked on my door one day. I only knew the youth by sight as he worked as a motor mechanic at 'my' garage. he asked me if I was interested in buying 'a couple of boat engines'. As I was not in need of such an item I declined his offer. I informed him that I would 'ask around' for him and casually asked where the engines were from. As I was aware that he KNEW that I was a Police officer, I was amazed when he informed me that the engines were 'knock off'. Needless to say he was despatched forthwith. I immediately telephoned my local CID colleagues who duly confirmed that two such marine engines had been stolen recently from the Hoylake Sailing Club. My colleagues didn't waste time in visiting the home of the youth. After questioning, the youth admitted having offered me the stolen engines (which were recovered) and he was arrested. On his appearance before the Magistrates' Court he was fined for his criminal participation involving the stolen engines.

Some of those I dealt with in the course of my duties in Cheapside included prisoners who were infected with various highlycontagious diseases.

One night, on retiring to bed after completing a late shift, I was telephoned by the Bridewell Surgeon, Dr 'Morrie' Kirwan. The doctor asked if I had any physical contact with a particular prisoner I had dealt with earlier. I confirmed that I had indeed, and was promptly informed that the prisoner was highly infected with scabies. It transpired that I too had been infected. Fortunately and thankfully, my wife had not. Acting on doctor's orders, Marje and I, there and then, bathed, scrubbed and thoroughly disinfected ourselves and although we were instructed to thoroughly wash and disinfect the bedding, I decided to destroy this to eliminate any possibility of further infection. This was not to be the only occasion that a dirty prisoner had infected me with scabies. Once it had been established that a prisoner is suffering from the disease, he or she is immediately isolated before being stripped, washed and disinfected. The prisoner is then kept in isolation and the cell is fumigated and sealed for 24 hours. Unfortunately, the risk from such diseases as scabies from an infected prisoner is one of the hazards of the occupation for a Police Officer.

One morning I was at the counter completing some administrative paperwork when the Bridewell doorbell rang. On looking through the steel hatch I saw that a Chief Superintendent was outside the door seeking admission. I recognised the Chief Super as being one of my colleagues from our CID days. He and I were Detective Constables on the same section and used to be mates. "Hiya Jim," I said as I opened the door and admitted him to our inner sanctum. Once inside Jim's face reddened and he glared at me. As I closed the door behind him Jim furiously tapped his rank insignia on his shoulder and snapped, "Jim! Jim! D'you know who I am?" I was taken aback at the Chief Super's verbal attack. As there was only my colleague, Constable George Emmerson, and myself present, I hadn't considered my greeting as being 'over familiar'. However, Jim obviously did, and it was painfully obvious that promotion had brought about a thick fog, which had eliminated the visibility of our past. Due to his high-handed attitude at such a small and unwitnessed 'breach of etiquette", I couldn't resist replying sarcastically as I turned to George, "Hey George, there's someone here who doesn't know who he is"! The Chief Super was furious at my sarcasm and he requested me to accompany him out of the hearing of my colleague. He then proceeded to give me one almighty dressing down, informing me that in future I address him as SIR! He also threatened me with the big stick of disciplinary proceedings should I ever so err again. Our previous friendship of some years' standing was to terminate there and then, for good.

I wasn't to endear myself to the Governor, or enhance my prospects, some days later whilst working underground preparing for the day's court hearings.

Answering a knock at the outer door I saw my old friend, the solicitor who obtains clients by throwing his cards into cells. He requested admittance to converse with his client before they appeared in court. My colleague inside heard his request and informed me that all three interview cubicles were at present occupied. I relayed the message and told him that he would have to wait outside until such time as he could be admitted. The solicitor then demanded admittance to consult with his client, as there was not much time before the courts started. I again told him that there was no room inside to admit him yet and added, "You should have got out of bed a bit earlier then, shouldn't you?" and closed the door. Yes, another visit from the Complaints Department.

The same solicitor attempted to drop me in the mire by reporting me to a Magistrate in open court for my refusing to allow one of his clients to have a cigarette in his cell. I was asked by the Magistrate if this was true. I denied this, informing the Magistrate that I had allowed his client a cigarette in his cell, but nobody had mentioned anything about a match! My attitude to welfare was not appreciated. Anyway, matches were not allowed inside cells and I didn't possess such an item, being a non-smoker. Furthermore, I was damned if I was running around after this particular man's clients! I had more important things to do.

During the occasional periods I continued with my cartoons of various colleagues and associates. I completed one of Mr Makin and was pleased to learn that he liked it so much, he had it framed and hung in his office where, as far as I am aware, it remains to this day. I also completed one of the Governor, Mr Mothers, and depicted him carrying a large two-bladed axe. Underneath I wrote, "The Axeman" indicating that he was always ready to give someone the 'chop'. Unfortunately, he did not appreciate my humour and made me fully aware that he was 'not amused'.

I now started to spend two evenings of my off-duty time attending night school. There, at Pensby Secondary School on the Wirral, I studied Welsh and learned to speak the language. I persevered until I could converse thoroughly with the 'natives' (it took two years' hard slog!). The relevance of my motive being that I regularly spent my holidays touring that beautiful part of the United Kingdom with my family. Having learned the language proved very rewarding and I was to find that many doors were opened due to my achievement.

It occurred to me that if I could master something as difficult as the Welsh language by relentless study, then I could equally persevere with a view to passing the so far elusive Sergeant's exam. I decided to make a genuine and concerted effort and applied to join the Promotion Study classes. I chose Wallasey Police Station as my class venue, as it was conveniently near to my home. I applied for 'facilities' to attend this once weekly class and the boss gave me a 'flexible' (almost reluctant) "Yes", provided I could be spared. (Suddenly I had become indispensable and might be missed!)

I attended the class every Wednesday afternoon. Officially the times of class were from 3 p.m. until 5 p.m. I can categorically say that I NEVER once missed a class. My class instructor was Sergeant (now Inspector) Mike Carr, a very able and efficient instructor indeed, who took a keen interest in those of his students who he considered to be genuinely keen to pass the exam (as always, we had a few time wasters among the class).

As time went on it was not uncommon for Sergeant Carr to ring me at home after he had marked my 'homework' to give me a telling off for giving what he described as 'silly' answers to some of his questions which he considered I should have got right! Eventually, I bought myself a tape recorder, which at first amused my classmates as I sat at the front of the class recording every word of every lecture. I still possess each of those tapes which contain very thorough and enlightening lectures, most of which is still current legislation. I took my promotion text books with me wherever I went (each one was not much larger than 'pocket' size).

One day I was 'dock officer' in court, sitting through a very minor (and boring) case of a simple drunk trial. I was reading my promotion handbook when the Governor, Mr Mothers, walked into court on a routine 'supervision' visit. On his discovering what it was that I was reading, he asked me to accompany him out of the court into the corridor. There he admonished me severely and instructed me to study in my own time in future, "not the firm's"! I must admit, I was, to say the least, a little upset by the boss's rebuke. Not only did I consider that I wasn't in any way neglectful of my duties, but I considered what I was doing to be (hopefully) beneficial to the job as well as myself, should my efforts ultimately bear fruit! I considered that Mr Mother's reason for my chastisement was nothing more than a 'clash of personalities'. It was not the first time that he had admonished me (usually in front of colleagues) for some petty reason that others were equally responsible for, but nothing ever seemed to be said to anyone else.

By and large, I found that trying to study at the Main Bridewell was difficult. At lunch time I would go into a room, settle down with my books, then in would come the card school. If they played quietly (as they did before I started studying) that would have been OK. However, when I was present, they would make one hell of a row. Due to this, I would sometimes move to another room, but the same would happen again. I was subjected to continual noisy banter and ridicule, and was continually being told that I was wasting my time as I'd never make it!

These comments were mainly from those whose ambitions were nothing more than to hang on to their jobs as 'unofficial jailors' and honorary staff' of the Vernon or Rose and Crown. Their conduct gave me added incentive to succeed.

Studying Hard for the Sergeants' Examination

There were times when I would occasionally deplete my valuable 'time due' to ensure my attendance at the Promotion class. This was not always possible due to staff shortages. These same 'staff shortages' never prevented the Rose and Crown or Vernon pubs being patronised at the same time as my class! .

After a month or so of promotion classes, I decided to attend Wallasey at lunch time and spend the extra time sitting alone with my books and tape recorder in the deserted lecture room. There, I would play a particular lecture over again in seclusion and digest particular points referred to at my leisure. I did this whenever I was on night duty, rest day, or on leave, and I utilised those particular off duty periods for that purpose. Although I was serving in another Division across the Mersey, nobody at Wallasey minded me being there alone in their lecture room, in the beginning.

Each Wednesday when I went to Wallasey I would call in and make a courtesy call to the station Sergeant and, with his blessing, I would proceed to the lecture room, take my place and revise last week's lectures with the help of my tapes, to my heart's content. All went well for some weeks, until one particular Wednesday, when I found the door to the lecture room locked. I returned to the station Sergeant who kindly gave me the key to admit myself to the room.

The following week, the same thing happened again. This time, however, I was informed that the janitor had the key and I should seek him out to get the lecture room door unlocked. The janitor was, in fact, a retired Sergeant who had served with the old Wallasey Borough Police many years earlier.

Eventually I found my 'quarry' and innocently requested that he unlock the lecture room door to allow me in. To my utter surprise he refused. He informed me that I wasn't supposed to be there until 3 p.m. which was as yet three hours away, so I would have to come back later. I couldn't believe it. I had got out of my bed especially (I was on night duty) to give myself those extra hours in the classroom. I asked him again to open the door for me. Again he refused. I became incensed by this ill-mannered man's behaviour. I didn't mince words and informed the ex-Sergeant that he was now "only the bloody lavatory cleaner" and demanded that he open the lecture room door.

Yet again this arrogant man refused me admittance. I saw a chain dangling from his belt to his trouser pocket. I grabbed the chain and wrenched it, pulling a bunch of keys from the obstructive man's pocket, tearing it as I did so. As he attempted to retrieve the keys I pushed him against the wall with one hand and detached the ring of keys from his chain with the other. After something of a minor struggle I wrenched the keys free and made numerous attempts with various keys before finding the correct one and unlocking the door. I opened the door then threw the bunch of keys down the corridor and told him that if ever he tried that sort of thing again, I'd keep the keys and throw him down the corridor instead!

I entered the lecture room and slammed the door. Eventually, after half an hour or so I had cooled down enough to get down to my studies. At 3 o'clock the rest of my student colleagues arrived, together with Sergeant Carr and our class began to get underway.

After about ten minutes or so, the telephone behind the Sergeant's lectern rang. Sergeant Carr turned and picked up the receiver. "Lecture room, Sergeant Carr," he said, then stood stiffly to attention and went on "Constable Turner? Yes, he's here sir!" It always amazes me why people stand to attention when addressing senior officers over the 'phone! Turning to me the Sergeant said, "It's the Chief Super, Swasie. He wants you in his office. What the hell have you done now?"

Although I had never met this particular Chief Superintendent personally, I was aware that he was considered by all to be somewhat eccentric. He was also known to be a keen botanist and recognised as somewhat of an expert on the subject. I donned my cap and left the class to make my way upstairs to the Chief Super's office. As I stood outside and knocked on his door, a voice from within commanded me to enter. I opened the door and entered his carpeted office. I stood to attention, saluted and said, "Constable Turner, sir" I was instructed to enter and close the door behind me. I did as I was told and stood in front of the Chief Super's desk.

The boss came on with all guns blazing! His broadside started with him asking me who the hell did I think I was talking to the station's caretaker the way I did, not to mention the fact that I had also assaulted him by taking his keys from him. The Chief Super was absolutely furious. As he ranted on and on, his face getting more red by the second as he worked himself into a frenzy, my attention was drawn to an unusually shaped cactus in a pot on a shelf behind him. As the boss continued with his tirade I stared, perplexed, at the plant behind him. I interrupted his ravings and asked, "Excuse me sir, I have one of those plants but I don't know what it is."

The Chief Super, knocked out of his stride, hesitated and, looking puzzled, he snapped, "Don't know what is?" I went on, "Behind you sir, isn't that a cactus of some sort?" The Chief Super turned to the potted plant. "Oh this?" He took the plant from the shelf and said, "A relative bought me this, it's a . . . " and went on to give me the full history and pedigree of that particular strain of plant: where it originated from, how to look after it, etc., and continued to educate me in the wonders of botany for a few minutes, rambling on about other similar strains for quite a while. "I'm very keen on botany sir" I lied, and went on to tell him that I intended to purchase books on the subject. The Boss then went on to advise me what were the best informative books to purchase to enhance my knowledge of the subject.

After a considerable time had elapsed, my education on the joys of plant life were finally terminated with the Chief Super saying, "Anyway, I must get on. Call in any time and let me know how you're getting on with your plants." "I will indeed sir," I assured him. Again I stood to attention, saluted him and thanked him for imparting such interesting and informative advice to me.

Closing the door behind me I returned to my class. As I had left my tape running, I could catch up on my missed lecture in my own time later. I intended to keep well out of the Chief Super's way after that, in case he realised that I had pulled a fast one on him. I never had any problems regarding my early attendance at the lecture room, or indeed, any further dealings with that particular janitor again!

I found time to enter some of my artwork in the form of a number of oil paintings I had completed into the Police Art Exhibition, at Fairfield. Amazingly, I won 1st and 3rd prizes in the oil painting section, and 1st, 2nd and 3rd prizes in the water colour section. I was presented with my prizes and certificates by the Assistant Chief Constable, Mr Wright (later to become a Chief Constable in another part of the country).

My main goal, however, was to pass the Sergeant's exam and I directed all my efforts and energy studying to achieve this end. I maintained at least two hours' study every day, irrespective of where I was, or what duty I was on. I studied on relentlessly. I took my family to Anglesey for a caravan holiday during my annual leave and even there, I would leave Marje and young Jo down at the beach while I returned to the caravan for my two hours of study, much to the amazement of those whose company we were in.

Finally, I applied to sit the examination, which was to be held in November 1980. Prior to the exam, I successfully applied for a two week intensive study course to be held at Well Lane, Birkenhead. This course was an absolute boon and I considered it very beneficial indeed. I attended this course, again armed with my cherished tape recorder. Each evening, at the conclusion of the day's lectures, I would go home and retreat to a quiet room and play those lectures over again, until each lecture penetrated my brain and (hopefully) stayed there. I would recite different aspects of legislation, definitions, powers of arrest, until I felt like a walking text book. Even crammed with all this knowledge and secretly, quietly confident, I became nervous and apprehensive as the November date for the all-important exam approached.

After completing my pre-exam intensive study course, and once again going over all that I had been told, the big day dawned. The night before, I retired to bed at 8.30 p.m., determined to be as fresh as possible for the exams. I arrived at Withens Lane College, Wallasey and took my place at the little desk allocated to me in the large lecture theatre. As well as the appointed adjudicators present, I also saw the familiar figure of our class instructor, Sergeant Carr. He was not going to be of any help now, I thought.

The old maxim now applied, "either you know it, or you don't"! Finally, at the appointed time, we were told to pick up our pens and start. The morning was consumed by sitting the first two of the day's three papers. Having spent a number of years in the CID I was reasonably confident with regard to the Crime paper. First we sat the Traffic paper (my worst subject!), followed by the Crime paper. I remained at my desk until we were ordered to put down our pens at lunch time. Per Sergeant Carr's advice, I felt reasonably happy with my morning's hard work, until the 'know all brigade' got to work. "What did you put for question so and so?" they would ask. I replied by quoting my answer to the particular question referred to. I would be greeted with "Oh no, you're wrong, it's so and so" they would say.

By the time I came to sit the final paper of the day (General Police Duties), in the afternoon, my morning's optimism had now evaporated, to be replaced with depression and pessimism. Again I remained at my desk until instructed to put down my pen. I thought I'd done OK but again, but the 'know all brigade' got to work! By the end of the day I wasn't sure how I thought I'd fared. Sergeant Carr and a couple of us from his study class adjourned to the nearby Queens public house in Liscard to perform a thorough post mortem on the day's proceedings (a bit late now, however!)

I decided to keep an open mind as to how I thought I had done. Fate alone would now decide if I had put enough effort into my endeavours.

I returned to work and carried on with my duties as normal. It would be quite a few weeks before the results became known and put me out of my misery.

The summer of 1981 saw the infamous riots erupt in a number of cities throughout the country. Liverpool certainly suffered its share of chaos, fear and anarchy. Many buildings were destroyed and there were numerous casualties; sadly, some fatal. During this time, all hands were mustered to the 'thin blue line' and assistance also came from many other forces. Many of us were absent from home for days.

Toxteth riots of 1981

Subsequently, and thankfully, order (and sanity) was finally restored and the City was eventually returned to some semblance of peace and tranquillity. Due to these riots, the courts were inundated with riot-related cases for many months after.

Finally, after continual scrutiny of the daily Chief Constable's orders, the exam results were published. As soon as the despatches arrived in their leather satchel at the Main Bridewell, I dived into its contents and retrieved the orders from amongst the rest of the morning's delivery. The orders were grabbed and opened out onto the Bridewell counter. Colleagues were jostling me and peering over my shoulder to see if anyone had passed that they knew (I was the only one from the Bridewell at that time who had sat the exam). I found my name - I had passed the Traffic paper. Looking further, I saw that I had passed the GPD (General Police Duties) paper. Now, what about the Crime paper? Would you believe it? I had failed it! I had failed the very paper which I had always considered to be my best subject.

Oh, I was so disappointed. There was one consolation, one comforting light visible at the end of the long tunnel. I had gained such excellent marks in the two successful papers that I would be allowed to re-sit the one failed paper the next November. If I were to fail at this attempt, then I would have to sit all three papers again twelve months on. That was a dejecting, chilling thought . I would be back to square one !

Police Art Exhibition. .Assistant Chief Constable Wright with Swasie.

Well Lane Police Station , Birkenhead.

Although I was grossly disappointed, I was more determined than ever to pass this one paper. There was no way that I was going to let it slip away and let success elude me on getting myself this far after all these years. Once again, I disciplined myself and got down to very serious and devoted study. Again I was to experience ribald remarks, mickey taking, noisy interruptions, the television being turned up loud as I sat in the far corner of the room.

I again applied for the next November's exam and again applied for facilities for attending Sergeant Carr's study classes. I also applied for the intensive study course to be held prior to the exam. All my requests were again granted and I attended at Wallasey once more. This time I experienced no hindrance or obstruction from the self-opinionated janitor! I was, however, threatened by Sergeant Carr that should I fail the one forthcoming paper, meticulous arrangements would be made for me to attend for treatment at an eminent taxidermist! Again, out came my cherished and trusty tape recorder.

The days, weeks and months went by - work and study, work and study. I used to spend my lunch periods either underground in a cold, deserted cell, or in the tranquillity of a quiet and empty courtroom, completely devoid of any form of interruption. I never ventured out in the evening and again, my leave period still included my daily two hours of study. Such was the paramount importance of my total concentration in my quest to eliminate failure again. Twelve months after my previous (partly successful) attempt, I sat my Crime paper again. This time the venue for the exam was Mather Avenue Training School. As the Traffic and GPD papers were being sat in the morning, I needed only to attend for the Crime examination paper after lunch.

I arrived over an hour early and sat in the seclusion of my car to once more go over my general notes. Eventually, the candidates for the day's exams started drifting past my car on the school's car park as they made to their classrooms for the afternoon's final paper of the day.

Many were genuine candidates like myself. Others were here for nothing more than a day's outing (as I shamefully had been on all too many previous occasions). I now realised how very annoying and distracting the latter category could be! These particular colleagues tried to encourage me to have a 'quick pint' as they had been doing during their lunch break. Just as if! And throw away two years of sheer hard work, just to be one of the boys? I should cocoa!

We all took our places for the afternoon's exam. I was sweating with concern and apprehension. I so much wanted to pass. I'd worked really hard and prayed that I wouldn't fail. Eventually, we were told by the adjudicator to start. I picked up my paper and studied it meticulously, and ever so slowly digested the contents of the paper. I liked it!

I settled down to writing my answers, remembering the very important lecture on 'exam technique'. Each question carried a maximum number of marks, sometimes as many as twelve marks for one question. Therefore, they must be answered very carefully. An example of how important exam technique is would be as follows.

A set of circumstances would be given and the offence outlined would be, say, an offence of Burglary. The particular question would be worth twelve marks. Assuming the candidate wrote down that the offence disclosed was "Burglary" he may receive 2 marks, as the answer was correct in essence. However, if the candidate were to disclose various aspects which caused him to arrive at his answer, such as quoting part of the definition which related to the criminal's actions, i.e. "as the person had entered the building or part of the building as a trespass (as per the definition contained in the Theft Act 1968)", he would gain, say 3 marks (we now have 5 marks). "Therein did steal or attempt to steal" (3 further marks) "or commit criminal damage therein" (3 marks) "contrary to section 9(1)(a)" (2 marks). It will be seen that we have now accumulated a total of 13 marks. The candidate would be given the maximum 12 for just that one answer. This is what is referred to in the lecture of 'exam technique'. It is obvious then, how important these lectures are"

My afternoon paper started well but after ten minutes or so, and every few minutes thereafter, proceedings were constantly interrupted by the sound of chairs scraping the floor and candidates selfishly clomping off to the toilet (accompanied by one of the adjudicators), as the need to relieve themselves of the lunchtime ale consumption manifested itself. I (and no doubt many others) found this to be very distracting and frustrating, as my concentration was broken many times due to these interruptions. So much so that finally, I threw down my pen, summoned an adjudicator and complained bitterly. My complaint fell on stony ground. How I cursed those selfish individuals who had gone to the pub during the lunch break and now found that they couldn't sit for more than a short time before they needed to use the toilet, on such an important day as this (for some of us). Even I, when I had made previous (not so genuine) efforts at taking the exams, was certainly not guilty of such inconsiderate conduct.

At the conclusion of the afternoon's exam I made my sentiments known to all those present, although the offenders had long since left, not bothering to utilise what time there was, only those of us who really cared stayed until the 'final bell'. Although one must never 'count one's chickens', I was quite happy with my effort and was reasonably confident of being successful, (however, let's wait for the results?) This time I avoided the 'know all brigade' and made my way home. Once home, I put the car away and went to my local for a long (and I considered) well-earned pint. In fact, I ended up somewhat inebriated after releasing all my pent-up tensions of the past two years and, quaffing considerable quantities of ale, I really looked forward to the results being published. If I failed this time I wouldn't bother attempting it again, I told myself. Again I returned to work hoping and praying that my attempts would be successful. If only to see the cynical grins wiped from the faces of my sceptical colleagues!

Only time would tell. I certainly wondered what my future held for me at this time?

Chapter Fifteen - Treading New ground

As I resumed work yet again, I tried not to think of the exams, but I found that I was becoming more impatient as I awaited the forthcoming results. All Police officers keep a pocket book in which are recorded their various duties, times, incidents etc. Being in the Bridewell, however, I considered that there was no real need to maintain meticulous entries other than on duty and off duty times. The case would be totally different when engaged with outside duties involving arrests or other similar incidents. Whilst in the Bridewell, I, no doubt like many others, sometimes allowed my note book entries to lapse, then I would need to spend a lot of time having to sit down and bring it back up to date. On one fateful occasion, my book became so far behind that when I made an arrest, I realised that I would need another book to record my evidence, as it would have been impossible for me to make a chronological record of every consecutive day since the last entry. It would be far easier to obtain a new book and start it off with my new arrest. (Failure to maintain one's notebook is a disciplinary offence!)

I approached one of the Sergeants, Sergeant Burrows, and requested a new book. I was issued with the item for which I signed. On being asked for my old book, I promised the Sergeant I would hand it in the following day, as I had left it at home! On receipt of my new book I entered details of my current arrest and prepared my evidence.

The following day, thinking (and hoping) that Sergeant Burrows would forget to ask me for my old book, I went about my duties. I was mistaken! As soon as he set eyes on me, the first thing Sergeant Burrows asked was "Have you got your old book, Swas?" I told him that I had inadvertently damaged the book (I had in fact singed it previously) and added that I thought that it had been burned and destroyed by mistake with the other household rubbish. Again, mistakenly, I thought that my explanation had been accepted. How wrong I was! Sergeant Burrows informed the Governor, Mr Mothers, who then sent for me and demanded an explanation regarding my failure to hand in my old note book. I explained to the Governor that I had inadvertently destroyed the book when I burned some rubbish. I considered it far better now to 'write the book off' than produce a singed and very out of date document. The Governor informed me that my explanation was not good enough. I was cautioned there and then, and told that I was to be reported with a view to disciplinary proceedings being instituted against me for 'Damaging Police Property'. This was now becoming a very serious matter indeed. For me to 'come clean' now, and produce the book, would reveal an equally heinous offence, that of telling a falsehood. As I had previously singed the book, my tale did have some semblance of truth I thought! I decided to leave matters as they now were and take whatever was to come my way regarding the matter. I pointed out to the Governor that I was sweating with anticipation of the forthcoming exam results, and added that if I were to pass the exam, a discipline hearing before the

Chief Constable would undoubtedly dash any hopes of my future promotion.   The blank expression on the Governor's face indicated to me that I was obviously wasting my breath and was 'piddling into the wind'! I do appreciate that my Police note book was an official document, but as it is usually only used as an 'aide memoir' at court hearings, or to verify hours worked or duties performed, the only entries that particular book contained were mainly my times of going on duty and going off duty. The one or two arrest cases it had contained had been dealt with long ago. I felt strongly that the Governor need not have been made aware of such trivia. However, now that he was aware, he was now about to eliminate any prospect of promotion chances for me, even before I knew if I had qualified or not.

I again asked the Boss to deal with the matter leniently as I stood to lose quite a lot. The Governor would not be moved. I left his office utterly dejected and hated him for his complete lack of compassion over such a minor matter. My sentiments were no different towards the Sergeant either, as he needn't have made an issue of it by reporting it to the Governor. Again, the issue certainly indicated the priorities held by some senior officers.

I was duly visited by the Complaints and Discipline Department and served with the appropriate forms. Normally I wouldn't admit that it was daylight at noon, but this time I decided to 'throw my hands up' and place myself at the mercy of the Chief Constable at my forthcoming disciplinary hearing.

Whilst awaiting my fate, the exam results were published in Chief Constable's orders. I had passed!! I had actually passed my Sargeant's exam! I was congratulated by some of my colleagues and received 'phone calls from officers (some of them senior) from other divisions. I hadn't divulged the fact that I was 'getting done' so I was continually being asked why it was that I looked so miserable when I should have been rejoicing at the news. I was pleased, I was jubilant: however, my joy was marred by the fact that I thought that all was now to no avail. All because the Governor couldn't have made a decision for himself over such a bloody silly matter. I did deserve a 'kick in the pants' for allowing myself to get into such an avoidable predicament, but to 'do' me on discipline was way over the top in my opinion.

Eventually, the dreaded day dawned. I was instructed to go to St Anne Street Police Station and there attend the Chief Superintendent's office for my case to be heard. With feelings of dread and trepidation I attended in my best 'bib and tucker'. I was ushered upstairs by a Sergeant who deposited me outside the Chief Super's door. I was told to remain there while he went inside and announced my presence. A short time later the Sergeant left the office, instructing me to remain where I was until the 'come in' sign illuminated on the Chief's door. I stood there in the corridor as colleagues and civilian staff (male and female) walked past me, all knowing that I had been a 'naughty boy'! I felt just like a delinquent schoolboy standing 'under the clock' outside the headmaster's study!

After what seemed an eternity, the 'come in' light flashed on. I knocked and entered, stood to attention and threw up a smart salute. The Chief Superintendent, none other than Alec Williams, my old CID boss, appeared to be sitting a mile away across the large, carpeted office. Acknowledging my salute, the Chief Super thanked me and gestured for me to close the door and stand at his desk. I stood in front of the Chief's large desk while he perused the papers compiled by the Governor, outlining my mortal sins. There was silence, broken only by the occasional sounds of activity from outside in the corridor. I stood there and gazed through the large window behind the Chief, admiring the wonderful, panoramic view of the City and the River Mersey beyond, looking towards the Wirral, sitting quietly on the skyline. Eventually, Mr Williams looked up at me and said, slowly, "Right" Before we go any further Swasie, either the Chief Constable can deal with this or I can. Which way d'you want it dealt with?" I had no hesitation in replying that I would like him (Mr Williams) to deal with the matter. Instead of the Chief Super tearing into me as I expected, he instructed me to remove my cap and sit down. "I don't think Mr Mothers likes you very much does he?" said the Chief, as he leaned forward and rested his chin on his left hand, as he gently puffed at his pipe held with the other. "No Sir, he doesn't." I replied. Mr Williams went on. "Perhaps if you were to roll down your shirtsleeves and hide those tattoos and trim that bloody monstrosity under your nose, it might help." I shrugged my shoulders. "I've told you to trim that moustache before," Mr Williams went on. Bloody hell, I thought, that was years ago; I thought he'd forgotten about that!

The Chief Super then changed tack. He congratulated me on passing my exams and added that if anyone deserved to pass, I did! He then informed me that he felt that this matter should never have gone beyond the Sergeant. He didn't agree that such a small issue should risk blighting my hard-earned chances of promotion as he , the Chief Super, was fully aware of my pedigree as a hard-working bobby. I was assured that the matter would go no further and I was told to go out and "concentrate on getting through my promotion boards". I felt choked by the boss's kind remarks. I stood up, donned my cap and again saluted smartly a man whom I respected very much. "Thank you very much indeed, Sir," I said. I was so grateful that common sense had prevailed. The Chief Superintendent dismissed me with, "You soft sod, now bugger off. Let's hope that the next time I see you, you will be wearing your stripes." I had no intention of 'gloating' as I appreciated the fact that I had certainly been the author of my own destiny by being so careless. I would, however, give the impression to Mothers that I had received at least a severe reprimand!

When the dust had settled concerning this little 'skirmish' and staff shortages started to occur among the Sergeants, due to sickness or annual leave, I eventually started to perform the duties of 'Acting' Sergeant. I was at that time the only one qualified to act as such. Later, I became responsible for identification parades. A very important step with regard to supervisory experience. I took this role very seriously. I started to stand in for any Sergeant who was absent for one reason or another. I was finding my new various acting roles very beneficial. In time, I occasionally accepted charges at the Bridewell counter as prisoners were brought before the charge desk. Now I was getting down to the real 'nitty gritty' duties of a Sergeant. Wearing my two (Acting Sergeant's) chrome chevrons on my epaulettes was the proud reward for my previous efforts and sacrifices. My next (and equally difficult) hurdles to overcome were those of my promotion boards.

Some of my spare time had now become occupied in assisting to run a local boxing club in the periphery of Toxteth. A fellow Sergeant (Bob Fisher) and I devoted a lot of our off duty time in helping to run the club. I attended each week and trained local youths in the noble art, assisted by some of the enthusiastic local residents and parents. Fixtures and tournaments were arranged at different venues, including Birkenhead and parts of the Wirral as well as Liverpool. I looked forward to each training session and used to spar with various (some very talented) youths, many of whom had potential and no doubt aspired to be budding future champions. Those lads at the Myrtle Boxing Club were a credit to the locality and all disciplined themselves to hard training for the benefit of themselves and their club. Most training nights commenced with Bob and I accompanying the older members out on a run before returning to the gym for further training on the bags and other equipment, and to assist the young boxers to perfect the art of 'ringcraft'.

At work, my duties continued to involve plenty of 'acting' (Sergeant) which made work once again interesting. I wondered what my promotion board would entail? We were joined at the Main by another 'passed' man, and old friend from the beginning, Constable Kenny Moore. Ken and I got on well together and shared the 'acting' duties.

One of our Sergeants, Derek Hough, was a very clever and able man with the pen. Derek wrote a very amusing tale of Ken and I attending our (imaginary) Promotion Board. This was circulated among the Bridewell staff, much to everyone's amusement, including mine and Ken's.

In the summer of '82 I successfully completed a computer course at Knowsley Hall. These courses were to train officers in the use of the PNC (Police National Computer). It was considered vital that as many officers as possible should become proficient in its use. To some, the course may have seemed easy. To me, however, computers were a new experience. The course was interesting enough and at its conclusion we all became qualified in the use of computers and returned to our various stations. I still carried on as Acting Sergeant in every department at the Main Bridewell.

One of my roles took the form of 'Regulating Sergeant'. This job catered for the handling of prisoners received from various prisons and remand centres, together with juveniles who were in custody, and the allocating of cells and courts, and eventually organising transport for their return to the various incarceration establishments. When performing as Regulating Sergeant, I found 'instant' popularity, as part of my job was to arrange escorts to man the prison transport. This included a lot of overtime working by those selected. Officers, hungry for any possibility of working overtime, would frequent 'my' office offering assistance, before casually requesting that they be selected as the day's escort. Quite often there was a certain amount of bickering among some of the men. Some would come and complain because so and so had done it yesterday and it was their turn now! I began to think that I should have a jar of Smarties on my desk to pacify those I had not selected! Some of the escorts abused the system by deliberately taking their time to return from the prison run so that they could book off late. I found it necessary to monitor some of these selfish individuals as their activities drew the unwelcome attentions of the Governor. I would then have to explain why certain officers always finished late from escort duty while others didn't. The later that one finished, the more one's allowances increased thus added to their already inflated overtime bill.

I was called urgently from the regulating office one morning and summoned up into court to assist a prison officer who was being violently attacked by his prisoner in the dock as he tried to escape. It was with considerable difficulty that the prisoner was eventually overpowered and taken down below and forcibly placed into a cell. The prison officer needed hospital treatment for injuries he sustained during the struggle. The incident was witnessed by all in court, including a number of solicitors, who were standing nearby, none of whom offered to assist the prison officer, prior to or following my arrival. Situation normal!

Another off-duty incident occurred one Sunday morning, as I was enjoying a lie in on my day off. This incident was NOT to assist my promotion prospects however!

My deep slumbers were disturbed by the ring of the telephone at 8 a.m. Bleary eyed and half-awake I picked up the confounded instrument and heard the distressed voice of a family friend, Barbara (Babs) Dodd. "Swasie, come quickly. Bill (her husband) and I have caught two men in the 'yard'!" Mr and Mrs Dodd were the owners of a large DIY store and building supply yard situated a mile away in nearby Moreton.

This Sunday morning, as usual, Mr and Mrs Dodd had gone to check the yard, which was closed for business for the weekend. On their arrival, they were curious to find a dilapidated old Ford Cortina Estate parked near to their premises. Inside the vehicle they saw camouflage jackets, black woollen ski masks, spades, nets and a black Labrador dog. They saw that part of the fence to the yard had been interfered with and was damaged. They opened up the yard and entered. On checking the premises they found two men in their early twenties, with another Labrador dog, hiding in a storage shed. Each man wore camouflage trousers and each was in possession of a spade. On being challenged by Mr Dodd and asked to account for their presence in his yard, one of the men stated that they were "after badgers"! Both men became abusive and threatened Mr Dodd. Mrs Dodd, fearing for her husband, immediately went and dialled 999 and called the Police. She then rang me, saying that Bill was in trouble and she was frightened for his safety.

After quickly donning tee shirt and jeans I was at the yard within 15 minutes. There, I was met by Mrs Dodd who by now was standing with her husband and the two men by the Cortina Estate. The two men were still being very abusive and intimidating to the couple, each of whom were well past middle age. I produced my warrant card and identified myself to the two abusive young men. Mr Dodd related the circumstances to me concerning their being found in his yard a short time earlier. I listened to Mr Dodd's tale then asked the two men if what Mr Dodd had said was true. One of the men replied, "We were only looking for badgers." I told them that I was not satisfied with the explanation given and was detaining them pending the arrival of the local Police. Again, both men became abusive, informing me (to no avail) that they "knew their rights"!

After what seemed a long wait (about 20 minutes) we were eventually joined by a Constable who arrived in his patrol car. The officer and I knew each other and Mr Dodd again related the full circumstances of the incident to the officer in the presence and hearing of the two men. The officer listened to Mr Dodd and after he had finished, the Constable asked the two 'offenders' if they had heard and understood Mr Dodd's allegations. Each man stated that they were "only looking for badgers". The officer produced a pad of 'document production' tickets (Forms HORT/1) and ascertained who was the owner of the Cortina.

One of the men admitted to being the vehicle's owner, but as he was unable to produce any documents relating to his use and ownership, the officer completed one of the 'tickets' from the pad and issued it to the owner, instructing him to produce the relevant documents within five days, as failure to do so would result in prosecution. The officer then wrote down the particulars of the two men on the cardboard back of the pad (instead of into his official note book)! He then gave the two men a telling off, threatening each that if they were to repeat such conduct they would 'find themselves in trouble'! Both men then made for their vehicle. Mr Dodd exploded. He insisted that the two be arrested for trespassing on his premises.

The Constable (to my sheer amazement) informed Mr Dodd that as there had been 'no offences committed', there wasn't anything he could do other than what he had already done, and reminded Mr Dodd that the two had been given a 'stern warning'. Mrs Dodd joined in her husband's verbal attack on the Constable. "No bloody wonder the public have no faith in the Police when you treat law-abiding citizens like this," she snapped. She went on to express her utter disgust at the officer's complacency and lethargic attitude. The Constable countered by insisting that he had dealt with the matter correctly, and added that he would not be told how to carry out his duties by members of the public.

I decided that I had seen and heard enough. I went to the officer as he was about to get into his car. I asked him why the two men were not being arrested. The officer curtly told me to mind my own business and reminded me that I was 'on his patch', as I was a Liverpool bobby and he was the man in charge here in Moreton. "Anyway," he went on, "what am I going to arrest them for?" I couldn't believe what I was hearing. The two men thought things were highly amusing and no doubt couldn't believe their good fortune seeing two bobbies arguing and appearing not to be conversant with the law. Mr and Mrs Dodd, however, were far from being amused.

I pointed out to the officer (who either didn't know or didn't WANT to know) what offences had actually been committed by the two men he was allowing to leave. Firstly, I informed him, they had damaged Mr Dodd's fence to the yard when they forced the corrugated sheeting apart, committing the offence of Criminal Damage. Once inside, they were then Found on Enclosed Premises. On their own admission, they were intent on Badger Baiting and being in possession of various items to facilitate their criminal activities (dogs, spades, nets, etc.) they were Going Equipped to commit such offences, as it could also be fairly assumed that they Intended to Steal due to their unlawful presence in a DIY establishment. Surely there were enough offences disclosed now to justify an arrest? The Constable shrugged his shoulders and again told me not to tell him how to do his job! He then got into his vehicle and drove off. The two 'offenders' left also, hardly daring to believe their good luck. This incident revealed one of the most blatant cases of 'neglect of duty' I was to witness throughout my entire career. I received a lot of flak from both Mr and Mrs Dodd as to the incompetence and sheer lack of care, not to mention utter laziness, by the Police, which indicated why the public was losing confidence in the service! Although I could certainly understand and sympathise with their frustration, I nevertheless was quick to sharply remind my two friends that I also was part of the Police service which they were referring to, and emphasised that I too ,was just as annoyed, and highly embarrassed, by my colleague's disgraceful conduct. I was equally quick to point out that the officer concerned did not represent the many, many enthusiastic officers that went about their duties diligently and thoroughly every day and who were not to be categorised in the same vein as he who had caused their vehement criticism of the Police.

They did agree with my sentiments and were extremely grateful for my assistance. Mr and Mrs Dodd could not be pacified, however, and they informed me that they intended to make an official complaint to the highest authority in the Police Service regarding the utterly irresponsible and contemptible way in which such a blatant criminal act had been dealt with. I must admit, I totally agreed with their sentiments whole heartedly and couldn't blame them one bit for being so angry and critical.

Mr Dodd did indeed write to the Chief Constable and complained bitterly at the treatment he had received. The Dodds were subsequently visited by a uniformed Inspector who unsuccessfully tried to resolve the problem amicably. Mr and Mrs Dodd both insisted on carrying on with their complaint against the Police. The Complaints and Discipline Department subsequently visited the Dodd's home in the form of a Superintendent. Both complainants gave very full and thorough statements in which both included my attendance at the incident. Consequently, I was now officially involved in a complaint against a colleague! As the matter went on I was eventually visited by the Superintendent also. The visit took place one evening as Marje and I were settled in front of the television. Although I didn't know this particular Superintendent very well, I did know him by sight and had already formed the impression that he seemed an arrogant individual. On the evening of his visit my wife admitted him into our home and told him to make himself comfortable. As he did so he looked around the room and critically eyed various items of Police memorabilia which adorned the walls and furniture. He looked at some wooden shields bearing badges of forces in which I had previously (and proudly) served, framed commendations and Shipwreck and Humane awards, and commented that the room looked like a "bloody Police shrine"! I didn't like his attitude at all.

My wife asked the Super if he would like a cup of tea or coffee. He politely requested the latter with one sugar. The Super's eyes then settled on my uniform cap, sitting on top of the television with its highly polished peak and 'quartered' top, its badge shining above the chequered band. The Superintendent criticised the position of the badge, telling me it should straddle the band itself and added that if I were under him, that's the way it would be! I hastily and curtly reminded him that as I wasn't under him the problem wouldn't arise, and the badge would be remaining where it was! (Clang! I sincerely hoped that in future I would never be posted to where he would be in charge!)

The Super then got down to business and pulled out a file from his briefcase. He read through his notes and then placed the appropriate blank statement forms onto the case in his lap. The Super went on to clinically inform me of the reason for his visit and outlined Mr & Mrs Dodd's complaints against the colleague concerned. After he did this I was asked if I was prepared to make a statement to confirm or rebut the allegations contained in the Dodds' statements, which, he reminded me, contained highly critical and defamatory comments about a 'serving colleague'! (placing emphasis on the latter). I confirmed that I would be prepared to substantiate all of the Dodds' criticisms, and was subjected to one or two uncomplimentary remarks for being so willing to "condemn" a colleague. This was both untrue and unfair, as the sole responsibility for the whole saga rested with the officer's failure to perform his duty properly.

Undeterred, I gave a statement concerning the unsavoury incident on that fateful Sunday morning, and had no qualms about backing my two friends; there was no way I was going against them to assist an idle, incompetent and unjustified member of the Police force! My wife, in the meantime, had been tactfully absent from the room, being engaged with various chores in the kitchen, including making coffee for us all. My wife entered the room and again asked if the Super took sugar. The Super confirmed he only took one sugar and then asked Marje if she would leave the room as what he and I were discussing was 'confidential'. I was furious at his cheek. How dare he ask my wife, in her own home, to leave the room. I stood up and told my wife that it didn't matter about the coffee

245

as the Superintendent was leaving. I reminded him that he was in my house, and under my roof, and I would make decisions, not him. I politely escorted him to the door and bade him good evening! After he had left, I returned to the room and there received a lot of flak from my wife, for ME being rude to HIM!

There was no doubt in my mind that due to my audacity in standing up for myself in my own home, plus my unpopular stand with the complainants, Mr and Mrs Dodd, the incident might have an adverse effect on any future promotion prospects. However, only time would tell. The complaint went on and eventually reached its conclusion, but not to the satisfaction of the Dodds. Fortunately, I was never called to give evidence in the matter, as I certainly would have found it very distasteful giving evidence against a colleague. However, I would not have shirked my responsibilities. Although the matter was eventually resolved, neither Mr nor Mrs Dodd would ever forget the treatment they received on that Sunday.

I plodded on at work and awaited my promotion board, wondering now, when that would be?

Chapter Sixteen - Signs of Movement

Further incidents, both on and off duty, occurred with regularity, one involving the prosecution of a 'reckless' driver who I reported for his inconsiderate and blatant recklessness whilst driving through the Mersey tunnel during a morning rush hour in heavy traffic. This particular man was heavily punished financially.

One morning, I received a buff-coloured, official-looking envelope in the morning's despatches. On the front, in bold type, it was addressed to 'Acting Sergeant 2425 Turner, Main Bridewell', and in the top left-hand corner was the word 'Confidential' in capital letters. Wondering what it was, I retreated to 'my' office and closed the door behind me. I opened the letter apprehensively, wondering if 'Mr Discipline' wanted to speak to me again! However, I was pleasantly surprised to read that I was to parade at Force Headquarters on Wednesday, 24 November 1982 at 11.30 a.m., to attend my Promotion Board!

My heart was pounding and although I was overjoyed, I was also a little nervous. Even though I had awaited this moment with impatience I now began to worry about various things, not least about who would be the senior officers on the board. Oh God, I sincerely hoped that the Super who I had deprived of his coffee at my home would not be one of them! I had three weeks to don my 'Promotion Board head' What would they ask me? Would the burned note book rear its ugly head? What about the Councillor and his Superintendent friend I had upset while I was at Lower Lane? All the things that could prejudice my chances now frighteningly manifested themselves to cause me torment. Well, I would have to take what came on the day. I would have to concentrate on making sure that I impressed those who were to interview me.

I busied myself asking those Sergeants and Inspectors whom I could trust what they would do in certain circumstances. I asked what they would do in hypothetical situations and 'picked' their experienced, supervisory brains to arm myself with as much ammunition as I could. I knew that it was almost certain that the favourite question concerning drinking on duty would be asked. I also knew that to give a narrow, and categorical answer without an accompanying explanation to such a question on that subject might be detrimental. It might appear that the obvious answer would be to say what the board wanted to hear, as opposed to giving a reasonable and logical answer that had been given some thought, before being offered. I tried to anticipate what questions would be asked of me and thought about what would be the most impressive answers to such questions.

At last the big day arrived. I cadged a lift to Headquarters in a patrol vehicle, ensuring that my arrival was at least half an hour before the appointed time. At 11.30 a.m. sharp I was marched into the interview room by a Sergeant. I saw the expressionless faces of the three senior officers who were sitting behind a large, polished, mahogany table, in front of which was a solitary chair. I was pleased (and relieved) to see that two of the officers were the familiar faces of ex-bosses of mine. The

Board consisted of Assistant Chief Constable Burrows, Assistant Chief Constable Crawford (Board Chairman) and Superintendent Hoole: the latter two I had previously served under and held each in high esteem. I certainly felt pleased and a little relaxed on seeing them. I considered (and hoped) that I had enjoyed a good relationship with each in the past. I didn't know Mr Burrows other than by sight.

I stood smartly to attention and saluted the Board. "Constable Turner, gentlemen" grovelled the Sergeant as he announced me, before smartly about-turning and leaving the room, closing the door behind him. Mr Crawford, being the true gentleman that he is, thanked me for my formal acknowledgement and instructed me to sit down and make myself comfortable, adding that I could remove my cap if I so wished. Both Mr Crawford and Mr Hoole knew my pedigree well!

The three men then huddled together and held a whispered conversation while they decided in which order they would address me. Mr Burrows started the ball rolling by asking me "why I wanted to become a Sergeant"! I wasn't expecting that one! To many, being asked why one wished to aspire to higher rank might seem an easy question. I found it hard to think of an appropriate answer which would impress. I sat for a moment and pondered. I wasn't rushing into anything! I finally decided that I would have to 'sell' myself, as if I were talking to a prospective purchaser. I rambled on about my capabilities (and virtues?) and rabbited on about how I considered my experiences would be beneficial to other younger and inexperienced officers should I be elevated to higher rank. I was allowed to prattle on for five minutes or so, informing all present how good I was and how I thought the service would benefit from my being made a Sergeant. Mr Burrows threw a few other questions, including one or two 'low balls' but I managed to maintain my 'innings' and keep up what I considered a 'mean score'!

Mr Hoole then took the reins. He was more gentle with me, although he was very thorough. Not for one moment did I think he was gullible in any manner or form. He was akin to a hospital consultant standing at a patient's bedside putting the young post-graduate doctor through his 'diagnostic' paces concerning the patient (in this case, the patient being the job, the 'young' post-graduate being myself). Mr Hoole appeared to be impressed with the way I was conducting myself and he seemed equally impressed with my answers to his questions and the way I put them over.

Finally, I was addressed by the Board's Chairman, Mr Crawford. He covered everything: foot patrolling, my opinions regarding the arming of the Police, my involvement with the Boxing Club (how the hell did he find out about that?) and other various aspects of my life on and off duty. I felt at ease with him, as I had with Mr Hoole. Finally, Mr Burrows decided that he wanted 'another go'. It had to be him who asked me the question which I had been waiting for since my interview began!

"Now Turner, you are on duty one night and you discover one of your men drinking on duty in the back of a pub. What do you do?! Again, to some the answer may appear to be simple. It is a disciplinary offence to drink on duty, full stop! Do you tell the Board what you think they want to hear (the text book reply, that it is a disciplinary offence and that the bobby should be suspended and reported forthwith?), or do you indicate to them that you have a mind of your own, capable of delving into the matter as to what had motivated the officer to contravene the regulations governing such conduct BEFORE reaching a decision? Either way, one could sink or swim by whichever answer he gave.

I decided to answer Mr Burrows' question head on with complete honesty, ignoring what a Sergeant 'should' do in the circumstances and concentrating on deciding what I 'would' do and, more importantly, why. I pointed out that having been a member of the CID, as he himself had, I had frequently drank on duty and respectfully pointed out that I considered many others in the force had done so at one time or another. I told him that I would address the matter on its individual merit. It would be very important to ascertain WHY the officer was risking his job by so imbibing. He may be under some form of pressure or strain, either financially or domestically. He may be indulging in 'concert' with someone he is trying to comfort due to some tragedy or other. If this were the case I considered that the matter could be dealt with at 'Sergeant' level by words of warning, even threats. If, on the other hand, it was revealed that the Constable was indulging purely for self-gratification and was blatantly neglecting his duties by doing so, then I would not hesitate to bring the 'big stick' of disciplinary proceedings out of the cupboard and use it accordingly. Again, I emphasised that circumstances would have to decide the appropriate action to be taken in each individual case.

I don't know if my 'sermon' impressed the questioner, Mr Burrows, but both Mr Crawford and Mr Hoole congratulated me on giving what they each considered to be a fair and impressive answer. Mr Burrows made no comment one way or the other!

After being questioned and conversed with for five minutes short of one hour, the Board concluded their interview. I was again politely thanked by Mr Crawford on behalf of the Board members as I stood to attention and saluted before taking my leave. I left Headquarters and took a leisurely stroll through the City centre and slowly (and pensively) made my way back to the Main Bridewell for my lunch. I thought that I had conducted myself well and sincerely hoped my efforts were good enough to have carried me through the first of my two Boards. I wouldn't know for some time yet.

I could never understand the philosophy of keeping candidates in the dark for so long before letting them know how they had fared. I was aware that Promotion Board passes were not to be taken for granted, as such passes were very much at a premium. I knew of many frustrated and bitter officers who had passed their exams only to be thwarted from further progress towards promotion by failing a Promotion Board. It was as if the promotional exam was the first fence of the infamous Grand National race, the two Promotion Boards were 'Beechers Brook'! The winning post was the promotion itself, the Sergeant's stripes being the ultimate 'accolade'! I sincerely hoped that I completed the 'course' successfully and eventually rode home the winner!

I continued as Acting Sergeant and ultimately appeared before my second (and if successful, my final) Promotion Board almost twelve months later. This time I was more prepared and confident. For some reason, I didn't have the feelings of trepidation that I had prior to my first Board.

My only anxiety before my second Board concerned who the Board members might be. I didn't want any hiccups now by facing anyone who may (rightly or wrongly) have an axe to grind for one reason or another, and be in a position to adversely decide my future. As it happened, I had no such problems and all went well. Again, at the conclusion of my interview, I was confident that I had answered all that had been asked of me in what I considered to have been an impressive and efficient manner.

Time went on and eventually I was informed that I had passed my final Board. I was now fully eligible to be promoted to the rank of 'most esteemed and illustrious' Sergeant! But would I be? And if so, when? From now on, I would be continually scrutinising orders hoping to see my name appear 'in lights', officially announcing that I had made it and being at long last promoted. I was to have a long wait! If patience is deemed a virtue, then by Jove, I became an ardent sinner!

Time passed ever so slowly and promotions were announced with frustrating irregularity at lengthy intervals. Each time a promotion or promotions were published, I was disappointed to see that it was always someone else, never me. Again, this brought ribald remarks from those of my colleagues who were pleased to point out that I would never 'get made'. Oh, how wonderful it would be for me to indicate the contrary to those jealous bastards! As time went on I started to worry when I saw names appear in the promotion list of those who had sat and passed the exams AFTER me, or, more frustrating still, those who had to endure their Promotion Boards again, after failing.

It began to dawn on me that being at the Main Bridewell, I was nothing more than a 'screw', a gaoler, an Acting Sergeant in a promotional cul-de-sac. It appeared that I may well be 'out of sight', and 'out of sight' as the saying goes could well mean that I was also 'out of mind'. It was becoming painfully obvious that there appeared to be only one remedy; I must get out of the Main Bridewell and go back out among the 'angry men'. This would certainly entail a large amount of risk, as, having lengthy service (twenty-odd years) under my belt, do I go back out onto the streets as a 'new' bobby amongst all the youngsters? And if I don't get promoted, milk padlocks on three shifts in all weathers for the remainder of my service, or do I stay where I am with an inside job and at least continue 'acting' as a Sergeant, and HOPE?

It was a decision only I could make. If I requested out and back onto the streets I could be sent anywhere throughout the County of Merseyside! I pondered the subject long and hard. The benefits of the Main Bridewell, in the role of Acting Sergeant, were now diminishing. I should really seek to gain further experience in this role in an 'operational' scale. Needless to say, those members of the 'very serious drinking squad' and others of their ilk, thought that I was stark raving mad to even think of going out, and back into the hard graft of street duty. One thing was certain, the very mention of 'street duty' scared the hell out of a lot of those working in the comfort of the Main Bridewell's confines (and no doubt still does)!

I discussed the possible advantages (and many disadvantages) of such a move with my wife. Although she was very sympathetic and understood my dilemma, she wisely left the ball entirely in my court as she did not wish to be blamed for encouraging me to make what could very easily (and probably) be the wrong decision if my gamble didn't come off. I spent a long time in the 'consideration department of the think tank', considering all the options for and against such an important move.

Once I had submitted my request for a transfer out onto the streets, there would be no turning back. Should I so decide, I would have to take pot luck as to where I would be posted. I could be sent to work in what was then the volatile area of Toxteth, or miles away to the 'sticks' in Kirkby or Huyton and learn to be a 'woollyback'! It was certainly not a decision to be taken lightly, but I would have to get my head into gear and try to decide what would be the best thing to do.

Eventually, I arrived back at the same, original conclusion. There was no further promotional advantage to be gained by my staying at the Main Bridewell, as I considered that by remaining there I was denying myself the experience of keeping abreast of operational procedures and becoming ignorant of the day to day workings of a 'front line' operational bobby. I decided to 'go for it' and take my chances! I duly set about typing out what I considered to be one of my most important applications, that of a request for transfer to 'street duties' (yet again)!

I furnished my report with all I could muster. I listed my (many) swimming and life-saving qualifications, first aid, and highlighted the various previous places and departments in which I had served, and what those duties entailed.

At its conclusion, my report must have read like an extract from Hans Christian Andersen! I was determined that I would leave nothing out, and sell myself to whoever was to decide whether to grant my request or not, and more importantly, to convince that particular person that I was definitely 'Sergeant material'.

My request for transfer was granted and I was pleased to learn that I was to be posted to "A" Division, and better still, to Copperas Hill (near my Boxing Club) where I would eventually again perform the duties of Acting Sergeant. Let's hope that I had made a right and sensible decision? At last I was going to become a 'proper' policeman again!

Chapter Seventeen - Between the Devil and the Deep Blue Sea

My last weeks at Cheapside soon drew to a close and I said my farewell to a place that had certainly given me much valuable experience, which could never be substituted anywhere else. During my last week I received a note instructing me to attend the Chief Superintendent's office at St Anne Street Police Station, the same office where I had been sent to 'stand under the clock' on a not too distant previous occasion; this time my new Chief Superintendent was to be Mr Parry.

At 9 a.m. on Wednesday, 3 April 1985, I again stood outside that same door, again awaiting the 'Come in' sign to light up. This time, however, I was to be welcomed, not scolded! My visit was short and sweet and after the preliminary 'Welcome to the Division' patter, I left to make my way along St Anne Street to my new base, Copperas Hill Police Station. I was there escorted up to my new boss, Superintendent Eric Bassender, an ex-County man.

Mr Bassender was a very outspoken man who didn't mince his words. He appeared to be very sure and confident. I liked him straight away. He impressed me with his competency. I formed the opinion that here was a man who could not only make a decision, but would stand by that decision come what may, not like all too many of his rank! The more that I got to know him, the more he came across to me as being scrupulously fair and also, one who would not tolerate laziness or inefficiency. He broke the ice on my first visit to his office by arranging for us both to have a coffee while we got to know each other.

We had a lengthy chat, during which I set out my 'stall', indicating the ultimate reason for my wishing to join him at Copperas Hill. He appeared to be fully aware of my ambitions and informed me that I would receive his total backing. He informed me that as soon as I had settled down and 'got to know the ropes' I would be performing the duties of Acting Sergeant on my own section. He went into detail as to what he would expect of me, telling me that one of his pet hates was officers drinking on duty. Any officers found so doing would be dealt with by him, ruthlessly. I assured him that I would start as I intended to carry on as a leader of my own section. The boss reassured me that if I were to encounter any problem whatsoever, especially once I started 'acting', I would receive all the help I needed from him personally.

I was very impressed indeed and looked forward to serving under him. He certainly appeared to be one of a rare species of senior officer. Although I had never met him before, I felt totally at ease with him and decided that he was a man who would reward those whose efforts warranted it, and on that score I was certainly to be proved correct. I considered that with his backing, so long as I played my cards right, I may well at last get somewhere.

My new section consisted mainly of young probationary Constables, although there were one or two with some service. We also had three

Policewomen on board. Most of the section knew me from the Main Bridewell, as I had helped them in the past (and they hadn't forgotten). I soon settled into the routine and at first I regularly accompanied one of the senior Constables (Tony Miskinnis) out on foot patrols round the City centre. Constable Miskinnis was always willing to avail himself should I need his help, as so many procedures and routines now differed since I last walked the beat. I will never forget Tony's assistance as I resumed my operational duties; nothing was ever too much trouble for him, and I remain eternally grateful for his selfless help. I was 'just another Constable' in the ranks at the moment. However, the lads knew the purpose of my joining them and most illustrated this by the respect that was shown. Some were understandably wary (those that needed to be!) as, although I was as yet a Constable, I was shortly to be their Acting Sergeant, one or two may well have resented this.

Once I had familiarised myself with the lads, the section and the various routines etc., and having notched up many foot and mobile patrols, during which I made a number of arrests, I seemed to be accepted and fully integrated back into the 'sharp end' of the job. I began to detect that some of the younger members of the section seemed loathe to visit the Main Bridewell, and were reluctant to take their prisoners there. I was informed that the reason for this was due to the attitude of some officers towards them when they took their prisoners in.

I was indeed aware that some of those did consider themselves somewhat above their station and were aloof to their younger counterparts, sometimes being quite rude. I assured them, however, that I would do my utmost to rectify the matter should any further similar treatment be afforded them in future. After a few weeks had elapsed, I arrived for duty one Monday morning and was instructed by the Inspector to don the silk, double chevrons of an Acting Sergeant, arm myself with a signalling stick (Merseyside Police are one of the few forces that have this type of equipment), and take the morning parade. I completed the form 107 (Duty state) and allocated my 'flock' their various beats and duties for the day. Later, I dismissed the parade and the 'troops' made their way out onto the streets. I completed the appropriate paperwork then decided to go out myself and 'peg' my men (visit them on their beats).

It was a strange feeling walking out onto the streets that wonderful sunny and warm morning as an Acting Sergeant on an 'operational' section. I felt ten feet tall carrying my 'status symbol' (signalling stick). This is a three foot long stick with a metal ferrule with which the Sergeant summons his Constable by striking the kerb with the ferrule. This can be heard a long way away. Now of course this procedure is rarely adopted as Officers now carry personal radios. I walked down past the Copperas Hill postal sorting office, on past the long line of parked Hackney carriages (black cabs) and down onto the well-known street of 'Maggie May' fame, Liverpool's Lime Street.

Eventually, as I walked among the early morning crowds making their way to work, I saw one of 'my' bobbies standing on a corner, near to Lime Street station. As I joined him I was greeted with the traditional

253

"All correct Sarge!" before showing him a visit by signing his notebook. Together we then walked his beat around the City centre shopping area. I now realised how much more I was enjoying the fruits of my labours and how I had definitely made the right decision in leaving the confines of the Main Bridewell down in Cheapside. As the young officer and I walked along the busy and bustling area of Church Street, we acknowledged the greetings from various shopkeepers as they opened up their premises ready for the day's business. This was the really pleasant side of policing; life was now becoming a different 'ball game'! I was impressed with the young officer's knowledge of his beat and its people. It showed that he had taken an interest in his job by getting to know his 'parishioners', many by name. He was aware of who everyone was and what they were doing. I was to find that this was the norm amongst those devoted young men and women who took their work very seriously.

Acting Sgt. with Police Carrier, Copperas Hill

Sadly, it was not long before I started to discover that some of the 'older' members of the section had hidden vices. No doubt I, myself, was continually being 'sussed out' (Police terminology for getting to know a new colleague) and was subject to constant scrutiny by those I had recently joined; this was to be expected. I was soon to discover who was difficult to contact, who always seemed to have a faulty radio or who was late in making a 'point' on his beat. I found that some of those I originally thought very charming and likeable were sometimes the wearers of 'two heads'.

The occasional failure to answer one's radio when called could be accepted when they explained the reasons for such failure, but let's not forget that I, too, was a young bobby once, and I knew when an explanation was feasible and when it was not! A certain one or two on the section were starting to give me cause for concern. There were occasions when I reluctantly had to admonish an officer for one reason or another and I found that once or twice an officer was 'testing' me! Sometimes I was shown resentment on the occasions when I had to exert my authority, so be it! This did not apply to the majority of the section, just a certain few. However, even a few was enough! I began to watch one or two closely. I was too long in the tooth to confide in the other Sergeants, as I didn't as yet know them well enough. Eventually, I was able to paint a picture of what was what and which Constable was 'friendly' with which Sergeant, and who 'liked their ale'.

As time went on one or two on the section started to become over-confident with themselves and due to this, their 'vices' were became more obvious. Some were beginning to show a mild form of contempt for my authority and one or two were becoming more than a little indiscreet! As I visited them on their beats during the latter half of a late shift, or the early part of a night shift, I started to detect the smell of alcohol, or, just as incriminating, the smell of 'Gold Spot' or strong mints, a dead giveaway to those who were drinking on duty. "Oh, so you think I'm daft enough to fall for that, do you?" I thought to myself. I remembered the Super, Bassender, emphasising his views regarding such behaviour. I was determined that no member of my section was going to put MY head on the block, as well as his own, just because he (or she) liked their pint!

At first, I made my views known during conversation, when I would casually switch to the subject of drink and how I thought it unnecessarily risky to consume ale whilst on duty, especially with the Superintendent that we had. All would agree with me and assure me that they would never indulge in such a practice and put themselves at risk! I eased my views on such matters into the conversation, indicating what action I would take if anyone were foolish, or selfish, enough to compromise ME by being caught drinking while I was in charge of the section. I hoped that my 'casual' approach and veiled warning would convey my distaste at anyone engaging in such activity, as I did NOT approve.

This particular activity has been going on in the Police no doubt since Robert Peel was a cadet, and no doubt is still an ongoing problem. However, I did not wish to be put to the ultimate test as to what I would or would not do in such circumstances. I considered that if anyone were to place me in such a predicament, then they could not have much respect for me; this would make it easier for me to deal with! It was not long before my hand was forced with regard to dealing with such matters.

The first incident of that nature occurred in the early hours of one

Sunday morning. One of the young bobbies on my section had found a door to one of the public houses insecure. He knew that there were no persons living there and decided to investigate and check that there were no intruders on the premises. He contacted control by radio and informed them of his find. I heard control direct a mobile to assist the Constable search the premises. As I was in the vicinity I too made my way along there to assist. On my arrival, ten minutes later, I saw a Police patrol car parked in an entry at the rear of the pub premises.

The vehicle was locked and was not displaying any lights. I entered the pub via the same insecure side door and made my way to the downstairs bar, following the sound of subdued voices. I entered the dimly lit room and saw the beat officer standing in the centre of the room making notes. Two other officers, the car driver and another beat man were standing behind the bar. On the bar counter were two pint glasses, one full and the other partly full, of beer. The partly full glass was at the elbow of the officer whose patrol car was parked outside.

As I entered the room the beat man making the notes saw me and confirmed that the premises had been searched and was 'all correct'! The young bobby informed me that the keyholder had been sent for and he was now awaiting his arrival. I asked the other two what they were doing behind the bar. The older of the two, the driver (who was one of those I had reason to watch), informed me that he and the other officer were just about to leave. I again asked him what they were doing behind the bar. He replied that he was just 'walking through' after having searched the premises. I indicated the two glasses containing ale and asked him what they were doing there. He denied any knowledge and insisted that they must have been there prior to his arrival.

I noticed that the untouched pint was still topped with a thick frothy head, and also noticed that the nozzle of the bar pump was still giving an occasional drip ! I dismissed the other officer who had been brought by the driver from his beat to assist, and told him to make his way back to his beat. I then instructed the beat man to remain where he was until the keyholder arrived. I accompanied the driver back to his vehicle and told him to give me a ride around the various beats so that I could 'have a word with him'.

Once inside the vehicle, I let the driver have it with both barrels. Remembering the saga of the Inspector and the pint of lager that night a long time ago at the Jack Sharp golf centre, I said, "D'you think I'm bloody stupid? I know bloody well what was going on.!"

By now the strong reek of Gold Spot filled the interior of the car. The driver cheekily informed me that he had answered the call and decided to pick another beat man up en route to add to their numbers. Fair enough, I accepted this, but insisted that I was no fool and knew damned well what I had interrupted. I told the driver that on this occasion I would overlook the matter, but would not forget it! I informed him that I was far from being naive and this would be the one and only time when I would be prepared to ignore the 'obvious' fact that he, or one of the others, had pulled two pints of beer and started to consume one of them. As he was about to reply I informed him of my observation regarding the 'thick', therefore fresh, head of froth, and the still dripping nozzle, and silenced him with the warning, "Next time, you'll all be for the chop!" I later met up with the officer who he had picked up, and accompanied him on his beat whilst I made my sentiments known to him also, assuring him that I had not just arrived on a banana boat! I didn't like telling the lads off but I found that a 'mild ticking off' went unheeded, and that kindness was interpreted as a sign of weakness. As it happened, the original beat man who had found the insecure premises later confirmed that my conclusions were correct. One of the other two had, in fact, pulled two pints of bitter (he himself had refused) and the driver had taken a mouthful just before my arrival. On that one occasion, I let the matter rest and hoped that I had made the right decision by making my views known, and hopefully eliminating the prospect of a repetition by them or anyone else on the section.

Due to this incident, I fell out with a fellow Sergeant on the section (who happened to be a friend of the driver), who informed me that he and others often 'indulged in the occasional pint' on night duty, and he didn't want me, a newcomer, 'rocking the boat'! He went on to inform me that if I continued to 'make ripples' on that score, he would make sure that I ceased to 'act' on the section. He and I had very strong words and I decided that I would have to watch my back from then on. Although I did not intend running to the Super, Mr Bassender, I did, however, bear in mind that if this sort of conduct continued or magnified among the section, this could surely reflect on my competency and I may ultimately need to take up his offer of help. I would wait and see how things transpired. I preferred to fight my own battles, if possible.

One afternoon, during our refreshment period, I was sitting at the table with one of the young recruits. The officer complained bitterly at having been grossly humiliated in front of his prisoner (a female shop-lifter) by staff at the Main Bridewell. I told him that we would both walk down to Cheapside after our meal and sort matters out.

The young recruit and I later attended at the Bridewell and the bobby pointed out the offending officer to me on our arrival. Just as I thought! The officer concerned was a stalwart of the 'very serious drinking squad', and one who was not known for his hard work or efficiency. He had spent many, many years in the Bridewell and no doubt considered himself quite indispensable. I went to my former Bridewell colleague and asked him to accompany me to a back room. There, I told him in forthright language that the young bobby standing in the front office represented the backbone of the Police service and should be shown the same respect that he himself expected. The duty Inspector, hearing my not too quiet rebuke, came into the room and immediately started to defend his subordinate. The Inspector didn't hesitate to point out that I was 'only an Acting Sergeant' and asked me who the hell I thought I was. His voice was raised louder than mine had been and my recruit could hear the Inspector's chastisement quite clearly. I stood my ground and replied defiantly that for too long the attitude here at the Main

Bridewell was nothing short of discouraging to young recruits when bringing their prisoners in for charging, and that he, as the officer in charge, should not condone it. I emphasised that if any more of my 'lads' were subjected to similar treatment, I would not hesitate to put my sentiments onto paper officially. Taking my recruit, I begrudgingly saluted my senior officer and took my leave. I was later informed that news of the incident had spread like wildfire throughout the 'grapevine' at the Main. Good! Perhaps I may have eliminated the problem. Due to this incident, I received some abuse from ex-colleagues at the Main Bridewell, but this was adequately compensated for by the amount of thanks and congratulatory comments I received from the younger element of the "A" Division bobbies, many of whom had also been the recipients of similar treatment at Cheapside. I didn't care who I offended on issues such as this, as I had total sympathy with those subject to such treatment by their own colleagues. Anyway, I had wanted to voice my sentiments on this particular subject for a long time! It was about time some of those in the Main Bridewell received a long overdue 'kick up the arse', or, better still, a transfer out of there and onto the streets. No chance! Eventually, the matter died a death and things carried on. However, I never received similar complaints from my recruits again!

I also did not like the way most shop-lifting incidents were dealt with by the store detectives at some of the large, well-established stores in the City centre. I considered that the procedure between the store detectives and the young Constables sent to deal with the incidents were anything but satisfactory.

Most of the store detectives were well established in their field and many were on familiar terms with the older officers of more lengthy service. These officers had set a precedent with regard to the procedure which they had adopted. They would attend the incident, listen to the circumstances offered by the store detective who would then furnish the officer with a 'statement', sometimes on an official form, sometimes on ordinary writing paper. The Constable, alone, would then convey the prisoner to the Police Station to be charged and documented. I didn't like this arrangement one bit! When any of 'my' young recruits were sent on a shop-lifting incident, I decided to accompany some of them. I was to make myself extremely unpopular among the store detectives by insisting that the store detective accompany the prisoner too, as I felt that it was the responsibility of the individual detective to relate the circumstances of THEIR arrest by outlining the reasons for the detention of that particular prisoner to the Bridewell Sergeant. I considered it appropriate that it was they, not the Constable (who had arrived AFTER the incident) who should justify the detention. I felt that if there was any dispute or allegation of 'wrongful arrest' then the store detective should justify his or her actions, not the bobby. Once this had been satisfactorily established, THEN the young officer could assist by processing the prisoner for any subsequent court appearance. This did not go down too well as it had almost become the established 'norm' to just hand the prisoner over with the store detective's statement. No, it was not good enough! We would do thinks the 'right way', whether they liked it or not.

My 'patch' at Copperas Hill included Liverpool's China Town. I found the Chinese population to be extremely friendly and a very hard-working and law-abiding people. They always showed the utmost respect to the 'cloth' and by and large were very obliging. I liked my Chinese 'flock' very much. I made many lasting friends among these fine Oriental people and always reciprocated by giving them my undivided attention whenever the need arose. My section arrested many local youths in and around China Town, especially in the evenings, when they would prey on the parked cars of patrons who were visiting the numerous Chinese eating establishments to sample their well-known and unique cuisine. We gave the area such undivided attention that we finally seemed to reduce the problem considerably, much to the delight of the restaurant mandarins as well as their customers.

It wouldn't be the first time that I and many other officers were invited to enjoy the wonderful cuisine at one or other of the many Chinese restaurants as invited guests, sometimes with our families, by the owner of the individual establishment.

As time went by, I was to spend quite a few bob dining in China Town when out shopping in the City centre. I can certainly strongly recommend so doing. China Town is well and truly worth a visit when wishing to sample the gastronomic delights of the Orient.

Life at Copperas Hill went on and I continued to train the youth of Myrtle Gardens and its surrounding areas at the local Boxing Club each week during off-duty periods. At work I was still monitoring one or two members of the section who I knew were intent on continuing with their on-duty drinking. It almost became a 'cat and mouse' game. At one stage things became so bad that I had no alternative but to confide in an Inspector who I trusted implicitly, Inspector Walker, who was an up and coming ambitious officer. Inspector Walker and I eventually managed to catch one of those we suspected. The officer was sent to the Chief Superintendent, who posted him from the section to another Sub-Division. I don't know if the Chief Super's action cured the problem, but it was never as widespread again. This did not enhance my popularity with some officers one bit, but it certainly had the desired effect!

It is amazing what an officer comes across when out on street patrol. At one o'clock one Saturday morning, I was patrolling along Bold Street on foot in company with a young Policewoman and we were heading up towards the well-known landmark, the bombed ruins of St Luke's Church. Our attention was drawn to a group of youths, including some females, who were laughing and cheering and behaving in a boisterous manner. On seeing us approach, however, they all ran away, with the exception of one poor unfortunate youth!

As we neared the youth we could see that he was totally naked. His hands were behind his back and we found that he had been chained to the iron railings surrounding the church gardens. The embarrassed youth explained that it was his stag night, and that he was to be married some hours later in the afternoon. He complained of the cold but there was no way that my colleague or I could release him. I summoned a mobile to bring a mac or overcoat to hide the young man's blushes as the City was as yet still teeming with late night revellers. I also had no alternative but to summon the Fire Brigade to release the hapless youth. My female colleague found the incident highly amusing. The youth understandably would not name those responsible for placing him in such a predicament, and I did not intend to officially pursue the matter.

Once he was released by the amused Brigade officers, I requested my mobile colleague to lend the youth a coat to cover his dignity and take him to his Anfield home which was only a short distance away. The youth thanked us all profusely and was whisked away to his home. He no doubt would have something to say later, after his wedding? I considered that no doubt we have all done something in the past which we bitterly regret and therefore acted accordingly regarding the amusing episode. Life would be so easy if the only crises we had to deal with were of a similar nature!

Some weeks later, after attending Liverpool Crown Court, I was walking along Dale Street with my ex-Main Bridewell Governor, Chief Inspector Beattie. As we neared the City Magistrates Court we came across one of our magistrates, obviously in distress, leaning against a shop door. He was struggling to loosen his tie. The boss and I went to the man, Mr Frank Molloy, a very well liked and respected member of the City's bench, and I asked him what the trouble was. The poor man was obviously in great pain and could only gasp that he felt unwell. Mr Beattie and I took an arm each and half-carried Mr Molloy into the nearby Police office at Cheapside. No sooner had we entered the sanctuary of the office when the man collapsed completely. His face was completely devoid of colour and I was alarmed to find that there was no sign of a pulse. I placed a hand mirror to his mouth but again there was no sign of any misting on the mirror. I removed the man's tie and began immediate mouth-to-mouth resuscitation and also pumped hard at the lifeless man's chest. An ambulance was summoned and quickly attended the scene. The ambulance crew administered oxygen while I continued relentlessly with my heart massage. I continued with my endeavours while the man was taken out to the ambulance and then throughout the hair-raising journey through the crowded streets to the Liverpool Teaching Hospital. I maintained my efforts right through to the treatment room in the hospital, where I was relieved, soaked in sweat and exhausted, by the medical staff.

After what seemed an eternity, the Casualty Doctor, Dr. Watkins, came out to me with the delightful news that, although the patient had suffered a massive heart attack and had in fact 'died' at one stage, my efforts had revived him. He was, however, critically ill. I notified the next-of-kin and the patient's wife and daughter arrived at the hospital a short time later.

Eventually, after cooling down and regaining my breath and composure, I resumed my duties. Although the patient, Mr Molloy, recovered enough to spend some time with his wife and family, sadly, he suffered another attack during that evening to which he tragically succumbed. I felt the loss of that particularly kind and well liked man very deeply. Only for that second attack, the medics were confident that he would have made it. Chief Inspector Beattie and I attended Mr Molloy's funeral some days later in full uniform.

An indication of Mr Molloy's popularity and standing in his local community and the high esteem in which he was held was indicated by the large numbers of people, from all walks of life, who attended to pay their last respects.

I was particularly moved as I stood to attention and saluted as Mr Molloy's flower draped coffin was conveyed from the church in Kirkdale en route to the cemetery. Suddenly the cortege stopped and I was summoned to Mrs Molloy in the leading car. Mr Molloy's tearful widow had taken the trouble in her hour of acute grief to stop the cortege so that she could thank me personally for the last precious hours I had helped her to share with her late husband before his tragic demise. Mrs Molloy leaned out from the car and embraced and kissed me to express her gratitude. The kind and selfless gesture by such a kind, wonderful and brave lady will remain indelibly imprinted on my mind for ever. Unknown to me, as well as the Chief Inspector (Beattie) submitting a report concerning my actions on that fateful day, a long letter of appreciation was written to the Chief Constable by the late Mr Molloy's family. Due to those kind sentiments being so expressed on paper, I was to be recommended for a Shipwreck and Humane Society Life-saving award.

I continued to 'enjoy' the strains and stresses of being an Acting Sergeant (piggy in the middle really!), patrolling and 'diligently sleuthing' around the City. As I walked around the City centre I was continually stopped by foreign tourists who asked if I would allow them to take a photograph of me (probably because of my large handlebar moustache.)

'Posing' with Foriegn Tourists, Liverpool.

261

Due to this I am in regular contact with some of these people world-wide, and I continue to write, and receive, letters and photographs from such far away countries as Australia, New Zealand, America and Germany. This is definitely one of the rewards of the occupation!

I was back to the seedier side of things whilst patrolling along the shopping area of Church Street with Constable Tony Miskinnis, in the early hours of a May morning. We saw a man crouching on the roof of Wades, a large departmental furniture store. I immediately summoned the Fire Brigade and requested the assistance of mobile colleagues. The Brigade arrived a short time later, together with the other patrols. The fire crew erected an extension ladder up to the roof where the youth was last seen. Once the ladder was in position and footed, I rapidly scaled it and climbed onto the roof of the building, followed by a young recruit, Constable Crew.

We soon discovered the offending youth. He was trying to secrete himself by hiding in the shadows underneath a broken window. The youth became very aggressive as my colleague and I discovered him with the aid of our torches, and threatened to push my colleague and me off the roof if we tried to arrest him. I instantly corrected the misinformed deviant by informing him that if anyone was to fall from the roof, It would not be my colleague or myself. Fortunately, he took my comments to heart and decided that it would be in his own best interests if he 'came quietly'. The youth was arrested and charged with attempted burglary and criminal damage to the window and on his subsequent appearance before the court he was sentenced to undergo a period of probation. Another of society's deprived and misunderstood 'casualties'.

I continued to engage myself in various arrests with my colleagues, many times taking a young recruit out 'hunting' for thieves or burglars, checking parcels at the end of the working day or late at night. As always, these efforts netted the unwary or over-confident of those who carried their 'loot' about the city. This procedure sometimes 'rubbed off' on some officers who then became good 'thief takers' themselves.

I frequently made visits to the pubs on my patch in the form of an official 'walk through'. Most licensees appreciated these visits, especially at those more renowned and troublesome venues, or when nearing closing time when such Police presence would ensure a quick 'empty out' and ultimately an early night for the staff. I made many friends among the licensing trade, but never to the point of being compromised in any way.

One night, well after closing time, I walked through a pub in Dale Street and caught the bar staff, and the landlord, still serving drinks. I gave the licensee a verbal warning illustrating my disdain at what he was blatantly doing. However, he must have thought that he was immune from prosecution and considered himself 'fireproof' as he had a number of bobbies (from the Main Bridewell) and one or two councillors and even Members of Parliament on his premises. The landlord obviously did not heed my warning, as a couple of weeks later, I discovered exactly the same thing happening again. This time, however, I didn't give him a warning. The Inspector and I organised a raid on the premises.

The licensee and a number of his customers (including an MP) were ultimately prosecuted for the sale and consumption of alcohol after hours. Some people just do not get the message, or, once again, interpret kindness as a sign of weakness! As a Member of Parliament was involved by being present during the raid, the incident received press coverage, which no doubt had a major influence in ensuring that the licensing laws were not contravened at those premises again!

Whilst at Copperas Hill, I was amazed to uncover some incidents of 'bullying'! A spate of this nature was certainly unusual amongst the Police. I found that young recruits were being made to cover for an older colleague on various occasions. He would take a 'prolonged' refreshment break, or unofficially get a young officer to cover while he went on an 'errand' (for a pint!). Understandably, those young officers concerned were reluctant to come out into the open over such a matter. Even so, I was to learn of these 'episodes' after having to chastise one or two young and vulnerable recruits whose paperwork was starting to lag behind.

I would instruct them to come into the station at certain times to get on with any outstanding reports. This was not getting done and a surreptitious check would reveal that they were still engaged as relief for the selfish individual concerned. When one or two plucked up courage to complain to him they were then subjected to threats or intimidation in one form or another. Eventually, I learned what was going on and made a point of taking the offending officer to one side . This man had almost the same length of service as myself. I made even bigger threats of severe retribution should this conduct not cease forthwith. Thankfully, my 'little chat' eliminated the nasty little problem on the spot!

I can categorically say that two of my 'virtues' are punctuality and smartness. Especially the former. I have never been one to tolerate lateness in any manner or form, unless, obviously, such lateness could not possibly be avoided. Since becoming an Acting Sergeant I was ALWAYS half an hour early for duty. One of my colleagues on my section lived near to me and was always last to arrive for duty. He would always cry that he had no transport. (I don't know what he would have done at Rose Hill in the early days!) Obviously it hadn't entered his head to leave home a little earlier to facilitate catching an earlier train. He asked me if he could travel to work with me one Sunday morning. I agreed and arranged to meet him at 6.15 a.m.. at a certain place when I would pick him up and transport him to Copperas Hill with me.

The Sunday came and I arrived at the appointed place to pick him up as agreed. I arrived at 6.10 a.m., five minutes early. I waited until 6.20 a.m. but of my colleague there was no sign. I made my way in to work and duly took the morning parade, minus our colleague. Eventually, the telephone rang and I answered an irate Constable who complained at having been left stranded over on the Wirral, as his transport had gone. I informed him that I had indeed waited at the pick-up point at the arranged time. "You didn't wait very bloody long" my colleague arrogantly complained, adding "I got there just before half-past." "Six-fifteen was the time!" I snapped and instructed him to get himself into work as soon as he could. I told him that in future perhaps he should vacate his bed a damned sight sooner and get his idle self down to the station to catch the appropriate train, assuming of course that the train driver would be good enough to wait should he be a little late! He was also informed that his future prospects of a lift from me were now zero. I think he must have 'got my drift' as from then on his timekeeping showed a marked improvement. He had obviously been allowed to get away with it for too long. In my book, lateness is akin to slovenliness. I was not prepared to accept the fact that I would always be early, but others could just please themselves, especially when I was eventually (and hopefully) promoted and would have my own section!

Remembering how we used to hold the occasional 'get together' when the section was off duty, I suggested that our section get their heads together and arrange a date when we could hold a beach barbecue one afternoon after we had completed our morning shift. My suggestion was accepted with great enthusiasm and a day was subsequently arranged for the Saturday of our next morning shift. Prior to the enthusiastically-awaited date, a number of us arranged for the purchase of meat, drink and other items considered necessary for our outing. When the Saturday arrived, a couple of us collected the goods from the butchers' and off-licence and took it to Copperas Hill ready for the afternoon's activities. The venue for our 'day out' was the quiet, secluded beach beneath the cliffs at picturesque Thurstaston on the beautiful Wirral peninsula.

After duty, the section went home to change before 'parading' down at the beach a couple of hours later. Most of us took along friends or members of our families and a wonderful party-like atmosphere ensued. During the somewhat boisterous activities, a couple of the girls from the section were unceremoniously thrown into the tide. We also received a visit from the local constabulary, who eyed us suspiciously through binoculars from the cliff-top. They must have thought it was an outing from an asylum!

The barbie was lit and when it was ready we got the lamb chops and pork sausages ready. To our horror, it was revealed that we had forgotten the most crucial of items. We had brought the fare, the paper plates, cups, drinks, barbie fuel, but nobody had brought any cutlery and - most important - knives! We did not have one knife between the lot of us! Sod it! We'd have to manage without a knives. A large bunch of fat, succulent pork sausages were presented, ready to be placed onto the grill. I had no alternative but to put them on as they were. In no time those on the outside were well and truly sizzling and soon became black and crispy.

We placed them onto a nearby table and had to try and separate them with our fingers! We were shaping like a right bunch of idiots. The sausages on the inside of the bunch were still completely raw! Next, the chops. These fared much better; at least they were all separate! The hilarity of the situation outweighed its shortcomings and we all enjoyed ourselves thoroughly. Some of us played rounders on the sand while others swam in the sea nearby. The party went on for several hours until all of the 'goodies' had been consumed and nothing was left.

Eventually the light started to fail and as it was now getting late, we decided to call it a day. We tidied up the beach as it resembled a medieval battle-ground. We removed all our litter and debris until the only indication of our presence was the rounders pitch, clearly marked in the sand. We all left for home as darkness fell, around ten o'clock. What a great day it had been. Everyone insisted that this must be repeated . There is no doubt that these 'get togethers' when off-duty certainly do wonders for morale.

Whilst on duty, one of my favourite patrol vehicles during the late evening or night shifts was the carrier. The large transit could accommodate several officers and was very handy when things were 'lively' in the City. During one night, I was driving the carrier along Dale Street with a number of bobbies (including a couple of Specials) when our attention was drawn to a noisy group of youths. They were obviously the worse for drink and were staggering along, shouting and swearing at innocent passers-by. I stopped the vehicle and went to the group. I told them to be quiet and make their way home in an orderly manner. The ringleader became more abusive and shouted to me, "Fuck off and get a shave." "Now, that's very naughty," I thought. I told the foul-mouthed youth once again (for the last time) to behave and go home, but he ignored my request and insisted on giving me verbal abuse, to the amusement of his friends and some of the passers-by.

There was no way this could be allowed. The offending youth was promptly arrested and placed into the back of our Police vehicle. One of his cronies was not at all pleased about this and lunged towards me shouting "Where my mate goes, I go!" Always willing to oblige, I replied "Certainly, Sir," and he too was arrested and placed inside the vehicle with his friend. The remainder of the noisy entourage obviously got the message as they rapidly made themselves scarce. Our two Drunk and Disorderly prisoners were transported to Cheapside to sleep off their inebriation and at Main Bridewell 'hotel', before their subsequent appearance before Their Worships the following morning!

Later, during the same shift, we saw another man who had obviously consumed more drink than he could cope with. He attempted to give his friends a demonstration of his skills in the martial arts. He lashed out with his leg and kicked in a large plate glass display window of Lewis's store. Unfortunately for him, in doing so he almost completely severed his foot. An ambulance was summoned and the budding Bruce Lee was taken with all speed to hospital where he underwent major and lengthy surgery in an attempt to save his foot. To add to this problems, he was also subsequently charged with Criminal Damage to the window!

Variety is certainly the spice of life and I certainly found a variety of jobs to keep me occupied. One morning, I was driving my patrol car up Copperas Hill behind a black cab. I could see the passenger in the rear seat and saw that the taxi was veering from side to side as it was being driven along. I pulled out and drew alongside the cab to see what was wrong. I saw the driver with his head completely tipped backwards drinking from a cup he was holding to his mouth, while he consumed its contents. I sounded my horn and signalled the driver to stop. When he did so I went to him and reported him for summons for the offences of driving his vehicle when not in proper control and driving without consideration for other road users. It would appear that some taxi drivers consider themselves immune from the law, as in no time, a deputation of taxi drivers arrived at Copperas Hill Police Station and a large number of taxis blocked the nearby streets in protest at such 'Police harassment! Superintendent Bassender showed his true grit when, once he had been informed of the reason for such protest, backed me to the hilt and even threatened to arrest any drivers himself who insisted on wilfully obstructing the highway by their futile protest.

The matter was resolved, and the offending driver was successfully prosecuted for his dangerous misdemeanours. I became a well-known (and disliked) figure amongst the City's cab drivers due to this incident. However, NO problem would ever be too big with a Superintendent like Bassender behind me!

I found also, when dealing with some politicians or other VIPs, they sometimes tended to have an air of arrogance about them. Some were very polite, but others were sometimes downright obnoxious. Once, when a couple of colleagues and myself were protecting the ex-Prime Minister, Ted Heath, whilst ushering him to his car from the University complex and running the gauntlet of a number of left-wing demonstrators, he didn't go out of his way to express his gratitude for our efforts, even though it was my colleagues and I that were hit by thrown eggs. I was not impressed with him at all. Likewise, when Mr Kinnock visited Liverpool I was crushed as I was assisting him from his car. The crowd were pressing me against his door as he was trying to alight from the vehicle. "Give me a chance to get out," he snapped at me. I snapped back, "Just show a bit of patience and you'll get out much easier!" There was no way I was prepared to grovel to them like so many other colleagues sometimes did. I was never impressed when dealing with most VIPs; many undoubtedly came bottom of their class where good manners were concerned!

I was always at loggerheads with a lot of my colleagues because of my benevolent attitude towards members of the Special Constabulary. Without doubt, I consider the majority of 'Specials' to be, like myself, dedicated to the cloth. This stupid, childlike anti-Special attitude which prevails in the service never fails to annoy me immensely. If the hierarchy of the service were to deal with the 'Special prejudice' in the same way as they do with instances of racial prejudice within the force, I don't doubt that the problem could well be eliminated. It has (wrongly) been said by generations of regular bobbies that the Specials take the overtime from the mouths of the regulars. Nonsense! This is a complete and utter fallacy. There are many, many serving Special Constables who would be an asset among the ranks of the regular force, even better than some I could certainly mention! Many young specials would like nothing more than to be able to join the regular force: many would undoubtedly give their eye teeth to do so, but cannot, because of some mild form of disability such as having a 'lazy eye' or maybe not being quite tall enough.

I do not in any way suggest that standards should be lowered for entry into the regular force, but to condemn Specials or sometimes ridicule them, or just plainly refuse to co-operate with or assist them, is a diabolical sin. This juvenile practice and ridiculous attitude is long overdue to be stamped out. Many times I accompanied a Special around his or her beat, and assisted them to find or make an arrest and encouraged them in any way I could by helping to advance their knowledge and training. Many has been the time that I have 'fallen out' with a regular colleague due to my 'collusion' with Special Constables. I consider them all to be very useful , extremely helpful and enthusiastic allies, and will always remain a very staunch member of the 'pro Special' lobby, irrespective of the sentiments and opinions of my regular colleagues .

I like to think (perhaps a little vainly) that due to my assisting many Specials in getting prisoners before the courts, I may have had a small influence in the amount of ex-Specials we now have serving in the regular Merseyside Police force. I sincerely hope that in this sphere, perhaps I was to them what the late Charlie Povall had been to me many years before.

During another busy night shift, I was called to the She Club in Victoria Street, one of the well-known clubs in the City. On my arrival I threaded my way through the throng of revellers inside the club and made my way to where a man was lying clutching his leg and groaning on the floor. The man had been shot with a twelve bore shotgun at point blank range and had received a severe wound to his right leg. Amazingly, the man refused to make any allegations, and even declined my offer of first aid. I accompanied him to hospital in the ambulance but he insisted that he did not wish to make a complaint!

Whilst in the Casualty Department at the hospital I was approached by one of the injured man's elderly relatives who was known to me. The old man apologised profusely for his injured relative's rudeness, explaining, "We all know about you at the Boxing Club, Mr Turner: it's just that he (the casualty) doesn't know what he's saying." I thanked the old man for his courtesy and after contacting the CID requesting them to attend, I left the matter with them. This particular matter was never brought to a successful conclusion due to the lack of co-operation of all concerned, not least the 'complainant'. Perhaps it was anticipated that the injured party would eventually deal with the matter himself, assisted by his relatives? Nobody at the Club saw or heard anything that would have assisted the Police in their enquiries!

Another incident which could well have adversely affected my promotion prospects occurred during the latter half of 1985 when my wife and I purchased a white and gold bedroom suite which consisted of two side wardrobes, between which was an illuminated, mirrored dressing table. We purchased the furniture from a well-known furniture store in the City centre. Our purchase was delivered as arranged and I duly set about fitting the items together and installing the completed unit into the bedroom. Once installed, the suite looked very attractive and certainly enhanced the room considerably.

There was one drawback, however. The store had sent the wrong handles for the drawers and doors! I contacted the firm, who apologised for their mistake and assured me that they had the correct handles which, if convenient, could be collected from the store the following day. This presented no problem as I was on duty the following morning, and as the store was on my 'patch', I would call and collect the handles. The following day I called as arranged. The manager was 'awfully sorry', but they had not had the appropriate handles delivered as promised (he must have forgotten that he'd told me the handles were on the premises). I was assured, however, that the handles would be delivered from the manufacturers the following day. Although I was annoyed at this set-back, I considered that twenty-four hours was not an eternity, so again, I arranged to call in the following day.

I called as instructed, but no handles! This procedure went on for two weeks. Things were getting silly now! Eventually I was given a parcel of handles and returned home to fit them. I attempted to fit the handles but found that they were for a completely different unit. The handles I had were totally useless for the model we had purchased. I returned yet again to the store and requested the correct items so I could fit them to my as yet incomplete bedroom suite. Unbelievably, the same problem reared its acutely annoying head again. The promises again continued to be broken for another couple of weeks. By this time the manager and I were on the point of really falling out!

Eventually, the manager categorically promised that I could collect the correct handles on a particular day. As it happened, I was on morning duty on that day and I informed the manager that I would call and collect the handles during my duty shift. On the day, I arrived at the store and parked my patrol car outside leaving my colleague sitting in the vehicle while I went to collect the handles.

As I walked across the pavement to the entrance of the store, I saw an identical suite to that of my own, on display in the window. As I entered the store the manager approached me apologising profusely as the handles had still not been sent from the factory. I reassured him and put him at ease by saying, "Don't worry. No problem!" The manager couldn't believe his good luck. He fully expected me to bring the roof down on his head! I went to the patrol car and returned with a screw driver from the tool kit. Returning to the store armed with the screw driver and a plastic carrier bag, I went in and made my way to a small door that led into the outside window display. The look of utter surprise and disbelief on the faces of my colleagues and those of passers-by as they witnessed the spectacle of me, in full uniform, kneeling in the window display and removing every handle from the units on display!

Finally, job done, I retreated back out of the display and into the shop. I was spotted by one of the female counter staff who frantically summoned the manager. Undeterred, I made my way out to our vehicle, hotly pursued by the manager, who by now had realised what I had done. The distraught and very irate manager spluttered his protests at my unappreciated initiative! The manager ordered me to hand back the bag of handles I had removed, informing me that he couldn't have an incomplete display in his window for all to see. "Ring the factory," I sarcastically suggested, adding, "You're certainly not borrowing mine!" The very angry manager threatened to ring the Chief Constable right away if I didn't give him the handles. I drove off, leaving him standing there on the pavement staring in utter disbelief and dejection at his handleless suite in the window. My colleague turned to me laughing almost hysterically, "You're one cheeky bastard Swasie. I don't believe what I've just seen," he said.

Before an hour had elapsed I was instructed by radio to return to the station and see my Inspector. I was asked by the Inspector to explain a complaint he had been asked to deal with (he didn't say by whom!) regarding my going into the store and removing items from a window display. I fully explained my frustrating situation and concluded that I was completely unrepentant, and anyway, there was no problem as the factory would deliver a new set of handles "tomorrow"!

The boss could hardly conceal his amusement and told me to resume my patrol, warning me to be prepared to explain myself on paper should the powers that be request a report. As I left his office, the Inspector said, "I don't know how the bloody hell you get away with it!" I didn't consider that I had done anything wrong, although maybe I shouldn't have been so blatant in full uniform. I didn't hear anything further regarding the matter and the handles now adorn our suite at long last! I have never dealt with that particular establishment since. In any case, I doubt if they would wish to serve me after that little episode, even though they were entirely to blame.

On Wednesday, 27 Nov, 1985, I received a 'phone call from a colleague at Headquarters. "Hi, Swas, Dave here. You're in orders tomorrow. Congratulations, you've been made!" I couldn't believe what I was hearing. Tomorrow was to be the day I had been waiting for, my promotion in orders! "Thanks Dave. I'll buy you a pint as soon as I see you." I offered enthusiastically. "I'll hold you to that," replied my informant and put the 'phone down. I was absolutely delighted with this pleasant (and long-awaited) surprise.

I wouldn't be celebrating yet until I had actually seen my promotion in official print. The following morning, I impatiently awaited the morning's despatches. As soon as they arrived, I dived into the correspondence rooting for the orders like an overjoyed and impatient little child opening his presents from Santa on Christmas morning! I spotted the Chief Constable's orders among the various parcels and other despatches and eagerly retrieved them. Yes! There it was for all to see, Chief Con's order number 2-28/11, "Promotions. To Sergeant. Constable 2425 Turner, from 'A' Division, to 'G' Division as from 6 January 1986." Fantastic!

Not only had I been promoted, but promoted over to Wallasey, near to my home.

I was absolutely ecstatic. That night, and many more, I 'pushed the boat out' on numerous occasions as I bought drinks all round and celebrated with friends, colleagues and relations both over in Liverpool and at my own local. I sincerely hoped those cynical colleagues down at the Main Bridewell had also read the order and inwardly digested it! I received congratulatory cards, letters and 'phone calls from friends and colleagues, including some senior officers who all wished me well. I was looking forward with relish to my new posting and couldn't wait for my remaining time at Copperas Hill to elapse so that I could get started with my own, new section!

One of the first jobs, was to get my uniform round to Joe, the tailor, at the stores in Kent Street, to have my new insignia of rank attached. Within the next week I collected my new Sergeant's uniform, signalling stick and chrome triple chevrons. Until the date of my new posting arrived, however, I was still acting Sergeant at Copperas Hill.

My Acting days continued with my involving myself in arrests and summonses as well as involving myself in similar incidents with my colleagues, and frequently resorted to my own 'unofficial' forms of initiative in the field of 'public relations'.

One such example occurred when I was called to a Chinese restaurant in Duke Street. As I arrived at the premises I was greeted by the excited proprietor. "Mr Turner, you come quick, man no pay," he said as he took me through to the dining area. He took me to a table where two waiters were detaining a man at one of the tables. Again, the proprietor informed me, "He order meal, eat meal, then no pay." The cocky individual looked at me and said, "I don't know what he's panicking for, I told him I'll pay. I didn't realise that I had no money on me." I established the penniless punter's identity via his driving licence. "So you do intend to pay then?" I asked. "Yeah, my sister lives in Hope Street, I'll borrow it from her." I was informed. As Hope Street was only half a mile away, I couldn't see any problem. Handing the man's driving licence to the proprietor I informed the customer. "Right, when you get back and pay the bill, you'll get your licence back, okay?"

The man was by no means happy with this arrangement, but became more enthusiastic when I explained that the alternative would be to explain all to the Magistrates the following morning. I allowed the man to leave the premises and make his way to Hope Street. In no time at all he was back with the money and paid his bill. The proprietor was pleased, I was pleased, and the man was given his licence back, and all ended happily ever after! Another one of life's little gems in how to keep everyone happy.

The days rolled by and before I knew it, Christmas was upon us. Our Section was on afternoon duty Christmas Eve (3 p.m. to 11 p.m.) and considering it was the time of festivities and good will towards all men, the latter half of the shift was busy with us all dealing with violent and domestic disputes, drunks fighting, and the proverbial disorderly drunks.

As I was finally making my way in to sign the section off duty, I walked past a British Rail mini bus which had stopped at traffic lights. The vehicle was full of revellers and the driver was still in his British Rail uniform. The over-enthusiastic passengers in the vehicle, some of whom were women, decided to start shouting abuse and take the mickey out of the cloth (me) as I walked by. All of them had obviously consumed more than their fair quota of alcohol and at first, I ignored their abusive taunts, allowing for the fact that it was Christmas. However, they decided to increase their crescendo of Yuletide blasphemy at my expense, so I went to the driver and asked him to get out of the vehicle, to the loud chorus of "All coppers are bastards, all coppers are bastards" from the interior.

As the driver alighted from the cab I asked him if he had any authority to have the vehicle on the road at that time of night. "Sorry about this, boss," he bleated, "I've only just finished. I'm allowed to take the bus home with me. These are just a few neighbours I'm giving a lift home to from a party as a favour." As he spoke I detected the smell of whiskey on his breath. "How many drinks have you had?" I asked. "Boss, honest to God, I've had one small sip of whiskey minutes ago when I picked the gang up." Pointing to his vehicle, he added, "Barney's got a bottle. I had a sip from that." By now the driver could no doubt see his Christmas, and his job, evaporating, should he be locked up. "Honest, boss, I'll pass the bag, no trouble, try me," he pleaded. "Never mind the bag. What's Mr Railway going to say when I tell him you've been using his minibus as a bloody taxi?" I said sternly. "If they find out I'll get the sack," he answered honestly. I asked him where they all lived and the by now frightened driver said, "We all live out in Huyton. I told them I'd pick them up from their party when I finished work."

I had established what was painfully obvious, that he had no right to be conveying any unauthorised passengers in his firm's vehicle. By now the driver was becoming a gibbering wreck. I was satisfied that he had only had a small drink and I accepted his explanation of his doing a favour for his neighbours and decided that I'd make sure that not only would he not be so keen to do the same again, but that his passengers would be extremely loathe to extract the urine from the cloth in future!" "Get this lot out of the vehicle, park it over there and lock it up, then give me the keys," I instructed him.

"Are 'ey boss, give us a chance will yer?" the alarmed driver pleaded, thinking he was about to be arrested. "Do as you're told," I repeated. The mini bus was emptied of its now not so boisterous men and women, who stood about the footwalk in their paper hats and tinsel, freezing in the cold night air. Once the vehicle was secure and the keys had been handed to me I said to the driver, "Right, now get walking to Huyton." (There were now hardly any buses and taxis were at an absolute premium.) "You can collect these keys from Copperas Hill Police Station tomorrow, AFTER dinner." Although the party had a long, cold walk ahead of them the driver thanked me profusely for my 'kindness'! "This wouldn't have happened if they hadn't been so bloody cheeky and cocky," I informed him. "That'll teach you all a bloody lesson," I added as they all started their marathon slog out to the sticks of Huyton. The driver was fully aware that his 'near miss' with the law was due solely to the belligerence of those in his 'party' and I giggled to myself as I could hear him chastising them all furiously for having put him in such a predicament after him having done them all a favour. The air was blue as he emphasised how cross he was! The sound of his angry rebukes echoed in my ears as I made my way into the station. As I hung the keys up in the station with a little tag, informing the staff that they were to be collected the following afternoon, I hoped that the driver realised how lucky he was, he had caught me on a 'good day'! The keys were indeed collected by a very grateful man as arranged and again, all ended 'happily ever after'!

Finally, as 1985 came to a close, I paraded for night duty on New Year's Eve, my last tour of nights at Copperas Hill, and my last tour of nights in Liverpool! Within half an hour of the New Year having dawned I had to assist a colleague to arrest three drunken yobos for damaging trees and uprooting shrubs as they rampaged through the City centre. The three louts were taken to the Main Bridewell to await their appearance before a special court later on New Year's morning.

After this incident, the section also dealt with a number of other drink-related incidents, assaults, damage, theft etc. "Here we go again," I thought. It appeared that the New Year was to be no different from the old. One drunken youth managed to climb the dizzy heights of a stone pillar at the entrance to St John's Gardens. However, due to his state of intoxication, once he had reached the top and stood on the plinth, he was unable to maintain his balance and fell the twenty-odd feet to the ground breaking a leg as he hit 'terra firma'. After such an horrific fall he was lucky to have only sustained the injury that he did.

For the rest of the week each shift had its number of incidents, until I finished my last night duty at 7 a.m., Monday, 6 January. From this day, I was now, at long last, a Section Sergeant! Although it was my rest day, I was to parade again at Headquarters later in the morning at 11 o'clock, together with the other newly-promoted Sergeants. We were to meet the Deputy Chief Constable, Mr Burrows, and also we were to receive our newly-updated warrant cards, bearing our new rank.

At 11 o'clock we were all lined up in Mr Burrows' office to receive his congratulations and best wishes on our promotion. He moved along the line, shaking hands with the single rank of men and women and offering his congratulations. He spent a short time with each one until he reached me. He just stood in front of me and gave me a nod of acknowledgement accompanied by an incoherent mumble before moving on to the next Sergeant and shaking his hand. Perhaps he just didn't like me? I was the oldest 'new' Sergeant there on that day. My chest swelled with pride so much that it is a wonder that my tunic buttons didn't pop off. Eventually, we were all dismissed and as I had only just finished a night duty , I went home to bed to catch up on some sleep, totally whacked, but deliriously happy! The following day was also a rest day but I spent the whole day getting my uniform into pristine condition ready for my first day as Sergeant when I would meet my new section.

Chapter Eighteen - The New Block Skipper

At 8-30 am, Wednesday, 8 January 1986, I drove my car into the car park at Manor Road Police Station, Wallasey. My feelings were of utter ecstasy, I was on top of the world!. I still found it difficult to believe that I had achieved my ultimate goal at long last and that I wasn't dreaming it all. Little did I ever dare dream that I would be a Sergeant in my home area, posted to the very station where a few years earlier I had been summoned before the Chief Superintendent for upsetting the station's janitor. I was now only too thankful that the Chief Super concerned had since retired!.

I left my car and walked to the rear entrance of the station, carefully carrying my tunic, still on its coat hanger, my new silk chevrons shining brightly in the winter sunshine. I could feel the stiffness of the 'soaped', razor sharp creases in my trousers as I walked. A young bobby held the door open for me as he entered and said cheerfully, "Morning Sarge, are you our new Sergeant?". As I entered my new domain I held out my hand and replied, "Good morning officer, Sergeant Turner, I'm the new Sergeant on A block". The young bobby shook my hand, "Pleased to meet you Sarge, my name's Mike Morgan, I'm on your block". Mike went on to give me a guided tour of the building, showing me where the locker, snooker and parade rooms were. He then took me up to the Sergeants' office where I donned my smartly pressed tunic. There, Mike left me and I started to make myself at home in my new environment.

Manor Road Police Station, Wallasey

A short time later another Sergeant, Bob Jones entered the office. Bob and I had already met. Indeed, I knew most of those officers with lengthy service at Manor Road. "Hiya Swas, welcome to the section mate", greeted Bob warmly, "I'll introduce you to everyone as soon as you've seen the boss". Bob then took me up a flight of stairs to the Chief Super's office. There I was ushered in to see my new boss, Chief Superintendent Richard (Richie) Adams.

Mr Adams and I had known each other for a long time. "Welcome Sergeant, come in and sit down" he said, thanking and dismissing my escort. As he closed the door, the boss gestured with his hand for me to sit in a comfortable chair near his desk. Sitting himself down he then buzzed for two coffees. "Well, well, well, you finally made it at long last eh?, well done Swasie, I'm pleased to have you aboard". I felt as though I was imagining the proceedings, it was hard to believe that it was me that he was talking to!.

As I sat there I couldn't help but remember the last time I had been in this very office, I noticed an acute lack of cacti in here now! I spent over half an hour with my new Chief Super and we talked about different matters over an enjoyable cup of coffee. Finally, the boss stood up and shook my hand. He suggested that I now go and meet my new 'lads'. "Should you ever need me Swasie, my door's always open" he kindly offered. I thanked him profusely for his kindness and hospitality and saluted him before leaving his office to rejoin Bob downstairs in the Sergeants' office.

Also in the office now were other Sergeants, all of whom were known to me. They all made a fuss of me and each welcomed me into the 'fold'. We all then adjourned up to the canteen for a brew before one of my co-Sergeants, John Murphy, took me back down to the locker room to show me my locker, before we returned to the Sergeants' office and I was shown my desk. Bob Jones then breezed in and said, "I'm just nipping to the Town Hall on an enquiry, 'fancy coming along Swas?". "I'd love to" I replied enthusiastically.

The two of us Sergeants then drove to the impressive Civic building in the centre of the town. Eventually we returned to the station where I was left to my own devices. I decided to put my gear into my locker and put bits and pieces into the drawers of my desk. These tasks took me up to lunch time and as I was to attend court in Liverpool in the afternoon I decided to go over and have my lunch in the canteen at Cheapside. After a quick lunch I attended number 7 court in Victoria Street for an outstanding motoring trial from Copperas Hill.

As I entered the witness box to be sworn, prior to giving my evidence, the chairman of the bench, noticing my new chevrons, congratulated me on behalf of the bench on my recent promotion. I was certainly feeling more than pleased with life and thanked the bench very much for their kind comments. On leaving court at the conclusion of the proceedings I decided to call at the Main Bridewell in Cheapside for a cup of tea with my former colleagues (the main reason was to pose really!).

Although I was welcomed by the lads, I could detect acute envy from some of them as I sauntered in carrying my new signalling stick. I enjoyed every minute as I sat there drinking my tea. They didn't have much to say now at the Main! I rang through to Wallasey and asked my co-Sergeant John Murphy, to book me off duty from court and told him I would see him the following afternoon on parade. As I left the Main Bridewell I realised that I was now assuming a new degree of responsibility. I wondered for how long I would be under the 'anaesthetic of promotional enchantment?. No doubt the time would soon come when the 'honeymoon period' would be over!.

The following day I paraded for afternoon duty and took the parade at 3 pm. During the parade I introduced myself to each member of my section in turn. My section consisted of mainly young officers, males and females, some of whom were only probationers (serving the first two years of their service). After being dismissed from parade they collected their radios and made their way out onto the streets. I settled down to familiarise myself with those files needing attention and completed other various items of an administrative nature before taking the supervision car and driving round my new 'patch'.

I settled in very quickly and found my new section to be a very keen and enthusiastic bunch. As usual, there were to be found one or two older members who, because of their lengthy service, didn't appreciate a newcomer arriving and telling them what to do!. Never mind, I could easily cope with that type!. As time went by I frequently walked the beats with my bobbies and in doing so befriended a lot of the local populace.

The bobbies always referred to members of Wallasey's public as 'TWRs, (typical Wallasey residents!). Due to my frequent 'long walks' with the bobbies I began to get somewhat of a reputation among them. After parade one day I overheard one of the drivers asking a beat officer if he wanted dropping off anywhere. The young Constable replied, "No it's okay. I've just been bloody captured by the Sergeant, Swasie walks the fucking legs off yer"!!. I would walk with one officer along his beat then meet another before walking his beat with him , oh !, they were pleased!.

During my first week I visited some of the local pubs for a 'walk through' in company with the beat man. On one such visit young Constable Magarvey and I entered the Twenty Row Inn and as we did so I caught a number of people gambling in the bar. The manager received a stiff telling off on my debut, a fine start!.

I soon came to know who was who on the section. The majority were conscientious and hard working, one or two however, I discovered had a reputation (which had been well earned) for being idle. By and large I was delighted with my new 'flock' and intended to give those that warranted (and deserved) it, my ALL. The section gradually accepted me and it soon became clear to them that I would be there any time they needed me and I would back them to the hilt in any crisis whatsoever, provided of course that they were in the right!. I did not intend to suffer shirkers.

One of my early 'claims to fame' occurred during a tour of night duty. As I drove round the division in the early hours of one morning I decided to have a cruise down to the beach and the nearby sandhills bordering the shore at Leasowe. As I made my way slowly along the coastal track my headlights picked out the roof sign of a Police car which was secreted behind one of the sandy mounds topped with tufts of Spartina grass. I stopped my vehicle and crept up to the patrol car which had its engine running but was not displaying lights.

I could hear the powerful hum of the vehicle's heater above the sound of the running engine. I shone my torch into the interior of the vehicle and saw the driver, fast asleep, his head against the offside window, his cap on the back seat. I thumped the roof of his car with my metal braced hand, BANG!!!. The young bobby nearly fell out of his vehicle as I wrenched his door open. "What the bloody hell's this" I asked the startled and still half awake cop. "Sorry Sarge, you've caught me good style, I throw my hands up" stammered the nervous officer wondering what fate now awaited him.

I stood there and lectured him, "The people of Wallasey pay their rates and want protection, not some lazy bastard sleeping the night away, when he's on good money"! I ranted. "S-sorry Sarge, it won't happen again promised the young Rip Van Winkle. "Make sure it doesn't, now get back on patrol" I said as I signed his note book recording my visit. No doubt he was apprehensive as to what I had put in his book. I didn't record anything other than my official 'peg'. Nothing more was said and I didn't mention the incident to anyone. I made no comment later as I signed the section off duty at 7 am.

The sandhills at Leasowe

During following night parade I called the section to attention as the Inspector entered the room. "Thank you Sergeant" acknowleged Inspector

276

Davies and I stood the parade at ease. After briefing the men, reading various items of importance from the 'reading out file' and allocating the section their various beats, patrols and other duties, I proceeded to hand out files and relevant documents for some officers' attention. I went to the previous night's 'tired officer'!, and discreetly handed him a pink alarm clock which I had borrowed from my daughter. "Here, take this. It's set for six thirty, so you should get off duty for seven" I said sarcastically. The young bobby took the clock from me and stood there open-mouthed, not knowing what to do or say.

Obviously the young errant had blabbed to his colleagues about the incident the night before, as the whole section fell about laughing hysterically at him standing there with an alarm clock in his hand. Inspector Davies in his ignorance asked, "What the bloody hell's going on Sarge?" I replied, "It's nothing sir, just a private joke" and recalled the section to order. My little 'jape' must have registered, as I never caught anyone sleeping on duty again.

After the parade, the young officer sheepishly entered the Sergeants' office and returned the alarm clock to me. "Point taken Sarge, I apologise for last night", he said, his face pink with embarrassment. "Okay" I grunted. The story of his sleep and the little clock spread throughout the sub-division (he should have kept his mouth shut!). I considered that I had dealt with the situation in an effective (and humorous) way which had delivered 'the message'!. To some it may seem that for such a 'serious' offence as sleeping on duty a more severe form of punishment should have been advocated.

Although I do not intend to diminish the gravity of the young officer's conduct during that night, my own vivid memory of the 'damaged' notebook is still paramount in my mind. I considered that by dealing with the matter in the manner I did not only (hopefully) cured the problem by means of humiliation, but may well have earned the loyalty and respect of a grateful officer for not resorting to the discipline code. I am satisfied that the message had been put across that any similar 'misdemeanour' would not be dealt with so lightly.

Another field where I considered the big stick should be wielded if my section failed to comply, involved those who insisted on NOT wearing their uniform caps when on duty in Police vehicles or when alighting from their vehicle to deal with an incident. This was conduct which I could not stand. If the driver of a vehicle found that by wearing a cap his driving was impaired, fair enough, although, being just on six foot tall myself, I always wore my cap, even when I drove the Mini Coopers which we once had. Eventually, I warned the section that if I were to catch anyone not wearing their caps without good reason, then they would be walking the beat wearing a helmet. I did not intend to budge one quarter on the subject.

I consider that an officer minus his hat (for no good reason) is improperly dressed. How smart and efficient is the impression given by Traffic officers who are very rarely seen minus their caps whether driving or not. I find this habit of shabby dressing is now becoming a regular sight among officers. This type of conduct not only manifested itself among the

Constables but sometimes officers of higher rank set a bad example too. I attended an incident with a number of patrols one day and shortly after, we were joined by an Inspector. On the Inspector's arrival, he alighted from his vehicle and joined me to assess the situation. Not only was he minus his cap, but he was puffing away at his pipe!!. Leaning over I whispered into his ear, "Excuse me sir, haven't we forgotten something"?. 'What's that Sarge'?, he replied. "Your cap sir, you're minus your cap", I pointed out politely. The Inspector turned to me and spat out venomously, "Don't you dare tell me what to do". I countered by asking him, "How on earth can I bollock the lads for not wearing their caps when you attend not wearing yours?"

The Inspector stormed off to his vehicle and donned his cap before returning to me saying, "There, satisfied"?. "No, not really sir, I don't let the lads wander about in public smoking either," I replied and got on with the matter in hand. The matter didn't end there, unfortunately. On returning to the station later, the Inspector called me into his office as I was walking past his door. On entering the office and closing the door behind me as requested, the Inspector laid into me with one almighty roasting. "Don't you EVER try telling me what to do again," he ranted, pointing out that he would do 'as he liked' and reminded me that he was senior in rank to me. "I wasn't telling you what to do sir, I was respectfully pointing out that you'd forgotten to put your cap on," I replied. The Inspector pointed out that he didn't take too kindly to a Sergeant giving him advice on how to dress. I again cut into his angry tirade, "While we're at it sir, you might as well bollock me for criticising your smoking as well because if I ever catch one of my bobbies smoking in public I'll stuff him"! Our verbal 'altercation' continued for a little longer and eventually ended in 'stalemate' as neither he, nor I would 'bend' on the matter.

My standards of discipline were widely known and I insisted on nothing short of punctuality and a smart standard of turnout. I indicated this by my own personal conduct and turnout!. As the matter was obviously not going to be resolved I saluted the Inspector and took my leave of him. I also received a 'mild' reprimand from the Superintendent for the 'unorthodox' way I dealt with one of the section who was starting to become a bad time keeper.

The particular Constable lived quite near to the station but would quite often arrive late for parade, irrespective of what shift he was on, he would then insult my intelligence by offering the most 'lame' excuse. During a tour of morning duty (7am to 3 pm) he was late TWICE in two days! The second time, he breezed into the Sergeants' office forty minutes late. The rest of the section had left the station and were now out on patrol. "Sorry I'm late Sarge," I cut him short as he was about to give me yet another pathetic reason for missing parade, "It's okay, you're not late!. I've put you on afternoon duty (3pm to llpm) today, so you can go back home to bed for a couple of hours." The officer stood there, his mouth agape. "B-B-But I've made arrangements to go out tonight" he bleated. I rounded on him and suggested that he ask the afternoon Sergeant for some 'time due' to facilitate his evening's revelry!

Years before, this type of procedure was not uncommon when dealing with persistent late arrivals, and many such 'offenders' were cured at Rose Hill by being so dealt with. The by now very disgruntled officer tried in vain to persuade me to rescind my decision but I was adamant, my mind was made up. "I'm sick and tired of your bloody timekeeping, If you don't like it, go and see the Chief Super" I said sternly. The officer left and made his way home hardly believing what had befallen him.

Later, on being relieved by the afternoon Sergeant, I informed him of the morning's incident and told him that he had an additional Constable on his afternoon strength! "Bloody hell Swas, you can't do that!" my colleague exclaimed. "I've done it" I replied, "I'm sick to bloody death of his bad time keeping, if I don't do anything about it now it might rub off on the others". The officer concerned paraded for duty in the afternoon but was allowed to go off duty early by having time deducted from what was owed to him. The officer was NEVER late for duty again (at least not while I was his Sergeant!!).

The following day, as I expected, I was summoned to the Superintendent's office. My Superintendent, Mr Lowe, was a man who I not only liked very much, but also deeply respected. He was a 'copper' through and through, and a man who worked tirelessly for the benefit and welfare of his subordinates, (a rare breed). I was asked into his office and told to sit down, then the Super started the ball rolling. "What's this I hear about you sending a bobby home because he was late?" asked the boss. Confirming what he had heard, I went on to elaborate upon why I had taken such action. I told him the story of my frustrated attempts to get the particular officer to 'toe the line', but until yesterday my attempts had so far proved futile. I added, truthfully, that I had NEVER been late for duty and although I was fully aware that circumstances occur which could adversely affect one's punctuality, I felt that this man was setting a bad example to the younger element of the section. "Well in future don't be so drastic. Send him or anyone else who needs 'talking to' up to me", the Super snapped. I appreciated that he meant what he said, but I didn't want others to do what I considered to be my responsibility. "Very well sir," I conceded.

Superintendent Lowe and I went on to have a lengthy discussion regarding my section, myself, discipline and police duties in general. I managed to air a few little 'grievances', knowing that, with this man, they would be listened to sympathetically and would not just fall onto stony ground!. "I've heard about your 'thing' concerning the wearing of caps (somebody must have been talking!) and footmen riding in cars" mused the boss, illustrating his intimate knowledge of everything that went on!. The subject of bobbies not being properly dressed when in view of the public and beat men riding in cars instead of walking their beats was a subject which I took very seriously. "Oh that sir, well I don't think it's right, bobbies walking about like bloody car park attendants, frightened of spoiling their coiffeur by having to wear a cap," I said, as I stood on my 'soap box'!. I agree with you entirely," said the Super. I was delighted,

I knew deep down that he was on my wavelength. For some reason I just couldn't go wrong in his eyes. These sentiments were totally reciprocated as I held him in very high esteem indeed. Our little chat was concluded with the Super saying, "Anyway, consider yourself bollocked for yesterday'!" I stood up, saluted and said, "Very good sir"! and left his office. Although the constable concerned was never unduly late again, his expression and attitude indicated that he never forgave me for what I did. However, this was never to cause me any loss of sleep whatsoever! I was utterly devoted to my section and would go through hell and high water for them if necessary, so long as it was justified, but if they were naughty, I could be naughty also!

I openly encouraged my officers to 'cultivate' tea specks by calling into shops or homes of 'vulnerable' people to assure them all of our undivided attention. On this score, I myself, certainly led by example as I am not ashamed to admit to doing the same thing. I considered such fraternisation justifiable in the interests of police public relations. Provided that the officer dealt with his tasks and listened to his radio, I was all for such reasonable (professional) intimate involvement with the public; after all, as rate payers, that is one of their entitlements, not to mention the psychological sense of security such action gives. Of course there were always some who would abuse this interpretation of P.R. but I was satisfied with my section's relationship with "Joe" Public!

A most tragic and determined effort of self-destruction was revealed to me when I was summoned to assist a young probationer who had attended a 'sudden death'. As I attended the scene, it brought back memories of the Athol Street tragedy of the distant past. I saw the body of a women who must have been severely mentally disturbed to have gone to such lengths to terminate her life. The poor lady had opened the gas oven to allow the gas to escape, then after slashing her wrists and cutting her throat, she had consumed a box of sleeping tablets before washing them down with half a bottle of whisky before lying down to die.

She was discovered by her distraught husband who turned off the gas and called the emergency services, who sadly could do nothing for his wife. The young bobby was certainly 'broken in' by having to deal with such a traumatic incident. He dealt with the matter in a most efficient, dignified and professional way, unlike the ex-navy colleague of mine so many years before. Scenes and tragedies such as this are indelibly printed on the minds of those who deal with such incidents, and this sad case was to be no exception.

One of my young recruits started to attract my attention. He was always 'hovering' about the station on some pretext or other and when challenged, was always 'engaged' in report writing. Even when he was out on the streets he could never be contacted. His radio always seemed to be 'faulty', but when tested, was found to be in full working order. I started to watch this particular recruit closely.

One day, I called into the station mid-way through the shift only to find the same officer wandering about the enquiry office when he should have been out on his beat, a considerable distance away. "What the hell are you doing in here?" I asked. "I'm catching up on some reports," he replied. As he was not renowned for his hard work, I said, "What reports? You never do bugger all so how can you have reports?" I went on to inform him that I would tell him when to come in from his beat to write his reports, and ordered him back out to resume his beat patrol. I began to wonder if he was apprehensive about being out on his own.

A couple of days later, I again caught him 'unofficially' inside the station. I asked him angrily, "What are you doing in here when you should be outside?". The constable replied, "Sergeant Hopewell said I could come in for reports". I wasn't at all pleased with this, as my co-Sergeant, Mal Hopewell, was equally concerned about this man's frequenting of the station and knew that I had told him to come in only when I said so.

There was nothing I could do for the moment as I was not going against a fellow Sergeant by countering his authorisation for the Constable's presence, but I decided to speak to the Sergeant and find out why he had reversed my original instructions to the probationer. Leaving the officer in the station, I took my patrol car and went out to meet my co-Sergeant. On meeting and discussing the matter, I was informed by my colleague that he had not seen the probationer during the watch, let alone spoken to him as he, the Sergeant, had been engaged on duties away from the station for the first two hours of the shift. The probationer was now getting himself into hot water as he had therefore lied to me. He had committed a blatant 'falsehood'.

I returned to the station post haste and on my arrival instructed the young bobby to attend the Sergeants' office forthwith in possession of his 'outstanding reports'. The young probationer Constable entered the office and I instructed him to close the door (I didn't want all and sundry listening in to what I intended to be the administering of one hell of an admonishment). Taking the paperwork from the officer I placed it on my desk and scrutinised it. As I thought, nothing important which was outstanding! Another lie. I threw the reports down and turned to the probationer. "You're a bloody liar," I snapped. "Sergeant Hopewell didn't give you permission to be in the station at all did he?". The recruit stood there not knowing what to say.

Finally he muttered lamely, "I thought he did Sarge". I went on, "I'm sick to death seeing you in the station. What's up?, are you too bloody scared to go out?" I threatened him with disciplinary proceedings if he ever lied to me again or was to be found anywhere other than where he should be. "Do I make myself clear?" I bellowed, reminding him that as he was still only a probationer he was putting his job on the line by his conduct. "I won't let it happen again", the young man assured me. I dismissed him and instructed him to get back to his beat and he left the office knowing exactly where he stood with me. Provided he made an effort and worked as hard as the rest of his colleagues, I would let the matter rest, we would have to see how he went on.

As the section lined up on parade the following day, I placed a saucer of milk on the floor at the feet of the admonished Constable, just to ensure that he had received my message 'loud and clear'. (Nobody else knew of his visit to my office the previous day.) Looking puzzled the Constable asked, "What's this Sarge?" I replied, "As you are the station cat, I thought I'd put your breakfast out Tibby!". The rest of the section were highly amused as they were all aware of his prolonged periods spent indoors. The young officer was known and referred to by that name from that day on. Although he managed to stay out of trouble, I found that he still, however, sometimes 'sailed close to the wind'. I consider that he was lucky to have been kept on the job, as much of his work left a lot to be desired.

I became the section's 'football' Sergeant and would take my contingent of men to assist the policing of matches at Everton, Anfield or Tranmere. I always looked forward to these 'outings' and quickly organised a particular routine for those days. I would take my 'gang' over to the ground and send one of them for fish and chips which we would then consume in the back of our personnel carrier. I decided this was better as, officially, we had forgone our refreshment period in order to get over to the ground early. There was method in my madness, as, on our return to the station at the conclusion of our tour of duty, I would tell the lads to make to a certain pub where I would buy them a pint after I had booked them off duty on the parade state.

One evening, I was leaving the station at 9 pm, after telling my lads to make to the nearby 'hostelry' after a particularly hectic and soaking wet duty at Liverpool's football ground. Our official duty for that day was 2pm to 10 pm. I was approached by the afternoon shift Inspector (whose shift was 3pm to 11pm). "Put a couple of your lads on the shopping precinct 'till ten will you Sarge?" he instructed. I informed him that this was not possible as I had sent them home off duty. The indignant Inspector then informed me sharply, "You've no right to have let them go, it's only nine o clock and you're not off 'till ten". I replied that we had not had a refreshment period as we were so busy and due to this I decided to utilise this period by allowing them to go home an hour early. The Inspector did not like this unofficial arrangement one bit!. 'Don't be bringing your Liverpool habits over here Sergeant, we don't do tricks like that at Wallasey". I wasn't going to argue with him but I did think "Here's another example of senior rank with no appreciation of initiative!"

I repeated this 'procedure' on all subsequent match days, much to the delight of my football section, they were more than pleased with the 'early dart'! Although other Sergeants performing football duty were at first reluctant to follow my 'example', the procedure became widely accepted as almost the 'norm'. I never once failed to ask my football section to make to the nearby pub where I would 'treat my lads' to a pint after each game, I always considered that to be my 'privilege'. Sometimes we made a night of it, most times we just had a couple before making our way home.

Many incidents occurred during those football duties, some more than a little amusing!. Usually the crowds, (especially the Merseysiders) were well behaved and the Scouse wit' was never far below the surface, and nearly always materialised in some form or other. There were of course the drink, fights, assaults, thefts or disorderly behaviour, there hardly ever failed to be some incident or other, whenever we were engaged at the big matches.

One Saturday match day, I arrived early at the station to prepare our personnel carrier for the journey over to Everton for the afternoon fixture. I found that our carrier had not been returned from undergoing its regular service and consequently, the only vehicle now available in the yard was our 'general purpose' van. This vehicle was a shabby Sherpa van, which was used mainly for the transporting and transferring of prisoners (mainly drunks and itinerants), carrying of traffic signs etc, and the collection and transporting of stray dogs. It had no windows and inside were wooden slatted seats which were fitted down each side of the van's interior, one of those seats being broken. The interior of the van smelled to high heaven, even though it was cleaned out regularly.

Obviously, I couldn't use this vehicle to take my lads over to Liverpool and back, the stink inside the vehicle was unbearable, and tufts of dogs' hair adhered to the seats. I rang the neighbouring station at Birkenhead to see if they could assist as they also had a personnel carrier. A young Constable answered the telephone and I asked him if his Sergeant would allow me to borrow the station's carrier to transport my section to the Everton match. Neither a Sergeant nor an Inspector were available, but the Constable told me that their carrier was being used by their own football section. However, the 'prison' van (a Transit van used solely for the transporting of prisoners to their places of incarceration from the courts) was parked in their yard. This van was clean and had proper cushioned seating in the interior. "That'll do, I'll borrow that then" I said, after the bobby informed me that the van was now idle as the courts had finished for the weekend.

I told the bobby to inform his Sergeant that I would collect the van then return it to their yard at the conclusion of the day's match duty. "I'll do that Sarge", confirmed the officer. I went over to Birkenhead, collected the van and returned to Wallasey to pick up my section. All went well until I was approached by a young Acting Sergeant halfway through the game. "Excuse me, Sarge, could you ring the Inspector at Birkenhead right away, please?" he requested politely. "Certainly", I replied, "What is it, d'you know?" The acting Sergeant grinned, "I've no idea Sarge, but he seems upset over something," he said with a chuckle! I made my way to the ground's Police office and rang the Inspector as instructed. I wasn't prepared for the verbal onslaught that I received. I was greeted by a torrent of angry rhetoric from a very irate Inspector!. "Who the fucking hell said you could take our van?" he raved. "I thought it would be okay as it wouldn't be required until Monday; ours is off the road," I replied. The Inspector could not be pacified, he was beside himself with rage. "I want a full, written report on my desk first thing in the morning!" he screamed. I was not prepared to be spoken to in this manner by anyone, however annoyed they were so I replaced the receiver and resumed my duties inside the ground. Later on during the game, I was informed by the 'football Inspector' that I was to submit a full report regarding my taking of the van from Birkenhead Police Station without permission, as the vehicle had been earlier reported 'missing' by the Birkenhead Inspector!

On my return to Wallasey I deposited my section and booked them off duty. I then arranged for the van to be returned to Birkenhead before going off duty myself.

As I paraded for duty at 7 am the following morning, my Inspector, Ken Stott, called me to one side and told me to complete a full typewritten report immediately after parade regarding my 'unauthorised taking' of the van from Birkenhead. This was becoming an absolute nonsense! The boss told me that the Birkenhead Inspector had been on the 'phone to him minutes earlier and explained the full circumstances of my sins. After the parade I rang the Inspector, a young 'whizz kid'. I had been longer on a message than he had been on the job! "What's this about a report sir?" I asked politely. "You had no bloody right to take our van yesterday, so get that report over here pronto!" he snapped. "I'll do better than that, I'll come over there myself, now" I replied as I angrily slammed down the 'phone. Thinking my own Inspector would agree with what I had done due to the circumstances which had prevailed, I said, "He's blown a bloody fuse, just because I used his van!"

I nearly fell over when my own Inspector replied, "He's quite right, you had no right to use their vehicle, why didn't you use our own van?" I turned to him and retorted, "You must be joking sir, it's full of shite and dog hairs, the seat's broken and it bloody stinks, I couldn't take the lads in that". "Why?, what's the problem? You'd be sitting in the front wouldn't you?" said the Inspector to my utter disbelief! What an attitude to have towards one's subordinates, I thought to myself. "Perhaps you don't give a monkey's for your men, but I certainly give a monkey's for mine and there's no way I was taking them over in that!" I said. Maybe that's the way he would have done things, I'm alright Jack - no way!

My Inspector then went on to say, "Well, you'd better get things sorted out because I don't want any hassle over a bloody van". 'I'd better sort it out? There was nothing to sort out as far as I could see: I'd borrowed a van that was otherwise not being used, full stop. I thought we were all in the same job?. What a load of petty minded red tape, all because I hadn't rooted out this individual Inspector. I had attempted to speak to my opposite number but there was nobody available, to ask him if I could borrow his confounded van (which was lying there idle) and to make matters worse, even my own Inspector didn't have the bottle to back me up. Two officers of equal rank? Surely they could have sorted out this 'little misunderstanding? No, he was prepared to let me stand on my own! What a childish storm in a ridiculous teacup. I drove over to Birkenhead on my own and made my way to the pompous little God's office.

I don't know how, but the staff at Birkenhead were buzzing with anticipation at the prospect of a forthcoming show-down between myself and their Inspector, who I knew to be about as popular as a fart in a 'phone box!. How they were aware of the up to date developments I don't know, but being bobbies, aware of the situation they certainly were!

I made my way up to the little despot's office and knocked on the door. I received an abrupt, "Come in!", and entered. Closing the door tightly behind me I then stood to attention and saluted before asking, "Now sir, What's the problem?" The Inspector looked at me and asked, "Where's the report I asked you for?" I replied courteously, "As we are alone sir, and have known each other for quite a long time now, may I talk 'man to man' with you, no rank involved?". He replied reluctantly, no doubt wondering what was coming next, "Okay Swasie, sit down and let's hear what you've got to say".

Birkenhead Police Station

I sat down and placed my cap, gloves and stick on his desk. "Right", I started, "Don't you ever speak to me as though I'm some new recruit or some piece of shit. I did what I did because I wasn't having my men travelling in a van that is normally used for the carriage of dogs, you didn't need your bloody van so as I considered I had no alternative, I borrowed yours. Why all the bloody panic, it was only lying there idle?" The Inspector looked at me, amazed at my blunt outburst. "Look Swasie, there's no need for us to fall out," he whimpered, "but you should have gone through the channels and sought permission from me!" "Sir", I interjected, "If the same set of circumstances were to arise again, I would do the same. There is no way my lads will be transported about in a bloody dog van", and added, "and there's no way I'm sitting down to type out a bloody extract from Gone With The Wind when you know very well why your van was used."

The Inspector looked at me and said slowly, "Okay Swas, let's both beg to differ. We won't fall out over this, after all, we're on the same side aren't we?". "Exactly, my sentiments entirely sir", I replied.

After resolving our differences the Inspector and I then had a cup of tea and a natter before I eventually left and made my way back to my own station. Ironically, that particular Inspector and I were to remain the best of friends after that (silly) little incident!, my own Inspector had made his position quite clear. I knew not to rely on his backing in future!.

On my arrival back at my own station I was met by Inspector Stott as he made his way out. "How did you get on with the Inspector at Birkenhead?", he asked inquisitively. I replied with as much respect as I could muster, "With respect sir, I suggest that you ask the Inspector!" My not too pleased Inspector then made off, hopefully, having been made aware of my dissent at his acute lack of 'bottle'!.

Again, the dogs were barking the little saga between the Birkenhead Inspector and I, all over the division, perhaps some of them were standing with their ears pressed to his office door during our 'altercation'?, it wouldn't be the first time ! I continued to enjoy life at Wallasey and as time wore on the section and I (hopefully) eventually seemed to have 'jelled'. We always seemed to be busy. How well I remember referring to my colleagues on the Wirral as woolley-backs when I worked in the city! Little did I realise then how wrong I was and how busy things were for those officers, I certainly realised now!

One morning I was requested to attend a local firms' premises by one of my policewomen. On my arrival I asked my officer to enlighten me. She informed me of a tragic incident involving a 15 year old boy, who had only started work there that very morning, having just left school. The poor lad had been assisting another employee to carry out some work on the roof of the premises and had slipped and fallen through the roof onto the concrete forty feet below. The policewoman had given what first aid she could to the youth and she and I then accompanied the ambulance to the hospital at Arrowe Park, where, sadly the youth was pronounced dead on arrival. As there was no need for me to remain I left the officer at the casualty department to enable her to continue dealing with the incident.

As I left the hospital I was directed by radio to fort Perch Rock, the well known landmark standing off New Brighton under the watchful eye of the equally well known lighthouse. I was asked to go and speak to the fort's owner, Mr Kingham, who had earlier rescued two little girls after they had been cut off by the incoming tide. I collected the two eight year olds and took them back to their homes. I returned the children to each of their frantic parents and strongly advised them to keep a sharp eye on their offspring in the future. The little duo had wandered for half a mile before going out to the fort along the narrow causeway across the sands. Only the timely intervention by an observant Mr Kingham prevented another tragedy occurring on that day.

Being a seaside town, one of our important duties when storms hit the area, was to close the New Brighton promenade to traffic. This was necessary during high 'spring' tides as the angry seas would crash over the sea wall flooding the immediate area and rendering the vicinity unsafe to both pedestrian and vehicular traffic. These duties were performed only when there was such a danger, and a special procedure was adopted to ensure that these duties were carried out correctly, and set guide-lines were adhered to. The special procedure was officially known as "Operation Neptune". Although there were the occasional idiotic motorists (or pedestrians) who insisted on tempting fate by driving or walking around the barricades, most people appreciated that such actions were taken for their own safety. Apart from one or two of those mindless people who were sometimes caught and soaked by the waves or their vehicles rendered useless by the huge torrents of water that cascaded over them, there were never any tragedies during such storms due to the deployment of 'Operation Neptune'.

Fort Perch Rock, New Brighton.

Near the sea wall, nestling near the sandhills, where once stood the large open air swimming baths, Derby Pool, stood a small concrete Police 'hut'. This served as a 'refuge' for lost children, first aid post, and was regularly visited by officers wishing to complete reports in the quietness of the hut's interior or to use the toilet and washing facilities it offered, especially during the night. We would call in during our shifts and 'hit the book'; sometimes the lads would spend their refreshment period in the quiet serenity of the surroundings. I regularly visited the 'hut' to endorse the station book and report any malfunction to any of the hut's equipment. Sadly, someone on high, in their ultimate wisdom, was to eventually decide to have the hut closed down and demolished, thus depriving the area of an important amenity, especially during the busy summer season. No doubt someone in authority decided to cut costs by allowing the loss of more of the area's heritage?.

One of the Inspectors who I served under was a very mild-mannered and quietly spoken man, who was also an extremely competent and efficient police officer, Les Davies.

One morning Les and I were out on a routine mobile patrol when we were directed by radio to attend at a local MIND centre (battered wives' hostel). We were met at the entrance to the premises by the lady in charge, the 'manager'. She informed us that a husband of one of her temporary 'residents' was inside assaulting his wife and breaking furniture.

On entering, the sounds of breaking glass together with a woman's screams could be heard. All of a sudden a man appeared from one of the rooms, dragging a very distressed woman by her hair. I couldn't help thinking how the spectacle resembled a cave man dragging his woman away to his lair! Inspector Davies, being the true diplomat that he is, managed to calm the man down and persuade him to release the woman, who then beat a hasty retreat out of sight.

"Now then what's the problem Tommy?" asked the Inspector in his usual calm manner after having ascertained the man's name. 'Tommy' replied by shouting, "My wife's not staying in here, she's coming home with me" and gesticulated furiously with his hands. The agitated Tommy then picked up a Spanish guitar which was leaning against a wall and proceeded to tunelessly strum the instrument. The three of us were surprised when he then asked "D'yer wanna hear me sing?" He appeared somewhat strange in manner by the demeanour which he now adopted. "Not particularly," replied Inspector Davies. 'Tommy' continued to strum the instrument with no semblance of rhythm whatsoever.

The Inspector moved towards the untalented maestro and told him to put down the instrument and leave the premises. He was then met with a torrent of abuse, "You're gonna hear me fucking sing!" snarled Tom, as he continued with his tuneless strumming and started to 'sing' some form of rendition. The Inspector once again politely asked Tom to put down the guitar and leave the building. Inspector Davies was completely taken by surprise when the budding 'Hank Marvin' threw down the instrument and punched him in the face.

The centre's 'manager' tended the temporarily stunned Inspector as I tried to grab his assailant. Realising what he had done, Tom then ran through the building with me in hot pursuit. We ran through a television room, much to the surprise of the viewers present, some of whom were small children. There was no way out for him now! I had him cornered. To my amazement, as I took hold of my quarry by his jacket, he jumped through a large plate glass window, taking the lace curtains, AND ME, with him! We both landed on the grassy area in front of the building in a tangle of arms, legs and lengths of lace. Fortunately, I landed on top of 'Tommy' who lay there badly winded by the fall (and possibly my weight?) which rendered him unable to resist further.

My Inspector was not badly hurt and the lady in charge of the establishment had informed him that she did not wish to instigate any proceedings with regard to the damage caused to the window, as she considered the whole circumstances surrounding Tommy and his wife's domestic problems needed help and sympathy to resolve. Their problems were so acute that it necessitated her temporary residence at the home with her child until the matter was resolved. The boss and I were persuaded to let the matter rest with her and as a result the matter was reported as 'advice given' at scene! (As it happened the couple were eventually reconciled and their domestic problems were brought to an amicable conclusion.)

As we left the scene, the boss grinned and said, "Swasie, it was worth a smack in the gob to see the two of you fly through that window wrapped in flowing lace!". Looking back, I also could see the funny side when I imagined how it must have looked!

New Brighton has its share of night clubs which are heavily patronised at weekends. Nightclubs, crowds and drink obviously bring their share of problems in the form of drunks showing off, fighting (including women), drink driving and many more ancillary incidents.

One such incident occurred in the early hours of one morning when a young man was stabbed and seriously injured at one club in the resort. I attended the scene with a number of officers. The injured man was lying unconscious inside the entrance of the club. He was bleeding profusely from a nasty wound to his abdomen. My colleagues and I rendered first aid as we awaited the arrival of the ambulance.

A crowd of hysterical young women had gathered, hindering our attempts to treat the young man. Taking no chances, I decided to treat the matter as one of a 'potential' murder. I posted an officer to every door of the building and requested the attendance of the O.S.D. to assist, together with the CID. I needed as many officers as possible to ensure that the identity of everyone present was obtained and verified before anyone was allowed to leave. This procedure is paramount should the incident turn into a murder enquiry. As being an ex-detective, I was fully aware how important this would be and despite howls of protest from those who demanded to be allowed to leave the premises, I stood firm and refused permission for anyone to leave until their identity had been ascertained. Pressure would be eased as soon as officers from the OSD (Operational Support Division) arrived and assisted to complete this task.

A short time later I was joined by a woman Sergeant. She didn't help matters by arguing with me in front of my subordinates and members of the public, informing me that I couldn't just keep three hundred people inside the premises against their will. This particular woman Sergeant had no previous CID experience and therefore could not grasp the gravity of the need to do so. It was imperative that all in the club should be identified. It was most embarrassing to be told by a colleague, who obviously had no experience of dealing with such a serious matter as this, not to mention the added incentive it gave to those protesting at their 'detention'. Her attitude could well exacerbate the already volatile situation so, not mincing words I whispered into her ear, "Will you piss off and leave it to me to deal with it!" My actions were gratefully acknowledged by the CID Inspector on his arrival, as the situation was being contained. The injured man was removed to hospital and at this time we were only aware that his condition was 'serious'.

The OSD arrived and assisted those already engaged in the laborious task of taking and verifying the names and addresses of all those present in the club. My female colleague was still uttering comments of dissent until she was adequately put in her place by the Detective Inspector and the night Superintendent, both of whom confirmed my original procedures as being totally correct in such circumstances. Although at first it had the makings of a very ugly situation, things were 'defused' by the arrival of the studio and SOCO (scenes of crime officers), whose very presence indicated to all present how serious the situation was. They accepted that the sooner our enquiries and tasks at the scene were completed, the sooner they could leave for home. One or two who were drunk and disorderly were arrested and taken into custody for the night.

Eventually things quietened down and after all work was completed at the scene everyone was allowed to leave. As I left the club in company with one of my Constables we came across a young couple leaning against a wall engaging in sexual intercourse. The woman's skirt was up about her waist and the man's trousers were about his ankles.

My colleague and I quickly brought proceedings to an abrupt halt with the threat of an overnight stay in the cells and a subsequent appearance before the court if they continued their actions. Both were moved on and as they made off, each adjusting their attire, the woman muttered, "Christ, yer can't even fucking screw in peace!" I realised that she must have been on home leave from finishing school at Rodean College. As there were no other persons about to witness the spectacle, I allowed the couple to continue on their way By the look of them both as they staggered off, indicating an obviously adequate liquor consumption, I was amazed at their capabilities to indulge in such activity!

A well known first division football player and I fell out due to his nocturnal misbehaviour as he frequented the New Brighton club scene. He and I crossed swords on a number of occasions . Finally, his chickens came home to roost! He was suspected of a number of early morning high speed car chases, each time managing to escape and later denying all knowledge and reporting his car stolen when we found the vehicle damaged, having been involved in a collision (usually with a wall or lamp post), before being abandoned.

Unfortunately for him, however, during the last chase he was positively identified by one on my officers, Constable (now Sergeant) Dave Peers, although he again managed to escape on the night. Constable Peers and I arrested him the following evening as he was taking part in a darts match in one of the riverside pubs. The footballer was arrested and on his subsequent appearance before the court was sentenced to a term of imprisonment for his erring ways. The player concerned now leads an exemplary life and is back in his team playing first division football .

There is a well known theatre in New Brighton next to the indoor fairground, where many well-known national (and international) performers have trod its famous boards, the Floral Pavilion. In the early hours of an otherwise quiet night shift as my colleague and I were on mobile patrol in Victoria Road, New Brighton, we drew alongside a car stopped at traffic lights. I saw a well known face sitting behind the wheel of the car, who was also known personally to me, the well known and well liked comedian, Stan Boardman. Stan is known for his generosity to charitable causes as he gives a lot of his time (and money) to such. He and I first got to know each other when he used to attend boxing tournaments involving my youths from Toxteth, Liverpool. "Hiya Stan", I greeted "How are ya Sarge?" replied Stan.

The Floral Pavilion Theatre, New Brighton.

The lights changed and Stan suggested that we pull across the junction to continue our little chat. I alighted from our vehicle and then stood chatting to Stan as I leaned against his car. Just then a voice from the rear of Stan's car said gruffly, "Why don't you fuck off copper." Stan looked at me and said, "Sorry about that Sarge, it's Reedie (Oliver Reed). He's pissed". I shone my torch into the rear of the car and, sure enough, there was the drunken figure of that well known man sitting slumped in a drunken stupor. He and Stan were both returning to their hotel a short distance away after finishing a show and having a 'few' drinks? The drunken back seat passenger became more abusive as his colourful language and drunken threats filled the still night air. He was obviously embarrassing Stan by his behaviour. Ignoring Stan's apologies I opened the rear door and poked my face into the face of the obnoxious drunk. "Listen, you. I don't like drunken bullies, and more to the point, I most certainly don't like you. If you don't shut that big foul mouth of yours, I will get the utmost pleasure in taking you in for the night"! I said in utmost earnest. I turned to Stan and said, "Stan, get this obnoxious, self-centred drunken bully out of my sight before I arrest him". Stan looked at me and a cheeky grin spread across his face as he said, "I take it you don't like him Sarge"? "Like him? I can't bloody stick him or his ilk at all," I replied. Stan bade me goodbye as our conversation was so rudely brought to an end. I didn't want to make an issue of things as no doubt Stan would have been compromised and his 'friend' was just not worth it. As my colleague and I resumed our patrol, my colleague expressed the fact that he too, was not a fan of the back seat drunk.

One of the jobs I disliked most was that of Bridewell Sergeant (Custody Officer). This entailed being responsible for the day to day running of the station, accepting charges, housing and bailing prisoners and catering for their well being while they are in Police custody, together with ancillary station duties. I never did consider myself to be 'welfare orientated' towards the criminal element and much preferred outside duties to those of the station's confines.

Being in the station did, however, have its variety of incidents involving staff, 'inmates', and of course the inevitable TWRs! As at the Main Bridewell, as soon as duty commenced, a thorough check was carried out (to eliminate any prospects of the 'Brown, O'Coat and Devlin saga!!), and ensure that all was in order. Checks of the cell state, prisoners and their property, 'found property' and 'stray dog' book entries inspected and daily orders read.

Bridewell Sergeant at Wallasey

This was a very busy period, and all was the total responsibility of the Bridewell Sergeant.

Matters were not helped by the daily arrival of my favourite Superintendent, who would come behind the counter and proceed to read every entry of every book before endorsing each individual item entered. He would reach under the counter and disrupt proceedings, even if I was dealing with a prisoner. "Where's the dog book Sarge?", Where's the property book?" Where's this?" Where's that?" He became such a pain. If he wasn't happy with anything, (and he usually found something amiss), he would grunt, "Should'a done this!" "Should'a done that!" Finally we christened him 'The nine o'clock shudda'! This title remained with him until his eventual retirement.

One morning, as I was up to my eyes in the general 'nine o'clock mayhem' in the Bridewell, I hadn't noticed the Super creep up behind me. As I was concentrating on what I was doing I felt someone push me as they tried to reach under the counter to retrieve one of the station's books. Thinking it was one of the lads not wanting to wait until I had finished what I was doing I snapped, "Will you fuck off! I'm up to my eyes here!" Everywhere went deathly quiet until the voice of a 'reprimanded' Super (no less than the nine o'clock shudda) was heard to say meekly, "Sorry Sarge, I'll come back later when things have quietened down". As he left, those others present tittered and giggled nervously.

Later, various colleagues, Sergeants and Inspectors, asked me if it were true that I had told the Super to "fuck off". Pretending that I knew it was him all the time, I shrugged my shoulders nonchalantly and replied, "Well, I was too busy to stop and look for books to be signed." This became another little episode that swept the station for a day or two, adding a little spice to my already 'tarnished' name among some.

I became a PSU 'commander' (Sergeant in charge of a Police Support Unit contingent) whose duties mainly entailed that of being engaged in public disorder confrontations. The training for a PSU officer was very physical and demanding. The regular training was very thorough and rigorous. We were trained to combat riotous situations, when missiles, petrol bombs etc were anticipated. During such training, injuries were sustained with worrying regularity.

During one training period at the former U.S.A.F. base at Burtonwood, one of my section was struck by a slab of concrete and sustained a broken wrist. We were subject to a simulated attack by 'defenders' of a building we were trying to forcibly enter. I managed to splint the officer's arm and place it in a sling while we were still 'under attack'. The Constable was moaning with pain and I ordered him back out of the way while I organised his removal to hospital. "Where should I go Sarge?" asked the injured officer. "Find a Superintendent and stand next to him, you'll be quite safe there!" I shouted sarcastically. "I heard that, Swasie!" boomed the voice of the 'nine o clock shudda', who was one of the observers of the operation. I looked across to him and grinned,

"Sorry sir, I didn't mean you, you're alright"! I cheekily grovelled. "Cheeky bastard," replied the Super, hopefully having taken my banter in good spirit. Broken arms, injured backs, cuts and bruises were par for the course during PSU training. It never managed to diminish the enthusiasm of those officers from such units however.

After collecting my breakfast from the counter in the canteen one morning, I went to join two of my section at their table. They were both deep in conversation, one, a member of my P.S.U. section was crying that his Saturday rest day had been cancelled as he was required to perform PSU duty (as I was myself) due to a forthcoming event where possible confrontation was anticipated. His colleague, who was considered as somewhat of a 'barrack room lawyer' was agreeing with his friend's annoyance and was encouraging his friend to contact the police federation (the bobby's union) over the matter.

I sat at the table and started to eat my breakfast. My colleagues' conversation intensified (for my benefit) as I sat alongside them. "I wouldn't mind, but I've arranged to go with the wife to a friend's wedding on that day," complained my PSU officer. "I wouldn't have that" said his colleague, mixing the bottle, "I'd be right on to the federation about it."

Their whinging and perpetual whining went on and on. It obviously didn't matter that I too had my rest day cancelled, being the PSU Sergeant. In the end I could stand their crying no longer. I stood up and snapped, "I'll go and see the Chief Super and ask him if you can be spared for that bloody wedding", and stormed off up to the Chief Super's office. After being admitted I asked the boss if my crying Constable could be spared on the forthcoming Saturday, explaining the reason for my asking, adding, "He's crying into my bacon and eggs downstairs." The Chief Super dismissed my request out of hand, "No chance, we'll need every officer we can spare," he said. "That's fair enough sir, I just thought I'd ask. His mate's mixing a bottle by winding him up telling him to go to the federation", I added.

The Chief Superintendent looked up and said slowly, "Sergeant, tell the dissident officer that if he doesn't like it here, I'll have him posted over to Toxteth as from tomorrow." I grinned and said, "It will give me great pleasure to convey your message to him sir." I thanked the boss and returned to my breakfast. As I sat down I addressed the PSU officer, "I've been up to see the boss and there's no chance of you getting off on Saturday." I told him curtly. "Thanks for trying anyway, Sarge", he replied gratefully. I then turned to his colleague and said,"The boss has told me to tell you personally that if you don't like it here, I've to tell him so and he will have you posted over to Toxteth as from tomorrow!"

The young officer sat there not knowing what to say. Finally he said, "I DO like it here Sarge, I was only trying to help. I'll keep my mouth shut in future". "Good, then let's hear no more moaning from now on", I said and tucked into my (now cold) breakfast. Our 'barrack room lawyer' never gave 'advisory consultations' in my presence again, as there was no doubt that such a posting would take place forthwith if the Chief Super were to hear of such.   •

Wallasey was not immune from the activities of some of those 'weirdos' who persistently visit and hang around public toilets, especially those conveniences situated near to parks and the sea front. Whilst out on patrol with my men I frequently came across these people during all hours of the day and night. As a Constable and I passed one such toilet during our walk along the promenade, we decided to check inside the premises.

On entering the toilet we saw a young man standing at the urinal, his camouflage trousers round his ankles, as he masturbated himself. "What the bloody hell's going on?" I asked abruptly. The terrified man stuttered and stammered, "S-sorry, Sarge, give us another chance will you? I'm a soldier home on leave." As there were no other persons about to be offended by the soldier's behaviour, and realising the repercussions if the services were to become aware of his deviant activities, I decided on 'instant justice'. I gave him one almighty verbal onslaught, threatening him with dire consequences should I, or any of my officers ever catch him hanging around the area again. I was always concerned for the welfare and safety of children when near to such places, and children were frequently out and about in the vicinity of the sea front. Instead of the young soldier accepting the admonishment, he burst into tears and started sobbing "Pull yourself together, man" I snapped. "I'm sorry Sergeant, I just can't help myself," he sobbed. I advised him to seek medical help if he considered that he had an uncontrollable problem, and told him to make his way home (he lived locally and was home on leave from his unit).

If I thought the matter had ended there, I was mistaken! An hour or so later my personal radio crackled into life. "Golf sierra one six, over!" (My call sign, GS 16). "Golf sierra one six, go ahead," I replied. "Golf Sierra one six, will you call in at the station, there are two people here requesting to see you urgently." I was informed. I summoned a mobile patrol to collect me and transport me to the station. I wondered what this would be about, as I hadn't a clue. I arrived at the station and made my way through to the enquiry office. As I entered and stood behind the desk I saw two men sitting in the foyer. I saw that one of them was the young soldier, who was holding a handkerchief to his eyes and was still crying.

"Can I help you, gentlemen?", I asked. The two men stood up and approached the desk. It was an unusual sight. The soldier, short and slim, wearing his camouflage trousers and jacket, in complete contrast to his friend, who was 6 foot three inches tall, weighing about fifteen stone, wearing a long, belted, camel haired coat and wide brimmed felt trilby. The big man said angrily with an effeminate lisp, "Look at the state of him, what did you make him cry for?" The young policewoman manning the enquiry desk stared in wonder as she was unaware of my dealings with the soldier earlier. I wasn't going to stand there justifying my actions to a complete stranger. I pointed to a nearby interview room. "Let's go in here," I directed. I was very brief as I said, "I think you'd better both leave gentlemen, before I start putting pen to paper." The young soldier obviously caught my drift. "C'mon Gordon, we don't want a scene," he said. Both men left the station, and nothing further was heard of the incident.

I was pleasantly surprised to receive a 'phone call at home one morning from my Superintendent, Mr Lowe (the nine o'clock shudda!). He informed me that a presentation ceremony had been arranged for me to be presented with a Shipwreck and Humane Award concerning the incident in Liverpool involving Mr Molloy. The award would be presented by His Worship the Mayor of Wirral, Councillor David Williams and his wife, the Lady Mayoress, in four weeks' time. The boss informed me that I could take my wife and daughter, plus two guests. Mr Lowe then congratulated me and rang off. I was delighted and looked forward eagerly to the day. As well as my wife Marje and daughter Jo, I decided to take a close friend and his wife.

On the day, I attended at Wallasey Town Hall with my family and friends, and we were eventually introduced to the Mayor and Mayoress. Also present were the local press and my Chief Superintendent, together with other recipients of the award. After the formalities were over and the presentations had been given and official photographs taken, we all chatted informally over drinks. A buffet was also laid on and we tucked into our lettuce and cucumber sandwiches in the spacious room overlooking the ships as they glided up and down the river outside.

All too quickly the happy day's events came to an end. I felt very proud as I stood with the Mayor during the ceremony, but also sadness at the reason that I was there, my near successful attempt to save a man's life. The Mayor was a thorough gentleman and he and his charming wife bade me and my family and friends goodbye after we had chatted informally for quite some time. It was well worth the wait to have my award presented in such a formal ceremonial way by such a nice couple as the Mayor and Mayoress. I would certainly treasure those proud moments. The following day the photograph and accompanying article appeared in the local and provincial newspapers, the Liverpool Echo and Wirral News.

The people of Wallasey were very appreciative of our efforts and I found that here, more than any previous postings where I had served, members of the public tended to put their appreciation on paper in the form of a letter to the Chief Constable, or Chief Superintendent. The individual's sentiments were not only acknowledged in the form of an official reply but their thanks were then formally conveyed to the officer concerned.

Of course the opposite also applied ! There were letters of complaint when it was thought that some of us had failed them and it was considered we had not carried out our duties correctly in one way or another, or some form of inefficiency had allegedly come to light. I was named in one kind letter addressed to the Chief Superintendent at Wallasey from the local Warren Drive Golf Club. The Club Secretary (Mr Lyon) wrote, courteously advising the Chief Super of the club's forthcoming 75 th anniversary celebrations which were to be held at the clubhouse and its grounds on a forthcoming date. The letter also informed the Chief that an occasional licence had been applied for via the local magistrates, as they were erecting a large beer tent on the day.

The Mayor of Wirral, David Williams, Who presented me with my Shipwreck and Humane Award.

With my wife Marje and my daughter Jo at the Mayoral Presentation.

One paragraph of the letter read, "I understand that our local bobby is a chap called Sergeant Turner, and from conversations I have had with local people, he seems to have earned a tremendous amount of respect from young and old alike. Perhaps if Sergeant Turner is on duty on the 22nd (June '86) he might like to pop into the club." This type of letter was most gratefully received and was typical of such letters written by Wallasey residents concerning members of the force.

Wallasey is a pleasant town and its people are warm and friendly, the vast majority of whom are very law-abiding. The town lies on the North West tip of the Wirral peninsular and contains pleasant beaches and lengthy promenades. Until a few years ago it also sported a pier which enabled fully laden ferries to bring in hordes of day trippers to the resort at New Brighton.

Sadly, with the demise of the pier and its large outdoor fairground, such bustling activity is no more. However, serious efforts to rectify the situation and bring the resort back to its previous popularity are now bearing fruit. During the summer season there is plenty of beach and boating activity. Many residents and visitors alike, take to their boats, which come in all shapes and sizes. The resort also boasts a large indoor fairground where many generations of parents and children have enjoyed themselves over the years.

One such occasion which proved immensely popular, drawing capacity crowds to the area was the 1986 International Power-boat racing event. This event certainly brought a lot of business and finance into the area. The week the event was hosted was blessed with hot and warm, sunny weather, just like all summers seemed to be in years gone by! All along the New Brighton promenade were various tents, stalls and marquees. Some of these were 'hospitality' tents, erected and manned by big name sponsors, and those who were either contributing or participating in the events.

The big event also featured an air display which included the famous Red Arrows, and a life-saving demonstration by the New Brighton lifeboat. As I made my way along the crowded sea front, past the crowds of children (and adults) standing in awe while they inspected the large, powerful seagoing beasts from all over the world, as they stood gleaming on their trailers prior to being placed into the water, I was invited into one of the sponsors' tents and offered a large glass of chilled, draught lemonade. It was such a hot day and the cool, refreshing drink hardly touched the sides as I gratefully gulped it down. Thanking my generous host I asked if it would be possible for some of my section (who were on duty, sweltering nearby) to call in for a glass during the day.

My cheeky request was enthusiastically granted with the utmost kindness and I arranged for the bobbies to each call in for a chilled glass of pop. "Here Sarge, take this," said one appreciative Samaritan (one of the sponsors) and held up crate of bottled beer. As some of my section were having a ten minute break in our carrier, parked nearby, I gratefully accepted the item and it was delivered to my thirsty flock. I made an exception to the rule with regard to drinking on duty, as I was already aware that some senior officers had been consuming glasses of champagne in one of the tents and one small bottle of pale ale wouldn't do any harm. A benevolent baker offered me a tray of pies and pasties and these also found their way into the carrier. Officially, we didn't have a set meal time due to the extremely busy day's duties. I therefore organised regular ten minute breaks, when the lads and girls of the section went to the carrier for their drink and a pie.

On Duty at The International Powerboat Day, Summer 1986.

All went extremely well during the whole event. A very friendly and enjoyable atmosphere was generated by all those present. There were no arrests and no trouble was encountered during the whole period, which speaks volumes for the way the whole event was organised and handled by all concerned.

During the event, whilst out and about, 'pegging' my section, I came across one officer who needed a 'flea' in his ear! I couldn't believe what I saw. There, sitting on the top of the concrete sea wall at Harrison Drive, a mile along from the main activities, was 'Tibby'! No helmet, no tie and minus his shoes and socks! There was always one who would take advantage of a little informality! He was immediately 'advised' to take himself out of the public view when he wished to do a spot of sunbathing, or, get himself back to his allotted post. I appreciated that it was very hot and I was quite happy for any of the section to 'cool off' during their break, as long as they used their discretion as to how they went about it. It was little wonder that the erring 'Tibby' was always getting himself told off, as he continually insisted on 'leading with his chin !'

On this particular day, the whole world was watching, not to mention the possibility of the Chief Constable, Chief Superintendent, the Mayor and Mayoress and many other local civic dignitaries who were attending the event. "D'you think there's any chance of you getting dressed, or is this the new issue?" I asked. "I was just sitting in the sun Sarge." 'Tibby' replied. He was promptly instructed to return himself to his former ,formal state and resume his promenade patrol.

Some days later I was walking through Wallasey Village, calling in to each shop and asking if all was well. Although I sometimes 'turned a blind eye' to parking on double yellow lines, I would not tolerate any parking within the limits of a pedestrian crossing (within the zig zag lines). This was definitely 'taboo'! On this day, one such offender had parked his vehicle almost next to a crossing and went shopping. As I could see no signs of the driver, I called into each shop in the immediate vicinity, I noticed that the vehicle displayed an orange 'disabled' badge. I entered each shop and after greeting each proprietor, asked those others present if they were responsible for parking the (named and numbered) vehicle in such a dangerous place. All those asked denied any knowledge whatsoever.

My last call was to the local post office. Again I asked if the offending vehicle belonged to anyone present, again a negative response! RIGHT! I knew what would draw an instant response! I went to the vehicle and took a pad of 'fixed penalty' tickets from my pocket and started to make out a traffic violation ticket. Within seconds an elderly man approached me who I had noticed standing in the queue inside the post office. "It's alright Sergeant, I'm going now" he said with a friendly smile. "Not so fast sir", I said, "why didn't you say it was your vehicle a minute ago when I asked" ? "Oh come on Sergeant, I was only in there a minute getting my pension," was the indignant reply, adding, "Can't you see the badge?" indicating the orange badge in his windscreen. I continued to make out the ticket. "May I have your name and address sir?" I asked politely.

The offender's attitude changed dramatically. As a number of people were staring at us the old gentleman started to 'play to the gallery'. "I'm an alderman of this borough. I fought in the last war for the likes of you!" he shouted for all to hear. "May I have your full name sir?" I again asked calmly and politely. "Your Superintendent is a friend of mine," the Alderman retorted, adding, "I'll be ringing him about you!" I replied, "When you ring him, tell him it was Sergeant Turner that 'did' you," and again asked, "Now, are you refusing your name and address?"

By now the furious gentleman was becoming flustered and, looking to his 'audience' he shouted, "You're a shithouse, I have influence. I'll have those stripes off your arm for this!" Pointing to the silver chevrons on my arm I corrected him quietly, "SERGEANT Shithouse sir, if you don't mind!" Eventually I managed to complete the ticket and to make matters worse I confiscated the gentleman's driving licence to send with the form so that the appropriate endorsement could be entered thereon as this particular offenc carried driving licence 'penalty points'. I received a lecture concerning how he had been driving since "Henry Ford was an infant" and "It was the likes of me that got the Police a bad name". The man promised to 'disrupt' my career as he left, as he intended to report me for my 'oppressive' conduct!

Some time later, when I returned to the station the young bobby manning the enquiry desk informed me that the Superintendent wished to see me on my return. I made my way upstairs to the boss's office. I saw him sitting behind his desk through his open door. He heard me approach and looked up from the papers he had been perusing on his desk, pen in hand. "Come in Swasie" he said. I stood before him, saluted respectfully and said, "Before you ask sir, it was me who 'did' the Alderman!" The boss grinned and said, "I know bloody well it was you. He's been on the 'phone bending my ear. To be honest, he's a pain in the arse!"

Ready for Foot Patrol, Wallasey

I knew that I could rely on the full backing of this particular Super (the nine o clock shudda'), no doubt he would have done the same thing himself, such was his complete impartiality. "I had no option sir, he was parked on the 'zig zags' in Wallasey Village," I said. "You don't have to explain Swasie, it shows that you're doing your job," complimented the Super.

.The same Super had cause to summon me to his office yet again the following day! This time he had received a 'phone call from a local shopkeeper who had a fruit and vegetable shop and persisted in taking up most of the footwalk outside his shop by stacking rows of boxes in front of his window, displaying fruit, vegetables, plants, plus empty cartons and paper bags. As well as having previously instructed the beat bobby to have a word with the shopkeeper, telling him to clear the footpath, I myself had instructed him to refrain from obstructing the pavement by removing the empty boxes and bags together with the 'outside display'.

All such repeated requests were to no avail. He blatantly carried on obstructing the free passage along the footwalk against my repeated requests. People sometimes gathered outside the shop to peruse the goods on open display and the shopkeeper sometimes conducted sales there adding to the obstruction. People wishing to pass had to step out into the roadway, which added danger to the situation.

One morning after again witnessing the usual spectacle, I went into his crowded shop as he and his staff were engaged serving customers. "Excuse me sir, may I have a quiet word with you please?" I asked. Turning to me the shopkeeper replied, "The stuff's staying where it is (indicating the goods etc outside his shop), you'll have to come back later. Can't you see I'm busy?" All present in the shop couldn't fail to hear his rebuke. I allowed him to finish serving an old lady and after he had given her change I took hold of his sleeve and drew him to me. In a loud voice I said, "If you don't clear that pavement NOW, I will arrest you for wilful obstruction!" He decided to call my bluff. "You can't arrest me for putting stuff outside my shop," he said, with a knowledgeable grin on his defiant face. Speaking into my personal radio I said for all to hear, "Golf Sierra one six, could you send transport to (the address) as I may be bringing in one male prisoner. Over!"

This had the desired effect. The shopkeeper called a young lad from a back room of the shop and instructed him to remove all empty boxes and bags from the pavement outside. The proprietor himself then proceeded (under protest) to remove all goods from the pavement and transfer them all into the confines of his shop. These proceedings caused bedlam in the already crowded shop. I remained outside on the footwalk until it was totally bereft of anything other than pedestrian traffic. Finally, when he had completed his laborious task, I said, "Thank you sir". I walked away to the dulcet tones of the now very annoyed and most indignant proprietor as he informed me of what was to befall me after he had complained to the Chief Superintendent!

This time the 'Nine o'clock shudda' greeted me with, "Christ Swasie, you're causing bloody murder out there!" I wouldn't mind if those wishing to complain told the truth and reiterated the circumstances causing their dissent as they happened. I was quite happy to stand and justify my actions. However, it was nearly always the case that the truth was completely distorted and blatantly interspersed with malicious fiction and innuendos, to add 'beef' to the complaint. In the case of the 'obstructive' greengrocer, he alleged that I had entered his shop and in full view of his customers, I had humiliated him by grabbing his lapels and threatened him with arrest! Nearly true, but not quite! Yes, I was again visited by Complaints and Discipline.

302

However, matters went precisely nowhere as none of those 'many' witnesses, in front of whom the 'complainant' was 'assaulted' could be found to substantiate his grossly exaggerated and malicious allegations. Not one person came forward or could be traced. The Super did, however, tell me to 'go a bit easy' as complaints like this didn't do me any good, as, when mud is thrown, some always sticks, as the saying goes! The pavement outside this particular shop remained clear from then on. As long as the particular greengrocer 'toed the line' and remained within the law, he had nothing to fear and could rest assured that he would receive my undivided and courteous attention should he ever require my services.

As well as my Constables, I also continued making arrests for an assortment of offences, including many for offences of an indecent nature Due to these 'unsavoury' arrests I was asked by a certain senior officer to 'ease off' as I was drawing attention to a local problem that so far had been 'kept under wraps'!. These particular type of offences were unfortunately regular and occurred in or near to the resort's seafront toilets and parks.

An offence of this nature was discovered when Constable Hart (now Sergeant) and I were directed by radio whilst on a night mobile patrol, to a rear entry between two streets of terraced houses off Poulton Road at 2 o'clock one morning. We were informed that a resident had heard noises coming from the entry at the rear of her house and she feared that burglars were about.

Constable Hart and I made our way to the scene. Parking our vehicle nearby the two of us crept silently along one of the streets and made our way cautiously into the entry. We switched off our radios and surreptitiously tiptoed along the entry keeping ourselves pressed tightly against the entry wall. Eventually we heard gasps and whispers ahead of us. We stopped. My heart was beating so heavily, I thought the sound of its beats would give us away as we stood silently and listened. Yes! There it was again, gasps, and somebody was whispering ten feet away in the darkness. I suddenly switched on my torch, its powerful beam illuminating a young boy masturbating a huge man who was leaning against a wall gasping in ecstasy at the boy's actions. On realising that they had been detected the youth, a boy of about fourteen years, ran off, hotly pursued by Constable Hart. I was left with the big man who was trying frantically to fasten his trousers to hide his erect manhood. "You're too late mate, I've seen all I need to see, you're locked up," I said as I grabbed his arm. "I wasn't doing anything," protested the big man. He was one big fellow alright! He was well over six foot and must have weighed about seventeen stone.

As we were in a dark entry with no witnesses, I anticipated violent resistance as I fully expected the man to attempt an escape. "Come on, we'll sort this out where there's some light and for your sake, don't try anything as you're in enough trouble!" I warned. "I won't try anything 'cos I 'aven't done nuthin," insisted my brazen prisoner. I walked him back to the main road, still anticipating an attempt to escape, I wasn't taking any chances. When we reached our locked car the big man made his move and tried to break free but I was ready! I spun him round and forced him over some ornamental spiked iron railings on top of a two foot wall in front of a house. To support himself he had to place his hands on the flower bed and protect himself from the iron spikes. "Stay as you are," I instructed. I warned him that if he moved he would not only injure himself, but I would charge him with the additional offence of assault on Police as well as the original one of gross indecency. Just to make sure he stayed where he was I held him by the scruff of the neck over the wall.

After what seemed an eternity I was rejoined by an exhausted and very dishevelled Constable Hart. "Where've yer bin, Harty?" I asked impatiently. "Phew!" gasped my colleague, "The little bastard got away." I consoled him by saying, "Never mind Brian, we've got one of them." "What are you on about?" asked our cheeky partner in crime of the juvenile escapee. Telling him not to be so clever, I said, "I'm arresting you for an offence of gross indecency."

He was placed into our car and conveyed to Manor Road. There, the circumstances of his arrest were related to the Bridewell Sergeant. It transpired that the man was a deck hand on the Mersey ferries and it was established that he was 'partial' to the company of young boys. He was documented, fingerprinted and photographed. In the meantime I obtained a plastic syringe (minus needle) from the medical room and Constable Hart and I returned to the scene for a more detailed search, as our detainee was still adamantly protesting his innocence and denying any knowledge of the young boy who had made his escape.

Eventually I found what I was looking for with the assistance of our two torches. There on the ground were two tell tale drops of semen. Thank goodness it was a dry night. Placing the tip of the syringe against the drops of seminal fluid I gently and carefully drew back the plunger as my colleague held his torch, and managed to obtain a small specimen of semen from the cobbled entry floor. I was delighted with my bright idea and although the specimen was only small, I considered it adequate enough for forensic analysis should I be required to go to such lengths. I returned to the station and informed the confident and self-assured prisoner of what Constable Hart and I had done. After placing the sample into a specimen bottle, I showed the labelled container to the prisoner and told him that I was sending it to the Forensic science laboratory for analysis, which would then enable me to present such indisputable evidence to the court, thus substantiating his night time activity in the entry. The prisoner then decided it would be futile to continue with his charade. "Okay boss, the kid and I were at it, but honest to God I don't know his name."

Our deck hand was pressed as to the identity of the young boy but he would not be moved. The big man started to cry, "Honest, I only met him last night. All I know is that his first name's Terry!" The prisoner elected to make a full and frank admission in the form of a written statement. He admitted to having committed other similar offences with men and young boys over a lengthy period. He was later charged with the original offence for which he had been arrested and others were 'taken into consideration'. On his eventual appearance before the Liverpool Crown Court he received a suspended prison sentence. The youth who had successfully eluded the clutches of Constable Hart was never traced.

The following week a very sad incident occurred involving an infant boy at Queensferry, on the Welsh border. The little toddler had wandered off from his home near the banks of the river Dee. I became aware of the incident while watching the evening news on television at home. It was said that a thorough search of acres of agricultural nurseries along the river banks would be continued at first light the following day. As I would be off duty on rest days for the following two days I contacted the North Wales Superintendent Mr Jones, who was in charge of the operation, to volunteer my services. My offer was gratefully accepted and I was asked to parade at a given venue the following morning. A friend of mine, Graham Rothwell, kindly offered to accompany me. The more eyes the better! I rang my own station and left a message to inform the Superintendent of my actions involving another force.

The following morning at the crack of dawn my friend and I attended the head office of Bees' nurseries near to Queensferry. I was one of only two Sergeants present, the other being my North Wales opposite number. The Superintendent gathered all the volunteers, including a number of RAF personnel from the nearby base at RAF Sealand, together with large numbers of civilian volunteers. The other Sergeant and I were each allocated a number of Constables, Servicemen and others to instigate a 'line' search.

The search was organised and we all spread out to conduct a thorough search of the vast area of nurseries, grasslands and marshes, as we slowly and painstakingly made our way towards the river Dee approximately a mile and a half away. Every ditch, shed, hut, outhouse, copse and hedge was meticulously combed in an effort to find the little boy, whose description and photograph had been circulated to us all. We even combed neighbouring farmland each side of the busy Queensferry trunk road. After two days our unsuccessful search was scaled down and I resumed my own duties back at Wallasey.

Tragically, our worst fears were sadly confirmed when the toddler's body was recovered from the river Dee many days later. This sad, tragic incident gave me the experience to organise an effective search party should similar circumstances arise again. This, in fact, almost happened in Wallasey one Sunday morning some weeks later when we received the dreaded message, 'little girl missing' a message which makes everyone's heart miss a beat! This little child had also gone missing near to a river, the River Fender which flowed through the estate where the child lived, and I feared a repetition of the Queensferry tragedy. Without further ado I attended the scene and commenced urgent enquiries as to exactly where the little girl had last been seen and by whom.

Situated near the scene was a public house, the notorious 'Oyster

Catcher'. This pub was certainly not renowned for its leanings towards the Police to say the least! "Right, we can't waste any time, we'll have to organise a line search," I said to my accompanying colleague, again, Constable Hart. Summoning what other officers I could muster (what with sickness, rest days and annual leave, my section was quite depleted) I instructed my Constable to carry out a quick search of the immediate area while I visited the pub to seek volunteers. "You must be joking Sarge, you'll be lucky if you get out of there in one piece" said the pessimistic Constable . I knew from past experience that when children were in danger, the roughest place in the land would guarantee help in any way requested and this time was to prove no exception.

I entered the crowded, smoke filled bar to taunts and jeers, and was advised many times to visit the 'Foreign Office'!

As I needed everybody's undivided attention I struck the bar with my signalling stick making one almighty bang! "QUIET!" I shouted. The noise abated and I said, 'Listen lads, I need volunteers to help me find a little girl who's gone missing." Without further ado, every single person present volunteered their services. I stressed to everyone that time was of the essence, as I was fearful of the nearby River Fender claiming the little girl's life. A burly spokesman stepped forward, "Tell us what to do boss and we'll do it," he said concerned and keen to get the search under way. "Give me five minutes lads and I'll be back," I said, as I wanted to obtain a detailed description of the girl and the clothing she was wearing, and also a recent photo if possible, from her home nearby. "Okay boss, we'll be here," said the pub 'spokesman'.

I then set out to make to the girl's home but was intercepted en route by Constable Hart. "It's okay Sarge, I've found her. She was wandering round the golf course!" he announced proudly. "Well done Harty," I replied. I breathed a sigh of relief because the River Fender meandered through the golf course. What a lucky break for Harty to have found her when he did! I returned to the pub and as I entered, the place became absolutely silent. I stood in the centre of the crowded bar and said, "I've come back to thank you all and to tell you that we have found the girl safe and well." I was deafened as a loud cheer was sent up by the potential volunteers. I received slaps on the back from one or two and one patron said, "You'll do me boss, have a pint!"

I was indeed privileged, I had trod new ground by being the first police officer to receive such friendly hospitality in that particular establishment. I intended to keep it that way. I politely refused the offer of a drink and thanked everyone by moving among the tables and shaking a few hands as I did so. I really was grateful to know that help was there when I needed it. Uttering my sentiments of gratitude to various individuals (many of whom were known to me!), I took my leave.

One local 'tough guy' , who appeared to enjoy some notoriety with his gang was still uttering comments of dissent. I decided to increase his notoriety. I said to him , in a loud voice, "Thanks very much for the tip off Jacko ,we'd never have caught that bastard, but for you." total silence decended. Our cocky youth now started stammering to his mates, "take no notice of him, I don't know what he's on about." However the seeds of doubt were sown and his image seriously tarnished.

Continuing to the door I saw two small children sitting at a table with their parents, each consuming a bag of crisps, their glasses of pop were on the table alongside their parents' glasses of beer. I leaned down and grinned. I whispered into the father's ear, "I haven't seen them" indicating the children, making it look as though I was doing him a favour by turning a 'blind eye'. "Cheers boss, you're a good 'un," he said. I was quite willing to pay such a small price in the interests of P.R.! I also thanked the licensee and left. I made my way back to the station and immediately sat down at my typewriter and typed a long letter of thanks to the licensee and customers of the Oyster Catcher pub.

The Oyster Catcher Pub

In my letter, on official Merseyside Police headed paper, I emphasised that all too often many of his customers had been subject to the unwelcome attention of the Police, but I now considered that the Police were indebted to those same people. I took it upon myself to be only too willing to acknowledge his customers' kind, willing and immediate response to my request for help. I felt that the least I could do was to put my gratitude , on behalf of the police, down on paper for all to see.

I stressed the point that even 'wrongdoers' can have good points, and when these come to the fore they should be acknowledged without hesitation. Having completed my letter, I placed it into an envelope and went out, purchased a stamp, and posted it off to the licensee of the Oyster Catcher.

The following Sunday I was out in company with an Inspector on a routine lunchtime patrol. As we were about to pass the same pub I suggested that we call in to show a visit. (I really wanted to, first, test my reception, hoping my welcome still held good, and second, I wanted to see if my letter had been received). The Inspector was not at all keen to enter the premises. "D'you want to get lynched?" he asked apprehensively. "C'mon, let's go in," I insisted.

We entered the pub, which was packed with Sunday lunchtime drinkers, and were greeted by, "Christ, here's Jimmy Edwards. Where've yer parked yer Spitfire?" from a half- sozzled patron. "Fuck off you, he's okay him, he's the one wot wrote the letter," chastised his equally inebriated pal. Ah, so it had been received! We approached the bar and threaded our way through to the counter. The landlord had just finished serving a customer   I greeted him with, "Good afternoon, landlord, everything alright"? I then introduced him to the Inspector. "How d'you do sir" said the landlord and, looking at me added, "Thanks for the letter, Mr Turner," and indicated my typewritten letter which had been framed and now adorned the wall on display near the bar. I was again receiving slaps on the back and offers of a pint from those who remembered my efforts of a week ago. "He's alright him, sir," said one bleary-eyed customer to the Inspector, and continued, "there'sh not many who'd take the trouble to do that," pointing to the framed 'trophy'.

The Inspector looked at me and said, "Now what have you been up to?" as he stood and read the letter, which had obviously been accepted with pride by all present. After a few minutes we left to continue our patrol. Once outside, the Inspector asked, "Who the hell authorised you to write that letter?" "Nobody sir, but I thought it right to acknowledge their offers of help," I replied. Nothing more was said with regard to the matter, BUT - the following day I was sent for by the CHIEF Superintendent! As I entered his office and closed the door behind me, the Chief Super's face told me that all was not well! Now what?

As I stood there in front of the boss's desk, he looked up icily and said, "Now, what's all this about sending unauthorised correspondence on behalf of the Police to such a notorious pub?". "I just thanked the customers for volunteering to help me sir, I replied meekly. "You should have requested my permission before undertaking such a task," the boss retorted angrily. "If I had sir, would you have granted permission?" I asked. "NO I would not!" snapped the boss. "With respect sir, that's why I sent it myself," I said, and, hoping to please him I added, "It certainly enhanced relationships between ourselves and the patrons there." My comments were rebuffed with the Chief Super telling me, "Don't EVER pull a stunt like that again Sergeant!" as he dismissed me from his office. I left his office thinking how nice it was of the Inspector to have gone and 'snitched' to the 'teacher'! There is no doubt that my little 'blunder' enabled me to visit the pub at anytime thereafter and be assured of at least a reasonable 'welcome', which would never be afforded to any of my colleagues!

Not all police work consists of doom and gloom, there are regular light-hearted moments. The proprietor of one of our local restaurants was notorious for ringing for the police and demanding urgent, immediate attendance 'to eject violent customers'. Many times officers arrived only to find that the reason for the call was due to someone not having paid their bill. Eventually, after I had attended many such calls, I informed the restauranteur in very forceful tones that my officers were not there to supervise the smooth running of his business, nor were they to be expected to perform the duties of debt collector.

I told him that if circumstances warranted our attendance, we would attend, but not just to ensure that some drunken yob paid his bill. His late night calls of this nature ceased forthwith. However, as I was about to leave the station in the early hours of one morning, I passed through the enquiry office to make my exit when I heard angry shouts and saw the young officer at the desk as he listened to an excited member of the public demanding the attention to which he was entitled. It was none other than our restaurant proprietor. He was very angry.

"What's the problem officer?" I asked my patient colleague. I was informed by the officer that earlier, two young women had been brought into the station by a bobby who had been summoned to the restaurant by our 'friend', who complained that the women had consumed a meal and tried to leave without paying. On duty, as the Bridewell Sergeant, was a particularly fiery individual who was already extremely busy with a number of violent, drunken prisoners when the two women were brought in. The Bridewell Sergeant, like myself, was fully aware of the restaurant proprietor's pedigree for 'crying wolf' and did not particularly relish the thought of being used as the proprietor's debt collector.

After hearing the reason for the females' detention, he allowed them to leave, as he considered the matter to be nothing more than a 'civil' debt, because they were not happy with the food. On learning of the Sergeant's actions, the irate restauranteur stormed round to the station, demanding that the women be prosecuted by the Police. I calmed the man down and told him I would go and speak with the Sergeant concerned. I went through to the busy Sergeant and told him of the presence of the very angry proprietor. My colleague informed me that it was a 'civil debt' and he was too busy to see the proprietor. I relayed the Sergeant's message but the man again became very angry and demanded to see the Sergeant, stating that he would not leave the station until he had done so. "I know the law!" he shouted. "It's not a civil debt!" To help calm him down, and to the amusement of the desk bobby, I said sarcastically, "You're quite right, it's burglary dinner"! "Yes, yes, it's burglary dinner," agreed the proprietor. "I'll go and get the Sergeant," I said, and told the temporarily pacified man that the Sergeant had only just joined the police and didn't quite know the law yet! "I'll go and get him for you, but you'll have to shout very loudly in his ear because he's extremely deaf," I said as I left the enquiry office. "Thank you very much," replied the grateful man, thinking he had a staunch ally who knew the law as well as he did!?

Reluctantly the Bridewell Sergeant allowed me to persuade him to see the proprietor. As the Sergeant leaned on the enquiry office counter, the restauranteur leaned over and in a very loud voice shouted down the ear of the shocked Sergeant, "It's not a civil debt, it's a burglary dinner!" The amazed Sergeant's eardrum must have damn near ruptured by its broadside of decibels from such a loud verbal outburst. The Sergeant put one hand to his 'attacked' ear and pushed the informative proprietor away violently with his other hand, sending him reeling backwards. By now we were joined by a number of colleagues from the nearby radio room and Constables' writing room. None of us could be of any assistance whatsoever as we witnessed the spectacle of the absolutely fuming Bridewell Sergeant leap over the counter and eject the hapless restauranteur from the station, threatening him with arrest if he returned. We were hardly able to stifle our suppressed hysteria at the unbelievable saga!

I was becoming well-known throughout Wallasey for my persistent prosecutions of adult pedal cyclists who insisted on riding their machines along the town's pavements and through pedestrian thoroughfares. I like to think that I even managed to curtail this offensive, selfish and dangerous trait by my continual pursuit of these offenders. I consider that this problem could be eliminated altogether if each offender was put before the court. I remember only too well an incident many years ago when a twelve month old girl was struck by an adult cyclist as he rode along a Liverpool pavement and collided with her buggy. The little child received injuries which resulted in permanent brain damage. I have never forgotten that tragic and totally avoidable 'accident'. I would NEVER deal with those selfish and inconsiderate offenders who completely disregard the law by doing this, by any method other than prosecution. Every day this continual selfish abuse continues to put young children and elderly people at risk of serious injury as they walk what should be the safe sanctuary of our footwalks.

One Saturday my football section and I were travelling towards the Wallasey tunnel in our carrier en route to Goodison Park to police an Everton home match when I saw a man riding his bicycle along the busy pavement, weaving in and out of pedestrians as they made their way along. Eventually we drew alongside the offender and I ordered him to stop and dismount from his machine. He was quite indignant at being stopped and humiliated in front of everyone for such a 'minor' infringement!

One of the lads in the back recognised the offender, who was a cellerman employed at a nearby pub, which was a regular 'watering hole' for numerous bobbies and CID personnel. No doubt the offending cyclist thought the convivial greeting from my colleague would eliminate any possibility of retribution for his 'minor' breach of the law. How wrong he was!

I alighted from the vehicle, noticing my colleagues glancing at each other as I did so. Perhaps some of them could see free ale evaporating before their very eyes? After obtaining and verifying the man's details, I formally informed him of the good tidings that he would be summoned for proceedings which I would instigate for his riding on the pavement. "Can't you give us another chance, I won't do it again," he pleaded. His pleas fell on deaf ears. If I catch you or anyone else riding on the pavement, you will end up in court every time," I said. The disgruntled cyclist put his cycle in the roadway and as he mounted his machine I got back into the carrier to resume our journey to Liverpool. One of my lads in the back, no doubt one of the patrons from the cyclist's pub, piped up with, "He's alright; he's a good skin, Sarge: you're not going to do him are you?" I turned and told all in the vehicle, "I expect ALL of you to summons those clowns when you catch 'em, not just me!" No further comment was forthcoming.

My name was taken in vain by many colleagues who frequented the pub, when they were told of the incident involving the unlucky cellerman. I was already unpopular with this pub's licensee as I had recently had cause to admonish him for a minor infringement of the licensing laws. The cyclist was eventually fined £75, plus £25 costs. Hopefully he received the message loud and clear, not to do it again!

Another one of my pet hates, selling cigarettes to children, reared its ugly head one morning when I was sad to see a pretty young schoolgirl of about twelve years puffing away on a cigarette as she made her way to school with her friends.

On seeing me the girl hid the weed behind her back but I had already seen her first! "Come here young lady," I said sternly, "I know what's behind your back." It was obvious that the young girl hailed from a good home by her extremely smart turnout. "I'm very sorry, sir," she said dejectedly. She was a well spoken girl, which again indicated that she came from a good home. "Where did you get the cigarette from?" I asked. She admitted to having just spent some of her dinner money on the purchase of two cigarettes for five pence each. I asked for the name of the shop and she pointed along the road to a sweet and tobacconist shop. "We all get them from there," she said.

I took the partly smoked cigarette together with the other one, and, dismissing her friends I took the girl back to the shop. As she and I entered the shop, the proprietor, who was serving a customer, looked at me and his face drained of colour. "Good morning, sir", I said. I waited for the customer to leave the shop and then showed him the two cigarettes I had in my hand. "Why are you selling cigarettes to children?", I asked. "I wouldn't dream of doing that," the shopkeeper replied. "This young lady tells me that you sold her these two ciggies a few minutes ago," I said. "No, not me," insisted the shopkeeper. "Well somebody's telling me lies, so we'll have to let the court decide who to believe then won't we?" I said angrily, as I was convinced that the girl had told the truth.

The little girl broke down sobbing, "I'm telling the truth sir, my mates can prove it 'cos they were with me," she cried. I believed her. I nodded my head indicating to the shopkeeper to follow me to the rear of the shop. There, I said to him quietly, "If you make me take this matter to court, I'll throw the bloody book at you"! "Okay Sarge, I did sell them to her, but I don't do it a lot," he whinged, realising I meant what I said. "I'm taking the girl to her parents, then I'll decide what to do," I informed the worried shopkeeper. "Can't we just forget this Sarge, I won't do anything like this again", he promised. "I'll be in touch", I said as I took the girl and left the shop.

I felt sorry for the girl as she was showing genuine remorse for her folly. I was informed by the contrite little girl that she lived with her mother, she had no father, and her mother would now be at work. To prevent the girl further distress I allowed her to make her way to school. I would call and see her mother the following evening as I would be on afternoon duty then.

The following evening I called at the girl's home, a neat, clean, semi-detached house on the outskirts of Wallasey Village. The mother was a very nice, caring lady who showed real concern on learning the reason for my visit. I straight away put her and her terrified daughter at ease by informing them both that my visit was purely informal and I would be leaving the matter with them. The girl again started to cry and I reassured her, "Come on sweetheart, don't cry, I'm not going to do anything. I'm more annoyed at the man who sold the cigarettes." I said. I told the mother that I was concerned for her daughter's welfare and angry at the shopkeeper for trying to make money from his despicable little trade with children.

"Sit down Sergeant, I'll make a cup of tea", said the grateful lady. The girl and I made friends over our cup of tea and I told her she was silly to start such a filthy habit. After a nice friendly chat over our cuppa, the three of us were all pals again. I left the house with the lady thanking me profusely for my concern for her daughter. Three days later I was asked to note the contents of a letter which had been received by the Chief Constable from the girl's mother, who had decided to put into writing her gratitude for my having probably steered her daughter from a possible path of drug taking by my timely and caring intervention of her daughter's clandestine habit. I was only too pleased to oblige. I went back to the shopkeeper and told him that he had escaped prosecution 'by the skin of his teeth', on this occasion! "I promise you Sergeant, there won't be another occasion"," said the relieved tobacconist.

One job I was very proud to perform each year at the insistence of the Superintendent, was to lead the Band of the Royal British Legion to the war memorial and to lay the wreath on behalf of the Police. I was complimented by the fact that Superintendent Lowe personally insisted that I perform this duty, even if I had to change rest days to do so.

At 10.15 am on the day, I marched ahead of the band to ensure that they and the contingents of army, sea and air cadets, as well as veterans of both World Wars, were uninterrupted during the march from Legion Headquarters to the memorial and back. During the ceremony, I marched forward and laid the wreath and was immensely proud as I stepped back, stood to attention and saluted before returning with the 'troops', back to Legion Headquarters where the parade was stood down. I was invited to join my senior officers and the local dignitaries, by Mrs (now Baroness) Chalker who I came to know well during my service at Wallasey. I would sit and chat with her and others, over tea and biscuits after the parade. I was amazed at how much of my pedigree Mrs Chalker was aware, I had many meetings with her, as my colleagues and I looked after her home, which was on our 'patch'.

At Rememberance Day Parade , Wallasey.

I maintained my contact with those Special Constables who regularly paraded at Manor Road. Many times, I would go out on patrol with one of them or organise a number of them to ride in the carrier or other mobiles, or accompany members of my section on foot, as did my partner, Sergeant Kenny Glass. Whenever any of the lads had been told off by Ken, the section were quick to coin the phrase, "I've just been 'glassed!" Each time the specials held a function or dinner, my wife and I, together with Sergeant Glass and his wife, would always be invited. Their gesture was always very much appreciated by us . I was very impressed with the efficient section of Specials at Wallasey, who all gave devoted service to the division and were always there when needed. When dissent was shown by the few who resented working with specials, they were made instantly aware that I, their Section Sergeant, had been a special at one time!

One of my enterprising young officers, obviously not realising that, having been born and bred in the vicinity, I was fully conversant with the local coastline, offered to drive me along the sea wall from Wallasey to Hoylake. We had a slow trundle along the four mile front alongside the sandhills and on past the well known Leasowe Golf Club and the adjacent, historic Leasowe Castle, while we admired the wonderful panoramic views and colourful seascape.

As we drove along the top of the sea wall my driver drew my attention to something bobbing about in the sea which was halfway up the concrete embankment, it was now almost high tide." What's that Sarge?" enquired my colleague, "STOP!" I said, "It's a body!" "Stop messing about Sarge, what is it though?" said my young colleague - he obviously thought I was joking. "It's a body," I repeated, I'd seen too many before to be mistaken! We stopped our vehicle and I went to the water's edge to verify what, sadly I knew already. Sure enough, the naked body of a young man was being gently pushed up the embankment by the incoming swells. I contacted our control room and requested the attendance of both the inshore lifeboat and the body removal service. I also requested the presence of the Police Surgeon.

The Coastal Track along the sea front at Wallasey

A short time later I was joined by my old friend, Dave Dodd, the deputy coxswain of the Hoylake lifeboat. By the time the inshore lifeboat had arrived, Dave and I had managed to wade in to the surf, retrieve the body and await the Police Surgeon to sanction its removal to the mortuary. The body was that of a young sea angler, one of two young men who had been swept out to sea during bad weather, when they had ventured out on their fateful journey a few days before from Colwyn Bay.

They had put to sea in a small open boat in the early hours, without adequate warm clothing or means of communication. Gales blew up and they were never seen alive again. The other man's body was recovered two days later off the Formby coast. Many times at Wallasey I dealt with 'near misses' involving sea anglers and small boat fishermen. Some of these 'near misses' were only averted due to the sharp-eyed public or the keen observations of myself, my section and the local coastguard. Many a time I chastised an inexperienced or ill-equipped boat owner as he was about to set off to sea, sometimes the weather itself should have been enough to deter such trips, but this was not so, and an additional 'word in their ear' was needed to get the message across!

I have seen many instances of sheer, life-threatening complacency, where, but for our intervention (and sometimes insistent prevention!) certain calamity would have ensued. Only too often do some boat owners put to sea with no means of communication, secondary power, life-jackets, flares or adequately protective clothing, all the ingredients of a 'Kami Kazi' mission. Some instances even provoked me to real anger at such blatant and selfish stupidity, which could well have caused a tragic repeat of our sea wall recovery, or unnecessary risk to searchers and rescuers.

My 'troops' and I continued to police the football matches when there never seemed to be a dull moment! Just prior to one Everton match I was walking along one of the streets adjacent to the ground, the crowds hurriedly making their way to the ground to secure their 'specks', every one seemed happy and friendly. Suddenly I came across a man standing on the pavement urinating against the newly-pebble-dashed wall of one of the many neat, terraced houses that back onto the ground at Goodison. He had obviously consumed a quantity of liquor at one of the many nearby pubs and decided to relieve himself before going onto the crowded terraces.

At this time I was joined by one of my Constables and as we made our way to our man, he was warned of our approach by the crowds, but not soon enough! My colleague and I were on him before he had time to finish what he was doing. "Sorry bosh, I wash taken short!" he said. I told the Constable to hold him as I knocked on the newly-painted front door of the house. A wet stain was up the wall and a pool of urine had gathered on the pavement beneath.

The door was answered by a young housewife clutching a baby to her ample bosom. "What's the matter?" she asked with alarm, seeing us both standing there together with our inebriated friend. "It's alright love, I just want to borrow a mop, scrubbing brush and a bucket of disinfected water," I replied, and informed her of the man's actions. Putting her other hand to her mouth she gasped, "My husband'll go mad, we've just had the house painted and pebble-dashed." I hastily assured her, "It's okay love, he's going to scrub and mop everywhere clean again," and told the unfortunate man that the alternative would be him being arrested and charged with 'drunk and disorderly' behaviour. "Fair enough bosh!" he said, grateful at the opportunity to retain his freedom, and not miss the match! A bucket of water containing a large quantity of bleach was supplied by the young housewife, together with a scrubbing brush and mop.

The man knelt down and scrubbed the pavement and wall before mopping the area clean, much to the amusement of the throngs of match goers, as it was obvious by our presence why he was so engaged!. Eventually, 'mission completed', he stood up, emptied the contents of his bucket down a grid and as he was handing his 'street cleaning kit' back to the lady, a young man approached (her husband) and asked, "What's goin' on 'ere"?

The remorseful pavement cleaner quickly explained what he had done but before he had chance to apologise, he received a cuff round the ear from the angry husband. "You dirty bastard, it's just cost me a bleedin' mint to have all the house done!" he said angrily. I pacified both parties and allowed the cause of the trouble to make his way to the match while I 'ticked off' the angry householder, telling him that 'justice' had already been done! The husband grinned as he saw the funny side, "Not only did the dirty bastard have to clean up his mess, but he got a clout as well, that'll do me", he said with a satisfied smirk. As we walked away I said to my colleague, "I bet he'll look for a bog (toilet) next time!" I considered that the matter had been far better dealt with than via the lengthy and costly way of the courts.

A similar form of 'justice' occurred when I had cause to admonish a group of youths who were trying to disrupt a church youth club's activities one evening. After being told to behave and go home, those requested did so, with the exception of one cocky fifteen year old youth. "You can't make me go, I'll stand here if I want to." I wasn't going to argue the toss, I grabbed him and placed him into the carrier and told him I was taking him home. The youth, realising that I meant business, sensibly gave his name and address. I asked the youth for his father's Christian name. "Ted, but his mates call him Eddie" replied the youth. Nothing further was said and when I arrived at the youth's home, my knock was answered by his father.

To give the impression that I knew 'Eddie' well (and thus ensuring his cooperation!), I said, "Hiya Eddie. Long time no see." I then said earnestly, "Nothing to worry about, seeing as it's you, I've brought your lad home instead of taking him in, 'cos I know you'll deal with 'im properly." "Why, what's up?" asked the concerned father. I informed him that his son had been causing trouble outside the local church youth centre and to make matters worse, he had uttered obscenities to one of my policewomen. I went on to emphasise that as I knew the youth's father, and knew that he would deal with his offensive son 'properly' I decided to take him home to his dad. I informed 'Eddie' that on being told his dad would sort him out, the youth replied, "There's fuck all my 'owl 'fella can do about it." "Oh did he now?" said Eddie. "Bring him in Sarge", he instructed. I escorted the cocky young man from the carrier and into the house and as we entered the hall BANG! the lad was hit by Eddie and sent sprawling the length of the hall before ending in a painful heap near the stairs. "Gerrup t'yer room, NOW!" shouted Eddie, "I'll show yer what I'll do about it. Thanks Sarge, leave it with me, you'll 'ave no more trouble with 'im," he promised as he showed me out.

No doubt the youth was about to receive a good hiding when we had departed, "Good, that'll teach the cocky little sod," I thought as I got back into the carrier! I found that most times when youths tended to be 'cocky' and cheeky when showing off in front of their mates or girlfriends, a quiet word with most of their parents normally solved the problem to the satisfaction of all concerned (except the youth!) A little 'gilding of the lily' never did any harm, when describing the actions of the offspring concerned!

An unusual incident occurred at 10 o'clock one morning when I was summoned by a member of my section to attend an ambulance in Grove Road which had sustained damage in an accident the officer was dealing with. I arrived at the scene to be met by the officer, Constable Cantillon, and the ambulance crew. The ambulance crew showed me the front and nearside of their vehicle, which had sustained damage, but they insisted that they must now leave as they had to collect an elderly patient. All had been explained to the officer prior to my arrival. The ambulance left the scene after the crew arranged to see the officer later, as they wished to furnish statements. Constable Cantillon had required my presence to advise and assist him.

The incident was caused when a man carelessly reversed his car out of his driveway into the main road striking the ambulance as it drove past. The ambulance crew detected the smell of alcohol on the offending driver's breath and attempted to detain him while the police were summoned. The man told the crew that after replacing his car in his driveway, he would provide them with the appropriate details of his insurance and driving licence. However, after returning his car to the path, the driver then went into his house and locked the door behind him, refusing to answer the knocks of the ambulance crew.

"He's still in there now, but won't answer the door Sarge", said my officer after putting me fully in the picture. "RIGHT!" I said, "there's been a traffic accident and you suspect that the driver who caused the accident had been drinking and driving?" "Yes Sarge," replied Constable Cantillon. "Okay, Steve, that's it then," I replied. We wandered down the path and inspected the badly-damaged rear end of a red Metro. The dents and tears bore white paint, obviously from the ambulance. Just then the flushing of a toilet could be heard from the bathroom above.

I took a ladder that lay alongside the fence and placed it up against the wall under the bathroom window. I climbed up and tapping on the frosted glass I shouted, "It's the Police, I know you're in there, open the front door!" I could see the shape of a figure within. The figure remained still, not a sound! I descended the ladder and my colleague and I went to the front door. I shouted through the brass letter box, "Police, open the door!" Again, no response! I then shouted through the box, "We'll give you one minute to open the door, otherwise we're coming in!" Steve looked at me puzzled. I think he thought I was just bluffing. "What'll you do if he doesn't open up Sarge?" he asked. "I'll show you in one minute," I replied.

The minute elapsed and after repeated requests for the door to be opened, 'CRASH!' I shouldered the front door and it gave way first time. I ran up the stairs and knocked on the locked bathroom door. "Police! Open up!" I shouted. Silence! "If you don't open this door, I'LL open it," I said sternly. After a lengthy pause, there was a loud click as the door was unlocked. The bathroom door opened slowly to reveal a red-faced, portly man dressed in a white shirt, burgundy bow tie, pin-stripe trousers and sporting highly-polished shoes. He looked every inch a professional man. The strong smell of whisky emanated from the room before he did. He was unsteady on his feet and he said, "How dare you come in here like thish, I'm going to report you!" He staggered out of the bathroom and almost fell into my arms. "He's well and truly pissed, "I remarked to my colleague and said to the inebriated householder, "You'll get your chance to complain at the station".

Our 'merry' prisoner tried unsuccessfully to attack my colleague and I but was too drunk to do any harm. "I know my ritshe!" he slurred as we ushered him downstairs and out to the patrol car. I ensured that his door was returned to its former condition by replacing the forced screws in the brass lock with bigger ones, and the man was arrested and taken into custody. It was revealed that he was in fact THREE times over the legal limit to drive, (at that time in the morning?!). He was charged with drinking and driving and ultimately appeared before the court, when, as well as being heavily fined and disqualified from driving for a lengthy period, he was also ordered to pay for the repairs to the damaged ambulance.

During a cold spell a poor old lady was rendered homeless one day due to her attempts to keep warm. After lighting a portable gas fire together with an electric fire, she inadvertently caused the ignition of nearby furniture by heat radiation, as the fires were placed too close to the chairs and settee. A fierce fire quickly ensued and as a result her home was almost completely destroyed and rendered totally uninhabitable. Constable Dave Ashworth and I attended together with colleagues of the Fire and Ambulance Services.

Although the lady was removed from the house, she was insistant upon returning, and I and others had to forcibly prevent her from doing so. At this early stage, it was obvious that the lady would be homeless and Social Services were contacted to assist her. We even had to force the old lady into the ambulance, but she flatly refused to be conveyed to hospital until I retrieved a metal box she had hidden in her house. She told me where to go to find the box.

After searching the charred remains beneath what was once the staircase, I found her metal box. One of the fire crew doused it with water to cool it off sufficiently for me to pick it up and take it to the old girl. She produced a key and unlocked the blackened box. Lifting the black, sooty lid, there inside, unharmed, were revealed her life savings, over £4,000 in bank notes. It was no wonder she was reluctant to leave! The lady was taken to nearby Mill Lane Hospital, thankfully suffering nothing more than shock, smoke inhalation and singed hair.

Some weeks later I attended another house fire, this time however, the outcome was far different! My presence had been requested by a senior fire officer, A.D.O. (Assistant Divisional Officer) Harris, as he was concerned about the cause of the blaze. On my arrival at the semi-detached house near to the river front, ADO Harris met me and said, "Come and have a look at this Sarge, I think the fire was started deliberately." I saw that one of my Policewomen had also arrived. A large crowd had gathered outside on the pavement to watch the fire-fighters extinguish the blaze, which had consumed most of the upper floor and roof of the dwelling. Fortunately the adjoining house had escaped damage. ·

Leaving the policewoman outside to keep an eye on the onlookers, the fire officer and I entered the house and with considerable difficulty managed to make our way up what was left of the burned and blackened stairs. The seat of the fire had been established as being in the corner of the bathroom, an empty petrol can lay amongst the worst of the damage. "There's no doubt it was arson," said the ADO.

Next to the bathroom was a bedroom, the contents of which were totally destroyed. We carefully made our way down and returned to the front garden. I was introduced to two men by the fire officer. "These gentlemen live here. They were bloody lucky because they were in bed when the fire started!" he said. I spoke to one of the men and asked him if he knew how the fire had started. Pointing to a woman standing nearby holding a large black and tan Alsatian dog on a choke chain, the man said, "It was her! She's fucking crackers!" He informed me that the woman was in fact his ex-girlfriend. They had parted with extreme animosity and she still had a key to the house which she used when she continually returned at all hours of the day and night to harass him. He and his co-householder were both in their beds when they were woken by the noise of the fire and made a hasty retreat from the house. As they made their way out of the house they saw the woman standing by the gate. When the ex-boyfriend went to her he could smell petrol on her clothing. I went to the woman with the two men and my policewoman colleague. I asked the man to repeat his very serious allegation in front of the lady concerned. On his doing so I asked the lady if she had heard and understood what had been said. "I heard," she replied. I asked her if it was true and if so, give an explanation for such conduct.

The 'spurned' woman hissed venomously, "Yes I did it; serves him right 'cos he burgled my house!" I told the woman that she would be arrested and taken to Manor Road Police Station as the offence we were now talking about was one of attempted murder as well as arson. The lady threatened to set her dog on my colleague and I, so, taking a chance, I grabbed its chain and in as friendly a voice as I could muster, I said apprehensively, "C'mon fella, there's a good boy," and was amazed when the animal allowed me to pull him away from his mistress and drag him down the path to place him into a shed in the back garden before securing the door .

The woman was arrested and taken into custody. On her eventual appearance before the Liverpool Crown Court, it was accepted that the lady was mentally unbalanced at the time of the offence and that she would benefit from psychiatric treatment. She was put into the care of the appropriate mental health authority for the help and treatment required.

I continued to make many friends on into my second year and during that time I had transferred to another equally good section. Like my old section, I had old, young, male and female officers, most of whom were very enthusiastic and capable officers. I always took a keen interest in my section, both on, and off, duty. If I found that any of my 'chicks' were suffering domestic or other problems, I would visit them or their spouses and offer what help I could. On one occasion, a young Constable's wife gave birth in our local hospital and my co-Sergeant, Ken

Glass, and I went to a local florist and purchased a large bunch of flowers before we both went to the hospital and together, walked into the ward carrying our large, congratulatory tribute to her. The sight of two uniformed Police Sergeants, one at each side of her bed, certainly raised a few eyebrows! Both Ken and I genuinely cared for the members of our section very much. Unfortunately, as usual, there were the inevitable one or two older, often disenchanted members who were downright lazy and were prepared to be 'carried' on the backs of their more energetic and enthusiastic colleagues.

One such man, who had quite a few years' service, tried to portray himself as 'Mr Efficiency', but this was a sham to hide his inefficiency. I was later to find that he was a prolific drinker (on and off duty!), but I was never able to catch him actually partaking! This was the very man who was keen to divulge places where I might find his colleagues 'hiding' when he said, "I'll take you round and show you where some of the lads sneak for a pint". As my views concerning the demon drink were widely known I immediately thought, what kind of man would 'shop' his fellow constables to a Sergeant? I would certainly watch this fellow!

Due to his pin-pointing of various venues to me I did in fact catch one or two of my section in licensed premises, but not once in possession of an alcoholic drink, (perhaps they had been made aware of my approach?) On being found they would receive a rocket if they could not justify their presence. They wondered how I had found them. They were informed that a colleague had 'grassed' (informed) on them, although I never divulged my source, (in hindsight, perhaps I should have done).

Fortunately, such occasions were rare, but I never trusted my 'informer' after he so willingly 'snitched' on his colleagues. In collusion with another man of more lengthy service (and equal lack of enthusiasm for police work) he and his mate were not a good influence on the younger element of the section, although it took some time for me to suss this out! I had cause to admonish these two on many occasions due to their attitude and dress. Eventually I managed to get through to them although I knew that under the surface I did not command their loyalty. One of the two attempted to usurp my authority on one occasion by continuing to smoke a cigarette as I entered the parade room to commence the afternoon duty parade. Watching closely, of course, were the rest of the section.

Glaring at the smoker I said, "Would you extinguish your cigarette please?". I placed the parade's documentation onto the table and we were then joined by the Inspector. As he entered the room I called the parade to attention. After acknowledging the parade I stood the section at ease. I then noticed smoke curling up and out from the cupped hand of the officer who had been requested to extinguish it. Halting the proceedings I said, "Excuse me sir", and walked over to the officer concerned. Leaning over I whispered into his ear, "Put that bloody fag out, NOW, and see me in my office after parade!" I then returned and allowed the parade to continue. Looking to my puzzled Inspector I said, "Just a small disciplinary matter sir."

After the parade the officer came to the Sergeants office and sauntered in. "You wanted to see me Sarge?" he asked with an arrogant air. "Close the door," I instructed. The Constable closed the door and stood there. "Yes I bloody do want to see you!" I said with a snarl. I told him to sit down as I had something important to say. As he sat down there was a knock at the door as a policewoman opened it to enter the room. "Not now!" I bellowed. The door closed instantly!

I placed my chair strategically in front of the Constable and sat down. Looking him straight in the eye I started. "I don't know what your game is or who you are trying to impress, but you and I had better get one thing straight, NOW!" I said. "I don't know what you mean Sarge," the Constable replied. I laid into him verbally, "What kind of a bloody man are you? First you try to endear yourself to me by trying to drop your mates in it by telling me what they are all up to and where, then you try to show the recruits how you will defy me. Don't you dare try to undermine my authority again, do I make myself clear?!" The officer was now beginning to see the light! I went on, "When I tell you to do something, bloody well do it!" He was advised to go and see the Chief Super if he didn't like the way I was running the section.

The reticent Constable was undoubtedly taken aback by my verbal ferocity. Just to make sure that the message was getting through I threw in, "If you wish to transfer, I'll gladly sort that out for you! "You've got it all wrong Sarge, I'm happy here," the constable whimpered, "Sorry about the ciggie - you won't have to tell me again," he added.

The Constable again profusely apologised for having 'given me the wrong impression' and assured me that I would have no cause to criticise him again. Although I knew that a leopard never changed its spots, I said, "Okay, we'll leave at that then. I rely on the likes of you to set an example to the younger members of the section." I allowed the Constable to leave and commence his patrol, but I knew that from then on I would have to watch him, and his mate, and more importantly, my back! After my little sermon, things seemed to improve, for a while!.

As I was driving around on mobile patrol early one evening in company with Constable (now Sergeant) Vincent-Lloyd, my radio sprang to life. "Golf Sierra One Six. Over!" Lifting the microphone I replied, "Golf Sierra One Six. Go ahead. Over." Back came the reply from control, "Yes Sarge, could you make the Farmers Arms, Wallasey Village. Report of two bombs planted in the premises. Over." "Golf Sierra One Six, en route," I acknowledged. My colleague and I, assisted by the licensee and his staff, cleared the building of customers and made a meticulous search of the pub but thankfully found nothing.

As I was leaving the premises I noticed a man standing nearby having just alighted from his car. The man appeared to be 'strange in manner' by his demeanour. He seemed to have a 'vacant' stare.. By this time I had been made aware that the telephone call to the police informing them of the 'bombs', had been made from a nearby public telephone kiosk at the junction of Grove Road and Claremont Road. The vehicle had just come from the direction of the kiosk, so I went to the man and asked him what he was doing in Grove Road near to Claremont Road.

Although he did admit to having been in the vicinity a short time earlier he denied having been near the 'phone box. "Who mentioned anything about a 'phone box?" I asked. I informed him of the reason for my questions and the man became very agitated. I asked him for his name and address and he shouted, "Fuck off. I'm not telling you, I'm not well." I insisted that he identify himself to me or I would be obliged to convey him to the station to ascertain his details. He then supplied me with his full name and address which I subsequently verified as being correct. I was still not happy with this man. His conduct and demeanour gave me cause to think that all was not well with him, although I couldn't put my finger on what it was. As I had no 'evidence' at this stage that he had perpetrated the incident, I allowed him to go. However, I decided to vigorously pursue the matter with regard to this man in an effort to bring it to a successful conclusion. I consulted with the Inspector in the Force Control room at Headquarters in Liverpool and made arrangements to attend there the following day.

I attended as arranged and listened to the tape recorded voice of the previous day's bomb hoaxer regarding the Farmers Arms. After hearing the voice, I identified it as being that of the man who had aroused my suspicions at the scene. Being satisfied beyond all doubt of this, I, together with a colleague, Acting Inspector Derek Bebington, saw the man at his home in the presence of his sister. At first our man strenuously denied being involved in any telephone call to the police regarding bombs in a pub. However, as I was in possession of a duplicate tape recording of the actual call, I played this over to the man and his sister.

The Farmers Arms Pub. Wallasey. Scene of the bomb hoax.

322

The man broke down sobbing uncontrollably and had to be comforted by his sister who said, "For God sake tell them the truth Nigel (not his real name), it's your voice and you know it." 'Nigel' sobbed, "It must be me, but I can't remember doing it." Due to the obvious distress and apparent acute depression of 'Nigel', the Police Surgeon was summoned to attend.

After the doctor had examined 'Nigel' and had a lengthy talk with him, the doctor diagnosed that the poor man was suffering acute mental illness. 'Nigel' had been a psychiatric nurse for many years, but sadly, after caring for mentally ill patients for so long, he himself had succumbed to severe mental illness and was admitted to hospital for treatment, thus terminating his career. It was obvious that it would not be in the public, or his interest to instigate proceedings and drag the man before the court. I filed a full report outlining the whole incident, together with 'Nigel's' pedigree and suggested that there be no further police action in the matter as the man was again undergoing psychiatric treatment. My recommendations were accepted and there the matter was laid to rest.

I continued to enjoy my days (and nights) at Manor Road and dealt with many problems of various magnitudes. Not all problems that had to be dealt with involved 'Joe Public'. Problems arose amongst my own officers on occasions, some of which were either quite serious or they could be delicate and sensitive, but all, for the sake of morale, had to be sorted out. As a section Sergeant I often found myself in an awkward position when dealing with internal matters concerning my men (and women).

I was really put 'on the spot' during one night shift when I drove round the town at midnight visiting my 'troops'. I decided to 'peg' one of the Specials as she patrolled the town centre shopping precinct on foot. I spotted her as I drove along the row of shops. I drew up alongside her and saw that she was crying. "What on earth's the matter?" I asked. "Nuthin," she grunted. I told her to get into the car as I was not having a uniformed officer walking around crying her eyes out for all to see!

As she sat in my vehicle I again asked, "Now, tell me what's up with you". The girl broke down and sobbed out her story. She informed me that a regular colleague on an adjacent beat had met her behind the shops as she was checking her property. As they both stood in the shadows, the male Constable not only put his hand down inside her tunic and under her bra to squeeze her breast, but he also exposed his penis to her and invited her to fondle him. I couldn't believe what I was hearing! I listened patiently to her frightening tale then decided to take her into the station and calm her down with a cup of tea, before asking her again to repeat and elaborate her story in the confines of the Sergeants' office.

After again listening to her amazing story concerning what, at this stage, was an allegation of a serious indecent assault on her by an officer from my section, who was also alleged to have indecently exposed himself to her I then decided to have the officer concerned, into my office to hear his side of the story before taking further action. "Oh no, Sarge, don't tell him I told you, I don't want it to go any further", cried the young woman. "Well, what DO you want"?, I asked, astonished at her 'misplaced loyalty'! "I just want to make sure he doesn't do it again," said the officer.

I glared at her and said, "You must be bloody joking young lady. You accuse a fellow officer of committing heinous crimes whilst on duty, and don't expect me to do anything about it. I'm getting him in here NOW"! The policewoman's tears again started to flow. "Get yourself off to the rest room 'til I send for you again," I ordered. She left for the rest room, no doubt now realising that her grave allegations could well cause absolute mayhem for all concerned, not least the Police service in general. I dispatched a mobile to collect the male beat officer and return him to my office right away.

A short time later there was a knock on my door. "Come in," I commanded. The door was opened and in stepped the rain-soaked bobby. "Close the door, take your wet coat off and sit down 'Alan' "(an alias) I said. "What's up Sarge? "asked Alan'. "I'm afraid there have been very serious allegations made against you by a colleague," I said, and went on to reiterate in detail the story that the young, tearful policewoman had told me a short time earlier.

When I had finished, 'Alan' said nervously, "That's not true, Sarge. I'm a married man. Your daughter and my daughter go to school together and are playmates; our wives know each other as well. I wouldn't do that." "Nevertheless, that's what's been said," I replied. I pointed out that if all the young policewoman had said was true, then I would have no alternative but to bring the Inspector in on the matter as charges would have to be preferred and the officer's suspension from duty would be necessary. 'Alan' was now a very worried and frightened man, his face went ashen. Again he denied improper behaviour towards his female colleague. For some reason I had a nagging doubt at the back of my mind that all was not as had been made out. As it was now approaching 1.30am, I decided to discreetly 'sound out' the rest of the section and see what I could find out about each officer before making a final decision before we went off duty at 7.00 am. I allowed the bobby to continue his duty assisting in the Bridewell, and sent the policewoman home.

Patient 'ferreting' among the section as I accompanied each of them on their patrols, revealed that the constable had been having an affair with the young policewoman for a very long time. He even had his own key to her house and made regular visits for 'passion' when on his way to or from duty. She had quite a reputation in the locality, as well as among the members of the section, and neither officer was very popular.

This now threw a totally different light on the matter! I returned to the station and had the Constable back into my office and again questioned him about the previously denied allegations. This time I told him bluntly, "I know quite a bit about you and her so don't give me any bullshit! Either I get the truth or the whole issue goes down on paper to the Inspector and Chief Super." The Constable spilled the beans and opened up. He told me everything, 'warts and all'. "I've been knocking her off for ages Sarge, but I wanted to finish it. We had a row when I tried to end our relationship yesterday and she met me during the night at the back of the shops to talk it over." He went on to tell me that there were tears and eventually things got carried away as they pacified each other! 'Alan' denied that anything was done without mutual consent and cooperation. "Yes we did finish up having a grope and a cuddle behind the shops, but we were both doing it to each other," he bleated.

I believed him and inwardly gave him credit for not initially exposing her adulterous relationship with him. However, such conduct on duty was abominable. "This isn't a bloody dating agency for Christ's sake", I snapped, "You're supposed to be protecting the bloody public, that's what you're getting paid for!" I informed 'Alan' that I could not deal with the matter totally myself as I considered that the Inspector would have to know. "Can't you deal with this yourself Sarge?" pleaded 'Alan'. "I'll try and prevent it reaching the top but the Inspector will have to be told," I said . I would speak to the Inspector after we paraded for duty on our next shift. In the meantime 'Alan' would have to spend the day worrying as to what his destiny held for him. During the following tour of duty I consulted the Inspector and we decided that there was no alternative but to put the ball in the court of the Chief Inspector. Eventually the matter was resolved by the woman being asked to leave the ranks of the Special Constabulary and the male officer being transferred to 'other' duties. To many, this may seem to be a scandalous 'let off' for both, but they were just two of many in the job who were 'at it'! Others (of all ranks) who have never been caught due to being a damned sight more discreet than the two who had revealed their activities by their own stupid behaviour , were more lucky!

An equally important role I considered to be my responsibility, was to make sure that officers receive the recognition they deserve for their efficiency and efforts. During one tour of night duty EVERY officer on the section arrested a villain for one type of offence or another. I was so impressed that I submitted the following report to the Superintendent for his observations:-

"During this last night shift, every officer without exception became involved throughout the night with various arrests and detentions, all of equal importance, including the Acting Inspector and myself. As the degree of involvement by 100% of the section meant there would be deprivation of police cover to the local area, I wish to bring to your attention the fact that each individual officer, of both supervisory and subordinate rank, to a man volunteered to forego his or her refreshment period. On completing each of the individual jobs concerned, each then went straight out to maintain cover. Due to this, not a single officer had any refreshments (or refreshment period) at all. This report is in no way any form of a complaint, indeed to the contrary. I only wish to emphasise the quality of the young officers concerned, and compliment each of them, respectfully, via yourself, on the high standard of selfless zeal and initiative each man and woman displayed."

My effort was rewarded by a subsequent personal visit to our next parade by the Super himself who complimented my section on their endeavours. Such personal attendances to the parades by senior officers were rare and therefore were much appreciated by the young men and women who saw that their efforts were being acknowledged by those in senior command.

Serious offences such as assaults and woundings were not always perpetrated by men. Sadly, many such serious assaults on fellow beings are all too regularly made by women. One such offence, a serious wounding, was revealed when myself and a policewoman, 'Barby Doll' Marsden, were directed to a nightclub where a fight had broken out. As we arrived the club's patrons were making their way home. The trouble had ceased but we were confronted with the sad sight of a young lady in a cotton print dress being comforted by two of her friends as she sat in a chair holding a towel to her face.

My colleague and I removed the towel; her pretty face was covered in blood which was oozing from a large gaping wound in her cheek and running down the front of her dress. We replaced the towel to staunch the flow of blood and were told that an ambulance was en route. The young lady had been attacked by another woman who had pushed a broken beer glass into her face. How any human being could do such a thing to a fellow being is beyond comprehension; for a woman to inflict such a serious wound on another woman is even more horrendous!

The injured woman was conveyed to hospital where a number of stitches were inserted to close the large, open wound. Unfortunately the poor girl now bears a permanent long, ugly scar down the side of her face. Policewoman Marsden and I commenced enquiries into the vicious attack and as the result of my colleague's diligent sleuthing, we went to a house in Birkenhead's North end the following day and there arrested a 25 year old female who was responsible for the savage attack. The woman was charged with the wounding and was subsequently dealt with by the Crown Court. A good piece of relentless police work by the lady officer.

Late one evening some weeks later, I was again in company with the same officer when we were called to a disturbance at a fish and chip shop. Inside the shop a man in his twenties was shouting obscenities to customers and staff. The man was an ex-amateur boxer who had obviously been drinking and was known locally as a bit of a bully. My colleague told the young man to be quiet and go home. The fact that it was a woman who told him incensed him further and he persisted in behaving in a drunk and disorderly manner. He lunged at the policewoman, threatening to 'break her nose' and started to grapple with her.

I grabbed the aggressive young man and a violent struggle ensued. The policewoman and I managed to get the fighting drunk outside and made for our vehicle. Not one person inside the shop offered any help! During the struggle my colleague was punched in the face and with difficulty the man was finally placed into our Police car. On arrival at the station the man again became violent as we tried to remove him from our vehicle. He kicked my colleague violently in her chest with his both feet as he lay on the back seat of the car. He was finally dragged from the car and taken to the charge office where he punched me in the face drawing blood from my mouth.

Due to his violent behaviour he was forcibly placed into a cell. The Police surgeon was sent for and later arrived to treat my colleague and I. The prisoner himself needed treatment also due to my striking him in self-defence. My woman colleague had to go off duty suffering from severe bruising to her face, arms and chest. The man responsible for the drunken violence was charged with a number of assaults on police for which he was rightly given a custodial sentence.

Another incident which could so easily have ended in tragedy happened in broad daylight one day as Constable Cantillon was driving me along the sea front at Harrison Drive. We were travelling along the roadway on top of the sea wall near to the Leasowe Golf Club while we checked recent storm damage and life-saving equipment on the sea wall.

As we made our way along we saw a motorcycle being driven towards us with two persons aboard. On seeing us, the motorcycle stopped and turned round. Its pillion passenger jumped from the machine and ran off into the nearby grounds of the Leasowe Castle. The rider then drove off at a fast speed towards Hoylake. We drove after the machine as he had no right to be on the sea wall and a check revealed that the bike had in fact been reported stolen. We pursued the machine at high speed along the narrow roadway. The rider eventually turned off from the sea wall and drove down towards the Leasowe lighthouse, with us in hot pursuit.

As we approached the lighthouse, travelling along the narrow roadway which had built in a number of 'sleeping policemen', the machine stopped and turned round to face us. The rider then drove his machine directly at us. My colleague braked violently and tried to avoid the oncoming machine. The motorcycle, however, crashed into the front of our vehicle as my colleague was unable to prevent a collision. The rider was catapulted from the machine on impact and thrown over the front of our vehicle to land in a heap. Amazingly, he got to his feet and ran off across fields, making good his escape along the nearby electrified West Kirby to Liverpool railway line. A subsequent, thorough search of the area failed to trace the very lucky offender. Neither my Constable or I were injured in the incident, the collision being completely beyond my colleague's control, despite his skilful attempt to avoid it. However, we did at least recover some poor individual's motorbike, unfortunately a little the worse for wear!.

As the year drew to a close, a tragic incident befell me which was to have disastrous consequences.

Chapter Nineteen - The End of the Road

At half past five on a dark, wet and windy December evening I was on foot patrol with a beat constable as we walked down a drizzly Victoria Road, New Brighton . We made our way past the well lit shop fronts as they were preparing to close at the end of the day. Suddenly, my attention was drawn to the sound of a powerful motor cycle making its way up towards us from the direction of the old pier. The machine appeared to be travelling at a fast speed, and the roads were still busy. The street lighting was on and although it was raining, visibility was good. I stepped into the centre of the road and signalled the motor cycle to stop. The motor cyclist decelerated, braked and steered towards the kerb as though he was stopping.

As I walked towards the large machine and was just a few yards from him, the rider gave the big powerful machine (a 1200 cc Kawasaki) full throttle after engaging a lower gear. The machine shot forward like a rocket. The half-ton vehicle and its well-built rider crashed into me, the engine's large, protruding cylinder head striking my right leg at the knee with full force. I was knocked back flat on my back, ten feet into the centre of the roadway and felt excruciating pain in my right leg. I had also injured my right arm and shoulder. How the rider stayed on his machine I'll never know. The machine mounted the kerb and scattered a bus queue of elderly people, amazingly missing each one as he roared off through a set of traffic lights showing red against him at a major junction a short distance further along the road before vanishing into the evening's darkness. I lay there momentarily stunned.

My colleague, Constable Morgan, called in frantically on his radio informing control what had happened (all in the blink of an eye!). Within what appeared to be seconds I was gently placed into a police vehicle and before I knew it I was being treated and X-rayed at Arrowe Park hospital within a very short time. My right knee was swollen as the main ligaments of my leg were badly torn and splinters of bone would later have to be removed from inside my knee. My injuries rendered me unfit for duty. After four months I attempted a come-back but my knee was still giving me trouble as walking was very painful.

One of the most important duties of my whole career was shortly to take place. The parade when I would be formally awarded my Police Long Service Metal. The ceremony would be held at Mather Avenue Training School on Friday, 5 February 1988. I was determined that I would be on that parade, even if I had to crawl there on my hands and knees! My wife, daughter Jo, brother Tom and his wife Maureen, would all accompany me on my big day.

I was up at 8 o clock then down to the dry cleaners at 9 o'clock sharp to collect my cleaned and pressed uniform as the shop opened. We spent the morning getting ourselves ready and at lunch time we all set off to Liverpool for the big occasion. What a fantastic day it was. What a wonderful ceremony.

Although my leg was giving me a tremendous amount of pain I was determined that it was not going to spoil anything. I limped into the parade room to join my colleagues as we were lined up into our allotted ranks. I stood there on the front rank alongside my colleagues, some of whom I had not seen for over twenty years. The police band played the 'Eton Boating Song' as we stood in our disciplined ranks before our proud, seated relatives, as they popped off their flash bulbs to record the day's events on film for posterity. The official police photographer was present as were his colleagues from the press. The pain in my leg was overruled by the deep sense of pride I felt as I stood there.

Eventually the parade was brought to attention as the Queen's representative, the High Sheriff of Merseyside, Colonel M. Creagh, O.B.E., T.D., D.L., graced the parade with her presence, escorted by the Chief Constable Sir Kenneth Oxford and his senior aides, before the High Sheriff presented those on parade with their coveted medal from the Queen. This medal was awarded by Her Majesty to those officers who had completed at least twenty-two years of exemplary police service.

Long Service Medal Parade, spot Swasie !

After the ceremony Colonel Creagh approached me and asked me to introduce her to my family. I was highly honoured to oblige. The Colonel had a lengthy chat with my wife and was interested to know how she managed to endure all those traumatic years of being a policeman's wife. Eventually we all adjourned to the main lounge after all the photographs, official and unofficial, had been taken. There, everybody chatted over drinks and enjoyed a very substantial buffet.

Our wives were presented with large bouquets of flowers, courtesy

With wife Marje , daughter Jo and 'Ma' am ' at Medal Parade.

Swasie with two of 'his' Constables. Long Service Medal Parade.

of the Police Federation and a happy time was had by all, and many old friendships were rekindled. I met my old room mate from L block, our billet at Bruche, Ian 'Jock' Walker. He was then a Southport Borough officer, but after amalgamation, he was now in the ranks of our Merseyside force.

'Jock' and I were then joined by Sir Ken, the Chief Constable (who was recovering from a recent back injury). Mr Oxford was not renowned for having a sense of humour. "How's your injured back sir?" asked 'Jock'. "It's bloody painful, I wouldn't mind, but I injured myself in the same place when I walked into the tail fin of a Lancaster during the war." replied Sir Ken. "That was a bit clumsy of you wasn't it sir, hurting yourself twice in fifty years in the same place." I was mortified at Jock's sarcastic quip. I thought Sir Ken was going to explode!. He glared at my ex-room mate and stormed away. I fully expected the following day a Chief Constable's order to announce, "The following posting to outer Mongolia will take place . . .!"

Ian ' Jock' Walker with Sir Kenneth Oxford after Long Srevice Medal Parade.

As the afternoon's pleasantries drew to a close I showed my family around the police kennels and stables, a special treat for my daughter Jo. After saying goodbye to my old friends and colleagues (I wondered how long it would be before our paths crossed again) we left for home. I will remember that day with pride and affection for the rest of my life.

After an operation to clean my knee of 'floating bits and pieces' I was sent down to recuperate at the Police Convalescent home at Hove. There, as before, I made a lot of new friends among my fellow patients and local residents as I spent many hours sitting outside the beach hut on the sea front . I befriended one family, the Baxters, as they walked along the prom from their nearby home. I still visit them to stay for short periods to this day. My period at Hove was very pleasant but unfortunately my ability to walk without difficulty continued to deteriorate. A further operation didn't ease the problem and again I spent a pleasant, mentally therapeutic period at Hove beside the sea. I was now beginning to suffer acute bouts of deep depression and my regular anxiety states were giving cause for concern both to my family and my doctors.

I was beginning to see my job vanishing before my very eyes and had difficulty accepting the truth, that there was no way I would be able to continue as a front line Police officer. I was again off duty and was now having to walk with the aid of a stick. As well as being treated for my painful leg injury, I was also receiving counselling in an attempt to get me to come to terms with the inevitable. To make the pill even more bitter, I had successfully applied to become a drill instructor at Bruche, but now, due to my permanent injury and subsequent disability, my posting had been cancelled.

During my last term at the convalescent home, as we sat outside the beach hut, many of the local residents would stop and chat as they went about their 'constitutional' or when out exercising their dogs. The majority of them expressed their gratitude at the way we performed such hazardous duties whilst protecting them, and their real concern for the injuries we sustained whilst performing such duties.

One such man and his lady wife even invited those patients who so wished, and were able, to visit their nearby home in Pembroke Crescent, and join them in a meal and a few drinks. This offer was gratefully accepted and a number of us were transported in the Home's minibus to their house one sunny afternoon where we imbibed and ate well on the lawns of their large detached house, secluded amongst the trees. I still visit Jenny and Herbie Parkhouse when I venture down to their part of the country, and my welcome is as warm today as it was when it was first extended.

Parade of 'Broken Bobbies', in the Parkhouses' Garden, Hove.

One day, whilst I was sitting pensively outside the beach hut contemplating what my future held. I sat staring at the powerful surf as it crashed angrily onto the pebbled beach. The sea was very rough due to high winds. I saw a frail, elderly lady standing on the beach as she waited patiently for her miniature terrier to relieve itself on the pebbles. Suddenly a huge wave crashed up the beach before receding back into the surf. The powerful undertow had sucked the old lady and her dog into the sea. I was horrified,

I struggled to the water with the aid of my crutch and threw myself into the foamy sea. I eventually managed to get myself out about thirty yards to try and find the lady. I dived under the water and at my fourth attempt felt what I thought was a clump of seaweed. It was the old lady's hair! I tried to make my way back to the beach hoping the heavy surf would do the job for me. I thought I was going to pass out with the pain in my leg. It was only by the grace of God that a powerful wave took us back up the beach as I tried to swim ashore with the semi -conscious woman.

We were unceremoniously dumped in the shingle and thankfully managed to avoid being dragged back by the undertow. We both lay there on the pebbles, the poor old girl was half-naked and muttering incoherently. I felt myself being dragged to my feet by a fellow patient, Andrew Kinsella. Boy, was I thankful to see him.

The lady was taken to hospital and I was helped back over to the home. I was pleased to learn later that the lady had made a full recovery and was none the worse for her horrendous ordeal. Sadly, the dog perished. The following day the lady's grateful husband called into the home to express his gratitude for what I had done, which is only what anyone else would have done if they had been there at the time.

The Home's Superintendent informed my force of the incident, for which there was no need. Sadly, not long after my return home from Hove, that wonderfully therapeutic establishment at the well known and immensely popular venue was closed down for good after those in authority, in their ultimate wisdom (many of whom had never been police officers) transferred the Police Convalescent Home (against the wishes of the majority of those at the sharp end) from beautiful Hove to Goring on Thames, although I am aware that facilities at the latter venue are a vast improvement to those at the former establishment!

I underwent yet another operation to my knee and was informed that the damage was such that I would need a complete new knee joint. To make matters even worse, the knee had now also become arthritic. I was sent to my force medical officer, who was very sympathetic and at first he postponed judgement to allow time to elapse in the hope that something could be done to save my career.

Alas, after a further twelve months it was obvious that by now my disablement would prevent my continuing in the force. I was once again sent to the force medical officer and on my second visit, he sadly broke the news to me that my disability had become more acute since his last examination and he had no alternative but to recommend that I be caste (invalided out of the service). My career was over!

After all the trials and tribulations, the scars and broken bones, the laughter and the tears, the job I loved so passionately was now being taken from me. Hardly able to speak, I dressed and left the medical centre to rejoin my wife and son who had driven me over for the medical, each of them knowing that the miracle I was hoping for would not materialise.

Not a word was spoken as we drove along Scotland Road towards the tunnel approach road, where once had stood Arden House. The memories came flooding back of those distant days, which only I could picture through my misty eyes, memories that I would cherish for ever.

The following day I went to Manor Road to perform the painful task of clearing my locker and desk before handing in various items of equipment, including my warrant card.

The loss of the job which had consumed my everything for over a quarter of a century was akin to a bereavement and I felt the loss very deeply indeed. I left the station feeling totally dejected and morose. As well as surgery to my knee, I certainly needed major surgery to remove the large chip that I now had on my shoulder!. I felt very emotional at having to prematurely leave my section and would certainly miss my 'chicks'. Whether they would miss me may well be subject of conjecture?

Unknown to me my colleagues (of all ranks), in collusion with my wife, arranged for me to attend the station on a date arranged "to clear up some administration regarding my pension etc"! On the day, my son came along 'for the ride' (he also was in on it) and when we arrived the three of us were told to make for the canteen for a cuppa until I was sent for.

As we sat at the table, the Superintendent, Mr Lowe (the nine o'clock shudda) breezed in. He greeted us 'in surprise' then asked the three of us to follow him through the dividing doors and into the lounge bar of the social club. As we followed him through I saw that the lounge was full of senior officers, colleagues and civilian staff from the station. Also present were the press, including a photographer. A buffet had also been meticulously laid out. What a pleasant, and touching, surprise. I now realised that I had been 'conned' into attending.

Mr Lowe presented my wife with a large bouquet of beautiful flowers and myself with an engraved silver salver on behalf of all present to mark my retirement from the force. The Super gave a very touching and complimentary speech outlining my service and the tragic cause of its premature end before I was presented with further gifts and cards from my section and colleagues. The press compiled their article and photographs were taken. One of the gifts presented to me was an expensive sea fishing rod, (I intended to 'christen' this as soon as I could!) I was overwhelmed! We all enjoyed a very convivial afternoon over a number of drinks when my colleagues assured me that they would keep in touch, (and they still do).

A photograph and accompanying article appeared in the local

Superintendent Lowe (The nine o' clock Shudda) presenting me with a Silver Salver from my collegues

Saying goodbye to my beloved section at Manor Road upon my premature retirement.

papers some days later informing the residents of Wallasey (and Wirral) of my retirement, and its cause. To add icing to the cake, the shopkeepers and their customers of Wallasey Village, assisted by my son Ron, arranged a farewell drink at their local pub, the Lighthouse.

I had certainly been given a 'fond' farewell by my colleagues and the people of Wallasey. This was very much appreciated by myself and my family, and due to the kind sentiments of these people, no doubt the blow of my leaving the force was softened considerably.

Although I would need further operations, and would have to come to terms with having to use a stick to assist my walking, (the legacy of my cherished career). I have no regrets whatsoever and would unhesitatingly recommend those keen men and women wishing to join the ranks of the profession to do so.

Since leaving the service I decided to try and chronicle my life in the Police force, by writing of my exploits, ' Off the cuff ' of course!. I hope that you have enjoyed it as much as I did.

Swasie Turner 1994